# Land, Law and Chiefs
## in Rural South Africa

# Land, Law and Chiefs
## in Rural South Africa

Contested Histories and Current Struggles

Edited by
William Beinart, Rosalie Kingwill and Gavin Capps

WITS UNIVERSITY PRESS

Published in South Africa by:
Wits University Press
1 Jan Smuts Avenue
Johannesburg 2001

www.witspress.co.za

Compilation © Editors 2021
Chapters © Individual contributors 2021
Published edition © Wits University Press 2021
Cover image © Gavin Capps, Cattle being herded near a platinum mine shaft in a traditional authority area in the North West Province

First published 2021

http://dx.doi.org.10.18772/22021056796

978-1-77614-679-6 (Paperback)
978-1-77614-680-2 (Hardback)
978-1-77614-681-9 (Web PDF)
978-1-77614-682-6 (EPUB)

All rights reserved. No part of this publication may be reproduced, stored in a retrieval system, or transmitted in any form or by any means, electronic, mechanical, photocopying, recording or otherwise, without the written permission of the publisher, except in accordance with the provisions of the Copyright Act, Act 98 of 1978.

Project manager: Elaine Williams
Copyeditor: Colin Bundy
Proofreader: Alison Lockhart
Indexer: Elaine Williams
Cover design: Hothouse
Typeset in 10 point Minion Pro

# CONTENTS

| | | |
|---|---|---|
| MAP | | vii |
| ACRONYMS AND ABBREVIATIONS | | ix |
| PREFACE | *William Beinart* | xi |
| INTRODUCTION | Land, Law and Chiefs: Contested Histories and Current Struggles<br>*William Beinart* | 1 |
| CHAPTER 1 | Constitutional Court Judgments, Customary Law and Democratisation in South Africa<br>*Geoff Budlender* | 21 |
| CHAPTER 2 | Was 'Living Customary Law' There All Along?<br>*Derick Fay* | 35 |
| CHAPTER 3 | When Custom Divides 'Community': Legal Battles over Platinum in North West Province<br>*Sonwabile Mnwana* | 60 |
| CHAPTER 4 | Chiefs, Mines and the State in the Platinum Belt: The Bapo-ba-Mogale Traditional Community and Lonmin<br>*Gavin Capps* | 81 |
| CHAPTER 5 | Mining, Graves and Dispossession in Mpumalanga<br>*Dineo Skosana* | 104 |
| CHAPTER 6 | The Abuse of Interdicts by Traditional Leaders in South Africa<br>*Joanna Pickering and Ayesha Motala* | 121 |
| CHAPTER 7 | Resisting the Imposition of *Ubukhosi*: Contested Authority-Making in the Former Ciskei<br>*Thiyane Duda and Janine Ubink* | 141 |
| CHAPTER 8 | Black Landlords, Their Tenants and the Native Administration Act of 1927<br>*Khumisho Moguerane* | 164 |
| CHAPTER 9 | Customary Law and Landownership in the Eastern Cape<br>*Rosalie Kingwill* | 186 |

CHAPTER 10  A History of Communal Property Associations in South Africa
            *Tara Weinberg*                                                          208

CHAPTER 11  'This is Business Land': The Hlolweni Land Claim, 1983–2016
            *Raphael Chaskalson*                                                     229

CHAPTER 12  Restitution and Land Rights in the Eastern Cape:
            The Hlolweni, Mgungundlovu and Xolobeni Cases
            *William Beinart*                                                        247

CONTRIBUTORS                                                                         266
INDEX                                                                                271

*Location of key sites mentioned*

## ACRONYMS AND ABBREVIATIONS

| | |
|---|---|
| ACC | AmaHlathi Crisis Committee |
| ACLA | Advisory Commission on Land Allocation |
| AFRA | Association for Rural Advancement |
| ANC | African National Congress |
| AnCRA | Association for Community and Rural Advancement |
| BEE | black economic empowerment |
| BRC | Border Rural Committee |
| CLARA | Communal Land Rights Act |
| CNIP | Ciskei National Independence Party |
| CNP | Ciskei National Party |
| COBACO | Concerned Bakgatla Anti-Corruption Organisation |
| CONTRALESA | Congress of Traditional Leaders of South Africa |
| CPA | communal property association |
| D | account development account |
| DAFF | Department of Agriculture, Forestries and Fisheries |
| DLA | Department of Land Affairs |
| DRDLR | Department of Rural Development and Land Reform |
| GRC | General Royal Council |
| ha | hectare(s) |
| IBMR | Itereleng Bakgatla Mineral Resources (Pty) Ltd |
| IPILRA | Interim Protection of Informal Land Rights Act |
| JSC | Judicial Service Commission |
| km | kilometres |

| | |
|---|---|
| KTC | KwaGcina Traditional Council |
| LARC | Land and Accountability Research Centre |
| LGTA | Local Government and Traditional Affairs |
| LRC | Legal Resources Centre |
| MARTISA | Mining and Rural Transformation in Southern Africa |
| MKLM | Moses Kotane Local Municipality |
| MLRA | Marine Living Resources Act |
| MPA | Marine Protected Area |
| MPRDA | Mineral and Petroleum Resources Development Act |
| NFA | Native Farmers' Association |
| NGO | non-governmental organisation |
| NHRA | National Heritage Resources Act |
| NLC | National Land Committee |
| NPS | North Pondoland Sugar |
| PGS | Professional Grave Solutions (consultancy) |
| PP | Public Protector |
| PTO | permission to occupy |
| SADT | South African Development Trust |
| SANCO | South African National Civic Organisation |
| SANNC | South African Native National Congress |
| SCOPA | Standing Committee on Public Accounts |
| SPP | Surplus People Project |
| SWOP | Society, Work and Politics Institute |
| TA | Traditional Authorities or Tribal Authorities |
| TDC | Transkei Development Corporation |
| TLGFA | Traditional Leadership and Governance Framework Act |
| TRAC | Transvaal Rural Action Committee |
| TRACOR | Transkei Agricultural Corporation |
| UDM | United Democratic Movement |
| ULTRA | Upgrading of Land Tenure Rights Act |

# PREFACE

**William Beinart**

This edited collection illustrates contestations over land, law and political authority in South Africa's rural areas, focusing on popular rights. The chapters were initially presented at three workshops that addressed the theme of Contested Histories in the rural areas. The first was convened by Gavin Capps and Peter Delius in October 2015 at the University of the Witwatersrand.[1] It was prompted by the recognition that historians and social scientists were increasingly being drawn into legal contests over land and political authority in the contemporary South African countryside, both as expert witnesses in court cases and through the provision of research to government, communities and lawyers. The workshop sought to create a space to compare such engagement in applied research work.

Participants discussed the specific cases in which they had been involved and the broader context of research. Some reflected critically on their experiences of providing court testimony, as well as assisting lawyers, non-governmental organisations and communities. Some participants had been directly engaged in policy formation and legislative processes. A common theme concerned the importance of historical and anthropological research about land, chiefs, governance and custom in these debates. Participants agreed to continue the conversation through future workshops and to encourage younger researchers in this field, working at the interface between academic scholarship and public engagement.

A second workshop was organised in May 2016 by Aninka Claassens, with the assistance of Rosalie Kingwill and other colleagues at the Land and Accountability Research Centre (LARC), University of Cape Town. This was a larger event that honed in on the role of law and the impact of the Constitution (Act 108 of 1996) with regard to strategically pressing issues of land ownership and property rights in the former homelands, as well as the increasing significance of customary law. This workshop sought also to promote a positive exchange between academics and practitioners, especially lawyers. The LARC workshop assessed the research priorities necessary to mount a legal, historical and discursive challenge to the current government policy of prioritising the authority of traditional leaders and councils over land and rural governance. Detailed discussion was directed to the land rights of ordinary occupants and users. There were a number of outcomes, including a focused discussion of land legislation that led into recommendations to the High Level Panel that reported to Parliament in 2017.

A committee was also chosen (William Beinart, Gavin Capps, Thiyane Duda, Michelle Hay, Rosalie Kingwill, Khumisho Moguerane and Wilmien Wicomb) to promote further academic initiatives under the Contested Histories banner. This committee held a third workshop at Wits University in November 2017. About 15 people participated, most of whom presented papers that were discussed in detail; we included both established academics and those still completing their degrees. The primary purpose was to facilitate publication of case studies that illustrated the themes emerging in the first two workshops. These papers have been reworked and form the basis for this collection. Responsibility for the publication was devolved to William Beinart, Rosalie Kingwill and Gavin Capps. William Beinart did the bulk of the editing.

Thanks to Roshan Cader for her patience in steering this collection through the publication process and to Colin Bundy for his meticulous contribution to editing.

NOTE

1   This was hosted by Mining and Rural Transformation in Southern Africa (MARTISA) project, funded by the Ford Foundation and located in the Society, Work and Politics Institute (SWOP) at the University of the Witswatersrand (2013–2018). Thanks to these institutions for their financial and academic support.

INTRODUCTION

# Land, Law and Chiefs:
# Contested Histories and Current Struggles

William Beinart

## BACKGROUND

The past two decades have witnessed growing competition for landed resources across much of sub-Saharan Africa, generating pervasive conflict over the ownership and control of communal property and the systems of customary authority that typically mediate access to it (Peters 2004, 2013; Ubink and Amanor 2008; Capps 2016; Buthelezi, Skosana and Vale 2019). This collection brings together a range of essays that explore the ways in which these struggles are unfolding in the South African countryside. They focus particularly on the intersections between law, history and academic research in current efforts to advance popular rights to land. They also examine political conflicts, above all in relation to the powers of the chieftaincy within and beyond the areas of customary or communal landholding, largely in what were formerly defined as the 'black homelands' or 'Bantustans'. The backdrop to the collection is shaped by the confluence of two important developments in the post-apartheid era, which are simultaneously redrawing the contours of the rural political economy and intensifying contestation over its future direction.

The first of these developments arises from the distinctive character of South Africa's national land reform programme. After the official end of apartheid in 1994, the new African National Congress (ANC) government adopted a multipronged approach to undo the gross racial inequalities in access to and control over land arising from white political domination and apartheid. Laws were passed and policies developed providing for: the restitution of land to black people who had been forcibly dispossessed by the state after 1913; the subsidised redistribution of land from willing white sellers to black landholders; the reform of land tenure in the communal areas to clarify rights of occupation, ownership and use; the protection of informal and customary landholdings; and new instruments of collective ownership called communal property associations (CPAs). Since local land management in the Bantustans had typically (though not exclusively) been placed under chieftaincies or tribal authorities during apartheid, these interventions inevitably raised questions about the future role and powers of those institutions in the new dispensation.

The 1996 Constitution enshrined democracy, the rule of law and universal rights. It also recognised customary laws and practices, to the extent that they were compatible with the Constitution more broadly. This raises complex issues in relation to land reform and tenure. If customary law and landholding is to be retained and developed, it will be necessary to engage in historical and grassroots research in order to identify rules and practices. Given that many of the latter are inadequately recorded and currently contested, this is a challenging task for legal as well as historical and social research. Land reform and tenure upgrading within and beyond the areas of customary tenure has thus provided a rich field for contestation over historical evidence and interpretation. It has also proven an inherently political process – one intricately tied up with the shifting terrain of political competition and conflict as South Africa has wrestled with efforts to build a stable, inclusive democracy that simultaneously respects and amends inherited forms of custom and chiefly authority.

A second major development has been the changing economic status of the former homelands themselves. Under apartheid, they were largely cast as labour reserves for the mines, factories and farms located in 'white' South Africa, and as dumping grounds for the black populations whom the apartheid authorities attempted to remove from white-owned farmlands and the cities. While there were initiatives to promote a degree of local economic activity, such as irrigation projects and decentralised industries, particularly towards the end of the apartheid era, these rural zones largely remained residual to the wider national economy. When the ANC came to power they were the poorest and least developed parts of the country.

In recent years, however, the areas with customary tenure have increasingly been identified as repositories of valuable resources, both under and on the land, including high-demand minerals (platinum, chrome, titanium and coal), fertile soils, wildlife and marine reserves, as well as areas of outstanding natural beauty. Some are located close to the boundaries of rapidly expanding cities, such as Durban, where peri-urban land is at a premium. In other cases, land in Limpopo with valuable plantations of macadamia nuts and subtropical fruits has been transferred to collective ownership. Spending power in some of the former homeland towns, now regional hubs, has escalated. This has a stimulated a wave of investment by mining, agribusiness, construction, retail and tourism concerns, both local and multinational, which is beginning to transform pockets of the former homelands from rural backwaters to new growth frontiers in the post-apartheid economy. As land values have risen, so have struggles for its control, with new avenues opening for accumulation by chiefly and other local elites, while growing numbers of the rural poor are threatened with displacement and dispossession.

These conflicts have been given further impetus and direction by the manner in which the constitutional imperatives of tenure reform itself have been translated at the policy level. After a brief experiment with democratising rural relations in its first term (1994–1999), the ANC government has increasingly turned to chieftaincy as a means of governing the former homeland areas, reproducing apartheid-era jurisdictions (Claassens and Cousins 2008). Under President Mbeki (1999–2008), the Traditional Leadership and Governance Framework Act 41 of 2003 (TLGFA) gave chiefs formal recognition and the Communal Land Rights Act (CLARA) of 2004 made it likely that administration and control of land in these areas would fall under the traditional councils established in the TLGFA. CLARA was subsequently overturned by the Constitutional Court in 2010, largely on procedural grounds, and by 2019 it had not been replaced. While the direction of ANC's tenure reforms remains uncertain, government policy under President Zuma (2009–2018) was sympathetic to chiefs (Weinberg 2015; Beinart, Delius and Hay 2017; Buthelezi, Skosana and Vale 2019).

This pro-chieftaincy thrust has been reinforced under President Ramaphosa (2018 # to the present) by the Traditional and Khoi-San Leadership Act (Act 3 of 2019) and parallel legislation defining the juridical powers of chiefs. Although there are differences within the ANC and some government departments, traditional authorities are often seen as the prime representatives of rural community interests in relation to land-use decisions. Mining companies and the state tend to turn to them first as local business partners. Major new laws like the Mineral and Petroleum Resources Development Act (MPRDA) of 2002, and subsequent policies, are helping clear the way for such developments by requiring black economic empowerment (BEE) deals in new mining investment. Local chiefs and traditional councils have been in advantageous positions to become intermediaries. At the same time such interventions can further weaken popular land rights. Parallels can be seen more broadly elsewhere in Africa where relatively weak states devolve functions to corporate enterprises that connect with localised power structures (Comaroff and Comaroff 2018). In the South African case, the central state retains considerable control of mining development and seems to encourage such links.

Questions about how land should be governed are equally significant in areas that have been restituted or redistributed to black communities. Rights over such land, and economic developments on them, have also sometimes become contested in disputes that invoke historical and customary precedent. The courts have become a frequent recourse for such conflicts. This has in turn drawn in key actors such as public-interest lawyers, non-governmental organisations (NGOs) and rural activists, as well as academics who have expertise on the history of specific areas or on custom and social change.

This volume draws on the research and experiences of such people. While it cannot claim comprehensiveness in the choice of the cases it considers, either geographically or thematically, it nevertheless provides a rich snapshot of some of these issues as they have been rehearsed in key parts of the country, at different juridical and administrative levels, and with an eye to their deeper historical contexts.

## FOCUS AND THEMES

As noted, our main focus in this collection is on the regions of South Africa that fell under the Bantustans or homelands in the apartheid era. While they comprised at their height about 14 per cent of the country's area, they still include around a third of the country's population. The boundaries of the Bantustans are no longer statutory, and in certain respects are fluid, but their institutional legacy remains in the systems of landholding and local authority, which are substantially different from most of the rest of the country. They are largely still dominated by forms of customary, non-private or off-register land tenure and many of them still have chiefs and traditional councils as part of local governance.

A few chapters also consider the land that has been transferred from white private ownership, and from the state, to black communities. Most of these areas now fall under forms of collective ownership, either trusts, or CPAs that were established under Act 28 of 1996. Recent government figures (The Presidency, South Africa 2019) suggest that about 8.5 million ha or 10 per cent of the agricultural land in South Africa has been transferred through government land reform schemes of restitution (about four per cent) and redistribution (about six per cent). The state is keeping direct ownership of an increasing amount of redistributed land, and leasing it to beneficiaries, rather than transferring it directly to CPAs.

At the outset it is important not to create rigid boundaries in thinking about the white-owned farms and the former Bantustans, nor urban and rural zones. These are not disconnected spaces geographically nor in the lives of many people. We should think about these issues outside of silos and in the context of wider processes of economic and social transformation now facing South Africa. Historically, many people have moved between these areas, as migrants, as workers and as the victims of forced removals. In some parts of the country, privately owned farmlands, communal areas and peri-urban settlements are juxtaposed and their social networks are meshed. The former homelands include growing cities and large peri-urban settlements. The issues addressed in this volume impinge on all South Africans. Nevertheless, poverty still remains most persistently entrenched in the areas of customary landholding and traditional systems of authority. Protecting the rights of poor families and communities in these areas is a priority. So too is new thinking about effective landholding and governance in addressing poverty and marginalisation.

There are four main interlinked and overarching concerns in the chapters of this volume. Firstly, several chapters assess the recent history of landholding and rural authority in South Africa. They demonstrate wide diversity in both, reflecting historical continuities and the uneven impact of apartheid. While chieftaincy often features as a central element in present claims and disputes to authority, some chapters show that rural communities developed new forms of organisation and landholding where traditional leaders featured only marginally. Contributors explore hybrid forms of local authority and landholding institutions that involve in varying degree the state, chiefs, communities and private landholders.

Secondly, with regard to the theme of the chieftaincy, the chapters discuss somewhat contradictory trends. On the one hand, they provide evidence that chiefs and traditional councils are becoming entrenched in the rural areas and are trying to assert control over land, rural resources such as minerals, and local politics. On the other hand, they show push-back from groups that reject the central role of chieftaincy in land administration and local government. They also discuss recent court judgments that have applied the Constitution to uphold the rights of communities, families or individuals where they are threatened by chiefs or external agencies such as mining companies.

Thirdly, chapters illustrate and debate customary law. The South African Constitution recognises customary law and the courts are attempting to incorporate and develop this branch of jurisprudence. The Constitutional Court has accepted that customary law is not static and has begun to evolve a 'living customary law'. Although still a fluid area, the Constitutional Court, in contrast to some regional courts, tends to favour a view of customary law that accords with the rights and protections of all South Africans as specified in the Constitution. This has resulted in judgments that run counter to traditionalist hierarchies and gender inequality. A number of chapters explore the dynamic character of land tenure on the ground, which may influence the content of living customary law.

Fourthly, chapters analyse the deployment of history in contemporary struggles and debates around these contested issues. A few discuss in some detail historical antecedents to current conflicts over land. More generally, chapters focus on different versions of local histories and their promotion in claims over land and chieftaincy, not least in the platinum belt. The ANC government instituted an official inquiry into chieftaincy disputes through the Nhlapo Commission, which was tasked with discovering legitimate succession. In these disputes, historical evidence about incumbency as well as rules and practices of succession have been central.

The Restitution of Land Rights Act (22 of 1994) also put a premium on historical and legal research to provide evidence that communities or individuals were deprived of their land by racial legislation after 1913. When such cases come to court, research is inevitably required to identify the history of landholding and the process of dispossession. The composition and boundaries of claimant communities are also sometimes contested because they can result in decisions that exclude some families from the benefits of land claims.

## ACADEMICS, APPLIED RESEARCH AND COURT CASES

Land reform has been a central issue for academics in South Africa and issues of tenure became of particular importance in relation to the legal challenge to the Communal Land Rights Act of 2004 (Hall and Ntsebeza 2007; James 2007; Walker 2008; Claassens and Cousins 2008). As the chapters in this volume record, historians and social scientists have frequently contributed research to the land restitution process in South Africa, as well as to claims and cases around the resolution of tenure disputes, overlapping rights, chieftaincy and customary law. We have encouraged contributors to illustrate and analyse their engagement, or at least to acknowledge how their ideas have developed in relation to public policy, claims and court cases. Contributors do not agree on all points and some differences can be discerned in the chapters. Each expresses the individual views of the contributor, and although they have been discussed collectively, we have not tried to impose uniformity. All, however, share a concern with democratic processes, with equality and with popular rights in South Africa. The chapters are critical both of the state and chiefs when they are judged to have worked against such outcomes.

In court cases and investigations that have arisen around such issues, academic historians and other experts are sometimes called upon to give evidence. In the *Salem* land claim case,[1] two noted historians appeared for opposite sides (Ross 2018). This case also demonstrates a trend where white landowners are increasingly hiring their own archival researchers to defend their land against claims. Courts, land commissioners and lawyers weigh evidence but often require expanded research and the seal of expert authentication. While courts seek certainty in a system that is still largely premised on conceptions of ownership rooted in common law, 'living customary law' is increasingly being recognised, introducing an element of legal flexibility. As the public-interest lawyer Geoff Budlender notes, decisions by courts, commissions and administrative bodies are taking into account a complex range of histories and rules. There have not, however, been sufficient judgments to provide decisive precedents in all areas of law and living customary law remains elusive in many areas. A number of chapters raise further questions about the relationship between legislative and customary law.

Derick Fay analyses the role of experts in some detail, showing how their contributions are shaped by the requirements of cases but also have the potential to influence legal arguments and court decisions. Their engagement in legal processes also defines their research in particular ways and brings them into new kinds of relationships with lawyers, officials, their research subjects, and with one another. This poses questions about the nature of their expertise: how did they develop their knowledge and what are the configurations of research and writing that underpin its production? Fay notes that during his anthropological training, the idea of 'custom' was considered outdated and static; anthropologists focused more on social practice and social change. However, the invocation of living customary law by South African courts has both necessitated working with this concept and provided a vehicle for rethinking customary practices as dynamic. Broadly speaking, experts have to operate within the conceptual ground rules being set by legislation, lawyers and courts, though they can try to introduce alternative approaches. Interpretation of the term 'community' is a case in point and its meaning is by no means identical in different legislation and judgments.

Research and evidence for court cases can present problems for academics. Historians, for example, have the freedom to explore multiple vantage points, to illustrate different interpretations and to qualify their arguments. Although they try to develop arguments consistent with their evidence, this is sometimes less uniform, less complete or messier than they would like (Ross 2018; Fay, Kingwill and Beinart in this volume). Lawyers deal with similar evidence and in many respects develop similar modes of argument. Lawyers also need to consider different interpretations in order to anticipate how their opponents may be thinking. But in general, they are compelled to avoid explicating alternative lines of argument that may be useful to their opponents. Lawyers need to ensure, as far as possible, that their evidence and argument is consistent with a version of the law as it stands, or a convincing development of the law. Academics working on court cases and claims have sometimes to be guided by lawyers both in the specific focus of their research and in constraining perspectives that could disable the case of the clients they are supporting.

Communities develop their own understandings of history. These are usually based largely on oral material, although some have access to archives and books that they use to strengthen claims. Their access to such materials is usually limited and for professional historians, their versions of history are often incomplete or inadequately contextualised. Sometimes they are clearly self-serving, but they also throw important light on historical processes that have not been adequately reported in the archives or in dominant regional narratives (Mager and Velelo 2018; Mnwana, and Duda and Ubink in this volume). Vernacular and oral evidence may also be mobilised to good effect in restitution claims and court cases. In this context, training and interviewing experience in such disciplines as history and anthropology, where extensive oral material is often recorded, is valuable. Academics can sometimes explain how memories and narratives are established, and become powerful vehicles for community claims and identities, even when they may not accord fully with other evidence.

Discussion in the workshops where these chapters originated illustrated the complexities faced by academic researchers acting as experts. Those contributing to this collection have nevertheless been keen to play this role, because they perceive it to be assisting processes of change in South Africa. The hurdles set by legislation such as the Restitution Act were perhaps higher and more demanding than many expected – both in relation to the law and the scale and complexity of evidence required. Academic researchers may also have policy agendas, or at least wish to support pro bono lawyers, such as the Legal Resources Centre (LRC), who have taken up cases on behalf of impoverished communities and worked creatively with the Constitution. The LRC and associated lawyers have undoubtedly influenced the direction of judgments, such as the *Richtersveld* case (2003),[2] and urged the courts to take account of socio-economic rights. Together with attorneys such as Richard Spoor, they have also been at the forefront of challenges to mining developments that threaten community land rights.

## POST-APARTHEID CHIEFTAINCY

With the transition to democracy, chiefs succeeded in ensuring that traditional leadership was recognised in the 1996 Constitution (Section 211) 'according to customary law' (Oomen 2005; Ntsebeza 2011). Though constrained by the Constitution, their influence on the government has increased considerably, particularly through the vehicle of the Congress of Traditional Leaders of South Africa (CONTRALESA). The TLGFA (2003) formalised the status of 'senior traditional leaders' and traditional councils. With the recognition came an influx of applications for, and disputes around, chieftaincy positions, some submitted to the Nhlapo Commission, established by the 2003 Act.

As mentioned above, the Restitution Act has further levered and mobilised chiefs to claim land on the basis of authority over landholding. Raphael Chaskalson shows how a chief claimed control of land in Bizana, in the former Transkei, following a successful restitution case from which the traditional council had had been excluded. Chapters by Mnwana, Pickering and Motala, and Duda and Ubink argue that chiefs have asserted power through effective political mobilisation at local, provincial and central government level. The TLGFA recognised many apartheid-era boundaries, but simultaneously tried to make traditional councils more democratic by introducing the requirement that 40 per cent of their members should be elected and one-third women. Traditional council membership requirements have, however, often been ignored (Buthelezi and Skosana 2018; Capps in this volume).

Provinces that contained former homelands passed their own laws, recognising the role of chiefs, who were also represented in provincial houses of traditional leaders; this and parallel developments in the legal sphere were a further carry-over from the Bantustans (Claassens and Budlender 2013; Delius 2019). The TLGFA and its provincial iterations did not devolve control over land and other administrative functions to traditional councils; this has to be specified in legislation. But at the local level, chiefs have often succeeded in inserting themselves as intermediaries between the central state and rural people. In certain respects, they run a parallel system of governance to elected local authorities. The ANC sees them as valuable in delivering the rural vote and the institution does have some grassroots support, especially where local government institutions are ineffective or corrupt.

As Thiyane Duda and Janine Ubink note, chiefs were associated with unpopular apartheid policies in much of the former Ciskei area of the Eastern Cape. But the Eastern Cape provincial government has been sympathetic to their political revival, even in contexts where local communities strongly contest this model. For example, a major legal case in Cala focused on the right of people of a particular administrative area to elect their own headman in line with historical practice, rather than accept a nominee of the local chief, who was supported by the province. Drawing on detailed evidence from University of Cape Town academic Lungisile Ntsebeza, the judge ruled in favour of the community. He argued that the Framework Act did not give this power to chiefs and the customary practice of the area should be accepted. This was an important example of a court being guided by the constitutional provision that traditional leadership should operate democratically. However, the legal victory was to a significant degree dependent on research by academic experts and the work of pro bono lawyers. Nor was it immediately enforced. In their chapter on a parallel case in Keiskammahoek, Duda and Ubink find evidence of an alliance between the Eastern Cape government and traditional leaders. In KwaZulu-Natal, especially, this authority seems to be spreading beyond the former homeland area over land transferred to CPAs (Hornby et. al. 2017).

Speaking of South Africa as a whole, Delius (2019: 8–9), who has been researching land restitution cases in Limpopo and Mpumalanga for the Land Claims Commission and Court, sees 'growing ethnic mobilization and conflict at local levels with long submerged identities being resuscitated by individuals and groups in pursuit of office' and notes how such processes 'have also contributed to a growing emphasis on and debate about which groups are "indigenous" and/or were the original rulers'. Duda and Ubink provide a specific example in the former Ciskei. Imposing chiefs against popular wishes and strengthening their control over village communities can have far-reaching political consequences within areas of customary landholding and beyond. The issue is not whether individual chiefs are 'good' or 'bad', but the structural problems that arise by extending controls over land, resources and administration to such intermediaries.

Sonwabile Mnwana, and Joanna Pickering and Ayesha Motala illustrate that in some cases, and particularly in the Bakgatla-ba-Kgafela area of North West Province, chiefs attempted to control protest against their authority by banning meetings. When challenged, they went to court to get interdicts prohibiting meetings that were considered hostile, ostensibly on the strength of their customary powers. While a lower court granted these interdicts, the Constitutional Court struck them down in *Pilane* (2013) on the grounds that they violated constitutional rights to freedom of expression, association and assembly; living customary law should come into line with constitutional principles.[3] The judgment was considered a major legal victory for constitutional freedoms and customary rights. However, evidence again suggests that the judgment has not been uniformly respected. Interdicts and other court orders continue to be sought and obtained by traditional leaders to silence and restrain their critics, thus enabling them to avoid dialogue or customary dispute resolution forums. This has other consequences, also, in that such restrictive political authority can inhibit open party politics in the villages.

## MINING AND CONTROL OF LAND

Mining in South Africa was initially highly concentrated, especially in the gold mines of the Witwatersrand and Free State. It largely fell within areas of private property in 'white' South Africa; or, historically, the process of colonisation resulted in private property being demarcated where land was seen to have promise for minerals. This pattern has changed in recent decades. The MPRDA of 2002 eliminated private ownership of mineral rights and vested it in the people of South Africa under the custodianship of the state – 'common property and subjected to the disposition of the state' (Capps 2012). Under the MPRDA, mining and production rights are governed by state permits. Mining has become increasingly decentralised in search of newly valuable minerals such as platinum, in which employment overtook gold by 2010. By chance major platinum deposits fell within the former homelands, particularly Bophuthatswana – now in North West Province. The resulting competition for resources and contestation over land administration in mineral-rich areas has drawn in chiefs, communities, lawyers and academics and was a significant element in the decision by Gavin Capps and the Society, Work and Politics Institute (SWOP) at the University of the Witwatersrand to convene the first Contested Histories workshop.

In this volume, Capps focuses specifically on the Bapo-ba-Mogale case in the context of the political economy of chiefly reassertion in North West Province. He argues more generally (Capps 2010: 27–34, 2016) that Mahmood Mamdani (1996) places too one-sided an emphasis on the political role of modern chieftaincy as 'decentralised despotism'. A feature of the democratic era in South Africa has been the increasing economic role played by chiefs as a form of landed power, especially in areas where mining takes place under their jurisdiction. Chiefs' capacity to retain administrative control over mineral-rich communal land has placed them in a strong position as intermediaries to negotiate with, and benefit from, mining corporations. The latter need access to land and natural resources and find it easier to deal with an apparently representative and single-entry institution. In cases like the Bafokeng and Bapo-ba-Mogale, this has enabled traditional authorities to appropriate mineral revenues and in some instances demand rewards for facilitating access. In the Bapo-ba-Mogale case (the collective membership of which is colloquially referred to as 'the Bapo'), this involved working with provincial officials and politicians who were also able to take advantage of divisions within the ruling lineage and the complex transactions involved. These new processes of accumulation have generated conflicts over the control of the monetary rewards of mining, with credible evidence pointing to the disappearance thereof. Chiefs are not, however, private landowners and are unable to benefit exclusively: the income is to some degree redistributed for public projects and to cement political support in order to reproduce their effective control over this property. There is a tension between accumulation by those in position and the remaining 'communal' elements in ownership.

In these cases, the rapid development of mining created competition for resources in the shape of chieftaincy disputes and also land disputes.

Mnwana also discusses post-apartheid laws regulating mineral rights, particularly the MPRDA and its accompanying regulations. He focuses on the Bakgatla-ba-Kgafela Traditional Authority on the platinum belt that has significant control over revenues from platinum mining in the area. In seeking to redress past injustices by transforming relationships between the mining companies and local communities, this legislation included greater state control over licensing, BEE, mine-community partnerships and social labour plans as requirements for mining companies. The state has encouraged communities who previously received royalty compensations for loss of land due to mining to convert their royalties into equity shares (see also Capps in this volume). These initiatives have reinforced the position of chiefs, as assumed custodians of communal resources and as mediators of mineral-led development and mining deals. The Traditional and Khoi-San Leadership Act (2019) seems potentially to enhance their power in contracting with outside enterprises.

Chiefs enter into mining contracts and receive royalties and dividends on behalf of rural residents who live in the mineral-rich traditional authority areas. This traditional-elite-mediated model of community participation in the mining industry has received increased academic and media attention, particularly since the 2012 Marikana massacre. In the face of protracted labour unrest in the platinum sector and the decline in platinum prices between 2011 and 2018, Mnwana argues that the dominant view propagated by the government, mining companies and the chiefs is to secure stability through the existing arrangements. This has reinforced land dispossession as local chiefs attempt to gain control over mining revenues by claims to land on the basis of 'tribal' identity. Claimants whose ancestors jointly bought private land, only to see it subsumed under chieftaincies during the era of segregation and apartheid, have tried to reassert these historical rights. In some cases, they see no alternative but to shift their meaning of land towards exclusive group claims and histories. The court battles highlighted in Mnwana's chapter address this link between national policy, control over land and rural political authority.

The history of mining in Bafokeng in the Rustenburg region of North West Province provides a parallel case that is not discussed in detail in our chapters. Capps (2016) notes that the Bafokeng and the Rustenburg region as a whole was distinguished by a particularly high concentration of African land-buying syndicates (including mineral rights) in the late nineteenth and early twentieth centuries.[4] However, the land was progressively registered to the state 'in trust' for a recognised chief and 'tribe'. This fusion of the legal apparatus of land title with broader notions of both 'state' and 'tribal' trusteeship over Africans produced a hybrid form of tenure. When these areas fell within Bantustans, proprietorial control was frequently contested between chiefly authorities and the Bantustan regimes, as 'tribal' and 'state' trustees respectively, particularly as the latter became increasingly reliant on the tax and royalty revenues generated by mining.[5]

Following the democratic elections of April 1994, the homelands were formally abolished and their territories reincorporated into the new unitary South African state. However, some of the laws that governed them remained in place at the provincial level. The courts effectively established the Bafokeng chiefs as intermediaries, who gained a significantly improved royalty and an equity stake in platinum production. In 2007, the Traditional Council became the largest shareholder in a major platinum producer and the Bafokeng chieftaincy corporatised its mining assets into a holding company that diversified into banking, telecoms and construction. As John Comaroff and Jean Comaroff (2009) argue, ethnic identity has been commercialised in parts of South Africa. In the Bafokeng case, financial dealings were highly professionalised, but in the case of the Bapo, where this was not achieved, Capps shows how provincial administrators and rival chiefly factions were able to siphon off a great deal of money by exploiting the continuing administrative ambiguities around 'tribal' and 'state' trusteeship. Mnwana and Capps illustrate how disputes over resources become entangled with issues of legitimacy, succession and competition for office. They can also involve some communities attempting to secede from the traditional authority to which they have historically been connected. Discussions of customary land law in this context (Peters 2004; Moguerane in this volume) attest to its negotiability and adaptability.

Dineo Skosana focuses on another element of contestation in relation to occupation of land for mining. The issue of grave sites has been significant in community claims to land (James 2009). At Tweefontein coal mine in Mpumalanga, multinational mining company Glencore removed graves in order to pursue mining operations. The African families affected felt that they were inadequately consulted and compensated. There was not opportunity to conduct appropriate ceremonies and relocation exacted a heavy psychological and physical toll on the families. Neither Glencore nor the state recognised the significance of ancestors in the arrangements made for the removal. This question became further complicated by land claims.

Skosana argues more generally that the National Heritage Resource Act (1999), under which such removals are regulated, is inadequate in catering for intangible heritage and particularly for the issues that are raised in this case. At the same time the MPRDA provides for strong rights by the holders of mining licences, as opposed to those who might be affected by mining, and tends to override the protection of heritage and specifically graves. This results in further marginalisation of those who already had weak legal rights to land and resources. For those who are dispossessed, the graves matter both because of their connection to their ancestors and because their removal is seen to perpetuate historical injustices.

## LIVING CUSTOMARY LAW

South African constitutional jurisprudence has incorporated and developed the notion of 'living customary law'. Budlender analyses major constitutional court judgments and argues that this has become an increasingly diverse and sustained legal field where popular rights are generally accepted and developed. He suggests that the judiciary is developing some degree of consistency on a case-by-case basis by interpreting the Constitution and applying it to the field of customary law. There is also evidence of the development of a body of law based on precedent. In certain respects, the precepts of living customary law are being developed through the courts rather than in legislation. But there is also evidence of courts and legislature moving in some diverging directions – particularly in relation to the powers of traditional leaders.

Fay explores the operation of living customary law in the *Gongqose* case (2012) near Dwesa-Cwebe reserve on the Eastern Cape coast.[6] Fay became an expert witness because of earlier ethnographic fieldwork in the area, so that he could attest to the nature of customary practice before the issue came to the courts. The *Richtersveld* land restitution claim (2003) and the *Bhe* judgment (2004),[7] which concerned the rule of male primogeniture in customary law of succession and inheritance, were key to the Constitutional Court's jurisprudence in this field. Aninka Claassens and Geoff Budlender (2013) noted that judgments were informed not only by old authorities but by contemporary everyday practice with an eye on socio-economic rights. These ideas were developed in Claassens and Ben Cousins (2008) who argued for a customary law that should not be formulated in ways that might support authoritarian or top-down rural hierarchies.

The *Gongqose* case concerned rights to marine resources under customary law at Dwesa-Cwebe, for those whose ancestors had long resided in the area. Those who were accused of contravening the law regulating fishing won their case in the Constitutional Court after judicial disagreement at lower levels. The LRC found funding to take this matter to the highest level in order to establish a legal principle and precedent. The question arose as to whether conservationist legislation designed to protect such natural resources negated customary rights. An expert witness for the state argued that the legislation should have priority and that fishing, especially with newer technology, could not be seen as customary and could not continue unregulated by the state. But the ethnographic evidence showed that such rights had been exercised over a long period of time and the court focused on the recognition of living customary law rather than the precise practice of fishing. The judgment gave the community continued access to marine natural resources, although this does leave open important issues in relation to the commercialisation of customary rights and the limits of conservationist controls.

## WHO OWNS THE LAND? THE NATURE AND STATUS OF CUSTOMARY LANDHOLDING

Living customary law might also apply to landholding in the former homelands but this has not yet been decisively established by the courts. Chaskalson explores some of the issues in relation to the *Hlolweni* land claim in Bizana, former Transkei, settled in court in 2010.[8] Following annexation, land was regulated by government proclamations that gave the state overarching power, but during the apartheid era there was a tendency to accept increasing control by chiefs. Chaskalson and Beinart discuss an alternative interpretation based around the writings of Alastair Kerr (1953, 1990), Professor of Customary Law at Rhodes University, who was one of the few to publish on this question. He saw the role of both chiefs and the state as largely administrative. Land once granted could not easily be confiscated and in regard to residential plots and arable fields, rights amounted to a form of ownership. Budlender and Johan Latsky (1991) adopted this idea, not so much because they wished to equate customary and private ownership, but in order to emphasise the strength of rights accorded in customary tenure. Claassens and Cousins (2008) emphasised the security of rights in such systems as well as the rights to exclude outsiders. However, they placed more emphasis on collective controls, particularly over commonage and natural resources such as forests or, Fay would add, fisheries. Beinart emphasises the strength of family rights and limitations on chiefly and collective community authority. He argues that living customary law should be defined to recognise and prioritise such rights.

Chaskalson, however, drawing on Sara Berry's *No Condition is Permanent* (1993), argues that local understandings of landownership and tenure in the former homelands are not static. The *Hlolweni* case shows that three different understandings of rights to the same piece of land evolved over a relatively short period, sometimes at the expense of household entitlements. The case arose over a restitution claim for about 10 000 ha that had been carved out of Bizana district for a sugar plantation and smallholder scheme under the Transkei government. The claimants were those displaced by the scheme but the sugar smallholders also contested their right to the land. The claimants were successful, based on their rights as previous holders of residential and arable plots with rights to grazing land. After they had won their case, the local chief claimed the land should come under the traditional council. All three parties seemed to agree that the old, family-based rights in the land had lapsed. These ideas were not necessarily imposed from above by a chief, but were generated by the claimants who wished to use the area as 'business land' for large-scale commercial agriculture, a shopping mall and other developments. Living customary law becomes particularly complex in this context.

Moguerane adds deeper historical context by exploring the nature of landholding in the early twentieth century. She shows how privately owned farms in the Barolong, Tswana-speaking areas became increasingly communalised. In part this was a result of government intervention and segregationist legislation that was, at that stage, intent on breaking down the control by chiefs over the land. However, Khumisho Moguerane also makes an innovative argument to the effect that ordinary landholders, who had previously paid rent to the chiefs, asserted their claims to land. Thus the making of the commonage in the Barolong Molopo reserve was in part a result of this pressure from below, in the period after colonisation. Her chapter again shows historical contestation over land, and over ideas about property. It suggests that caution should be exercised in assuming the customary law has remained static and has long been entrenched in all the former homeland areas. Private property became increasingly barred to African people after the Natives Land Act (1913) and the Native Administration Act (1927). This analysis is echoed in Chaskalson's chapter, which also explores changes in landholding that were generated from below, rather than simply being imposed from above. Simultaneously, those commoners who gained access to land increasingly established a form of ownership in practice. In this respect, her arguments tie in with Beinart's about the significance of family-based property on customary land.

Rosalie Kingwill examines another variation of the history and character of African landholding. Her cases are based on land that was allocated in individual title in the nineteenth century Cape (Kingwill 2014). Over the course of time it continued to be held by the successors in the form of family property in private tenure. The land was seldom sold and usually regarded by families as a long-term asset. Elements of African customary norms and concepts of property were infused into the ownership of private, titled landholdings. In the examples provided, the definition of family membership for the purposes of access to land includes all categories of kin, without having to be named or quantified. The argument formed around the case studies suggests that it takes more than title to create practices of private ownership that involve alienation, or narrow systems of inheritance and exclusion. Kingwill explores such hybrid forms of ownership and develops a gendered approach in analysing access to such land.

Simultaneously, after 1994, the Department of Land Affairs moved away from the permission to occupy (PTO) certificates, which had been the most general recognition of land rights in the homelands. These were problematic in several respects: they were dependent on government proclamations and Bantustan legislation of increasingly dubious validity and they were also very largely registered to men. But the absence of any central system of record has been a major change, leaving a legacy of uncertainty in the rural areas. The early attempts to develop new legislation governing customary forms of tenure under the new Constitution were informed by democratic, communalist ideas. But attempts to legislate these failed with the termination in 1999 of Minister Derek Hanekom's tenure at the Department of Land Affairs. CLARA, the alternative legislation passed in 2004, placed greater emphasis on traditional authorities and was declared unconstitutional in 2010. Replacement Bills were circulated in 2015 and 2017 but have not yet been finalised.

Tara Weinberg discusses how some of these changing ideas were formulated in the Communal Property Associations Act 28 of 1996. The Act made provision for group or community control of land that was transferred under the land reform programme and also in effect provided a vehicle for living customary practices. She argues that this was not imposed from above by the new state but emerged also from community mobilisation and debates as the prospect of new land became available through restitution and redistribution. The CPAs, as collectivities, became private owners of land with title. But rights within the farm depended on the CPA constitution and the practices developed by such landholding groups. Thus, land reform established a new hybrid form of landownership, drawing on some the customary practices, but different from them both in the formal rights of collective ownership and the capacity of communities to make their own rules.

Collectively the chapters on tenure argue for the importance of hybrid forms and ideas, whether resulting from long-established title, as in Kingwill's case, or land held in customary tenure. They all emphasise that chiefs have not been continuously in control of land allocation – and some lay emphasis on the strength of family rights, akin to ownership. Ideas about customary landholding are diverse and changing. But Beinart suggests that we are left without a clear statement in law about the nature of customary land rights held by families and that this is an urgent priority in a context where such rights are increasingly threatened. While the Interim Protection of Informal Land Rights Act (IPILRA) of 1996 provides a legal defence again dispossession of informal and customary landholdings, it has little bureaucratic support and makes certain exceptions. The recent judgments in the *Maledu* and *Baleni* cases, both handed down in 2018, may seem to have established that full and informed consent by the relevant customary landholders is now necessary before mining can take place.[9] Agreement by the chief and traditional council is not sufficient. The landholders, by implication, should also be beneficiaries of development, if they agree to it, and receive full compensation. Yet it has taken cases funded by pro bono lawyers, opposed by the state, to achieve this outcome and government responses to these judgments suggest that they are not entirely secure. The courts and the executive again seem to be pursuing different priorities. Nor do these judgments give a clear statement about the content of customary and informal land rights.

Some argue that it is best to leave customary land tenure, properly protected against dispossession, to be regulated at a local level. This is also an attractive route for those who are opposed to the commodification of land and titling, which may lead to alienation. However, there are many examples in our chapters of external intrusions on customary land or threats from chiefs and local accumulators. Customary practices do not always seem to provide sufficient protection against dispossession. The passing of the 2019 Traditional and Khoi-San Leadership Act may reinforce these dangers of accumulation from above. In this context, there is increasing advocacy of a form of land registration at the level of the family. The High Level Panel report (Parliament 2017) and the Presidential Advisory Panel on Land Reform and Agriculture (2019) both supported this route. We hope that the chapters collected in this volume may help to inform this continuing debate about land, customary law, contested history and local political authority. Although the chapters are not in agreement on all points, and do not all specifically focus on policy, collectively they offer an alternative approach to current routes being pursued by the government.

NOTES

1. Salem Party Club and Others v Salem Community and Others (CCT 26/17) [2017] ZACC 46 (11 December 2017) ('*Salem*').
2. Alexkor Ltd v Richtersveld Community and Others (CCT 19/03) [2003] ZACC 18; 2004 (5) SA 460 (CC) 2003 (12) BCLR 1301 (CC) (14 October 2003) ('*Richtersveld*').
3. Pilane and Another v Pilane and Another (CCT 46/12) [2013] ZACC 3; 2013 (4) BCLR 431 (CC) (28 February 2013) ('*Pilane*').
4. The following draws on Capps (2010: 153–80, 252–62). See also Capps (2012: 71–2) for a more condensed version.

5   See Gavin Capps, 'Full Research Report on Land and Political Histories in Bafokeng', commissioned by the Legal Resources Centre. Submitted as Third Respondent's Answering Affidavit in the Matter of Royal Bafokeng Nation v Minister of Rural Development and 15 Others, 999/2008 [2008] ZANWHC, April 2011.
6   S v Gongqose, Elliotdale Magistrate's Court E382/10 (unreported 2012) ('*Gongqose*')
7   Bhe and Others v Khayelitsha Magistrate and Others [2004] ZACC 17 ('*Bhe*').
8   Hlolweni, Mfolozi and Etyeni Communities v North Pondoland Sugar [2003] LCC41/03 [Judgment 2010] ('*Hlolweni*').
9   Maledu and Others v Itereleng Bakgatla Mineral Resources (Pty) Ltd and Another (CCT 265/17) [2018] ZACC 41 (25 October 2018) ('*Maledu*'); Baleni and Others v Minister of Resources and Others (73768/2016) [2018] ZAGPPHC 829 (22 November 2018) ('*Baleni*').

REFERENCES

Beinart, William, Peter Delius and Michelle Hay. 2017. *Rights to Land: A Guide to Tenure Upgrading and Restitution in South Africa*. Johannesburg: Jacana Media.
Berry, Sara S. 1993. *No Condition is Permanent: The Social Dynamics of Agrarian Change in Sub-Saharan Africa*. Madison: Wisconsin University Press.
Buthelezi, Mbongiseni and Dineo Skosana. 2018. 'The Salience of Chiefs in Post-Apartheid South Africa: Reflections on the Nhlapo Commission'. In *The Politics of Custom: Chiefship, Capital and the State in Contemporary Africa*, edited by John L. Comaroff and Jean Comaroff, 110–133. Chicago: University of Chicago Press and Johannesburg: Wits University Press.
Buthelezi, Mbongiseni, Dineo Skosana and Beth Vale, eds. 2019. *Traditional Leaders in a Democracy: Resources, Respect and Resistance*. Johannesburg: Mapungubwe Institute for Strategic Reflection.
Budlender, Geoff and Johan Latsky. 1991. 'Unravelling Rights to Land in Rural Race Zones'. In *A Harvest of Discontent: The Land Question in South Africa*, edited by Michael de Klerk, 115–138. Cape Town: Institute for Democratic Alternatives in South Africa (IDASA).
Capps, Gavin. 2010. 'Tribal-landed Property: The Political Economy of the Bafokeng Chieftaincy, South Africa, 1837–1994'. PhD. Diss., London School of Economics and Political Science.
Capps, Gavin. 2012. 'A Bourgeois Reform with Social Justice? The Contradictions of the Mineral Development Bill and Black Economic Empowerment in the South African Platinum Mining Industry'. *Review of African Political Economy* 39, no. 132 (2013): 315–333.
Capps, Gavin. 2016. 'Tribal-Landed Property: The Value of the Chieftaincy in Contemporary Africa'. *Journal of Agrarian Change* 16, no. 3 (2016): 452–477.
Claassens, Aninka and Geoff Budlender. 2013. 'Transformative Constitutionalism and Customary Law'. *Constitutional Court Review* 6: 75–104.
Claassens, Aninka and Ben Cousins, eds. 2008. *Land, Power and Custom: Controversies Generated by South Africa's Communal Land Rights Act*. Cape Town: UCT Press.
Comaroff, John L. and Jean Comaroff. 2009. *Ethnicity, Inc*. Chicago: University of Chicago Press.
Comaroff, John L. and Jean Comaroff, eds. 2018. *The Politics of Custom: Chiefship, Capital and the State in Contemporary Africa*. Chicago: University of Chicago Press and Johannesburg: Wits University Press.

Delius, Peter. 2019. 'Mistaking Form for Substance: The Disjuncture between Pre-Colonial Dynamics and Post-Colonial Policies in Relation to the Role of Chiefs'. Draft paper presented at the conference 'Citizenship and Accountability: Litigating Customary Law and Traditional Leadership under South Africa's Constitution' 17–18 June 2019, Bonavero Institute of Human Rights, University of Oxford.

Hall, Ruth and Lungisile Ntsebeza, eds. 2007. *The Land Question in South Africa: The Challenge of Transformation and Redistribution*. Cape Town: HSRC Press.

Hornby, Donna, Rosalie Kingwill, Lauren Royston and Ben Cousins, eds. 2017. *Untitled: Securing Land Tenure in Urban and Rural South Africa*. Pietermaritzburg: University of KwaZulu-Natal Press.

James, Deborah. 2007. *Gaining Ground? 'Rights' and 'Property' in South African Land Reform*. Abingdon: Routledge-Cavendish.

James, Deborah. 2009. 'Burial Sites, Informal Rights and Lost Kingdoms: Contesting Land Claims in Mpumalanga, South Africa'. *Africa* 79, no. 2 (2009): 228–251.

Kerr, Alaistair J. 1953. *The Native Common Law of Immovable Property in South Africa*. Durban: Butterworth.

Kerr, Alastair J. 1990. *The Customary Law of Immovable Property and of Succession*. Grahamstown: Grocott and Sherry.

Kingwill, Rosalie. 2014. 'Papering over the Cracks: An Ethnography of Land Title in the Eastern Cape'. *Kronos* 40, no. 1: 241–268.

Mager, Anne K. and Phiko Jeffrey Velelo. 2018. *The House of Tshatshu. Power, Politics and Chiefs North-West of the Great Kei River c. 1818–2018*. Cape Town: UCT Press.

Mamdani, Mahmood. 1996. *Citizen and Subject: Contemporary Africa and the Legacy of Late Colonialism*. Princeton: Princeton University Press.

Ntsebeza, Lungisile. 2011. 'Traditional Authorities and Democracy: Are We back to Apartheid?' In *The Fate of the Eastern Cape: History, Politics and Social Policy*, edited by Greg Ruiters, 75–92. Pietermaritzburg: University of KwaZulu-Natal Press, 75–92.

Oomen, Barbara. 2005. *Chiefs in South Africa: Law, Power and Culture in the Post-Apartheid Era*. Oxford: James Currey.

Peters, Pauline E. 2004. 'Inequality and Social Conflict over Land in Africa'. *Journal of Agrarian Change* 4, no. 3 (2004): 269–314.

Peters, Pauline E. 2013. 'Conflicts over Land and Threats to Customary Tenure in Africa'. *African Affairs* 112, no. 449: 543–562.

Parliament of South Africa. 2017. *Report of the High-Level Panel on the Assessment of Key Legislation*.

The Presidency, South Africa. 2019. *Final Report of the Presidential Advisory Panel on Land Reform and Agriculture*.

Ross, Robert. 2018. 'The Wizards of Salem: South African Historians, Truth-Telling and Historical Justice'. *South African Historical Journal* 70, no. 4: 633–653.

Walker, Cherryl. 2008. *Landmarked: Land Claims and Land Restitution in South Africa*. Johannesburg: Jacana Media.

Weinberg, Tara. 2015. *The Contested Status of 'Communal Land Tenure' in South Africa*. University of the Western Cape: Institute for Poverty, Land and Agrarian Studies.

Ubink, Janine and Kojo S. Amanor, eds. 2008. *Contesting Land and Custom in Ghana: State, Chief and the Citizen*. Leiden: Leiden University Press.

CHAPTER

1

# Constitutional Court Judgments, Customary Law and Democratisation in South Africa

Geoff Budlender

In the *Hyundai* case (2000),[1] Chief Justice Langa said that the Constitution is located in the historical transition from a society based on injustice and exclusion from the democratic process, to one that respects the dignity of all citizens and includes all in the process of government.[2] The concept of transition captures two elements of the legal change brought about by the interim Constitution, which came into operation in 1994, and the 'final' Constitution of 1996. On the one hand, this was not a process of revolutionary change: the interim Constitution was adopted by the apartheid parliament, and there was legal continuity. The courts continued to exist, the judges stayed in office and existing laws remained in place. But on the other hand, a fundamental transformation was intended: the constitutional transformation aimed to change the nature and purpose of the legal system, so that it would achieve fundamentally different ends from those it pursued under apartheid.

The Constitutional Court was a new apex court, very differently constituted from the existing courts. It was to be the fulcrum of this change in direction. From the outset, the Court repeatedly emphasised the transformational nature of the new Constitution. In the first case the Court heard, *Makwanyane* (1995), Justice Mahomed emphasised that the Constitution was a decisive break from, and a ringing rejection of, that part of the past that was racist, authoritarian, insular and repressive, and a vigorous commitment to a democratic, universalistic, caring and aspirationally egalitarian ethos.[3]

This dual task – retaining part of the past, but rejecting 'decisively' that which was unacceptable – has given rise to a tension between continuity and rupture. The difficulty of this project is aggravated by the fact that law and legal systems tend to be conservative. When you ask a lawyer, 'What is the law today?', the lawyer first tries to find out what it was yesterday – not what it should be tomorrow. Precedent is fundamental in common law legal systems such as ours. It plays an important role in promoting predictability and stability. And so we look to precedent – the past – to find out what the law is today. While we now seldom look to the very distant precedents of Roman and Roman-Dutch law, we still look to precedents developed by the courts, mainly over the last century. The inherently conservative nature of a precedent-based system is self-evident. Although reliance on precedent is a core and necessary element of the legal method, the reflex reversion to precedent is conservative in its consequences. Precedent needs to be reconsidered.

The difficulty of transformation was compounded by the fact that in 1994, the lawyers who operated the legal institutions and profession had been trained within the system that operated during the apartheid era. The law they had studied and practised was not based on the Constitution. Only those who went to law school after 1994 studied constitutional law with reference to the new Constitution. The judges – including the new judges who were appointed – generally had no training in the legal implications of the Constitution. They were required to create new precedents and to develop a new body of law that would permeate all of the fields of law. Even those fields traditionally regarded as 'non-political' – for example the law of contract – embody assumptions about power, property and justice that have to be re-examined to see whether they are consistent with the intended new ethos, and the need for law to give effect to it. And of course, the judiciary and the legal profession were overwhelmingly white and male. If the legal system was to be transformed, those who ran it needed to be transformed – yet the starting point was the existing judiciary and profession.

The duality of continuity and rupture is reflected in the Constitution's approach to customary law. Section 211(3) of the Constitution requires courts to apply customary law where it is applicable, 'subject to the Constitution'. Section 39(2) requires the courts to develop both the common law and the customary law so as to 'promote the spirit, purport and objects of the Bill of Rights'. In the field of customary law, the task has been more complex and far-reaching than simply reconsidering existing precedents in the light of the new constitutional order. First, the courts have questioned whether what was previously accepted as precedent truly represented the customary law. Second, they have had to ask whether that correctly reflects current customary law. And third, they have had to consider whether the current customary law is justified in the new constitutional order.

## JUDGMENTS AND NEW DIRECTIONS IN CUSTOMARY LAW

I start with an overview of how this process has evolved. It took a surprisingly long time for customary law to reach the Constitutional Court. *Richtersveld* (2003),[4] a land restitution case in the Northern Cape, was the first major customary law case the Court considered. That judgment laid down far-reaching principles. *Richtersveld* was followed by the *Bhe* case (2004),[5] which dealt with women's rights to succession to property, another key issue in customary law; this judgment endorsed and expanded the *Richtersveld* principles.

Since then a string of decisions have applied and extended these first judgments: *Shilubana* (2007) dealt with chieftainship;[6] *Gumede* (2008) dealt with marriage and divorce;[7] *Tongoane* (2010) dealt with customary land rights;[8] *Pilane* (2013) dealt with the right of dissent and free association in customary communities;[9] *Sigcau* (2013) addressed issues of traditional leadership;[10] and *Mayelane* (2013) was concerned with marriage.[11] Together, they amount to a wide-ranging consideration of key legal questions in customary law: land, marriage, divorce, inheritance, leadership, dissent and association.

When one stands back and looks at what has happened, those judgments arguably constitute the most radical project that the Constitutional Court has undertaken. Ten important principles emerge from the judgments. For present purposes I focus on the Constitutional Court, as the apex court. The principles also find expression in judgments of the High Court and the Supreme Court of Appeal.

1. The judgments establish firmly that customary law and traditional leadership derive their force and authority from the Constitution, and are subject to the Constitution and the rights in the Bill of Rights. The Constitutional Court repeatedly pointed out that the Constitution is the supreme law, and all other law must be consistent with it. Thus, for example, Justice Chaskalson pointed out that there could not be two systems of administrative law, one under the Constitution and the other under the common law: 'There is only one system of law. It is shaped by the Constitution which is the supreme law, and all law, including the common law, derives its force from the Constitution and is subject to constitutional control.'[12] The same necessarily applies to customary law. Even now, however, we are not altogether clear

about the reach of this principle, because section 36 of the Constitution provides that all rights may be limited by law of general application 'to the extent that the limitation is reasonable and justifiable in an open and democratic society based on human dignity, equality and freedom'.

2. Customary law must not be viewed through a common law lens. When one reads the judgments of the courts over the years, one sees judges and lawyers attempting to fit the principles and processes of customary law into common law concepts that they can recognise. For example, when it comes to land rights, lawyers dealing with cases or disputes over customary law repeatedly try to apply concepts that derive from the South African and Roman Dutch law of ownership. Whether they are looking at trusteeship, or the landholding itself, they tend to take the concepts with which they are familiar, and attempt to fit the relevant customary law concept into that category. The Constitutional Court indicated in *Richtersveld* that this is inappropriate.[13]

3. Customary law evolves and develops to meet the changing needs of the communities in which it is embedded. The Constitutional Court observed *Bhe* in that the formal rules of 'official' customary law have failed to keep pace with changing social conditions, as a result of which they are no longer universally observed. These changes have required that customary rules adapt, and therefore change. The Court has adopted the concept of 'living customary law', which is interpreted, applied and, when necessary, amended or developed by the community itself or by the courts. This will be done in view of existing customs and traditions, previous circumstances and practical needs, and the demands of the Constitution as the supreme law.[14] (We tend to forget that the common law also changes over time, as social circumstances change. However, it changes at a glacial pace. I will come back to this later, when I deal with how one knows what the customary law is at a particular time or in a particular community.) The concept of a living customary law recognises that the law may reflect social changes and adapt to circumstances. This is a powerful tool in the process of transformation.

4. The Constitutional Court has reinforced this approach by admitting local practice as a central element of evidence of what the specific content of customary law is. Again, I will come back to this later.

5. Textbooks, old authorities and judgments help to establish the content of customary law. But this is subject to a fundamental and far-reaching qualification initially introduced by the Court in the *Bhe* judgment: the Court found that customary law had been distorted in legislation, textbooks and court decisions during the era of segregation and apartheid. The Court made plain that these sources have to be dealt with cautiously, because they may reflect distorted versions of customary

law. Deputy Chief Justice Langa concluded in *Bhe* that customary law had been distorted in a manner that emphasised its patriarchal features and minimised its communitarian ones.[15]

6. The problem of a distorted account of customary law is aggravated by the static or 'ossified' account of customary law in the 'official' sources: they do not have regard for the living nature of customary law, and as a result may not reflect what the Court has called 'true customary law'. As Deputy Chief Justice Langa expressed it in paragraph 86 of *Bhe*: 'True customary law will be that which recognises and acknowledges the changes which continually take place'. Justice Mokgoro pointed out, in a prescient passage in her judgment in the early *Du Plessis* case (1996), that the customary law had degenerated into 'a vitrified set of norms alienated from its roots in the community'.[16] This form of 'customary law' is reflected in old textbooks and court decisions. At best, therefore, and even assuming that there was no distortion at the time they were written, these sources reflect the law as it was at a particular time.

7. For both of these reasons, rules accepted and enforced during an era of authoritarian government may have been inappropriate, outdated, ossified and simply wrong. This has a potentially radical consequence: the old judgments are not necessarily right and are not automatically to be followed; they are to be looked at critically. For example in 1908, in the case of *Petlele* (1908),[17] the then Supreme Court pronounced itself on the limited ways in which, it said, Africans could hold land under customary law. That was accepted as the law and the judgment was followed in other cases. Now it is possible to say that this position is wrong – either because it was distorted and wrong at the time, or because even if it was correct at that time, the true customary law has changed as social practice and circumstances have changed. This is a radical approach because it calls into question the power of precedent, to which I have already referred. It opens up possibilities of transformation. We can now explore customary practices and gather evidence from communities about current grassroots views of 'the customary'.

8. The judgments build on what the courts call a contextual approach to the realisation of rights. The Constitutional Court looks at customary law not in the abstract, but in relation to its consequences. The judges ask: what are the consequences on the ground? What are the consequences for inequality and poverty? A version of customary law may be questioned because of its consequences. If the law inevitably has an unlawful consequence, then it is likely to be invalid.

9. The Court has said that you do not lose your rights as a citizen when you are a member of a traditional community. Thus, all people have full rights of freedom of speech and assembly, and these are not limited by the authority of a traditional leader or council. That principle was established in *Pilane*. On application by the

chief, the High Court had interdicted members of the community from holding meetings to discuss whether they should secede from the community. The majority of the Constitutional Court set aside that interdict. They confirmed that dissent and debate are the essence of South Africa's democracy, and you do not lose the rights of freedom of assembly and speech by being a member of a traditional community.

This is of course very important for establishing democracy and accountability within customary communities. A traditional leader who claims the authority to control meetings and assemblies in his or her area on the basis of custom – which was part of the practice under apartheid – now faces multiple legal challenges in trying to uphold that claim: it will now be asserted that this practice was an apartheid distortion of the true customary law. In any event, even if it was part of the customary law, that is no longer the case, because the law has developed. Even if the law did not develop under its own processes, it has to be developed now under the Constitution, because members of customary communities are in the first place citizens of South Africa, who enjoy all of the rights in the Bill of Rights.

10. The final principle relates to the position of traditional leaders. This requires a little background. Many traditional leaders are recognised and paid by the state under the Traditional Leadership and Governance Framework Act of 2003 and its provincial iterations. While we should be critical of the Act and its political intentions, there is an important element of the legislation that has largely been neglected. It is this: the core concept in the legislation is the concept of *recognition*, not *appointment*, of traditional leaders. The president is given the power to 'recognise' traditional leaders, but not the power to appoint them.

There is a clear contrast here between the current legislation and the Native Administration Act of 1927, section 2 of which provided that the governor-general and his various successors could recognise *or appoint* a traditional leader. Similarly, section 5 of the 1927 Act empowered the governor-general and his successors to *create* tribes. Now, the statutory power is a power to 'recognise' a traditional community. It seems to me that this has significant legal consequences. When you 'recognise' something, you say 'it exists, I see it and I recognise it'; you don't say 'I create it'. The difference between recognition and appointment is fundamental and opens up space for expanding the democratic process in the development of customary law.

The Constitutional Court has accepted that there are traditional leaders who are not recognised in terms of a statute but are accepted locally in accordance with custom. In *Sigcau*, the Court pointed out that the dispute over competing claims to the paramount chieftainship was 'statutorily settled', but 'not settled customarily', when one of the claimants was recognised under the Black Administration Act.[18] In *Pilane*, the Court held that the statutory authority accorded to traditional leadership does not necessarily preclude or restrict the operation of customary leadership that has not been recognised by legislation.[19] In the context of our recent past, in which the state and Bantustan governments decided who was a 'traditional' leader, this can have far-reaching consequences. The fact that the president has not said 'I recognise this person' does not necessarily mean that the person concerned is not in fact and under customary law a traditional leader. It seems that such a person may be a customary leader with customary law powers, even though not recognised under the statute, and therefore having no statutory powers.

The implications of this remain to be tested. Most customary leaders will seek recognition by the state, because this formalises their position, provides statutory powers, facilitates access to the state, and provides a right to a stipend and to participation in the houses of traditional leaders. The new approach creates scope for the legitimacy of recognised traditional leaders to be challenged. The president cannot 'recognise' as a traditional leader, someone who is not in fact such a leader according to custom. This represents a radical change.

Taken together, these ten principles represent a surprisingly radical project in the development of customary law. It was embarked upon without any overarching statement of intent. Under the broad guidance of the Constitution, the transformative project has unfolded in stages, in response to specific cases, each case building on its predecessors. The process has followed the incremental common law method, taking one step at a time, but the overall implications are profound.

I do not believe that anyone predicted this process. It has its source in the finding in the *Richtersveld* judgment that the Constitution acknowledges 'the originality and distinctiveness of indigenous law as an independent source of norms within the legal system' – and that it is 'subject to the Constitution and has to be interpreted in the light of its values'.[20] That has been the foundation of much of what followed.

## FINDING CUSTOMARY LAW

The flexibility and adaptiveness of customary law raises a difficult practical challenge: if customary law is changing and has to be developed to reflect social change, and if those changes may differ from one community to another, how do we know what the law is?

It is worth noting that the problem is not limited to customary law. The common law, as expounded by the courts, has also changed over time. It has done so by reference to the vague concept of 'the legal convictions of the community'.[21] Precisely which community that was, and how the courts established what its legal convictions were, was never explained. Now, the development of the common law (like the customary law) is anchored in the Bill of Rights, in terms of section 39(2) of the Constitution. This provides greater predictability – and also more rapid development – than was previously the case.

The development of customary law takes place by reference first to changes on the ground. The first task is to establish the 'true customary law' as it is practised by the community concerned. Thereafter, the law must be tested against the Constitution.

Up till now, there has been a very thin literature dealing with the interaction of history, social change and customary law. There are not many relevant written materials available. That is now changing. This collection represents an important step in that process. In practice, lawyers and the courts have found that experts in history and the social sciences can be very helpful. There is a need to establish, from the perspective of those 'on the ground', what the actual practices are – and also what in reality happened in the past, and whether it was inconsistent with the 'official' customary law. Those who can provide this evidence are of critical importance in helping the courts to determine the living customary law.

The older, more static and patriarchal accounts of the customary law tend to be associated with the apartheid past. But with the rejection of colonial and apartheid understandings of African societies, the way is now open to reinterpret both the past and the present. The academic experts are not there to dictate what the answers should be. They give evidence of research that elucidates complex historical processes, and they present customary practices as established through fieldwork research. They provide the results of research that lawyers could not undertake. They listen to evidence and interpret it in the light of their skills and knowledge. They are able to explain the impact of colonial and apartheid conceptions and rule, and the scale of change within African communities for whom customary law remains significant. Their evidence must also, of course, be viewed critically by the courts.

The Constitutional Court has on occasion struggled to determine the living customary law. In *Mayelane*, the Court had to decide whether a man in a customary marriage needs the consent of his wife in order to enter into a second customary marriage. Questions arose as to the precepts of Tsonga customary law and, depending on the answer, whether a second marriage without consent would be in line with the Constitution. The Court received conflicting evidence as to the customary law. Affidavits were filed by individuals who were living in indigenous marriages under Tsonga customary law; by an adviser to traditional leaders; by various traditional leaders; and by experts who drew conclusions from the available primary material. In the end, the evidence was not decisive – it did not produce a crisp and clear answer either about the past or the present. But the majority of the Court said that the customary law should be developed in such a way as to require that a second marriage should require consent of the first wife. The Court agreed that whatever the position in the past, it would be appropriate to develop such an expectation in order to advance women's constitutional rights to equality and dignity.

This is an example of the Court looking at the situation on the ground in order to identify custom and, if the custom is not clear, developing it in a manner which is consistent with the rights in our Constitution. That has also been done in a case decided by the Botswana Court of Appeal dealing with succession rights, *Ramantele* (2013).[22] In that case, the Court recognised that customary rules of succession may have largely excluded women in the past. The president of the Court of Appeal said rather caustically to the lawyer for the defendant: 'What you're really saying is that the wife could keep the pots from the kitchen'. The Court had regard for anthropological or sociological evidence of changed practice in this regard, and found that it was necessary to develop the law to meet both practice on the ground and the principle of equality in the Constitution of Botswana.

In such cases, the research becomes particularly important in order to show how customary law has changed, and what is actually happening on the ground. With respect to a number of issues, not least gender relations, social practice has advanced beyond what might have been written down when compilations of customary law were first made – for example in the case of Botswana by Isaac Schapera (1938). Social reality and custom may have been different then. Scholars argue that the earlier phases of colonial rule saw the enforcement of a strongly patriarchal version of customary law as the colonial state sought to cement rural control by shoring up the weakening authority of chiefs, and that chiefs themselves took advantage of the opportunity to assert themselves in this context (Chanock 2001). And we should not assume that the custom recorded in texts, or enforced by the courts in the first half of the twentieth century, represented an immutable version.

Sensitivity to the historical and social evidence is paramount for the effective development and recognition of a living customary law. Evidence can potentially be adduced for every aspect of the customary law. This is of particular importance in relation to land, where an ossified conception of top-down allocation and control still prevails. Land rights were of course affected by extensive legislation in this field, but most of that legislation has fallen away. There still is a degree of uncertainty as to how customary land rights are acquired and terminated, and what their content is – and who can make and participate in decisions in this regard. Extensive research has been done for academic purposes and for court cases. There has been some, but not sufficient, clarification by the courts of the living customary law in relation to land rights.

Lawyers and researchers have to identify what evidence might be relevant; assist in formulating the questions and identifying where the answers might be found; and then place this material before the Court and argue what its consequences are. In the *Richtersveld* case, the lawyers argued for the development of the law to recognise community ownership or 'communal indigenous ownership'. The Court's acceptance of some indigenous rights as 'akin to ownership' has influenced subsequent legal argument and judgments. Thus far, however, the courts have made only a modest start in the process of identifying and clarifying the content of customary land rights. (See Beinart in this collection, who argues that this judgment does not sufficiently clarify customary land rights in the post-apartheid era.)

The *Richtersveld* judgment was a profound starting point. It is an important example of the combination of historical evidence, contemporary social research, interpretation of customary law and the application of constitutional principles in expanding an important field of law. The role of the judges was to weigh the evidence; to take cognisance of precedent, legal argument and the Constitution; and to forge some certainty and (where certainty is not possible) a direction of travel that entrenches principles of democracy and the Bill of Rights.

In summary: we need to know what happens (and has previously happened) on the ground. This can only be adduced by interviews and meetings in the community at its various levels, starting with the household and the family. This is a highly democratic process compared with a strategy that involves looking only at law books and old cases. It involves a process of interrogating ideas expressed by those who are engaged with the current practice of living customary law and then testing that against the principles in the Constitution.

The answers are not easy, and very often they are disparate and even conflicting. In the *Mayelane* case, where such a divergence in opinion was evident, the Court in effect said: we can see that there are different ways of viewing customary law and we are now choosing the route that gives effect to the principles in the Constitution.

I have identified some of the important new principles that have emerged from this process. Potentially the most radical account emerged from the judgment in *Bakgatla* (2015).[23] In that case, the Court dealt with a dispute arising from the implementation of the Communal Property Associations Act (1996). Justice Jafta noted the principles that underscore the democratic nature of communal property associations (CPAs) established in terms of the Act. A CPA constitution must embrace fair, democratic and inclusive decision-making processes that afford members the opportunity to participate in the association's decisions. All members must have equal standing and CPAs must proscribe discrimination of any kind. Members must have fair access to the property of the association and the business of the CPA must be accountable and transparent. Having explained these principles, which are set out in the Act, Justice Jafta said: 'The Act is a visionary piece of legislation passed to restore the dignity of traditional communities. It also serves the purpose of transforming customary law practices.'

There have of course been many difficulties in implementing the CPA Act. These difficulties arise whether the property-holding entity is a CPA, a trust or another instrument of collective ownership. The judgment is of great importance, because it identifies practices and principles that should underlie the transformation of customary law. The judgment asserted democratic principles in the functioning of CPAs, rather than placing this particular CPA under the authority of a chief, and it reiterated the application of general democratic principles in the development of customary law. The court did not say the CPA Act is now part of customary law. But it seems to me that the judgment identifies the principles on which we can rely in the development of customary law: democratic process, fair and inclusive decision-making processes, equality, fair access to collectively owned property, and most importantly in many cases, accountability and transparency.

We cannot invent customary law. We should not adopt a romantic approach and argue that 'true' customary law, quite unlike anything else we know, is perfect. It is not. But these principles provide a long-term direction, in the same way that the Constitution provides a route of travel for legislation and the common law more generally. Where the details of customary law are disputed, these principles should provide guidance to judges in order to develop certainty around specific legal issues and practice. And where the law is plainly inconsistent with those principles, there is a strong argument for development of the law to bring it into line with these principles. They include transparency and accountability in the operation of customary law. These are of course issues of the greatest importance because in the real world, customary law operates mainly in local courts and non-judicial processes, often dominated by local powerholders, in rural areas where scrutiny by the media is not likely.

The Constitutional Court has thus established powerful tools for dealing with disputes under customary law and has pointed the way to the transformation of customary law. Transformation is facilitated by the fact that the Court starts from the premise of the fluidity of living customary law.

Sceptics will understandably ask whether these decisions of the Constitutional Court have made much impact on the ground. Especially in the former homelands, where customary law is most likely to be invoked, women are still discriminated against, people are still arbitrarily deprived of their land and unaccountable decision-making practices persist. But law and the courts do not by themselves change social institutions and practices. What the law can do is establish rights and provide a framework within which people can organise and defend their rights. The Constitution facilitates change by enabling organisation on the ground and through the enforcement of rights in the courts where other mechanisms fail.

The Constitutional Court has created a means and process for empowering people on the ground to change things. Lawyers and experts – historians, sociologists and anthropologists – can work with such processes. They can explain and give voice to the process of transformation when it comes to the courts. It has taken some time for customary law issues to come before the courts in any number, but this is now becoming more frequent and the Constitutional Court has developed some momentum and consistency in key judgments. Lawyers who support the development of democratic practices and an elaboration of constitutional principles have to make the most of the opportunity.

This is all the more important because the process is not entirely linear and consistent. Firstly, the government has made legislative efforts to reverse the democratisation project. We see it in the Traditional Courts and Traditional Affairs Bills, as well as in prospective land legislation. All show a desire to place greater power in the hands of traditional authorities and the implication may also be that those authorities will have a stronger voice in determining the content of customary law.

Secondly, not all of the decisions of the Constitutional Court have been unanimous. The minority judgment of Chief Justice Mogoeng and Justice Nkabinde in the *Pilane* case does not reflect the democratising project that I have described. It is a judgment that in effect says, of traditional authorities: these are very important institutions and the courts must support and encourage them. The implication in that case would have been to curtail dissent expressed against traditional leaders, by increasing their control over meetings. This in turn may have curtailed constitutional rights. Those rights are of course not absolute. The minority judgment implies that they should be given effect in the context of local social relations in which traditional leadership should be able to exert authority. The minority judgment reflects a conservative approach. It is also impossible not to notice that it is expressed in language that is unusual in our Constitutional Court. One can imagine, when one reads the majority and minority judgments, the heated discussions that must have taken place in the judicial conference.

The future direction of the Constitutional Court in the sphere of customary law will also be affected by new judicial appointments. The chair of the Judicial Service Commission (JSC) is the Chief Justice, so his voice carries weight. In the appointment of Constitutional Court judges, unlike other judges, the majority view of the JSC does not necessarily prevail. The JSC puts up a slate of candidates, which goes to the president, and the president makes a selection from that slate. The president has unusual power in the selection of Constitutional Court judges and it would not be surprising if he consulted the Chief Justice before making a decision. A consistent alternative and more traditional view of customary law is not yet being articulated and pressed. A president who is committed to a conservative version of the customary has significant opportunities in that regard.

These countervailing legal tendencies are seen in a context in which mining rights are becoming increasingly important to customary communities. Where there are minerals in the land, which is effectively the community's land, and mining rights are to be granted, questions of great importance arise: Who is entitled to the benefits of those rights when the old order mining rights are held not by those communities, but by mining companies? Who is entitled to participate when the old order rights are converted into new order rights under the Mineral and Petroleum Resources Development Act (MPRDA) of 2002? Who is entitled to participate when new rights are granted under the MPRDA?

Mineral discoveries have been made and are still being made in areas where there is customary tenure of the land concerned. A latter-day version of the gold rush has taken place since the MPRDA came into effect, and increasingly its focus has been on land occupied by customary communities. Disputes have emerged most vividly in the North West Province, affecting communities such as the Bafokeng, the Bakgatla-ba-Kgafela, the Bapo-ba-Mogale, and the Bakubung-ba-Monnakgotla – and the groups that form part of, or are affiliated to, these larger communities. In each case, there are disputes about who is entitled to the benefits of the minerals and who owns or controls the land under which they are mined. This has become a legal battlefield over rights and over the accountability of traditional leaders.

The claims and conflicts in relation to land, mining and accountability go to the heart of the democratising process. The disputes are heated, because there are huge vested interests at play and great benefits to be gained or lost, often including the land itself. At present, the approach of the Constitutional Court seems to favour democratic principles and broad access to resources. The Court is operating in a moment of widely expressed revulsion against corruption and the enrichment of the few at the cost of the many.

It is difficult to predict the character of the Court, or the political context, five or ten years from now. So this is an important moment for the further development of the living customary law. Legal and political struggles can be connected and impact on each other. The legal cases often emerge from local political and social struggles. There is a need for a closer dialogue between these strategies in the hope of cementing, defending and advancing the gains that have been made.

NOTES

1. Investigating Directorate: Serious Economic Offences and Others v Hyundai Motor Distribuytors (Pty) Ltd and Others In re: Hyunadai Motor Distributors (Pty) Ltd and Others v Smith NO and Others [2000] ZACC 12 ('*Hyundai*').
2. I participated as an advocate in the following cases mentioned in the chapter: Richtersveld, Gumede, Pilane, Ramantele, Shiubana and Tongoane.
3. S v Makwanyane and Another [1995] ZACC 3 para 262 ('*Makwanyane*').
4. Alexkor Ltd and Another v Richtersveld Community and Others [2003] ZACC 18 ('*Richtersveld*').
5. Bhe and Others v Khayelitsha Magistrate and Others [2004] ZACC 17 ('*Bhe*').
6. Shilubana and Others v Nwamitwa [2008] ZACC 9 ('*Shilubana*').
7. Gumede (born Shange) v President of the Republic of South Africa and Others [2008] ZACC 23 ('*Gumede*').
8. Tongoane and Others v National Minister for Agriculture and Land Affairs and Others ZACC 10 ('*Tongoane*').
9. Pilane and Another v Pilane and Another [2013] ZACC 3 ('*Pilane*').
10. Sigcau v President of the Republic of South Africa and Others [2013] ZACC 18 ('*Sigcau*').
11. Mayelane v Ngwenyama and Another [2013] ZACC 14 ('*Mayelane*').
12. Pharmaceutical Manufacturers Association of South Africa and Another: In re Ex Parte President of the Republic of South Africa and Others [2000] ZACC 1, para 4 ('*Pharmaceutical Manufacturers*').
13. *Richtersveld*, para 50, 51.
14. *Bhe*, para 154, *Shilubana*, para 81.
15. *Bhe*, para 89.
16. Du Plessis and Others v De Klerk and Another [1996] ZAA 10 ('*Du Plessis*').
17. Petlele v Minister for Native Affairs and Mokhatle 1908 TPD 260, at 271 ('*Petlele*').
18. *Sigcau*, para 3.
19. *Pilane*, para 44.
20. *Richtersveld*, para 51.
21. Minister van Polisie v Ewels [1975] (3) SA 590 at 597.
22. Ramantele v Mmusi and Others [2013] BLR 658 (CA) ('*Ramantele*').
23. Bakgatla-ba-Kgafela Communal Property Association v Bakgatla-ba-Kgafela Tribal Authority and Others [2015] ZACC 25 ('*Bakgatla*').

REFERENCES

Chanock, Martin. 2001. *The Making of South African Legal Culture 1902–1936: Fear, Favour and Prejudice*. Cambridge: Cambridge University Press.

Schapera, Isaac. 1938. *A Handbook of Tswana Law and Custom*. London: Oxford University Press.

CHAPTER

# 2

## Was 'Living Customary Law' There All Along?

Derick Fay

In recent years, South African constitutional jurisprudence has shifted to incorporate and develop the notion of 'living customary law' (see Budlender in this volume). Moreover, the concept has circulated outside the courts and legal profession, with the potential to reframe scholarly and policy discourses on struggles over land and other natural resources. This chapter examines the relationship between legal and analytic terminologies through a reflexive reading of the reframing of my own work as evidence of 'customary law rights' in the context of a 2012 trial. In doing so it engages a set of questions, the first of which forms the title of this chapter: was 'living customary law' there all along?

I conducted ethnographic fieldwork in Hobeni, near the coast of the former Transkei, Eastern Cape, in 1998–1999 and returned for follow-up research in 2009–2011. My findings predominantly revealed continuities in the practices around land tenure. Why should this now be labelled 'living customary law'? Had I failed to recognise it, or to name it correctly? If it had been possible to think about this material without reference to the concept of 'living customary law', what would be gained, or lost, or changed – analytically, legally or politically – by deploying the concept?

I was engaged as an expert witness in a 2012 court case (*Gongqose*) involving three fishermen arrested inside Dwesa-Cwebe Nature Reserve.[1] During the case I presented material written a decade earlier, prior to the 'living customary law' jurisprudence, from my 20 months of research in Hobeni. This was one of the seven communities adjoining the reserve and my earlier visit coincided with negotiations regarding a land restitution claim on the reserve. The court eventually found, legally speaking, that a customary system of resource regulation existed, thereby providing grounds for a series of appeals that culminated in a successful case in the Supreme Court of Appeal in May 2018.

In the course of the trial and the subsequent appeals, and in the work of my fellow expert witness, Jackie Sunde, my earlier work on land tenure was cited as evidence of customary law. In reflecting on references to my work in Sunde's dissertation (2014), I came to look back at how – and whether – I had engaged the language of 'customary law.' Revisiting the dissertation and its deployment in the 2012 court case and subsequent legal and scholarly texts, I was reminded that 'custom' and 'customary law' had not appeared as analytic concepts in the earlier text.

In reflecting on these shifts, I draw on efforts to theorise the roles of anthropologists and historians as expert witnesses. I am trained as a sociocultural anthropologist. The literature on anthropological and historical approaches to evidence at trial is rich but inconclusive. James Clifford (1988: 340) draws the differences between the disciplines starkly, arguing that 'the distinction between historical and ethnographic practices depends on that between literate and oral modes of knowledge', but comparative studies highlight interactions between the fields that refute this simple dichotomy. For example, Arthur Ray (2016: 65; cf. Bens 2016) shows how anthropological engagement with the U.S. Indian Claims Commission in the 1950s catalysed the formation of ethnohistory, leading to 'increased use of documentary records to supplement archaeological and ethnographic sources', while anthropologists as well as historians engaged the 'so-called history wars' in Australia and New Zealand (Ray 2016: 23).

In South Africa, the impact of Marxist historiography in the 1970s and 1980s on anglophone anthropology (Gordon and Spiegel 1993), the boundaries that Clifford draws between historical and ethnographic knowledge do not appear so stark. Likewise, the effects of written and oral evidence on courts are open-ended. Paul Burke (2011) provides examples where judges questioned written evidence, because of their familiarity with the documentary form, while Ray (2011: 158) observes that judges may underplay the role of interpretation and expertise in handling historical materials, treating 'historians [as] essentially clerks', charged with collecting masses of primary and secondary sources. Burke notes instances where judges deferred to anthropological expert presentations of oral testimony, but others have highlighted concerns about 'hearsay' (Thuen 2004: 274–275). Ray (2011: 15–16) notes that anthropological participant observation offers the possibility that unanticipated questions in court can be answered on the basis of the anthropologist's direct fieldwork experience.

A significant literature on 'the anthropologist as expert witness' encompasses works that aim to advise the prospective anthropological expert (Rosen 1977; Kandel 1992b). This highlights the contrasts between anthropological and legal reasoning and epistemology (Kandel 1992a; Sapignoli 2009; Thuen 2004; Bens 2016), it illustrates tensions between expertise and advocacy (Stewart 1979; Ramos 1999; Zenker 2016), problematises temptations towards 'strategic essentialism' (Thuen 2004; Zenker 2016), reveals anthropological critiques of legal process as an 'explanation for judicial failure' (Edmond 2004: 213), and discusses 'bias, stereotyping, and racism [in different] legal orders' (Miller and Menezes 2015: 392).

Burke (2011), who had practised as a lawyer on four land claims in Australia prior to entering anthropology, builds upon Pierre Bourdieu's (1986) notion of the social field to theorise the way that social action is shaped by 'the structure and … the characteristic activities of an entire professional world' (Terdiman in Bourdieu 1986: 806). Developing this idea in relation to anthropology, Burke argues that as an expert witness, an anthropologist is faced with the prospect of triangulating 1) the direct evidence provided by claimants in the course of the trial, 2) the anthropological archive, comprised of existing literature and the anthropologist's own work, and 3) the relevant legal doctrine. In doing so, he argues, the anthropologist will likely face disciplinary and interpersonal pressures towards advocacy on one hand and the norms of expert independence on the other.

Burke (2011: 30) concludes that 'the anthropologist must manage this triangulation in a way that achieves maximum compatibility between the three elements, while projecting expert independence'. As he also notes, the claimant's lawyer is also undertaking to triangulate the same three elements, creating potential for discord between the expert and counsel – ideally managed in pre-trial discussions (Scheffer 2010: 82–84; Kandel 1992b). Finally, he observes that while an anthropologist *could* present ethnographic data as complex, polyvalent and approachable through multiple theoretical perspectives, *in practice* this rarely happens: 'because of … expectations that the facts will always favour one interpretation over another and that the expert's role is to authoritatively resolve indeterminacies' (Burke 2011: 30). Ray similarly notes the 'the risks of bringing … historiographic discussions into the courtroom' (2011: 113).

Burke (2011) sets out a clear methodology, beginning with a review of the overall ethnographic archive potentially relevant to the case, including the theoretical orientations of the contributors. Subsequent stages analyse how ethnographic material becomes evidence in court: comparing the 'archive' with the anthropologist's report to the court, to clarify where decisions and choices were made by the anthropologist; interviewing the anthropologist regarding the same; and reviewing these against the transcript of the trial. I build on his framework to examine the 'triangulation' processes evident in *Gongqose*.¹ Burke's focus on 'the relevant legal doctrine' has helped me to separate the concept of 'living customary law', as deployed in law, from both ethnographic data and its theoretical presentation. I reflect upon my own research and written reports, the trial and the interactions between the court and the legal team.

In addition, I argue that Burke's framework understates the potential for the claimants, the legal team and the experts collectively to (re)define the actual legal points that must be proven. His first example, on the evidentiary hearings prior to the *Mabo v Queensland* case, is the most similar, concerning an important case that led to the development of 'native title' doctrine and the abandonment of the legal concept of *terra nullius*: 'The absence of any legal doctrine of native title at the time of the hearing of the facts in *Mabo* is a challenge to the general triangulation model of anthropological agency' (Burke 2011: 97). Likewise, in *Gongqose*, the case involved relatively innovative legal arguments about the status of customary law rather than engagement with a well-established legal doctrine.

## 'THE ANTHROPOLOGICAL ARCHIVE' C.1999

The legal construct of 'living customary law' came to be central to the criminal defence argument used by the Legal Resources Centre (LRC) acting for David Gongqose and the two other fishermen. The LRC was by this time highly experienced in providing legal assistance to communities in land rights cases and in working with academics.

Neither 'custom' nor 'customary law' were central analytic concepts with which I was actively engaged in my graduate training. As Burke's analysis of the field would suggest, to have focused on 'custom' in my dissertation would have cut against the grain of contemporary theory in anthropology. In all the papers I had written in graduate school, the sole paper that referred to 'custom' or 'customary' was from a required course on the history of anthropology in which I had criticised the static portrayals of custom in late nineteenth-and early twentieth-century works. Likewise, in my comprehensive exams, 'custom' only appears in a quote from Pauline Peters as an emic concept subject to ethnographic analysis, not an analytic term: 'Struggles to obtain exclusive rights over communal resources [in Botswana] have turned on reinterpretations of the terms custom and communal tenure' (Peters 1994: 2). Similarly, my grant proposals did not make use of the language of 'custom' or 'customary law', even as they set out a project that focused on the tensions between the newly established Hobeni Communal Property Association (set up to own the communal land and as a representative structure to the landowning trust which would own the Nature Reserve) and existing landholding practices.

The presentation of material in the dissertation itself similarly reflects the absence of an explicit framing in relation to custom or customary law. The sole reference to customary law per se was in a discussion of disputes over livestock trespassing in gardens, referencing Digby Sqhelo Koyana's (1980) note that a magistrate in the 1920s 'cited precedents in customary law requiring the fencing of gardens for claims to be upheld' (Fay 2003: 174). The few references to 'custom' and 'customary' in the dissertation were primarily as a gloss on the isiXhosa term *isithethe* and appeared primarily in discussions of ritual and ceremony, frequently in references to particular customs, not to 'custom' as an overarching body. *Isithethe* (pl. *izithethe*) refers in local classification to customs or ceremonies that, while seen as traditional, can be neglected without risk of illness; these are contrasted with *amasiko*, health-preserving life cycle and crisis rituals organised around agnatic kin, which may cause illness if neglected (Fay 2003: 172). Other references were in the titles of older texts (Cook 1927; Davies 1927; Soga 1931).

This framing reflects not only disciplinary expectations, but also the policy environment at the time, in the late 1990s and early 2000s, in which the notion of customary law was discussed primarily in relation to questions of ownership by traditional authorities and women's land rights. On the one hand, the discourse emphasised that apartheid structures did not reflect customary law: the 1997 Department of Land Affairs (DLA) White Paper, for example, highlighted that apartheid and homeland regimes had given chiefs 'land-ownership rights and far-reaching powers over land allocation, often beyond those normally sanctioned under customary law' (DLA 1997: 33–34). Elsewhere, customary law was itself seen as problematic: the White Paper argued for 'reform of marriage, inheritance and customary law which favour men and contain obstacles to women receiving rights to land' (DLA 1997: 72). It identified as a potential constitutional issue that 'traditional authorities... carry out land-related functions in terms of customary law' (DLA 1997: 38).

On the other hand, passages allude to what would come to be identified as 'living customary law', highlighting dynamism and local control in contrast to static and top-down formulations: 'The requirement that traditional systems adapt to accommodate the changing position of women is also not fundamentally threatening to customary law. There are many deeply traditional areas where these changes are happening spontaneously' (DLA 1997: 89). Likewise, it argued that its policy proposals were not 'in conflict with customary law ... [vesting] the ultimate ownership and control over the land with the members of a group as is the case under customary law'.

Notwithstanding the latter examples, overall customary law was primarily represented in policy discussions from the late 1990s and early 2000s as a patriarchal body of norms, particularly in relation to land, with 'the customary system of patrilineal succession' (Bennett 2004: 77) challenged by the opposition of women's groups. The recognition of customary law in the Interim Constitution 'was little more than a formality' and much of it was seen as 'threatened with constitutional review' (Bennett 2004: 77–78). As Aninka Claassens notes, the negotiations over the final 1996 Constitution rejected the argument of the 'traditional leader lobby … that the right to equality should be subject to customary law', and the Constitutional Court subsequently 'ruled against the chiefs' objections to the Constitution during the certification of the Constitution' (2013: 72; Albertyn 1994). While the principles underlying constitutional negotiations mandated that the drafters 'protect South Africa's diverse cultures' and 'guarantee application of customary law in the courts' (Bennett 2004: 78), the implications of these points were uncertain and there was little indication in the land policy literature of the framing in terms of 'living customary law' that would later emerge.

Policy-oriented research in the same period was oriented around 'practice', the everyday activities and justifications through which local people claimed land. Customary law might be part of the broader category of norms that shaped landholding practice, but it was not necessarily the central focus. In Ruari Alcock and Donna Hornby (2004: 17), to pick an example, all of the references to 'customary' are in the space of a page concerning gender equity, with the exception of a reference to 'legal and customary guidelines around property distribution after the death of a household head'. The only reference to custom is in the definitional statement that 'an institution is an established law, custom, practice, system or social organisation' (2004: 1). For Alcock and Hornby, the language of custom or customary is absent, but this does not preclude their central focus on the institutions, norms and procedures that regulate landholding and land administration. Likewise, as Claassens recounts, the 1997 White Paper focused on practice:

> The [White Paper] approach sought to recognise and protect … *de facto* use and occupation rights. It recognised both long established practice and 'customary precedents' as countervailing sources of land rights, which could be upheld against the nominal owner of the land, who in the former homelands was often the state. [It] sought, as the primary intervention, to bring the law in line with current practices as opposed to attempting to develop new law and expect current practice to change accordingly (2012: 7).

My ethnographic fieldwork took a similar approach, aiming to take up Catherine Cross's call for attention to 'the administrative gap between what the state and its bureaucracies prescribe and what people on the ground are actually doing by way of transacting land ... [and examining] how far the state has actually failed to control land practice itself in relation to its African population' (Cross 1991: 64). In this analysis, I used Cross's call for attention to state incapacity in South Africa to 'transcend the local through generalisation, comparison and the framing of local data in terms of wider academic debates' (Burke 2011: 7). As Burke would argue, this reflects the structures of the discipline of anthropology that compel claims of significance beyond the particular case. Contrasting my findings with a literature on the Transkei region that focused on state domination (Hendricks 1990; Haines 1984; Segar 1989; Ntsebeza 2001), I highlighted works from elsewhere in sub-Saharan Africa that demonstrated the gap between government policies and rural Africans' use of land (Fay 2003: 28, citing Berry 1993, Platteau 1996 and Shipton 1989).

My dissertation thus took shape partly as a critique of rule-focused accounts, showing how variation in landholding in Hobeni emerged in practice within broadly shared procedures and repertoires of argument about land allocation and administration. These practices were only loosely articulated and often at odds both with claims by traditional authorities and also the proclamations and regulations that had been enacted to govern land in the region. My dissertation documented norms, expectations and institutional practices that could be read as evidence of 'living customary law', but the overall argument was that these would give an incomplete account of land tenure. Focusing on the normative was insufficient, both because people would make different choices within a common set of procedural rules and because they would sometimes act in ways that defied or challenged local and legal norms. Instead, I argued that 'the institutions that enable access to land cannot be understood simply in terms of structured rules or norms', and aimed to show 'how local variations emerge despite common sets of rules' (Fay 2003: 1; Fay 2005, 2012).

## LIVING CUSTOMARY LAW JURISPRUDENCE

I turn here to the legal doctrine, showing how the notion of 'living customary law' emerged as a way to reframe what might have been called 'local practice' a decade before. Beginning with the *Richtersveld* (2003) land restitution case and *Bhe* (2004), which concerned succession and inheritance, the Constitutional Court's jurisprudence introduced the category of 'living customary law'.[2] Aninka Claassens and

Geoff Budlender (2013) summarise key points in the decisions, noting that customary law is subject to the Constitution, that it must not be viewed through a common law lens and it can develop as a living law. Elucidation thus should not depend on textbooks and old authorities alone and interpretations should take a contextual approach to the realisation of rights, foregrounding poverty and inequality (Budlender in this volume). Living customary law can be made by 'all those who engage with, and shape, custom through their daily activities' (Claassens 2013: 72).

Despite these precedents, the Constitutional Court was reluctant to rule substantively on the relationship between 'living customary law' and land and resource rights in the *Tongoane* (2010) decision,[3] which overturned the 2004 Communal Land Rights Act (CLARA). The court recognised that the provisions of CLARA affected 'indigenous law and customary law', but reached its decision on a narrow technical basis (Claassens and Budlender 2013; Mailula 2011), striking it down because it was passed using a procedure that did not allow provincial input. Notably, the court did *not* rule on the substantive arguments presented to the court that the CLARA would 'undermine existing security of tenure held by people living under customary or indigenous law; [and] very substantially impact upon the nature and content of customary law in South Africa'.[4]

The discursive and conceptual shift towards analysis in terms of 'living customary law' in land activist scholarship is especially evident in the court papers for the *Tongoane* case and in the related materials collected by Aninka Claassens and Ben Cousins (2008). The editors argued that '"living law" interpretations of custom are potentially a way of avoiding the danger that customary law will be used to subject some South Africans to an authoritarian legal regime' (2008: 25). Although these ideas were not so evident in the *Tongoane* judgment itself, they figured in the arguments that the LRC brought to the *Gongqose* case. Through the TshintshaAmakhaya non-governmental organisation (NGO) network, the arrests of the fishermen came to the attention of the LRC (which had not worked in the area previously) around July 2011.

At this time LRC lawyers Wilmien Wicomb and Henk Smith (2011) were preparing a paper on customary communities as 'peoples' and their customary tenure as 'culture' for a conference celebrating the thirtieth anniversary of the African Charter on Human and Peoples' Rights. They argued that an opportunity arose from the obligation of courts in terms of section 211(3) of the South African Constitution, which states that 'the Courts must apply customary law when that law is applicable, subject to the Constitution and any legislation that deals with customary law' (Wicomb and Smith 2011: 429). Their argument drew on the restitution case, in which Smith and the LRC had represented the *Richtersveld* community: 'In recognising the aboriginal title of the Richtersveld community… the Court held that the real character of the title that the Richtersveld Community possessed ... was a right of communal ownership under indigenous law' (2011: 8).

Likewise, in *Tongoane*, 'the Constitutional Court insisted ... that customary law systems are not invisible, but systems of law equal to statutory and common law' (Wicomb and Smith 2011: 432). Its decision read: 'the presence of living customary law as a form of regulation on the ground is not equivalent to a legal vacuum. It is rather a genuine presence that must be treated with due respect, even if it is to be interfered with.' Moreover, Wicomb and Smith (2011: 440–441) argued that rights established under customary tenure could be defended as an expression and practice of culture:

> In the case of communities on communal land adhering to living customary law ... the argument for the recognition of their rights to property is about the recognition of informal tenure rights as cultural activities and therefore the right to culture. In other words, the way in which these communities exercise their tenure rights within a communal system is an articulation of their culture.

Their conclusions in the article point to a set of principles they developed and deployed in the *Gongqose* case: communal ownership is associated with customary law and culture; customary community law is grounded in practice by the community; thorough investigation on a case-by-case basis is necessary to ascertain its content; and a community seeking protection of its communal land should define itself as adhering to customary law (Wicomb and Smith 2011: 443).

## LEGAL QUESTIONS IN THE *GONGQOSE* CASE

As Burke (2011) argues, both the legal team and the anthropologist are engaging in triangulation of the ethnographic archive, claimants' statements and points of law; indeed, as Randy Frances Kandel (1992b: 59) wrote, 'expert testimony is most successful when there is an understanding between the attorney and the anthropologist on ... the way facts will be introduced to prove some point of law'. The arguments highlighted above would shape the processes of triangulation that took place in the case. Inevitably, triangulation requires anthropologists to engage in a form of representation at odds with the 'thick description' of ethnographic writing, reducing the account to its legally significant aspects. In the course of serving in the case, I was asked to provide an affidavit and testimony in condensed form, largely tailored to the evidentiary requirements of the court and the planned arguments of the advocate for the defence.

In preparation for the *Gongqose* trial, Wilmien Wicomb of the LRC provided the two expert witnesses, Jackie Sunde and myself, with a memorandum that connected the jurisprudence around living customary law, the right to culture and the doctrine of aboriginal land tenure to the defence of David Gongqose. Critically, she argued 'there has never been an explicit extinguishment of the customary law rights of the community in the terms accepted in *Richtersveld* and therefore they remain entitled to access the resource in terms of custom'. In contrast to proof of custom under the common law, she argued that 'in proving custom under the Constitution, you prove more than a rule to fill a gap, but prove the existence of a system of law that is independent and develops on its own'.[5]

Wicomb then discussed the evidence required: proof of the existence of a set of uniformly observed, reasonable rules that regulated the 'social, political and legal existence of our community and in particular... use and access of all the common resources'. These should also define the user group and conditions for entry thereto. Moreover, the evidence should show that 'access to the resource is a mainstay of [the] community's culture' and that the right survived legislative interference, which would require showing that no legislation 'expressly extinguished the community's customary law right to fish', or 'rendered the exercise of... the indigenous law right to the resource unlawful' or 'granted limited rights... in circumstances where the only reasonable inference to be drawn is that the rights of indigenous law were extinguished'.[6]

Here, in the view of the LRC legal team, were succinctly presented the legal points that would need to be triangulated with the claimants' testimony and the evidence of the expert witnesses. The expert reports were brief and largely targeted to these requirements. (I also presented evidence regarding poverty in the area and the land claim negotiation process.) My statement on 'customary regulation' (even at this point, it appears, I was reluctant to use the language of 'customary law') comprised five paragraphs:

1. A system of customary regulation exists governing use of natural resources in the communities around Dwesa and Cwebe.
    1.1.1. Historical evidence describes fishing and collection of shellfish in the vicinity of Dwesa-Cwebe since at least the 18th century (Fay, Timmermans and Palmer 2002).
    1.1.2. Access to these resources was conferred by membership in a local community, acquired by birth, marriage, or through affiliation to a neighbourhood subheadman and headman. In practice, access was dependent upon knowledge and skills.
    1.1.3. Such knowledge and skills have been transmitted from generation to generation, as young people accompanied older experts on fishing

and gathering excursions. Family histories and genealogies recount the details of this transmission.

1.1.4. These rules were part of a larger body of customary regulation, still in practice in the present day, that governs access to local resources including residential, agricultural and grazing land, firewood and building wood, thatching grass and mud for brickmaking.[7]

Sunde's dissertation reflects a process of triangulation in which the author's starting point was more directly congruent with the points of law. Building on a history of activism, including working for recognition of customary law in the Department of Agriculture, Forestries and Fisheries (DAFF) and in a series of court cases in the Western Cape, Sunde's research at Dwesa-Cwebe (primarily in the communities of Hobeni and Ntubeni) was underway before and after her appearance in the *Gongqose* trial. Her statement was considerably longer, at 17 pages, and she presented a general historical background on use of marine resources by people along the South African coast, background on customary fishing communities internationally and the impact of statutory regulation. Most notably she explicitly deployed the language of customary law more directly; the key section on 'the use of marine resources by the Dwesa-Cwebe community in custom and culture' highlights some of the points I made above, but argues explicitly that 'access to natural resources is an integral part of the culture and constitutes the material basis upon which cultural identity is maintained'; ceremonial and ritual rights and obligations are tied to the ancestors and frequently involve seaside locations and/or marine resources. She described a number of specific rules concerning access to and harvesting of marine resources.[8]

## CUSTOM IN THE TRIAL

The transcript of the trial proceedings and the documentary evidence consist of some 800 single-spaced pages. I highlight here some of the ways in which the participants in the trial treated questions of custom and customary law, including the relative openness of the magistrate to hearing evidence and points from the defence legal team that went beyond triangulating with existing doctrine and instead aimed to introduce novel legal arguments.

Anticipating that the case would subsequently be heard on appeal, the defence team aimed to establish a factual basis that could support the constitutional argument regarding rights under customary law. As is not uncommon in court, the proceedings were often halting and non-linear in their structure, as the lawyers aimed to build up an evidentiary record, with an overarching logic that might be opaque and confusing to witnesses and observers. The evidence, however, constituted a potential resource for the closing arguments and a later appeal (Scheffer 2010). At a minimum, this meant going beyond the immediate facts of the presence of the three men inside the reserve boundaries, which was uncontested.

At the outset of the trial, the prosecutor presented the charges and the defence advocate, Jason Brickhill, responded with an admission of the facts and a plea explanation that 'the statutory regulation of marine resources has not extinguished our customary rights, of access to marine resources. Therefore our conduct was not unlawful in terms of the Marine Living Resources Act 18 of 1998 (MLRA) and/or the decree'.[9] Given the admission, the prosecutor decided not to call the four witnesses who had been brought to corroborate the facts and the trial proceeded to the examination of the accused David Gongqose by Brickhill.

Brickhill asked Gongqose to 'tell the Court about your family lineage, your descent'. Gongqose replied by listing his patrilineal ancestors going back about seven generations, listing names that I recognised from oral histories of the settlement of southern Hobeni. The state prosecutor immediately questioned the relevance of the evidence in the light of the admissions. Brickhill responded by explaining that the aim is to 'to establish the fact that the accused is part of this community, is part of this customary law system' and the magistrate allowed him to proceed 'in light of the very specific defence, and that being the customary law, access to resources, it would be incumbent upon the defence to establish that there is in fact such a heritage in the area'.[10]

In the exchanges that followed, Brickhill's questioning allowed Gongqose to recount both rules around fishing and the history of attempts to secure access to marine resources, focusing on the period since the 2005 closure of the Marine Protected Area (MPA). Immediately evident was a transition from a focus on factual and ethnographic questions to legal issues that would characterise the overall process from the initial trial to subsequent appeals. At the outset of cross-examination, the prosecutor asked, 'You were caught fishing illegally, do you agree with me?', immediately drawing an interjection from Brickhill, on grounds that it 'asserts a legal conclusion ... whether it's illegal or not is a matter for argument at the end of the case. We have no difficulty with the assertion that he was caught fishing ... but the conclusion of unlawfulness seems unfair to put to the accused.' The prosecutor rephrased the question to focus on fishing where 'you know you are not allowed' and questioning continued, focusing primarily on establishing that the marine resources had not been included in the Dwesa-Cwebe land restitution claim, which had been settled in 2001.[11]

The defence brought a second witness, Vuyelwa Siyaleko, and asked her to confirm that she was training to become a traditional healer. The prosecutor again objected:

'Those four charges [have] got nothing to do with the traditional healers in the area...to call a witness to say to come and tell this Court about the traditional healers and what they do in the customary law, doesn't relate to the charges with all due respect. One must at one stage draw a line and say but it is not relevant to the issue of fishing in the protected area.' Brickhill explained that 'she is affected in a spiritual dimension which the accused does not qualify' and is also a member of the mussel harvesting committee, reflecting women's interests in resource use. After a further interjection and discussion, the Court agreed 'to err on the side of allowing the evidence' while advising the defence to keep it as relevant as possible.[12] The witness was warned (at the request of the prosecutor) that discussions of mussel harvesting in a protected area may be self-incriminating. Brickhill's questioning and the cross-examination focused exclusively on traditional healing, which involves being called by the ancestors to perform ceremonies at particular locations on the coastline.

My testimony followed the written report quite closely but also supported Siyaleko's. In rereading the transcript, my reluctance to directly invoke 'customary law' is evident. Brickhill repeatedly asked about the 'system of customary regulation', and the 'customary system'.[13] I addressed the points without explicit reference to 'custom' or 'customary'; my sole use of the term 'customary practice' appeared again in reference to the distinction between *isithethe* and *isiko*. The only point at which I referred directly to a 'customary right' was in response to a question from the prosecutor in cross-examination:

P:  If the marine protected area is kept like it is at the moment, does that have an infringement on the customary rights of the accused?
DF: As I understand the customary rights yes.
P:  In which way?
DF: The customary right of access in utilisation of mussels and of shell fish.

In contrast, Sunde's testimony was framed explicitly in relation to custom: 'My doctoral studies focus on customary fishing systems and small scale fisheries governance'.[14] Her account invoked the framing of customary law both in describing local practices and highlighting international agreements that justified recognition of customary fishing rights.

## EDUCATING THE COURT

The *Gongqose* case differs from the cases examined by Burke in terms of the degree to which it engaged established legal doctrine. Working in the context of the second generation of land claims in Australia, where the legal points to be proven were relatively settled, Burke perhaps understates the way claimants' legal teams can also offer direction to the court in a less settled context. Unlike many of the cases examined by anthropologists working on aspects of indigenous rights, the defendants in the *Gongqose* case were not being required to fit into categories recognised by the state, statutory requirements or established legal doctrine (Thuen 2004; Nadasdy 2002); rather, they and their legal team were proactively working out the implications of existing statutory, constitutional and foreign law, and redefining the significance of customary law as a grounds for claims to resources. Wicomb (2015: 51) emphasises the novelty of the arguments in her own reflections on the case: 'My briefing to [Brickhill] ... set out the facts of the case and the idea of asserting constitutionally protected customary rights as a defence against the charge of unlawful fishing in the reserve ... Jason turned to our colleague and said, "Now that is making new law."'

The case was heard in a Magistrate's Court, where the state prosecutor and magistrate were not necessarily concerned with the constitutional questions brought by the defence. This gave rise to a situation where the state prosecutor conceded key parts of the defence arguments regarding customary law, even as the magistrate allowed a wide range of evidence, anticipating a later constitutional appeal. In the course of the cross-examination of Sunde, the prosecutor effectively – and perhaps unwittingly – affirmed key elements of the defence case. Part of his approach was to emphasise that the two expert witnesses brought by the defence were social scientists, not conservation specialists. In asking Sunde her areas of specialisation, he stated: 'We are not denying at all, the State is not denying, nobody has ever denied that there is a right of customary law.'[15]

At the same time, his statements suggested that customary law rights would not make the actions of the accused legal: 'The accused was found fishing illegally and it is illegal, do you agree? [JS:] I believe that the accused was operating within his customary legal system.' He would state later that 'to argue to this Court that the accused acted lawfully is a farce', leading Sunde to respond that 'there is a contradiction between our constitutional law and the way in which the marine living resources statute is being implemented'. The prosecutor engaged her on the relationship between customary and statutory law (an issue that would later be raised by the magistrate as well) and she indicated that in her understanding 'customary rights are protected in terms of the constitution which is above the Marine Living Resources Act'.[16]

The open-ended quality of the legal doctrine at this stage of the trial is evident from a set of questions that the magistrate raised both during the trial in a series of exchanges with Sunde, and in a letter to the legal teams on 16 March 2012. These sources offer the most direct insight into the magistrate's thinking; as Burke notes, '[judicial] interventions are revealing in a way that the tight formality of judgment writing never is' (2011: 159). Judges, he notes, also tend to rebuff attempts to interview them about cases.

One question pertained to whether the Magistrate's Court could apply customary law, given that a Magistrate's Court was forbidden (under section 170 of the Constitution) from ruling on the constitutionality of legislation. In fact customary law cases predominated historically in the magistrate's courts in the region, but the Constitution provided a new context (Kerr 1986: 527; Ndima 2004; Harris 1998; Mnisi Weeks 2016: 47–50). In response, Brickhill wrote:

> The Constitution provides, in section 211(3), that the courts must 'apply customary law when that law is applicable, subject to the Constitution and any legislation that specifically deals with it'. There is no indication that this section excludes the jurisdiction of the lower courts... The Magistrates' Court thus has the jurisdiction to apply customary law. In the matter at hand, the Court is asked to recognise and apply the customary law.[17]

The magistrate's questions continued with the more pressing issue of how to handle legal pluralism: 'Presuming that is argued that a lower court has such jurisdiction to interpret and apply customary law, which legal system supersedes the other where an act permissible in customary law is in conflict with conduct prohibited in terms of statutory law of the Republic?' In response, Brickhill reiterated:

> Customary law is only subject to legislation that 'specifically deals with it'... In addition, customary law may be regulated by statutory law... It might be suggested that the MLRA provides such regulation. However, regulation cannot amount to the complete extinguishment of customary rights unless it is done explicitly and if such extinguishment is not done in a manner consistent with s 36 of the Constitution... Customary law rights are directly recognised under the Constitution. Legislation, too, derives its force from the Constitution. Rights derived from the MLRA may therefore be considered to be equivalent to those derived from custom.[18]

His responses to further questions from the magistrate also affirmed the argument that defence of a customary right negates unlawfulness and clarified the scope of customary right as limited to members of Hobeni community, noting the evidence presented of shared rules that include rules regarding how rights might be acquired. The process here goes beyond triangulation, in Burke's sense: the defence team was not only aiming to present congruence between the facts presented by the claimants and experts, on one hand, and the law, on the other; they were also seeking to establish the legal points to be proven and actively shape the legal doctrine that the magistrate would use to interpret these facts.

## EVIDENCE IN THE COURT JUDGMENTS

Burke argues that when ethnographic evidence is incorporated into legal arguments and judgments, there is a tendency to focus on the factual information sufficient for the legal points, and not further:

> In academic anthropology there is, ideally, a relative openness to what counts as evidence, a heterogeneity of approaches, and the continuing expansion of evidence and revision of interpretations. In contrast, the judicial process is essentially about drawing boundaries around the totality of evidence and constructing an interpretative finality about the enclosed material (Burke 2011: 94).

The rulings of the South African Constitutional Court cases reveal this point, seeking no further 'interpretative finality' than the level of closure necessary to make a particular legal point. For example, in the *Mayelane* (2013) case,[19] the evidence regarding Xitsonga customary law was ambiguous and contested by various witnesses. Ethnographically incomplete, it was nonetheless legally sufficient for the court to rule and advance women's right to equality and dignity (Budlender in this volume).

Likewise, a decade earlier in *Richtersveld*, the court had sidestepped a set of questions regarding the existence and content of customary law, focusing on the evidence that was sufficient to resolve the case:

> In the course of establishing indigenous law, courts may also be confronted with conflicting views on what indigenous law on a subject provides... It is not necessary for the purposes of this judgment to decide how such conflicts are to be resolved... This case does not require us to examine the full range of problems concerned. In the present matter extensive evidence exists as to the nature of the indigenous law rights exercised by the Richtersveld Community.[20]

Questions that might seem urgent from an ethnographic or historical perspective may be set aside as the court sets out to rule only on the questions before it.

In this light, I turn now to the way the expert testimony was represented in the magistrate's judgment. For a magistrate to write a written judgment in a criminal case is extremely unusual, but he did so in this case, presumably anticipating an appeal. The document reveals both the reduction of ethnographic evidence to the minimum necessary to make the legal point, and the ways in which the magistrate was working out the implications of the constitutional recognition of customary law. It shifts the central concern from the content of custom and customary law – the focus of the two expert witnesses – to the legal question of their status in relation to statutory law.

The magistrate acquitted the accused on counts of possessing weapons inside a nature reserve and entering the reserve without a permit; he found them guilty of attempted fishing, but the sentences were suspended. In his written judgment, he summarised my testimony regarding custom succinctly: 'A system of customary regulation exists governing the use of natural resources in the communities around Dwesa and Cwebe. [Fay] described the authoritative structures including sanctions and remedies as developed and respected by those subject to them.' Sunde's testimony was also reduced to a few paragraphs:

> Ms. Sunde's evidence was that historically, many coastal communities have relied heavily upon marine resources for their survival and that this use was not merely a matter of subsistence or material need, but also constituted part of the culture and custom of many communities... Ms. Sunde detailed the long-standing and well-developed system of customary law in the Dwesa-Cwebe community and Hobeni in particular, which system comprised a system of rules relating to, and use of, marine resources. At the heart of this system is a customary norm entitling members of the community to have access to, and to use, marine resources for subsistence, ritual and other purposes.[21]

When he turned to discussing customary law directly, he drew heavily upon the work of Thomas Bennett (2004). Bennett's work provides a historically and ethnographically informed perspective on customary law that is already pre-digested in the recognisable form of a legal handbook, relatively accessible for a judge and focused on points of law above all. Notably, he quoted Bennett on the point that 'tradition may... be asserted to resist [state] policies' and a passage emphasising that courts may not be familiar with customary law as it 'derives from the practices of particular communities; these practices differ considerably from place to place, and they change constantly over time'. Finally, he cited Bennett on the relationship between customary law and the Constitution: 'With the inclusion of a justiciable Bill of Rights in the Constitution, the validity of a wide range of laws ... could now be tested against the standards of fundamental human rights ... due in part to the possibility of constitutional review and in part to the association of customary law with a right to culture'.[22] He went on to affirm that the evidence presented was sufficient to establish a system of customary rights: 'The accused persons have established ... that ... a custom of fishing within the coastal waters by the fishermen of the communities of Dwesa and Cwebe exists. This custom of fishing has subsequent to the enactment of the Marine Living Resources Act 18 of 1998, found itself in conflict with national legislation.'

He continued, recalling the defence argument regarding extinguishment: the 'complete extinguishment of the customary rights of the communities of Dwesa and Cwebe to practice these customs ... without consultation is ... irrefutable' and suggested that sections. 43 of the MLRA might not 'survive a test of constitutional validity', while adding that the magistrates' courts could not rule on constitutionality.[23]

For the purposes of this chapter, I do not consider the subsequent appeals to the High Court in Mthatha or the Supreme Court of Appeal in Bloemfontein in detail.[24] The leave to appeal was submitted in June 2012, but the case was only heard by the High Court in November 2015, with the judgment issued in February 2016, and the legal issues involved shifted from those at the Magistrate's Court. In addition to the defence arguments in the Magistrate's Court, the appeal added the argument that the minister had declared that the MPA was reviewable in terms of the Promotion of Administrative Justice Act 3 of 2000 in that it was unlawful, unreasonable and procedurally unfair.[25]

In relation to customary law, the heads of argument in the 2015 appeal cited the magistrate's finding that 'a custom of fishing within the coastal waters by the fishermen of the communities of Dwesa and Cwebe exists'.[26] Notably, in the High Court's subsequent judgment, the existence of rights under customary law was not contested; the questions hinged on whether the rights to practice one's culture (sections30 and 31 of the Constitution) might be balanced against the right to environmental protection in section24.[27]

In its February 2016 judgment, the Mthatha High Court presented a more detailed account of the case for customary rights than appeared in the Magistrate's Court:

> The record establishes that when the appellants were arraigned and eventually convicted they, and the rest of the members of the Dwesa-Cwebe com-

munities, had been accessing the MPA and fishing not only to sustain their families, but as an expression of the communities' culture and for economic reasons; they regarded the sea, rocks and coastline at and around the Reserve as sacred to them and the home of their ancestors; they claim to have known and used a range of fish and other inter-tidal resources since the time of their ancestors; they understood that nature had a way of protecting itself and this is what regulated their harvesting; the tides and the weather did not allow them to go fishing every day; they also had their own way of making sure that there would be enough fish for the generations to come, having been taught by their fathers and elders not to take juveniles and to put the small fish back. These rights were never unregulated, and were always subject to some form of regulation either under customary and traditional practices ... or through official state regulation.

Nonetheless, the High Court would go on the reject the claim, arguing: 'To contend that the mere existence of a customary right negates unlawfulness on a charge under the MLRA would serve not only to elevate the sections 30 and 31 rights at the expense of the right to the environment, but would make nonsense of the objects of the MLRA.'[28]

It concluded that the claimants should have sought an exemption to the no-take designation under the terms of section 81 of the MLRA. The Court glossed over the evidence on the record that showed the fishers had been engaging the relevant departments for recognition of their rights of access in terms of the MLRA consistently since at least 2001.

The Supreme Court of Appeal, in turn, deemed it unnecessary to consider the constitutionality of the MLRA or the review of the declaration of the MPA, instead focusing on the legality or criminality of actions under customary law. It ruled that 'the appellants have proved that at the time of the commission of the offence, they were exercising a customary right to fish. That right was not extinguished by legislation specifically dealing with customary law. Therefore, the appellants' conduct was not unlawful.' The judgment also noted in passing with dismay that the National Director of Public Prosecutions 'fail[ed] to file written submissions and present oral argument', which 'deprived this Court of the benefit of being able to canvass issues relating to unlawfulness and customary rights in criminal law, with the authority constitutionally responsible for the institution of criminal proceedings on behalf of the State'.[29] This passage again points to the way the court may shift the specific legal questions away from matters of ethnography or 'living customary law' towards a more internal legal discourse.

## CONCLUSIONS

The findings in the three judgments on the case to date have arguably answered the question with which I began the chapter. Although I did not previously use the term 'customary law' in my earlier research, the academic evidence could be construed, in the light of developing jurisprudence, to show that there were rights to marine resources under customary law for those who resided in the area. The subsequent questions concerned the relation of customary and statutory law: whether the existence of these rights negates unlawfulness under the MLRA; whether the MLRA may have extinguished these rights; how they might be 'balanced' against environmental rights in section 24, and whether the review of the decision to declare the MPA (an argument introduced at the appeal stage) could go forward. In terms of Burke's framework, the arguments of the claimants, the legal team and the experts 'triangulated' sufficiently to establish one of the key points of legal doctrine brought by the defendants' legal team, convincing the prosecutor and the courts that a right to fish exists under customary law. The Supreme Court of Appeal, in turn, agreed further that this right negates the charges of unlawfulness under the MLRA.

I want to highlight, however, the way in which the legal approach to evidence, which tends to engage the minimum necessary to address the legal questions (Burke 2011: 94), may leave uncertain the status of these rights as *living* customary law. What it means for these customary law rights to be 'living' in the view of the court has been largely left unanswered – in the 1054 page appeal record, the only references to 'living customary law' appear in the arguments of the LRC and the affidavits of the claimants; none of the courts engaged explicitly with this framing of local customary rights (cf. Burke 2011: 18; Tamanaha 1995).

The case can be viewed in the light of Canadian jurisprudence that was invoked in the arguments. The concept of 'frozen rights', which is 'the legal theory that aboriginal rights were limited to traditions of pre-European contact times' (Ray 2016: 87), was deployed in Canada to argue that only the technologies and techniques used for fishing in the pre-colonial period or at the time at which treaties were signed should be recognised by the state. Related questions around cultural and technological (dis)continuity were raised in the course of the *Gongqose* trial, by the expert witness brought by the state (marine scientist Peter Fielding), but were not directly addressed by the courts. In the *Gongqose* trial, the prosecutor asked Fielding, 'If I ... say that the Dwesa-[C]webe community is a fishing community ... how would you react to that?' He replied:

> A fishing community in terms of being a fishing community for ever and ever? ... on a historical perspective I would say no. People do fish here and they have been fishing here probably for the last 60 years but I think fishing activity has only occurred here since the availability of fishing gear ...

He reiterated this point a few minutes later: 'There has been a lot of pushing the point that ... they have always been catching fish. But I do not think that has happened until the development of modern line fishing.'[30]

In the Canadian jurisprudence, the 'frozen rights' doctrine was subsequently overturned in *Regina v Sparrow* (1990), which allowed for customary rights to be affirmed in their contemporary form rather than in their 'primeval simplicity' (Ray 2016: 215). Implicit in this ruling is a recognition of historical change that is compatible with the dynamic notion of 'living customary law'. In the *Gongqose* ruling, the Supreme Court of Appeal addressed the question of change only indirectly, with a statement that 'the validity of a custom is no longer determined according to the common law', footnoted with a reference to *Van Breda and Others v Jacobs and Others*, a precedent-setting case from 1921 that Bennett (2009: 23) considers 'the leading authority on how to prove custom' in the common law. *Van Breda* stated that 'to be recognised as law, a practice must be certain, uniformly observed for a long period of time and reasonable.'[31] The *Gongqose* ruling echoed the Constitutional Court's argument in *Richtersveld* that 'the approach adopted in Van Breda should not be allowed to inhibit' the development of customary law, and in *Shilubana*, in which the court noted that 'while change annihilates custom as a source of law, change is intrinsic to and can be invigorating of customary law' (Bennett 2009: 23). In the absence of tests for the existence and duration of custom that had developed from the *Van Breda* jurisprudence, the court accepted the existence of historical evidence of fishing on the Transkei coast without explicitly considering the question of technological and institutional change.

It does seem that there is a potentially unresolved set of questions in the *Gongqose* rulings, given that concerns analogous to 'frozen rights' were raised, but not addressed directly. There is no indication that the state intends to challenge the case further in the Constitutional Court, nor any indication that a 'frozen rights' argument would withstand further scrutiny. There is a possibility of a third party challenge, if conservationists and marine scientists were able to convince a court that they should have standing in the case. The omission reveals the ways in which the narrowly circumscribed legal ruling leaves open questions that are arguably important both for the legal doctrine around living customary law and for public perceptions of the justice of the case.

NOTES

1   S v Gongqose, Elliotdale Magistrate's Court E382/10 (unreported 2012) ('*Gongqose*').
2   Alexkor Ltd v Richtersveld Community and Others (CCT19/03) [2003] ZACC 18; 2004 (5) SA 460 (CC) 2003 (12) BCLR 1301 (CC) (14 October 2003) ('Richtersveld'); Bhe and Others v Khayelitsha Magistrate and Others [2004] ZACC 17 ('*Bhe*').
3   Tongoane and Others v National Minister for Agriculture and Land Affairs and Others (CCT 100/09) [2010] ZACC 10 ('*Tongoane*').
4   Hastings W. O. Okoth-Ogendo. Affidavit (2010) submitted in *Tongoane*, para 21.
5   Wilmien Wicomb, 'Memo on Legal Issues and Evidence: State v David Gongqose and Others', 29 January 2012, p. 8. Memo to expert witnesses in *Gongqose* (Wicomb memo).
6   Wicomb memo, pp. 9–10.
7   Derick Fay, Expert witness report, submitted to legal team in *Gongqose*, 27 February 2012 (Fay report).
8   Jackie Sunde, Expert witness report, submitted to legal team in *Gongqose* 26 February 2012 (Sunde report).
9   *Gongqose* (2012) vol 1, 13.
10  *Gongqose* (2012) vol 1, 25–27.
11  *Gongqose* (2012) vol 1, 42–43.
12  *Gongqose* (2012) vol 1, 74–77.
13  *Gongqose*, (2012) vol 2, 86–87, 89, 137–138.
14  *Gongqose* (2012) vol 2 133, 146–155.
15  *Gongqose* (2012), vol 3, 194.
16  *Gongqose* (2012) vol 3, 197, 217, 197–198.
17  Jason Brickhill, 'Heads of Argument on Behalf of the Accused'. *Gongqose*, 11 April 2012, para 12 (Brickhill 'Heads' 2012).
18  Brickhill 'Heads' 2012, para 15–16.
19  Mayelane v Ngwenyama and Another [2013] ZACC 14 ('*Mayelane*').
20  *Richtersveld*, 54–55.
21  *Gongqose* (2012) judgment 9, 10.
22  *Gongqose* (2012) judgment 19.
23  *Gongqose* (2012) judgment 23.
24  Gongqose and Others v Minister of Agriculture, Forestry and Fisheries and Others ZAECMHC 1 [2016] ('*Gongqose* 2016') and Gongoqose and Others v State ZASCA 87 [2018] ('*Gongqose* 2018').
25  Wilmien Wicomb, 'Notice of Application for Leave to Appeal', *Gongqose*.
26  Jason Brickhill and Michael Bishop, 'Heads of Arguments on Behalf of the Appellants in the Appeal/Applicants in the Review', *Gongqose* 8 April 2015 paras 69–70 (Brickhill and Bishop 'Heads' 2015).
27  Section 24 of the Constitution contains within it tensions between conservation and utilisation: it establishes the right 'to have the environment protected, for the benefit of present and future generations, through reasonable legislative and other measures that … (ii) promote conservation; and (iii) secure ecologically sustainable development and use of natural resources'.
28  *Gongqose* (2016) paras 23, 39.
29  *Gongqose* (2018) paras 64, 20, 34.
30  *Gongqose* (2012) vol 3 262–64.

31  Van Breda and Others v Jacobs and Others AD 330 (1921) cited in Shilubana and Others v Nwamitwa [2008] ZACC 9, para 55 ('*Shilubana*').

REFERENCES

Albertyn, Catherine. 1994.'Women and the Transition to Democracy in South Africa'. *Acta Juridica* (1994): 39–63.
Alcock, Ruari and Donna Hornby. 2004. *Traditional Land Matters: A Look into Land Administration in Tribal Areas in KwaZulu-Natal*. Pietermaritzburg: Legal Entity Assessment Project.
Bennett, Thomas W. 2004. *Customary Law in South Africa*. Cape Town: Juta & Co.
Bennett, Thomas W. 2009. 'Re-introducing African Customary Law to the South African Legal System'. *American Journal of Comparative Law* 57, no. 1: 1–31.
Bens, Jonas. 2016. 'Anthropology and the Law: Historicising the Epistemological Divide'. *International Journal of Law in Context* 12, no. 3: 235–252.
Berry, Sara. 1993. *No Condition is Permanent: The Social Dynamics of Agrarian Change in Sub-Saharan Africa*. Madison: University of Wisconsin Press.
Bourdieu, Pierre. 1986. 'The Force of Law: Toward a Sociology of the Juridical Field'. *Hastings Law Journal* 38, no. 5: 805–853.
Burke, Paul. 2011. *Law's Anthropology: From Ethnography to Expert Testimony in Native Title*. Canberra: ANU E Press.
Claassens, Aninka. 2012. 'Entrenching Distortion and Closing down Spaces for Change: Contestations over Land and Custom in South Africa'. PhD diss., Roskilde Universitet.
Claassens, Aninka. 2013. 'Recent Changes in Women's Land Rights and Contested Customary Law in South Africa'. *Journal of Agrarian Change* 13, no. 1: 71–92.
Claassens, Aninka and Budlender, Geoff. 2013. 'Transformative Constitutionalism and Customary Law'. *Constitutional Court Review* 30: 75–104.
Claassens, Aninka and Ben Cousins, eds. 2008. *Land, Power and Custom: Controversies Generated by South Africa's Communal Land Rights Act*. Cape Town: UCT Press.
Clifford, James. 1988. *The Predicament of Culture: Twentieth-Century Ethnography, Literature and Art*. Cambridge: Harvard University Press.
Cook, Peter Alan Wilson. 1927. 'Customs Related to Twins among the Bomvana of the Transkei'. *South African Journal of Science* 24: 516–520.
Cross, Catherine. 1991. 'Informal Tenures against the State: Landholding Systems in African Rural Areas'. In *A Harvest of Discontent: The Land Question in South Africa*, edited by Michael de Klerk, 63–96. Cape Town: Institute for Democratic Alternatives in South Africa.
Davies, C.S. 1927. 'Customs Governing Beer-Drinking among the Bomvana'. *South African Journal of Science* 24: 521–524.
DLA (Department of Land Affairs). 1997. 'White Paper'. Pretoria: DLA.
Edmond, G. 2004. 'Thick Decisions: Expertise, Advocacy and Reasonableness in the Federal Court of Australia'. *Oceania* 74, no. 3: 190–230. Pretoria: Land Affairs White Paper.
Fay, Derick. 2003. '"The Trust is Over! We Want to Plough!": Land, Livelihoods and Resettlement in South Africa's Transkei'. PhD diss., Boston University.
Fay, Derick. 2005. 'Kinship and Access to Land in the Eastern Cape: Implications for Land Reform'. *Social Dynamics* 31, no. 1: 182–207.

Fay, Derick. 2012. '"The Trust is Over! We Want to Plough!": Social Differentiation and the Reversal of Resettlement in South Africa'. *Human Ecology* 40 no. 1: 59–68.

Fay, Derick, Herman Timmermans and Robin Palmer. 2002. 'Competing for the Forests: Annexation, Demarcation and Their Consequences from c. 1878 to 1936'. In *From Conflict to Negotiation: Nature-Based Development on South Africa's Wild Coast*, edited by Robin Palmer, Herman Timmermans and Derick Fay, 48–77. Pretoria: Human Sciences Research Council.

Gordon, Robert J. and Andrew D. Spiegel. 1993. 'Southern Africa Revisited'. *Annual Review of Anthropology* 22: 83–105.

Haines, Richard J. 1984. *The Silence of Poverty: Networks of Control in Rural Transkei*. Cape Town: UCT School of Economics.

Harris, B. 1998. 'Indigenous Law in South Africa-Lessons for Australia'. *James Cook University Law Review* 5: 70.

Hendricks, Fred 1990. *The Pillars of Apartheid: Land Tenure, Rural Planning and the Chieftancy*. Uppsala: Almqvist & Wiksell International.

Kandel, Randy Frances. 1992a. 'How Lawyers and Anthropologists Think Differently'. *National Association for the Practice of Anthropology (NAPA) Bulletin* 11, no. 1: 1–21.

Kandel, Randy Frances. 1992b. 'A Legal Field Guide for the Expert Anthropologist'. *National Association for the Practice of Anthropology (NAPA) Bulletin* 11, no. 1: 53–81.

Kerr, Alistair. 1986. 'Customary Law in Magistrates' Courts and in the Supreme Court'. *South African Law Journal* 103: 526.

Koyana, Digby Sqhelo. 1980. *Customary Law in a Changing Society*. Johannesburg: Juta & Co.

Mailula, Douglas. 2011. 'Customary (Communal) Land Tenure in South Africa: Did Tongoane Overlook or Avoid the Core Issue?' *Constitutional Court Review* 4, no. 1: 73–112.

Miller, Bruce Granville and Gustavo Menezes. 2015. 'Anthropological Experts and the Legal System: Brazil and Canada'. *The American Indian Quarterly* 39, no. 4: 391–430.

Mnisi Weeks, Sindiso. 2016. 'Women Seeking Justice at the Intersection between Vernacular and State Laws and Courts in Rural KwaZulu-Natal, South Africa'. In *The New Legal Realism: Volume 2: Studying Law Globally*, edited by Heinz Klug and Sally Engle Merry, 113–142. Cambridge: Cambridge University Press.

Nadasdy, Paul. 2002. '"Property" and Aboriginal Land Claims in the Canadian Subarctic: Some Theoretical Considerations'. *American Anthropologist* 104, no. 1: 247–261.

Ndima, Dial Dayana. 2004. *The Law of Commoners and Kings: Narratives of a Rural Transkei Magistrate*. Leiden: Brill.

Ntsebeza, Lungisile. 2001. 'Land Allocation in South Africa's Former Bantustan with Specific Reference to the Role of Traditional Authorities'. Research paper prepared for the MWENGO Land Project, Harare.

Peters, Pauline E. 1994. *Dividing the Commons: Politics, Policy and Culture in Botswana*. Charlottesville: University Press of Virginia.

Platteau, Jean-Philippe. 1996. 'The Evolutionary Theory of Land Rights as Applied to Sub-Saharan Africa: A Critical Assessment'. *Development and Change* 27, no. 1: 29–86.

Ramos, Alicida R. 1999. 'Anthropologist as Political Actor'. *Journal of Latin American Anthropology* 4, no. 2: 172–189.

Ray, Arthur J. 2011. *Telling it to the Judge: Taking Native History to Court*. Montreal: McGill-Queen's Press.

Ray, Arthur J. 2016. *Aboriginal Rights Claims and the Making and Remaking of History*. Montreal: McGill-Queen's Press.

Rosen, Lawrence. 1977. 'The Anthropologist as Expert Witness'. *American Anthropologist* 79, no. 3: 555–578.
Sapignoli, Maria. 2009. 'Indigeneity and the Expert: Negotiating Identity in the Case of the Central Kalahari Game Reserve'. In *Law and Anthropology: Current Legal Issues*, edited by Michael Freeman and David Napier, 247–268. Oxford: Oxford University Press.
Scheffer, Thomas. 2010. *Adversarial Case-Making: An Ethnography of English Crown Court Procedure*. Leiden: Brill.
Segar, Julia. 1989. *The Fruits of Apartheid: Experiencing 'Independence' in a Transkeian Village*. Bellville: Anthropos Publishers.
Shipton, Parker. 1989. *How Private Property Emerges in Africa: Directed and Undirected Land Reforms in Densely Settled Areas South of the Sahara*. Cambridge: Harvard Institute for International Development.
Soga, John Henderson. 1931. *The Ama-Xosa: Life and Customs*. Lovedale: Lovedale Press.
Stewart, Omer C. 1979. 'An Expert Witness Answers Rosen'. *American Anthropologist* 81, no. 1: 108–111.
Sunde, Jacqueline. 2014. 'Customary Governance and Expressions of Living Customary Law at Dwesa-Cwebe: Contributions to Small-Scale Fisheries Governance in South Africa'. PhD diss., University of Cape Town.
Tamanaha, Brian Z. 1995. 'An Analytical Map of Social Scientific Approaches to the Concept of Law'. *Oxford Journal of Legal Studies* 15, no. 4: 501–535.
Thuen, Trond. 2004. 'Anthropological Knowledge in the Courtroom: Conflicting Paradigms'. *Social Anthropology* 12, no. 3: 265–287.
Wicomb, Wilmien. 2015. 'The Limits of the Law: The Struggles of the Traditional Fishers of Hobeni Village'. In *Human Rights in Minefields: Extractive Economies, Environmental Conflicts and Social Justice in the Global South*, edited by César Rodríguez-Garavito, 41–72. Bogata: Dejusticia.
Wicomb, Wilmien and Henk Smith. 2011. 'Customary Communities as "Peoples" and Their Customary Tenure as "Culture": What We Can Do with the Endorois Decision'. *African Human Rights Law Journal* 1, no. 2: 422–446.
Zenker, Olaf. 2016. 'Anthropology on Trial: Exploring the Laws of Anthropological Expertise'. *International Journal of Law in Context* 12, no. 3: 293–311.

CHAPTER
3

# When Custom Divides 'Community': Legal Battles over Platinum in North West Province

Sonwabile Mnwana

Land conflict has increased in sub-Saharan Africa, particularly in the context of land grabs, mounting scarcity, commodification of customary land rights and landed resources, competition and emerging inequality (Peters 2004; Chimhowu and Woodhouse 2006; Mnwana 2015).[1] In South Africa, perhaps more than anywhere else in the African continent, land has long been a major cause and outcome of racial inequality. With more than 17 million Africans still living in the former 'homelands' or Bantustans, whose land tenure rights remain poorly defined and insecure, South Africa's history of racial exclusion of Africans from landownership remains central to the ongoing struggles over land.

This chapter details the intense local land struggles over the platinum-rich land in South Africa's North West province. The central argument is that land disputes tend to be struggles over meanings of 'community' and 'property' at local level. Such struggles are mainly fought through contending versions of custom and distinct group identities. These disputes take the form of exclusive group claims over the platinum-rich land. Some of these claims have led to lengthy court battles between the groups of land claimants at village level and the local chief. I argue that since

African 'rights' and 'property' in rural land are defined through custom, custom has become central in how meanings of 'property' and 'community' are defined and redefined in contemporary struggles. Ironically, despite increasing reference to living customary law, the courts have quite often continued to define custom as a rigid set of rules, which remains unchanged and is carried on from one generation to the next. I argue that such a description not only fails to capture the complexities of South Africa's rural social milieu, it also perpetuates inequality and property disputes at village level, particularly when communal land is targeted for mining expansion.

## IDEOLOGICAL PREMISE

Far from being idyllic rural cultural enclaves, South Africa's former homeland areas are, and have long been, geo-political spaces of resistance and socio-economic marginalisation. These were the colonial 'native reserves' where the white minority governments (the colonial, Union and apartheid states) dumped millions of land-dispossessed Africans at different historical moments. As such, it would be limiting to describe rural Africans in these spaces as historically or even currently members of homogeneous political and cultural 'communities' whose interests could be legitimately represented only by local chiefs. The latter are often regarded as the rightful custodians of African custom and property rights in land and landed resources. Colonial dispossession and disregard of African indigenous landholding systems, denial of private property rights, enforcement of chiefly-mediated 'communal' rights and the ascription of tribal identities to Africans were the key elements of the system of indirect rule employed by the colonial state (Mamdani 1996).

This system was influenced by the demand for migrant workers and the need to enforce political control, and was justified by Social Darwinist thinking (Mamdani 1996; Delius 2008). Colonial officials perceived land rights in the African population to be 'communal' in nature since African peoples were seen 'as being at a lower level of social evolution'; private property was a mark of civilisation (Delius 2008: 213). Social Darwinism was applied vigorously in the colonial state's late nineteenth-and twentieth-century land policies that were directed at addressing the African land tenure question in South Africa. Of course, the effectiveness and the character of this application, particularly when it came to indirect rule and the power of chiefs, varied somewhat from place to place. In the Cape, for a limited period, Africans were permitted to purchase private property and a form of 'individual tenure' was pursued. But as indirect rule and segregation policy and ideology took hold in the early twentieth century, the faulty notion was promoted that all Africans were subjects of chiefs and thus members of tribes. In South Africa the colonially derived versions of customary rights and governance mechanisms, both legally ambivalent and administratively laborious, were to be kept intact and sustained through colonial declarations and legislation, especially the Natives Land Act of 1913 and the Native Trust and Land Act of 1936.

In the apartheid era (1948–1994), the South African state decided to entrench tribal authorities over the whole of the areas demarcated as Bantustans, thus rendering it impossible for the rural poor in the former homelands to have communal tenure without chiefs. African groups and individual families had held land and other property rights outside the boundaries of centralised chiefdoms, although in most instances not outside custom (Cousins 2008; Walker 2004). Moreover, the literature on the pre-colonial history of Africa offers some evidence that various factors limited the authority of chiefs, making it possible for people to leave the chiefdoms of despotic or weak chiefs and join other 'tribes' (Delius 2008: 15).

Some scholars observe that the escalating conflict on the platinum belt epitomises a resurgence of ethnic identities in post-apartheid South Africa (Comaroff and Comaroff 2009; Manson 2013). However, I argue that competing versions of custom and contrasting group identities that dominate these struggles reveal not just ethnic revitalisation, but serious divisions that challenge the very meaning and existence of 'tribal' or 'traditional' communities. Since rights to communal property are secured through group ('tribal') membership and defined through custom, custom itself has become a space for contestation.

## CHIEFS AND CUSTOM

In the first half of the twentieth century, as segregation became entrenched, the South African state increasingly abandoned a previously prevailing hostility to chiefs and sought to devolve limited authority to what they saw as a conservative and relatively accommodating local authority. Increasingly, local chiefs in the former homeland areas were assumed to be custodians of communal properties in the rural areas where Africans lived. Custom became an instrument of colonial administration, control and coercion over African masses (Channock 1985; Mamdani 1996). By and large, rural power during the apartheid era was organised at the level of a local institution – a 'tribal authority'. African authority at local level had to be legitimised and defended through the distorted versions of tradition and custom.

Mahmood Mamdani (1996: 109) argues that chiefs' power became solidified over 'communal' property to crush rural resistance against the state.

Where Africans had purchased landed property privately as families, syndicates and other communities that were not tribal, South African government policies from the 1920s increasingly enforced a requirement that they should constitute themselves as 'tribes' and register their properties under the names of a 'recognised' chief. Such a property would then be transferred to a state 'trustee' – a colonial official – who held the title deed in trust for the chief and his tribe (Capps 2010; Claassens and Cousins 2008). Central to the colonial mode of crystallising and enforcing customary law were the courts. For Mamdani (1996: 109), it was the courts – 'the torchbearers of that civilization' – who enforced customary law. Law was central to colonialism's chief claim of bringing 'civilisation' and 'the rule of law' to Africa. However, the colonial mandate could not align with 'civilizing' courts of law and the mandate shifted from 'the civilizing mission to law and order administration'.

The post-apartheid Constitution in South Africa recognises customary law and mandates the courts to 'apply customary law when that law is applicable, subject to the Constitution and any legislation that specifically deals with customary law' (section 211, 3). However, this mandate seems difficult to realise in the light of post-1994 legislation that reinforces the apartheid-style power and authority of chiefs. However, 'to determine the content of customary law by standards of "formal" law is to apply a distorted paradigm' (Claassens and Cousins 2008: 362). Generally, the courts in South Africa have increasingly categorised custom into two main categories: the 'official' and the 'living' law. 'Official' customary law is a product of the state and legal experts, while 'living' law refers to the law actually observed by the people who created it (Bennett 2008: 138). Official customary law is a product of colonial formalisation of indigenous peoples' law, which imposed rigid, Western, rule-oriented conceptions of law and order. Living law, on the other hand, evolves organically out of ever-changing African sociocultural processes of dispute resolution (Comaroff and Roberts 1991; Budlender and Fay in this volume). Therefore, it is through the process of colonial formalisation that African 'living law' became distorted.

The legal status and tenurial security of the land occupied and used by Africans, especially individual families in rural areas, remains unclear. At the root of this paradox lies the history of dispossession of indigenous communities and the imposition of significantly distorted versions of 'custom' (customary law) during colonial and apartheid periods. This issue is further complicated by the state and other actors in South Africa who generally define African property rights as 'communal' (Cousins 2008). As such, tenurial rights to land and other natural resources are generally conceived as communal – shared by groups who are defined as communities or political units – 'tribes'.

But the content of African custom was significantly reshaped or distorted by colonial and apartheid experience in South Africa and elsewhere in Africa. The colonial process of 'formalisation' or crystallisation of custom enhanced the power of chiefs. This is not to suggest that pre-colonial chiefs had no power at all. In fact, chiefs did allocate land and distribute other resources to members of their polities. But this power was significantly enhanced by the colonial system of indirect rule. For Mamdani, customary law became both 'all embracing' and divisive. It 'embraced' under the power of chiefs 'previously autonomous social domains [among others] the household, age sets, and gender'. Yet, the purpose of customary law, argues Mamdani (1996: 110) 'was not about guaranteeing rights, it was about enforcing custom. It was not about limiting the power [of chiefs], but about enabling it.' As such, the rigid, crystallised, ubiquitous version of custom, which conceptualised African custom as law – legally enforceable rules that governed all aspects of African life – has no pre-colonial precedent. Martin Chanock, for instance, maintains that in 'Africa, as elsewhere, much of life is lived outside of the law and involves values and patterns of behaviour which are different from these enshrined in the state's legal system. In these patterns may be found a repository of customary values which provide better building blocks than those which were legitimated by the colonial order' (1989: 87).

## PLATINUM MINING IN COMMUNAL AREAS

South Africa is the world's largest producer of platinum. Increasingly, land that fell under the former 'homelands' of South Africa has become the target of mining companies. Much of the area where platinum deposits are located – tagged 'the platinum belt' – spreads beneath rural communal land under the political jurisdiction of traditional (formerly known as 'tribal') authorities, mainly in the North West and Limpopo provinces. The two provinces include parts of former Bophuthatswana and Lebowa and bear the marks of the oppressive apartheid order: extreme poverty, massive unemployment, poor education and a lack of basic public services.

Since the early 2000s the state has enacted legislation that has not only legitimised the mediation of relationships between mining corporations and communities by traditional leaders, but has also enabled continuities in rural power relations in the areas that fell under chiefs and 'tribal authorities' in the homeland era. These laws are often interpreted to facilitate control by chiefs of customary land rights and distribution of mining revenues in rural areas.

Although the post-1994 African National Congress (ANC) government at first vacillated about defining and codifying the powers and status of chiefs, it eventually passed legislation that significantly increased the powers of chiefs in rural local governance. The Traditional Leadership and Governance Framework Act (Act 41 of 2003, TLGFA) is the main piece of legislation in this regard. The TLGFA empowers traditional (tribal) authorities to preside over precisely the same geographic areas that were defined by the apartheid government. Among other things, the Act potentially enables chiefs and their traditional councils to be granted powers over the administration and control of communal land and natural resources, economic development, health and welfare, and the administration of justice. However, the Act does not impose all of these powers – they have to specifically extended by legislation. The position is further complicated in that provinces have enacted their own versions of the Act. In theory the Act requires changes in membership if the tribal authorities are to become traditional councils but this process has not always been adequately followed (see Capps in this volume).

This legislation promotes a controversial governance role for chiefs. Other controversial laws that, so far, have been successfully resisted by rural citizens include the Communal Land Rights Act of 2004 (invalidated by the Constitutional Court) and the Traditional Courts Bill (Mnisi 2011). Post-apartheid laws regulating mineral rights, particularly the Mineral and Petroleum Resources Development Act (MPRDA) (Act 28 of 2002) and its accompanying regulations, also drive the inclusion of traditional communities in South Africa's platinum industry. In seeking to redress past injustices by transforming relationships between the mining companies and local communities, this legislation has adopted a range of measures, including enhanced royalty payments, black economic empowerment (BEE), mine-community partnerships, and social labour plans as requirements for mining companies. The state has encouraged communities who previously received royalty compensations for loss of land due to mining to convert their royalties into equity shares (Capps in this volume). Consequently, with the state's support, chiefs, as assumed custodians of communal resources, have become mediators of mineral-led development and mining deals.

As assumed custodians of rural land and other tribal properties, chiefs enter into mining contracts and receive royalties and dividends on behalf of rural residents who live in the mineral-rich traditional authority area. This traditional-elite-mediated model of community participation in the mining industry has received increased media attention, particularly since the 2012 Marikana massacre (Mnwana 2013; Botes and Tolsi 2013). Members of the South African Police Service shot at striking mine workers at the Lonmin Mine, North West province, and the massacre left 34 miners dead and many injured. In the face of protracted labour unrest in the platinum sector and the decline in platinum prices since 2011, the dominant view propagated by government, mining companies and the chiefs is that community control of mineral revenues mediated by tribal elites is crucial for congenial relations within the rural-based platinum sector.

Chiefs see themselves as legitimate mediators and gatekeepers through whom mining capital can gain 'easy access' to cheap local labour and communal land. However, this model has not yet led to tangible benefits for community members. Rather, it has enhanced the power of the chiefs and led to a lack of transparency, non-accountability, heightened inequality, deepening poverty and local tensions. Post-apartheid laws regulating and governing traditional leadership and mining reform have been criticised for promoting exclusion and corruption by using 'distorted constructs of custom' to 'impose contested identities' and 'undermining [rural residents'] capacity to protect their land and ... mineral rights' (Claassens and Matlala 2014).

## THE BAKGATLA AREA

This chapter stems from research that explores the multiple impacts of platinum mining in South Africa's former homeland areas. A research team comprising myself and two research assistants collected data in three stages between July and November 2013 in three villages in the Bakgatla area: Motlhabe, Sefikile and Lesetlheng. The first stage was local-level fieldwork. Our methods included in-depth interviews, observations and a second stage of analysing documents such as court case reports and archival records. The third stage was a detailed collection of oral histories. The main purpose was to focus on land and political histories and how they inform the present struggles in the Bakgatla area. The project is still in progress and I continue to make sporadic follow-up research visits to the study area. The ethnographic material presented here is based on semi-structured interviews with village activists. This material is corroborated by reference to archival documents in the South African National Archives in Pretoria.

The Bakgatla-ba-Kgafela community is one of the communities on the platinum belt that has significant control over mining revenues as a result of mining in the area. A product of South Africa's turbulent history of colonialism and racial oppression during apartheid, the eccentric confederation of 32 villages that constitute the Bakgatla area spreads all over the north-eastern and north-western foothills of the magnificent Pilanesberg mountains. This largely Setswana-speaking traditional authority area, under the leadership of *Kgosi* (Chief) Nyalala Pilane, is one of the largest communal areas in the North West province. It covers an area of more than 40 farms in the Pilanesberg region, about 60 km north of the town of Rustenburg. With approximately 160 000 residents the Bakgatla-ba-Kgafela area, which falls under the Moses Kotane Local Municipality (MKLM), is the epitome of a prominent tribal authority area with vast mineral resources (Mnwana 2015). As is the case in many rural areas in South Africa, the relationship between the Bakgatla traditional authority and the MKLM has not been smooth. This can be attributed largely to the lack of legal or administrative clarity about the role of traditional leaders in 'developmental' local governance.

Like other tribal authorities that were incorporated into Bophuthatswana, the Bakgatla chieftaincy had farms registered with the state in trust for the chief and his tribe. These farms spanned some of the richest mineral resources on the western limb of the Bushveld Complex. During apartheid, the Minister of Bantu Affairs, in his capacity as a 'tribal land trustee' mediated the contracts between mining companies and tribal authorities (Capps 2012). The powers of 'state trusteeship' regarding mineral and surface rights on tribal land were transferred to the Office of the President of Bophuthatswana when the latter gained its 'independence' in 1977. The Bakgatla chieftaincy began to receive mining royalties from the Anglo American Platinum (Amplats) Union Mine in 1982, deposited into Bophuthatswana state D-accounts (development accounts), held by the Office of the President (Mnwana 2015).

Due to the global upsurge in platinum demand in the 1980s and 1990s, the royalties payable rose significantly. From time to time, the chiefs would request funds from these accounts for various community development projects. If granted, funds would be deposited into a tribal trust account administered by a local state official. When this study was conducted in 2013 a 'tribal' account for the Bakgatla community existed at the District Office for Local Government and Traditional Affairs (LGTA), North West province in Mogwase, about 5 km from Sun City. This was where the monies from the Bakgatla D-account were supposed to be managed at a local level. According to the manager at this office, in the 1980s and early 1990s mining royalties in the Bakgatla Trust account amounted to between two and three million rand.[2] Under *Kgosi* Nyalala Pilane, the Bakgatla Traditional Administration has channelled various mining revenues to private business accounts that he opened in the community's name (Mnwana 2015).

After South Africa's first democratic elections in 1994, the D-accounts fell under the administration of the province's Department of Finance and LGTA. Since then, significant amounts of money have mysteriously disappeared from these accounts

(Capps in this volume). Since it took over the administration of these funds, the North West provincial government has been neither transparent nor accountable to the relevant communities.

The global boom in platinum group metal prices, which began in the early 1990s, ushered the Bakgatla-ba-Kgafela area and other rural communities on the platinum belt to centre stage of South Africa's post-apartheid mining economy. Several mining operations developed and *Kgosi* Nyalala Pilane entered into numerous deals and concessions with the mining companies and other investors. As a result of these deals, the Bakgatla-ba-Kgafela community became a huge business empire, estimated to be worth approximately R15 billion by 2012 (Khanyile 2012). This has heightened the chief's power and status.

Mounting resistance against *Kgosi* Nyalala Pilane has developed due to his lack of transparency and accountability in corporate dealings, and various allegations of corruption against him. The mining-related investments that the *Kgosi* has created through contracts with the mining companies are legion. They keep changing, making it extremely difficult for communities to keep up with them. *Kgosi* Nyalala Pilane is the director in most of the complex company structures that bear the Bakgatla name. Some village groups contest these mining contracts that are signed by the chief. They argue that their forefathers bought the mineral-rich farms as private properties and they should never have become tribal land. Most of the struggles in the Bakgatla area between the chief and various village groups have been fought in court. Furthermore, disputes over land and mineral revenues in the Bakgatla area are modelled through constructions of group identity and competing versions of custom.

The village level struggles and selected court judgments that are discussed in the next section demonstrate how disputes over control of mining revenues tend to underpin the power of local chiefs, particularly when the courts' interpretation of custom is rigid and distorted. The section below also demonstrates that the post-apartheid court judgments have ironically adopted an apartheid logic in their interpretation of customary law, which envisions all Africans as 'tribal' subjects whose property rights should be controlled and mediated through the office of a chief.

## DISPUTES, COURTS AND CUSTOM

Court battles between Bakgatla chiefs and their subjects predate the era of platinum revenues. During the rule of *Kgosi* Tidimane Pilane (Nyalala's predecessor), there were sporadic instances of resistance against the traditional authority. In one instance in 1953, *Kgosi* Tidimane imposed a levy of one ox per person on every adult male member of his tribe for the purchase of the farms Middelkuil No. 564 and Cyferkuil No. 372. Those who could not offer oxen were obliged to pay £15 (about R3 000 in 2020) per person. The combined price for the two farms was £14 000 (about R2.7 million in 2020 prices). In June 1956 a group of village residents, led by Jacob Pilane, a village activist and relative of the chief, filed a court petition accusing the chief of failing to account for the money he collected and 'wrongfully and unlawfully using and appropriating tribal funds for [his] personal benefit'.³

The native commissioner in Pilanesberg refused to grant permission to the private lawyers of the complainants to gain access to the tribal accounts of Bakgatla. He even denied them permission to visit the Bakgatla area in Pilanesberg. The hearing took place at the Transvaal Supreme Court in Pretoria on 28 June 1956. Jacob Pilane was listed as the only 'petitioner' against *Kgosi* Tidimane. Judge C. Bekker dismissed Jacob's application on 16 August 1956. His judgment was primarily based on the argument that the chief had no responsibility to account 'to anyone of his individual subjects' concerning the tribal accounts and that Jacob, although a member of the tribe, did not have *locus standi* to file a court application against the chief (see Pickering and Motala in this volume). Bekker continued: 'In native law the chief, in circumstances such as the present is held accountable only to the tribe acting in, or through a *lekgotla* or tribal meeting ... the petitioner [Jacob], in his private capacity is not, in my view of the matter entitled to the relief he claims – reliefs personal to himself and not to the tribe'.⁴

The judge also awarded costs against Jacob. The chief's loyalists in Moruleng subsequently sued Jacob's family for challenging the chief and accused him of trying to overthrow the chief. Jacob was unable to pay the legal costs, so Tidimane sent a group of men to his home to confiscate his cattle and agricultural tools by force. When this happened Jacob was in Swaziland, where he worked as a chef. One of his sons, who witnessed these events, said: 'The year was 1956 and I was doing Sub B when they came and took all my father's possessions. They came looking for my father's cattle. They took three cows together with all the ploughing equipment and left. They sold them to a white farmer called Piet Koos ... in Pilanesberg.⁵ Jacob never recovered his confiscated property.

The judgment against Jacob Pilane relied significantly on a distorted version of 'official' custom, which absolved chiefs from accounting to individual community members, thus providing them with enormous leverage to manipulate the downward accountability processes. As the only person entitled to call meetings (according to the 'official custom'), if a chief wanted to avoid accountability he could simply refuse to convene community meetings. The courts' use of distorted 'official custom' continues in the post-apartheid democratic era. Over the past decade, *Kgosi* Nyalala Pilane has filed several court interdicts against a number of villagers who challenged his power over the Bakgatla-ba-Kgafela community. This has intensified as more community members display displeasure with the chief's unilateral control over mining revenues.

In 2006 the regional court at Mogwase convicted *Kgosi* Nyalala and his close associate, Koos Motshegoe, on more than 40 counts of fraud and theft.[6] The fraud charges centred on the allegation that in 1998 *Kgosi* Nyalala had signed three loan agreements to the value of R13 million with the Land and Agricultural Bank of South Africa on behalf of the community, but without a community mandate. He pledged to repay this money through the annual royalties that the tribal authority receives from Anglo American Platinum. The regional court found that *Kgosi* Nyalala 'was not authorised to act on behalf of the tribe to enter into a loan agreement'.[7] Subsequently the court denied the *Kgosi* and his co-accused the right to appeal. *Kgosi* Nyalala's lawyer filed a petition with the judge president of the North West High Court, who in 2009 granted the chief and his co-accused permission to appeal against their criminal convictions.[8]

In September 2010 the high court upheld the application and acquitted *Kgosi* Nyalala Pilane and his co-accused of all criminal charges.[9] This ruling surprised and devastated the villagers. This blow was even more severe for members of the Concerned Bakgatla Anti-Corruption Organisation (COBACO), a village-based grassroots movement that had worked hard, with limited resources, to get the chief convicted. It had taken them from 1997 to 2006 to finally get *Kgosi* Nyalala Pilane to court.

In May 2008 *Kgosi* Nyalala filed an urgent court interdict at the North West High Court against a group of residents led by David Pheto. Identifying themselves as the 'Royal House', Pheto and other disgruntled community leaders had called an urgent general community meeting (a *kgothakgothe*) in order to oppose the mining transactions that the chief was about to sign on behalf of the community. The meeting was to be held on 21 May 2008. The dissenting group of residents also wanted to pre-empt another general meeting called by the chief on 28 June 2008 to co-opt the community into endorsing a murky mining transaction. Through this meeting *Kgosi* Nyalala intended to obtain a tribal resolution for a transaction between Itereleng Bakgatla Mineral Resources (Pty) Ltd (IBMR) (owned by the Bakgatla-ba-Kgafela) and Barrick Platinum South Africa (Pty) Ltd, a subsidiary of Barrick Gold Corporation.

The villagers opposed this transaction, mainly because they felt marginalised. They felt that the chief was unilaterally signing a mining contract that undermined their land rights without fully involving them. At the time, *Kgosi* Nyalala was facing a case about numerous instances of fraud and theft. Pheto and other villagers demanded that *Kgosi* Nyalala step down from his position. In response, *Kgosi* Nyalala interdicted Pheto and five other leaders of the dissent 'from interfering with a... general meeting', which was to be held on 28 June 2008.[10] In the North West High Court, Judge A.M. Kgoele consolidated the two interdicts and handed down the judgment, confirming both the interim interdicts by the chief against Pheto and others, on 3 December 2008.[11] The central argument in the judge's decision was that Pheto and five other community leaders did not have *locus standi* to call meetings of the tribe or to mobilise for the removal of *Kgosi* Nyalala from his position. Kgoele dismissed their claim that they were members of the 'Royal House' and refused them leave to appeal. The Supreme Court of Appeal also turned down their request for leave to appeal this decision.

Subsequent judgments at the North West High Court reinforced Kgoele's decision and helped to suppress opposition against *Kgosi* Nyalala. In September 2011 Judge R.D. Hendricks confirmed an interdict by *Kgosi* Nyalala against Pheto and other leaders, preventing them from calling community meetings. In line with previous judgments and the North West High Court, the judge found that Pheto and others were not members of the 'Royal Family', therefore they did not have *locus standi* to call meetings or to represent any group of villagers in Bakgatla-ba-Kgafela territory. Hendricks imposed punitive costs on Pheto and his fellow dissenters. He averred: 'It is quite apparent that the [r]espondents are doing everything within their means to unseat and undermine the authority of the [a]pplicants [*Kgosi* Nyalala and the Traditional Council] and to litigate as often as possible in an attempt to create confusion within the tribe. This behaviour borders on being vexatious. This, to my mind, calls for a punitive costs order.'[12]

Village-level disputes, whether over land, power or otherwise, are closely linked to struggles over mining revenues. In other cases involving local activists against *Kgosi* Nyalala Pilane, decisions at the North West High Court were no different. The court's decisions maintain the version of custom that ossifies the chief's power over communal property and endorses the tribal authority as the only legitimate authority with *locus standi* to represent village residents. For instance, a group of residents, calling themselves the Bakgatla-ba-Sefikile Traditional Community Association, claiming ownership of the mineral-rich farm Spitskop 410 JQ, sought a court order to compel the Minister of Rural Development and Land Affairs to transfer the ownership of the said farm to their names. This application sought to effectively remove *Kgosi* Nyalala's custodianship over this property and its mining revenues.

The North Gauteng High Court transferred the application to the North West High Court on 31 January 2011. Judge Leeuw handed down her judgment on the case on 1 December 2011. She relied strongly on the perceived 'customary' custodianship of chiefs over communal land, and made reference to the Constitution and post-apartheid legislation that empowers chiefs to act as trustees over communal land. In this land dispute case, the judge, citing the Constitution and customary law, argued: 'In this matter I am enjoined by the Constitution to recognise that land that is held by the *Kgosi* or traditional leader on behalf of a tribal community should be dealt with in terms of legislations that have been enacted for the purpose of regulating amongst others, the ownership thereof as well as the role and powers of the traditional leaders.'[13] The judge dismissed the application of the Community Association with costs.

Another land claim by a group in Motlhabe village has produced a secession move, which culminated in a protracted court case. The move to secede began with a notice in July 2009 from the leaders of land claimants calling themselves the Bakgatla-ba-Kautlwale addressed to the traditional council of Bakgatla. Ba-Kautlwale asserted strong claims over the mineral-rich farm Welgewaagd 515. They declared that Motlhabe village (located on Welgewaagd) was no longer under the jurisdiction and administrative control of the Bakgatla chieftaincy. In February 2010 *Kgosi* Nyalala's threats of legal action became real as soon as the leaders of the secession group circulated a meeting invitation. The invitation was addressed to 'The Residents of the Motlhabe Village' to discuss secession. *Kgosi* Nyalala filed an urgent High Court application to interdict the leaders. The interdict prohibited Bakgatla-ba-Kautlwale from convening any village meeting without the tribal council's permission.

This was the beginning of a protracted legal battle between the chief and the Bakgatla-ba-Kautlwale group. The battle went as far as the Constitutional Court. At the North West High Court on 30 June 2011, Judge Landman upheld *Kgosi* Nyalala's interdicts against the two ba-Kautlwale leaders and village activists Mmuti Pilane and Reuben Dintwe. The judge argued: 'Any action by a parallel but unsanctioned structure that is neither recognised by law or custom seeking to perform or assume functions that are clearly the exclusive preserve of recognised authorities ought to incur the wrath of law'.[14] The North West High Court and the Supreme Court of Appeal denied Pilane and Dintwe leave to appeal against this judgment. The lawyers who represented the two activists took the matter to the Constitutional Court, which set aside the three interdicts in February 2013 mainly on the basis that these 'interdicts adversely impact on the applicants' rights to freedom of expression, association and assembly'.[15]

It is striking that all of the lower courts found in favour of the chief and traditional authorities. The Constitutional Court judgment was thus a landmark victory for traditional communities: it affirmed the freedom of expression, assembly and association of rural residents. It granted the Bakgatla-ba-Kautlwale a significant victory by removing all of *Kgosi* Nyalala's interdicts and it also reaffirmed the right of the villagers to meet without having to seek permission from the chief to do so. Subsequent to this court victory, the Bakgatla-ba-Kautlwale leaders have filed applications to be recognised as an independent traditional authority in terms of the Traditional Leadership Governance and Framework Act of 2003. Some of these claims have been connected to the long-standing dispute over Motlhabe headmanship (Mnwana 2018 and Budlender in this volume).

## THE COMMUNAL PROPERTY ASSOCIATION

The Constitutional Court issued another landmark judgment on Bakgatla land disputes in August 2015. This involved the Bakgatla-ba-Kgafela Communal Property Association (the Bakgatla CPA) – a landholding entity established in terms of section 5(4) of the Communal Property Associations Act (CPA) (28 of 1996). Ordinary residents in the Bakgatla areas established the Bakgatla CPA in 2005 to hold land rights acquired through a restitution claim of seven farms. These communities were forcefully removed during apartheid. Most of these farms are now located within the famous Pilanesberg Game Reserve. The chief tried to oppose the formation of a CPA, in favour of a community trust. The claimant community prevailed in the end and a CPA was established. (For a similar conflict, see Chaskalson in this volume.)

However, the chief's objections were not without an impact. Instead of registering the CPA permanently, the Department of Rural Development and Land Affairs registered a provisional association. This 'provisional' status was to become a key impediment for the community members towards realising their rights. In 2012 the CPA tried to stop *Kgosi* Nyalala from giving away a piece of land that belonged to the community to developers for the construction of shopping mall in the Bakgatla area. *Kgosi* Nyalala immediately rejected the legitimacy of the CPA, arguing that this association was valid only for a period of 12 months, unless renewed. The Bakgatla CPA went to court to confirm its legal registration as a permanent association. This was to become a prolonged court battle, which went through the Land Claims Court, the Supreme Court of Appeal and ultimately ended up at the Constitutional Court.

In all these courts, the Traditional Council argued that the Bakgatla CPA no longer existed as it had not been turned into a permanent association in terms of section 5 of the CPA Act. The CPA argued, on the other hand, that, according to section 5(4) of the CPA Act, a provisional CPA does not cease to exist after 12 months if it is not renewed, although it may no longer be able to continue managing land. The Land Claims Court agreed with the CPA's interpretation and ruled in its favour. The court ordered the director-general of the Department of Rural Development and Land Affairs to register the Association permanently, since it had met all the requirements of the CPA Act. The Land Claims Court went further to argue that the reason for the Bakgatla CPA not being registered permanently was mainly the administrative failure of the state, particularly the minister's unlawful interference. The chief and the Bakgatla Traditional Council appealed this judgment and the Supreme Court of Appeal upheld their appeal.

After these opposing judgments at the Land Claims Court and the Supreme Court of Appeal, the Constitutional Court, in August 2015, reinstated the order of the Land Claims Court arguing that the Bakgatla CPA had met all the requirements of a permanent association stated in the CPA Act. The Court not only ordered the director-general to register the Association but went on to argue: 'The fact that a traditional leader or some members of the traditional community prefer a different entity to the association is not a justification for withholding registration and imposing mediation on the parties'.[16] This was a landmark judgment, not only for the Bakgatla CPA, but also for all the communal landholding entities in the country that are not under a chief.

## CONCLUSION

The expansion of mining on rural land has produced local struggles. One point of departure in my attempt to understanding mining-led conflict in rural South Africa has been to observe the character of the legal disputes. The latter, particularly in the context of the Bakgatla disputes, tend to highlight the role of custom. Why are the new rural struggles dominated by court battles? Is the customary law applied by courts so distorted that it has potential to divide a 'community'?

The distorted interpretation of African custom in judgments at a level below the Constitutional Court has amounted to a defence of the power of chiefs. The courts have not been consistent but the trend of judgments replicates the rural structure of power during apartheid. According to Mamdani (1996), this institutional power was defended and legitimised through custom. The institutions that enforced custom had authority to define it in the first place. The interpretation of custom by courts and their defence of institutional power epitomises this phenomenon.

These court battles have also to some degree shaped the character of resistance. Resistance seems to be rooted in contesting claims by traditional authorities, and particularly *Kgosi* Nyalala, over landed property and customary authority in the Bakgatla area. It must also be noted that the judgments discussed in this chapter come at an enormous financial and psychological cost, particularly for the ordinary community members. They require a great deal of time and consultation. They are dependent on lawyers who can act on a pro bono basis.

However, the Constitutional Court, which places primacy on constitutional rights, has overturned local courts on at least two key occasions in this discussion. The 'new' rural customary order enforced by the post-apartheid state hinders the flexibility and consensus inherent in the living law. It is this inflexibility in the way that the state and some of the the courts conceive custom – as a rigid set of rules – which perpetuates inequality and disputes at village level (see Duda and Ubink in this volume). Rigid custom renders rural disputes into zero sum games. Groups or individuals that can prove in court that they have the legitimate version of custom are likely to win. This phenomenon destroys the natural consensus inherent in the 'living' African custom.

Hence, I argue that the colonial crystallisation of custom made it difficult to 'bend' when people's social conditions change, but easy to 'break' when socio-economic conditions transform disputes over property. Both the chiefs and ordinary villagers compete to bring forward the most 'legitimate' version of custom in order to have exclusive control over communal property. By perpetuating a distorted interpretation of custom that protects and empowers chiefs, the courts not only leave the chiefs unaccountable, they also enhance marginalisation of ordinary rural residents, which makes residents lose faith in the justice system (Mnwana 2014).

A central feature of the village-level struggles described in this chapter are the diverse – and sometimes conflicting – group interests that run through them. This is in part explained by the fact that since rights over communal property are politically mediated by institutions of tribal authority, disputes over communal resources frequently take the form of power struggles at different levels in the tribal hierarchy. Moreover, in Bakgatla, land struggles tend to be fought through competing versions of history, custom and contrasting group identities, which in turn function as social markers of rights to power and control over mineralised land and its revenues. Even with the 'modern', fairly democratic landholding entity, the Bakgatla CPA, claims tend to draw on some of these diverse histories and identities.

The case of the Welgeval claimants epitomises this (Manson and Mbenga 2009). A group of Bakgatla claimants within the CPA claimed excusive ownership to the farm Welgeval 749, initially owned by Reverend Gonin (a Dutch Reformed Church missionary). In the nineteenth century it was the place where his converts lived – ostensibly not as subjects of chiefs. These were mainly former *inboekelinge* (African children abducted by Boers in a form of slavery at a young age) (Morton 1992). Some were Africans who were displaced during the *difaqane* (nineteenth-century forced dispersals) and Boer raids for cattle and slaves. They later formed a small community of African converts, whom the Dutch chose to call the *Oorlamse*. It was some elite members of the *Oorlamse* community who composed the nine-member syndicate that purchased the Welgaval farm for private use in 1912.

When some of the members of the original syndicate died, the remaining members could not keep up to date with the yearly instalment. When the farm was about to be resold again in 1932 the descendants of the original African buyers approached Chief Ofentse Pilane for help. The chief raised the outstanding amount from the villages in the Bakgatla area and placed a firm condition that the farm would then be a property of the Bakgatla 'tribe' (Manson and Mbenga 2009). The two families who were part of the buying syndicate who had fully paid for their portions of the farm (Moloto and Sefara families) tried unsuccessfully to prevent defend their portions on the farm from being declared tribal property together with the rest of the Welgeval farm in 1933. The claimants were forcefully removed from this farm in May 1980 by the Bophuthatswana government in collusion with Chief Tidimane Pilane (of Bakgatla) to make way for the establishment of the Pilanesburg Game Reserve. Although this farm was included in a 'successful' land restitution process of 2008, many residents felt that the restitution process had failed the historically dispossessed people. They felt that the financial compensation was inadequate and did not benefit all the relocated families. Such claims tended to intensify tensions and divisions within the Bakgatla villages and CPA itself instead of providing relief and realisation of land rights.[17] At the centre of the ongoing tensions was the fact that only the descendants of the original buying syndicate – mainly the Moloto and Sefara families – received direct compensation. If any form of benefits accrued to the rest of the disposed Welgeval claimants, the Bakgatla traditional authority administered the benefits on their behalf. This led to significant tensions among the claimants as many families felt unfairly excluded. An elderly woman (73 years old in 2013) in the new Welgeval village, whose family suffered significant losses during the forced relocation in 1980, explained

> In 1996, we claimed our land as the relocated families. In 2006, a group from with us called the *Bareki* [buyers – descendants of the buying syndicate] also claimed after us. They were successful in their claim. They were compen-

sated. Our claim failed. We are not benefiting from the Game Park. I think the only people who benefited are the descendants of the buying families. They are part of the Welgeval CPA.[18]

Elsewhere I have argued that the emergence of exclusive group claims over mineral-rich land in rural South Africa emanate from the fact that mining itself has led to another form land dispossession. Since local chiefs gain 'control over mining revenues through exclusive claims to land and "tribal" identity, the land claimants see no other alternative but to shift their meaning of land towards exclusive group claims and histories' (Mnwana 2018: 229). The court battles highlighted in this chapter reinforce this argument as well as disputes over different versions of custom.

At the pan-tribal level, the broader struggle to remove the chief could be simultaneously undermined by conflicting group interests between and within different villages. This, I suggest, is particularly likely in a context where power at these lower political levels has the potential to translate into exclusive control over mining benefits. A critical effect is that contemporary struggles over land and mining rights contain within them political impulses that could ultimately lead to the disintegration of the 'tribal' community, as defined in the law. This is most graphically illustrated by the secession move in Motlhabe, as well as the assertion of political independence by the land claimants in Sefikile. Indeed, rigid customary rules can be discriminatory and exclusive to other social categories. Pauline Peters (2004) attests that the very negotiability and adaptability of customary property rights tend to favour the local elite (chiefs and other power holders) who use the rules of customary law to assert exclusive claims over communal property. This argument illustrates some weaknesses within customary law and processes, but does not necessarily suggest that customary rights inherently reinforce inequalities.

As Geoff Budlender's article in this volume points out, the concept of the 'living customary law', which has been adopted by the Constitutional Court, is key to dealing with these challenges. The Constitutional Court has tended to make judgments against those who use arguments about custom to consolidate control of resources and local institutions in the hands of chiefs. If it is to effectively grapple with complexities of rural land struggles, the concept of living customary law should not only focus on changes in the content of custom over time, but should also take stock of shifting power dynamics. As argued, these tend to be reinforced when chiefs and traditional councils are able to act as intermediaries – especially when minerals or other major resources are found and exploited on land to which there are customary claims. Such an approach could help ensure access to land rights for previously marginalised social categories and limit the power of the local elite actors.

NOTES

1. This is an updated and expanded version of my article, '"Custom" and Fractured "Community": Mining, Property Disputes and Law on the Platinum Belt, South Africa,' *Third World Thematics: A TWQ Journal* 1 no. 2 (2016):, 218–234. It retains some elements of this earlier article.
2. Meshack Motswaeli, interviewed by Sonwabile Mnwana, Mogwase, Pilanesburg, 12 August 2013.
3. Pretoria National Archives (PTA), PTD, 1442/1956.
4. PTA, PTD, 1442/1956.
5. Sereti Pilane, interviewed by Sonwabile Mnwanga, Moruleng, 2 November 2013.
6. National Director of Public Prosecutions v Pilane and Others (692/06) [2006] ZANWHC 68 ('*Pilane* 2006')
7. S v Pilane and Another (CA 59/2009) [2010] ZANWHC 20 ('*Pilane* 2010').
8. *Pilane* 2010.
9. *Pilane* 2010.
10. Pilane and Another v Pheto and Others 1369/2008 [2008] ZANWHC ('*Pilane* 2008').
11. *Pilane* 2008.
12. *Pilane* 2008, judgment 3 December 2008.
13. Bakhatla Basesfikle Community Development Association and Others v Bakgatla ba Kgafela Tribal Authority and Others 320/11 [2011], para 42.
14. Pilane and Another v Pilane and Another ZANWHC 263/2010 [2011] para 43 (*Pilane* 2011).
15. Pilane and Another v Pilane and Another (CCT 46/12) [2013] para 70 ('*Pilane* 2013').
16. Bakgatla-ba-Kgafela Communal Property Association v Bakgatla-ba-Kgafela Tribal Authority and Others (CCT 231/14) [2015] ZACC 25, para 54.
17. Bridgeman Sojane, interviewed by Sonwabile Mnwana, Welgeval, Pilanesburg, 3 November 2013.
18. Bafedile Molefe, interviewed by Sonwabile Mnwana, Welgeval, Pilanesburg, 15 November 2013.

REFERENCES

Bennett, Thomas W. 2008. 'Official vs Living Customary Law: Dilemmas of Description and Recognition'. In *Land Power & Custom: Controversies Generated by South Africa's Communal Land Rights Act*, edited by Aninka Claassens and Ben Cousins, 138–153. Cape Town: UCT Press.

Botes, Paul and Niren Tolsi. 2014. 'Marikana: One Year after the Massacre'. *Mail & Guardian*, 12 September.

Capps, Gavin. 2010. 'Tribal-Landed Property: The Political Economy of the Bafokeng Chieftaincy, South Africa, 1837–1994'. PhD diss., London School of Economics and Political Science.

Capps, Gavin. 2012. 'Victim of its Own Success? The Platinum Mining Industry and the Apartheid Mineral Property System in South Africa's Political Transition'. *Review of African Political Economy* 39, no. 131: 63–84.

Chanock, Martin. 1985. *Law, Custom and Social Order: The Colonial Experience in Malawi and Zambia*. Cambridge: Cambridge University Press.

Chanock, Martin. 1989. 'Neither Customary nor Legal: African Customary Law in an Era of Family Law Reform'. *International Journal of Law, Policy and the Family* 3, no. 1: 72–88.

Chimhowu, Admos and Phil Woodhouse. 2006. 'Customary vs Private Property Rights? Dynamics and Trajectories of Vernacular Land Markets in Sub-Saharan Africa'. *Journal of Agrarian Change* 6, no. 3: 346–371.

Claassens, Aninka and Ben Cousins. 2008. *Land, Power & Custom: Controversies Generated by South Africa's Communal Land Rights Act*. Cape Town: UCT Press.

Claassens, Aninka and Boitumelo Matlala. 2014. 'Platinum, Poverty and Princes in Post-Apartheid South Africa: New Laws, Old Repertoires'. In *New South African Review 4*, edited by Gilbert Khadiagala, Prishani Naidoo, Devan Pillay and Roger Southall, 113–135. Johannesburg: Wits University Press.

Comaroff, John. L and Jean Comaroff. 2009. *Ethnicity, Inc*. Chicago: University of Chicago Press.

Comaroff, John L. and Simon Roberts. 1991. *Rules and Processes: The Cultural Logic of Dispute in an African Context*. Chicago: University of Chicago Press.

Cousins, Ben. 2008. 'Characterising "Communal" Tenure: Nested Systems and Flexible Boundaries'. In *Land, Power & Custom: Controversies Generated by South Africa's Communal Land Act*, edited by Aninka Claassens and Ben Cousins, 109–137. Cape Town: UCT Press.

Delius, Peter. 2008. 'Contested Terrain: Land Rights and Chiefly Power in Historical Perspective'. In *Land, Power & Custom: Controversies Generated by South Africa's Communal Land Act*, edited by Aninka Claassens and Ben Cousins, 211–237. Cape Town: UCT Press.

Khanyile, Gcwalisile. 2012. 'Bakgatla Tribes Men Facing Corruption Probe'. *IOL News*, 14 October.

Mamdani, Mahmood. 1996. *Citizen and Subject: Contemporary Africa and the Legacy of Late Colonialism*. Princeton: Princeton University Press.

Manson, Andrew. 2013. 'Mining and "Traditional Communities" in South Africa's "Platinum Belt": Contestations over Land, Leadership and Assets in North-West Province c. 1996–2012'. *Journal of Southern African Studies* 39, no. 2: 409–423.

Manson, Andrew and Bernard K. Mbenga. 2009. 'The Evolution and Destruction of Oorlam Communities in the Rustenburg District of South Africa: The Cases of Welgeval and Bethlehem, 1850s–1980'. *African Historical Review* 41, no. 2: 85–115.

Mnisi, Sindiso. 2011. 'The Traditional Courts Bill: Controversy around Process, Substance and Implications'. *South African Crime Quarterly* 35: 3–10.

Mnwana, Sonwabile. 2013. 'Are Communities Benefiting from Mining? Bafokeng and Bakgatla Cases'. *South African Labour Bulletin* 37, no. 3: 30–33.

Mnwana, Sonwabile. 2014. 'Chief's Justice? Mining, Accountability and the Law in the Bakgatla-ba-Kgafela Traditional Authority Area, North West Province'. *South African Crime Quarterly* 49: 21–29.

Mnwana, Sonwabile. 2015. 'Mining and "Community" Struggles on the Platinum Belt: A Case of Sefikile Village in the North West Province, South Africa'. *The Extractive Industries and Society* 2: 500–508.

Mnwana, Sonwabile. 2016. '"Custom" and Fractured "Community": Mining, Property Disputes and Law on the Platinum Belt, South Africa'. *Third World Thematics: A TWQ Journal* 1, no. 2: 218–234.

Mnwana Sonwabile. 2018. 'Private Property? Village Struggles over Meanings of Land and Mining Revenues on South Africa's Platinum Belt'. In *The Future of Mining in South*

*Africa: Sunset or Sunrise?*, edited by Salimah Valiani, 203–231. Johannesburg: Jacana Media.

Morton, Fred. 1992. 'Slave-Raiding and Slavery in the Western Transvaal after the Sand River Convention'. *African Economic History* 20: 99–118.

Peters, Pauline E. 2004. 'Inequality and Social Conflict over Land in Africa'. *Journal of Agrarian Change* 4, no. 3: 269–314.

Walker, Cherryl. 2004. '"We Are Consoled": Reconstructing Cremin'. *South African Historical Journal* 51, no. 1: 199–223.

CHAPTER

4

# Chiefs, Mines and the State in the Platinum Belt: The Bapo-ba-Mogale Traditional Community and Lonmin

Gavin Capps

This chapter arises out of the collective effort of the Mining and Rural Transformation in Southern Africa (MARTISA) research project at the Society, Work and Politics Institute (SWOP), University of the Witwatersrand.[1] My own involvement in researching Bapo history results from long-term academic engagement on the platinum belt. This has included work on legal cases that were brought to support community rights to land and resources, as well as for the Marikana Commission of Inquiry, particularly in relation to the Bapo case itself.

The land near Rustenburg on which the Marikana platinum mine is situated is that of the Bapo-ba-Mogale traditional community. Mining started on this land in the 1970s, yet the community has seen very little benefit. Conflicts between different branches of the chieftaincy have made it difficult for the larger community to become beneficiaries. The state and its officials have acted in such a way as to siphon off the income from the mines rather than return it to the community. This chapter explores the complex and shifting relationship between Lonmin, the mining corporation, the Bapo chiefs and the provincial government since mining began in this area. A particular focus is the multiple crises in legitimate community authority and representation, which have been affected by the interests of Lonmin and the government's interventions. This in turn raises larger questions about contested histories around traditional authorities when they become vehicles for the management of major resources. New legislative frameworks also underpin the experience of traditional councils, communities and 'empowerment'. These are issues of growing concern as they are increasingly replicated across the rural areas of South Africa.

The bulk of this chapter focuses on the long and troubled relationship between chiefs, mines and government. In particular it details the enormous financial losses, of over R600 million, suffered by the Bapo community. In 2012, Lonmin's corporate image was shattered by the Marikana massacre. In the commission of inquiry that followed, Lonmin's failure to meet its social obligations to the surrounding area – a condition of its licence to mine – was laid bare. The spotlight also fell on the dubious role played by Cyril Ramaphosa, a non-executive director on the board of Lonmin, and CEO of its main black economic empowerment (BEE) partner, Shanduka. As was widely noted at the time, the fortunes made by these companies during the recent platinum boom contrasted sharply with the endemic poverty in the rural villages adjacent to the mines.

In 2014 Lonmin sponsored a deal that was an opportunity to put things right, incorporate the Bapo community and salvage a little of its corporate reputation. A royalty previously payable to the community for mining platinum on its land was converted into a direct equity stake in the company, worth R564 million, together with a 'deferred royalty payment', and preferential opportunities to bid for mine supply contracts. This, said Lonmin, would enable the community to enjoy the full benefits of participation in the mining economy, and enable the company to meet the BEE requirements set by the South African government. Research concluded in 2016, when it seemed that attempts to resolve conflicts over traditional authority and the flow of funds was far from resolved.

## THE BAPO-BA-MOGALE AND EARLY MINING

In the 1960s,[2] Western Platinum Limited gained the mineral rights to a 6 791 ha block of land partway between Rustenburg and Brits.[3] It grew to become the primary platinum asset in the sprawling empire of the British multinational, Lonrho. The land comprised six farms that had been historically registered to the Bapo Tribal Authority, and which would soon be formally defined as the entirety of its administrative territory. The fates of the small Tswana chiefdom and nascent mining giant were thus inextricably entwined at the heart of the new platinum economy.

In 1969 the Minister of Bantu Administration and Development acted for the chiefdom in his statutory capacity as its 'trustee' to make a contract for mining. These farms had all been purchased, with mineral rights attached, by African groups during the late nineteenth and early twentieth centuries and, as elsewhere in the Rustenburg region, registered to a state official 'in trust' for the Bapo chief (Capps 2012b; Capps and Mnwana 2015). Royalties were paid into a dedicated 'tribal trust account' again controlled by the state. This method of administering tribal revenues – later known as the development, or D-account – proved particularly controversial in the Bapo case. The system of state trusteeship worked against the interests of the Bapo community before mining had even commenced.

The 1969 lease stipulated that the Bapo Tribal Authority would be entitled to a royalty rate of ten per cent of taxable income. But, as was the standard practice at the time (Manson and Mbenga 2003), both current and future capital expenditure were deducted from the mine's 'taxable income', meaning that the Bapo would only receive a stipulated minimum of R2 000 per annum until mining was fully operational. The company had unlimited access to the farms in order to develop whatever surface or underground infrastructure it considered necessary.

In 1977, the Bapo area was absorbed into Bophuthatswana, which had gained its fictive independence from South Africa. Aiming to expand Bophuthatswana's tax-base in the name of 'national development', the new homeland government informed Western Platinum that its rights would be ceded to a rival if mining did not soon commence in the Bapo lease area. Drilling duly began in 1985, but the only lease revenue paid into the Bapo trust account over the next two years would be the paltry guaranteed minimum of R2 000 per annum. In 1987, a new agreement was reached with the president of Bophuthatswana – in his inherited capacity as state trustee of Bapo land – that extended the lease by a further 50 years. This raised the minimum royalty to R200 000 per annum, but did not change the formula for reducing royalties by the amount of capital expenditure. Consequently, it was not until 2000 that the Bapo Traditional Authority received its first full royalty payment.

The advent of democracy in 1994 appeared to bring with it the promise of a new relationship (Bowman 2016: 28). Lonmin wanted to extend the lease while using the Bapo traditional authority to assist in the removal of 'unauthorised' people from its mining area and in opposing any restitution claims to it. In return the Bapo were offered an improved royalty formula. But Lonmin's approach also coincided with the onset of a boom in the global platinum price (Capps 2012b). Equally keen to claim their rightful share in the platinum bonanza, the Bapo appointed new lawyers to represent their interests in the impending negotiations.

Yet no sooner had they started negotiations than the rules of the game changed dramatically. The Minerals and Petroleum Resources Development Act (MPRDA) 18 of 2002 gave the state custodianship of all mineral resources in South Africa, abolishing mineral rights as a form of private property and replacing them with a centrally administered licence to prospect or mine (Capps 2012a). The state intended to transform the racial structure of mine ownership, both through the preferential allocation of 'new order mining rights' to black-owned companies, and by requiring historically white mining corporations to meet a prescribed black shareholding target. Eventually set at 26 per cent by an adjunct 'Mining Charter', this BEE component would now become a fundamental condition of attaining mining rights. All mining companies would have to pay a standardised royalty to the state. Rural communities that had previously been in receipt of royalties would be able to retain them subject to new forms of administrative regulation. But mining companies would also be encouraged to convert these 'community royalties' into direct equity stakes, thus moving closer to their black shareholding targets.

Lonmin devised an ambitious plan to win significant empowerment credits by creating an entirely new company – Incwala Resources – that would be transferred to black majority ownership to become the first major mining house of its kind. The portents for the Bapo in this venture initially looked good and it seemed they would get 'cornerstone investor' status. But they had to raise the finance for their Incwala stake and were informed in 2004 that they had 'missed critical deadlines' (Boyle 2014b; Swart 2012b). The 52.7 per cent empowerment stake in Incwala was to be split between three BEE entities with close ties with the Mbeki presidency.

The Bapo lawyers reacted to their client's exclusion by threatening to interdict the entire transaction. Lonmin's grudging response was to offer a minority 2.85 per cent stake at an upfront cost of R70 million, which it would finance through a short-term loan at commercial rates. In this arrangement, the Bapo shares would serve as collateral and be housed under the temporary administration of a new trust. The trustees were all selected by Lonmin and these appointees had the power to sell the shares without the Bapo Tribal Authority's consent (Swart 2012a). This posed the potentially explosive question of who really controlled the shares.

Boasting a coterie of high-profile BEE partners, who brought with them the promise of political influence, Incwala was lauded as an empowerment success and trebled in value by 2007 (Steyn 2012). Platinum did particularly well because of increased demand for catalytic converters in the motor vehicle industry; its price rose from under $500 per ounce in 2001 to over $1 500 in 2007. Lonmin could afford to be more generous and the company envisaged that good relations with the landowning community would secure social stability around its operations and burnish its corporate image. The Bapo secured beefed-up legal expertise through the attorney Hugh Eiser. In 2007, the Bapo team placed a number of grievances on the table concerning past royalty payments and calculations. Lonmin conceded on some items. The most significant of these was the royalties for the past mining of the Bapo farm Wonderkop. Lonmin not only commenced paying royalties on this portion of the Bapo reserve, but also issued an R18 million cheque for the portion it had already extracted. The amount of revenue involved was now becoming much larger.

In 2008, talks collapsed altogether. This, however, was not primarily the result of differences over mine economics, but rather the overspill of tribal politics (see Mnwana in this volume). A long history of factional disputes in the Bapo ruling lineage, and struggles to control the tribal authority and its resources, came to a head in 2008. This forced the legal team to request the suspension of negotiations until the situation had stabilised. Yet, such was the political turbulence in Bapong that, by December 2008, the premier of the North West Province had appointed an external administrator to run Bapo affairs.[4]

Platinum share prices dramatically collapsed in the wake of the 2008 global financial crisis, and many of the BEE deals constructed across the platinum belt now looked decidedly shaky (Bowman 2016). Incwala was particularly exposed as its black investors had relied on loans with a large portion drawn from private banks. Lonmin had fallen far short of the production targets on which their original repayment schedules had been based. With a R1.5 billion debt due to mature in September 2009, but no dividends with which to service it, Incwala teetered on the brink of insolvency (Steyn 2012).

This provided the opening for the Bapo lawyers. Eiser submitted an excoriating account of Lonmin's treatment of the community around the Incwala transaction and the motives that lay behind it. Lonmin had initially resisted the Bapo team's suggestion that part of the tribal royalty could simply be exchanged for Lonmin's own shares in Incwala during the 2007 equity conversion negotiations. The overarching impression was thus of Lonmin doing everything it could to maintain control of the BEE entity that it had created.

By 2009, Lonmin had repeatedly claimed that the Bapo leadership struggles meant that it 'could not put forward a legitimate authority' to assume control of the holding (Swart 2012b). However, Eiser argued that a legally empowered representative was now in place in the form of the provincially appointed administrator and Lonmin could no longer legitimate its control of the community's 2.85 per cent Incwala stake. In 2009 the Bapo team received a R38.2 million offer for these shares from Shanduka Resources, as part of a bigger play for the Incwala BEE holding.

Headed by former general secretary of the National Union of Mineworkers and African National Congress (ANC) luminary Cyril Ramaphosa, this was a serious proposition.

The Shanduka deal went ahead and in 2010, it was announced that Shanduka had taken control of Incwala. This involved R300 million of its own capital, plus a R2.5 billion loan from Lonmin to buy out the original BEE investors. As with the first Incwala transaction, the industry press hailed Lonmin's masterstroke in meeting BEE requirements and bringing the politically prized Ramaphosa on board. However, Lonmin's impoverished black landlords remained on the peripheries.

In 2012 the Marikana massacre cast a damning light on Lonmin's labour relations and practices. In the commission of inquiry that followed, its empowerment strategy was subjected to critical scrutiny, revealing the exclusionary logic of the elite bargain that underpinned it (Forrest 2015). Ramaphosa's infamous emails the day before the massacre – criminalising the labour dispute, and calling for 'concomitant action' – were a particularly graphic demonstration of his value to the British multinational as a means of pushing its agenda at the heart of the South African government, the ruling party and its allied unions.

In the three years leading to August 2012, the platinum slump led to the growth of Shanduka's debt to Lonmin (Steyn 2012). During the Marikana Commission, it also emerged that Lonmin had reneged on a pledge to build 5 500 houses for mine workers and local villagers around its mining complex – a responsibility that now directly lay with Ramaphosa as chairperson of its 'transformation committee'. This R665 million commitment formed part of the Social and Labour Plan that helped secure its New Order Mining Rights in 2006, in conjunction with the BEE credits. Yet by 2012 only three show homes had been constructed (Benchmarks 2012). Lonmin was technically in breach of its mining licence obligations and had prioritised its politically connected partner over the socio-economic development of its operational area. In 2014 the embattled Ramaphosa resigned from the Shanduka and Lonmin boards to resume his political career as deputy president of the ANC.

In 2009 the Department of Mineral Resources launched a review of its BEE policy, which concluded that the benefits of the empowerment deals to that point had accrued to 'a handful of black beneficiaries' (Bowman 2016: 13). An amended Mining Charter was released in 2010 with the aim of ensuring that future empowerment transactions were more 'broad based', not least by incorporating 'mine communities' as 'an integral part of mine development'. Lonmin fell short of the overall BEE compliance target. But if reviving the Bapo equity negotiations appeared to offer part of the solution, this would also necessitate dealing with the political instability within the community.

## A LEGITIMATE AUTHORITY? ELITE COMPETITION AND STATE INTERVENTION

The Bapo Tribal Authority had entered the new South Africa under the leadership of Bob Edward Mogale, its recognised chief (*kgosi*) of 11-years standing.[5] By 1998 it was apparent that he no longer possessed the 'mental capacity to discharge his functions', as the court judgment in *Mogale* (2010) later put it.[6] With the support of the premier of the North West Province, Popo Molefe, a decision was made in the royal family to reduce *Kgosi* Mogale's role to 'ritual matters only', and to call Radikobonyana Emias Mogale – a senior uncle from the second house – back from his job in Johannesburg to assist in running the community's affairs.

The *Rangwane*, or 'Uncle to the Chief', assumed effective control of the Bapo Tribal Authority in 2000 when the first full royalty of R12.7 million was paid into the trust account, transforming its financial situation. The *Rangwane's* early tenure is consequently remembered as one of modest delivery and improved organisation, at least by his closer allies in the royal family. But, despite the premier's support, it seems that the *Rangwane* role as 'acting chief' was never formally defined, creating the conditions for two rival centres of power, with competing forces and projects: close associates of the old chief and those of the new *Rangwane*.

In 2004, when the Traditional Leadership and Governance Framework Act (Act 41 of 2003) came into force, apartheid-era 'tribal authorities' could be transformed into constitutional-era 'traditional councils' and continue to administer the resources of specified 'traditional communities'. The Act's stated aim was to 'restore the legitimacy and integrity' of the institution of 'traditional leadership' in the democratic dispensation. But its principal effect was to reproduce the jurisdictions and structures of the Tribal Authorities that had been established by the notorious 1951 Bantu Authorities Act, and reaffirmed by subsequent homeland legislation (Claassens 2008; Jara 2011). Nevertheless, it did introduce the requirements that 40 per cent of the membership of the new traditional councils should be elected and that a third of the total should be women. A traditional council would only receive official recognition when the names of these members had been gazetted, and each would serve a maximum five-year term. In the interim, pre-existing tribal authorities would be treated as traditional councils for the sake of administrative continuity, but would have to comply with its requirements within a year of its commencement to retain their legal validity.

In practice, the result was confusion. Monica de Souza (2014) has shown that the traditional council elections that should have marked the formal reconstitution of all tribal authorities were only held a fortnight after the cut-off date of 24 September 2005, and it was a further three years before the results were ever gazetted.

Moreover, in Bapong, only 7 out of the 30 new council members were women, falling short of the one-third gender requirement. As elsewhere, this would leave the Bapo authority open to question, casting doubt on the legitimacy of its business transactions and legal standing. These uncertainties were further compounded by the promulgation of the North West Province's Traditional Leadership and Governance Act (Act 2 of 2005), which set out *different* timescales to those of the national legislation for the first five-year terms of the new councils in the province and neglected to provide guidelines for future council elections (De Souza 2014).

In 2008, *Kgosi* Bob Edward Mogale made a surprise appearance at a community meeting, called by the Traditional Council in Bapong. Brandishing legal papers, two of his associates took to the stage, declaring the Bapo administration to be malfunctioning and corrupt. The *kgosi* had therefore decided to dissolve the Traditional Council, all its members were dismissed forthwith, and the *Rangwane* was to cease acting in his place. The chief's supporters attempted to seize direct control of the council premises. In response, the *Rangwane* supporters, who were formally recognised by the province as leaders of the Traditional Council, applied to the North West High Court for an urgent interdict to declare the chief's actions invalid.

Since 2000, the inflow of mineral revenues and expansion of new mining activity had significantly increased the material stakes for the control of the Bapo administration and its resources. According to leading members of the *Rangwane* faction, the 'mentally infirm' chief had been captured by elements in the wider royal family, who were using him as the gateway to the 'community's very large cash-holdings, its assets and its business relationships'.[7] This included potentially lucrative procurement contracts with Lonmin, and a major deal with Skychrome, which was seeking to open a new open-cast chrome mine on a site in Bapong village, recently allocated by the Traditional Council for a health centre. With the sometimes covert, and sometimes overt, sponsorship of these mining companies, the chief's associates were accused of mobilising unemployed youth to divide the community and destabilise the administration, while at the same time manipulating him into signing business agreements, ostensibly on behalf of the tribe.

Whatever the veracity of these claims, they clearly made an impression on Acting Judge Sithole who ruled in July 2008 the chief's 'purported dissolution' of the Traditional Council to be 'unlawful'.[8] The chief and his associates were banned from entering the council's premises and ordered to desist 'purporting to represent' the Bapo community in dealings with Skychrome or any other commercial entity. However, Sithole reserved judgment on the critical question of the legal validity of the Traditional Council as it was currently constituted. Under the new legislation, it fell to the provincial government to determine whether the traditional council had met the requirements for official recognition. The Provincial Traditional Affairs Directorate had initially stated that the *kgosi* had no power to dismiss his uncle. Then, on 15 July 2008, the premier published a notice in the provincial gazette formally announcing the 'reconstitution' of all the traditional councils in the North West Province, including the one elected in Bapong in October 2005 (De Souza 2014). The provincial government now argued that, in the absence of the anticipated court decision on its legal validity, the Bapo community remained *without* a recognised traditional council.

The provincial government also had responsibility for the appointment of a suitably qualified person to assist a struggling council. This would be on the recommendation of its royal family, and subject to a review after a period of 180 days. On 12 December 2008, Abel Dlamini was deployed to Bapong by the province. An accountant by training, Dlamini bought a professional office staff with him and quickly established a constructive working relationship with both the *Rangwane* faction and their legal representative, Hugh Eiser. Over the course of his tenure of one year, Dlamini also made a concerted effort to establish sustainable administrative systems. But his services did not come for free. By the end of his term in December 2009, a total of R18 million had been paid from Bapo coffers to Dlamini's consulting company (Boyle 2016b). Dlamini helped organise a second traditional council election, in the hope of ending the uncertainty over its legal status. However, the province refused to recognise the result on the grounds that the dissolved council could not be replaced until the North West High Court had clarified the legal position. Dlamini also attempted to professionalise the traditional council by creating a post for a full-time CEO.

When Dlamini left, Makepe Jerimiah Kenoshi was appointed to the position of CEO. In contrast to Dlamini, he forged an alliance with *Kgosi* Bob Mogale and his associates. By January 2010, Kenoshi had stopped communicating with the Traditional Council and terminated Eiser's mandate. Later affirmed by the chief in writing, the significance of this 'decision' cannot be overestimated. Whether by accident or design, it came at the exact moment that Eiser was gearing up to challenge Lonmin's choice of Shanduka as its BEE partner. But Lonmin's lawyers were able to argue that Eiser no longer had the *locus standi* to bring a case.

In March 2010, it came to light that Kenoshi was preparing to 'invest' R234 million of the Bapo funds in a property development in the Hartebeesport Dam area (Manson 2013; Claassens and Matlala 2014; De Souza 2014). On hearing the news, the Bapo council opened disciplinary proceedings against Kenoshi, arguing that he did not have the legal authority to sign over the money. The provincial government backed Kenoshi and his associates around the Bapo chief, which suggested they had stronger connections with the ANC North West Province hierarchy. They obtained a court order against 26 members of the Traditional Council that banned them from the community offices. The Traditional Council filed a counter application for its own interdict against Kenoshi. Both the applications were heard on the same day, 29 July 2010, in different courts.

Each hearing turned on the key questions of whether the Bapo Traditional Council had been properly reconstituted, in line with the requirements and timelines of the provincial Act of 2005 and, if not, whether it still at least remained the lawful governing body of the traditional community. Both Justice Landman and Justice Legodi in their respective hearings found that the council had not met the requirements for reconstitution. However, Landman argued that the Traditional Council did not have the *locus standi* to administer the tribe, and hence institute proceedings against Kenoshi, while Legodi determined that the council continued to exist as a legitimate administrative authority and had a sufficient material interest to warrant *locus standi* in the Kenoshi matter. Indeed, for Legodi, the *locus standi* argument was 'nothing else than a smokescreen' to avoid the substantive issues raised by Kenoshi's conduct (Claassens and Matlala 2014).

The Legodi judgment proved sufficient for the council to dismiss Kenoshi. But, although both rulings were scathing of the province's attempt retrospectively to reconstitute the traditional councils under its jurisdiction in July 2008, and then intervene in the Kenoshi matter, their differences over the current status of the Traditional Council allowed the provincial government to cling to its position that the Bapo remained without a valid governing authority. Hence they would need to stay under administration until such time as new elections put a properly constituted traditional council in its place. This created the conditions for the wholesale looting of the substantial mineral revenues that had accrued to the Bapo.

The 2005 provincial legislation for traditional councils gave them the power to manage and administer the funds of 'their' traditional communities, but section 30 also held that the premier would 'cause' a 'trust account' to be opened for each council, into which all the revenues and proceeds benefitting that community would be paid, mining royalties included. Moreover, it would fall to the premier 'to approve estimates of revenue and expenditure' from these community trust accounts, explicitly authorising larger payments. Section 30 simply reproduced the old 'tribal trust' or D-account system, and, with it, the provincial government's ultimate control of such revenues in the North West. There was, however, an important proviso, aimed at holding the trustee state to account. Section 31 provided that the 'books and accounts' of every traditional community would have to be annually 'audited by the Auditor-General', and the results reported to both the premier and that traditional council. Not a single trust account in the province was audited after

1994, rendering all traditional authorities vulnerable to abuse by incompetent or corrupt officials.

During his term as administrator, Abel Dlamini had commissioned an audit of the Bapo deposits in the D-account by a private accountancy firm. This found that in 2009 there was R393 million to the tribe's name, which he duly reported to the community at large. Within three years almost the entire amount had 'disappeared' from the D-account, and no one seemed to know where. Leading figures in the Traditional Council appealed to the Office of the Public Protector (PP) to lead the hunt for the 'missing millions'. Advocate Thuli Madonsela, the PP, took up the Bapo case in January 2012, and first reported to the community that September (Swart 2012b). When the Auditor General last audited the D-account in 1994, the community was found to have R721 000 to its name (PP 2016). But, as the mining royalties rolled in after 2000, a total of more than R617 million - comprising R392 million in deposits and R224 million in interest earned – accrued by 2014. Yet, by 2014, only R495 000 of this remained. More than R600 million had now disappeared.

It is possible to identify some of the key mechanisms at work. When the new provincial government came to power in 1994, it inherited a D-account from the Bophuthatswana regime reportedly comprising some 800 sub-accounts, 101 of which were for traditional authorities (Stone 2013d). These remained bundled together, despite the requirements of the 2005 Act, making it virtually impossible to separate their individual funds. Worse yet, the myriad sub-accounts that formed the collective D-account had multiple signatories (Stone 2014a). The provincial government failed to produce the accounts annually required by the Auditor General, meaning that there was no external scrutiny of how much was in them, or how it had been spent (Boyle 2016a). The lines of accountability were further blurred by the delegation of the premier's fiduciary responsibility over D-accounts in 2009 to the provincial Department of Finance, 'creating confusion all over' as Premier Supra Mahumapelo put it (Stone 2014b). Eiser, the Bapo council lawyer, remarked that it was in the provincial government's 'interest to keep the account lumped up and ostensibly in a mess' (Stone 2013c).

The provincial government used the D-account as a private investment fund, putting money into speculative ventures (Stone 2013a). It did so without the permission of the traditional councils concerned and, when combined with the multiple governance failures, this created the conditions for massive financial mismanagement. Allegations are consequently rife that the D-account not only acted as 'slush fund' for senior ANC politicians and officials (Stone 2013a), but that it had also been systematically looted, 'with millions spent without approval and more taken into private accounts abroad', according to government sources, including a senior Treasury official (Boyle 2016a). Two years into her investigation Madonsela, the PP, stated that she sensed a 'cover up' (Stone 2014b). Both her inquiry and a parallel investigation by the North West Province Standing Committee on Public Accounts (SCOPA) were stymied at every turn by the intransigence of the premier and officials. The exasperated chair of SCOPA, Hlomane Chauke, remarked that 'we are not dealing with people who are fair and honest ... some of them belong to jail and not in government' (Stone 2013d). The SCOPA inquiry collapsed.

After Bapo had come under administration, a decision was made to build a fitting new residence for its *kgosi*, with an adjacent office block and debating chamber for his council. Majestically perched on a Magaliesberg hillside with commanding views of the Bapo valley, the budget for the 'Royal Palace', as it became known, was originally set at R20 million (PP 2016). The cost had risen to R115 million by 2017 (PP 2017). Some R68 million was spent on consultants and R2.8 million on décor (Tau 2016). The PP's findings revealed that R13 million had been paid for a community hall that was never built and R10 million to a construction company with no record of what the payment was for or who had authorised it (Boyle 2016a). Sizeable sums were also paid to administrators, councillors and royal family members, as well as to suppliers for services such as catering and security, and to universities and colleges as bursaries (PP 2017). These amounts account for some of the missing R600 million.

By 2014, four different people (in addition to Dlamini) had acted as administrators, typically on contracts of around six months with varying breaks between. At least two had been appointed on the request of the royal family, to fill the administrative vacuum left by continued infighting and the failure to constitute a traditional council. The foundational issue was the extraordinary range of discretionary powers afforded to the administrators by their terms of reference, including powers to authorise projects, appoint contractors, sign off payments, hire and fire administrative staff, and represent the Bapo in commercial negotiations and legal processes.

Complaints about unilateral decision-making and lack of accountability were consequently rife. The royal palace was a case in point. Provincial government officials had either failed in their oversight functions or actively colluded with administrators to siphon off funds. The overriding suspicion was that successive administrators were unaccountable and were on the look-out for money-making opportunities. According to the *Rangwane* faction, 'After five years, there is not even a single policy', because the administrators 'know that if I am capacitating the council then it means I am losing my job' (Swart 2012b). So long as the Bapo authority remained without a recognised traditional council, it would not have the *locus standi* to recover its 'missing millions' and hold the perpetrators to account.

Lonmin, however, did have an interest in securing an effective traditional council as BEE partners to formally negotiate and sign off the equity stake. The provincial government issued a circular in April 2011 warning traditional councils across the province not to undertake commercial transactions until they were 'duly reconstituted' through new elections, explaining that if they 'lacked legal standing at the time the said contracts/deals were concluded', they 'might be of no force and effect' (De Souza 2014: 48). For Lonmin the imperative was precisely to establish the conditions for the successful reconstitution of the Bapo traditional council.

## BAPO CHIEFTAINCY

At the heart of this problem were groups contesting traditional authority (see Mnwana and Chaskalson in this volume for the disabling effects of similar conflicts).[9] In 2011 the North West Province government launched a 'process of mediation and restoration of order and harmony among the royal elites of the Bapo community' (Khunou 2014c: 2). The politico-administrative imperative was to 'restructure' the institution in a way that was amenable both to its constituent lineages and thereby secure the foundation for a stable and functioning traditional council. A three-day 'retreat' was unsuccessful in resolving conflicts. Thus the province appointed one of its legal advisers, Thabo Lerefolo, to act as Bapo's third administrator. Lerefolo in turn appointed a legal academic from the University of the North West, Professor Freddy Khunou, to conduct an extensive 'review and validation of traditional structures and succession patterns' of the Bapo chieftaincy, and determine whether the 'current structure' of the royal family was 'the one envisaged' by the 2005 Act (Khunou 2014c: 1–2).

In effect, Khunou was being called on to play the same role as the professional ethnographers who had been deployed by the apartheid and homeland states. As John Comaroff (1974: 46) pointed out, the 'usual procedure' was for these ethnologists 'to consult the genealogies', which had 'been collected for each ruling dynasty and decide, in terms of the formal rules of succession, who the rightful office-holder should be'. Yet this approach misunderstood 'the very essence of Tswana politics', in which 'internal competitive processes' were 'ordered by the manipulation of genealogies and legitimized by exploitation of rules'. Recorded genealogies were not an infallible guide to the 'legitimate' incumbency.

In Bapong, government intervention along these lines had contributed to the long history of political turmoil (Malindi 2016). Government officials would back one candidate over another for reasons of administrative expediency and/or state control. But these decisions were often so devoid of popular legitimacy that they laid the ground for further succession challenges. Khunou's academic and professional training was not in Anthropology, but Law. He nevertheless had a strong record of involvement in these questions (Khunou 2014b: 3–4). He had contributed to the White Paper on which the National Traditional Leaders Framework Act of 2003 was based and developed policy documents and manuals on its implications for the National House of Traditional Leaders. He argued that the new traditional councils represented a genuinely democratic transformation of what had existed before. Mazibuko Jara (2011) was critical of this view.

Khunou's primary concern was to determine the 'membership and composition of the Royal Family in line with the legislative imperatives and customary law', with exclusive reference to documentary sources, rather than through oral interviews (Khunou 2014a: 2). He argued that his 'objectivity was not clouded with the views of the warring factions and those individuals who might have vested interests' (2014a: 3). This approach placed him in the tradition of state-sponsored ethnological research rather than opening up the local dynamics of office and power. He adjudicated from the exclusive standpoint of the 2005 Act, which defined the royal family as 'the core customary institution or structure consisting of *immediate* relatives of the ruling family', which could also include 'other family members who are *close* relatives' (2014a: 31–37). He decided that membership of the royal family should be restricted to the Mogale lineage, including the *Rangwane* but excluding some who had supported the chief. In the interests of 'peace and reconciliation', a second forum – the General Royal Council (GRC) – should be established to accommodate the members of the 'extended royal families' with functions strictly limited to traditional matters. Finally, the other key institutional structures that had collapsed under the weight of internecine strife – the Office of the *Kgosi*, Council of Headmen and Customary Court – should be revived.

Seen from the perspective of the *Rangwane* faction, who were from the Mogale lineage, this was a beneficial solution. Despite its previous shifts, the North West Province government at this point recognised the *Rangwane* as the acting chief on the basis of his familial relationship to the 'incapacitated' and hence effectively 'retired' Bob Mogale. The rival group that had cohered around Mogale during the early 2000s was a fading force and had lost various court cases. The provincial government decided to work with *Rangwane* and his Traditional Council in order to implement the findings of the report, treating Bob Mogale as a ceremonial figurehead. The *Rangwane* now held the primary power to determine the composition of tribal organs – including the 60 per cent of appointees in the Traditional Council – in conjunction with the ailing *kgosi*.

Implementation was outsourced to a consultancy called Nthontho Business Solutions. Its founding CEO, Lehlohonolo Nthontho, played a significant role in the restructuring of the Bapo royal family and forged a close alliance with the *Rangwane* and his son, Vladimir Mogale, who emerged as the 'spokesperson' of the revamped Office of the *Kgosi*. Whatever the processes at work, the final determination of the reconstituted royal family and GRC had been made by January 2014, and the requisite 60 per cent of appointees to the Traditional Council identified, with the formal blessing of the chief. All that remained was for the rest of the Traditional Council to be elected by the community. After a number of delays, elections were held across the province at the end of that month, and, for the first time in Bapong, the elected 40 per cent would meet the one-third gender requirement.

In February 2014, the then MEC for Local Government and Traditional Affairs in the North West Province declared that 'as a result of Professor Khunou's involvement' there 'is stability in the Royal Family', allowing the community 'to manage its own affairs'.[10] The *Rangwane* would continue to 'deal with and approve all necessary payments' in the interim. In April, a 'policy conference' was convened at the royal palace to ratify the new governance structures. At last, everything was in place to see through the royalty-to-equity conversion with Lonmin, and crucially just in time for the December 2014 empowerment target deadline.

## BAPO, LONMIN AND NEW DIVISIONS

When Eiser's mandate to act as legal representative was formally revoked, the second administrator, Julius Moloto, brought in a new 'advisory team' of Basic Point Capital, Nedbank and the legal firm, Bell Dewar. The last of these was of particular significance as it had represented the neighbouring Bafokeng chieftaincy. The *Rangwane* faction had itself long admired the 'corporatisation' model pioneered by the Bafokeng, in which all their economic assets were placed in a separate holding company, regulated by company law. Not only would this provide a vehicle to house any future equity stake, but it would also allow the Traditional Council to exploit a clause in the 2005 Act and, like the Bafokeng before before them, get out of the D-account system altogether.

Three million rand of the community's funds were paid to Bell Dewar and in November 2013, the council was informed that the conversion deal was imminent (Stone 2013b). By June 2014 the requisite Traditional Council was in place and administration consigned to the past. The new Office of the *Kgosi* launched a campaign to mobilise the necessary consent for the equity conversion deal amongst the Bapo. That month, around a thousand unemployed youth were deployed on a 'community consultation' exercise, at a reported cost of R1.2 million (Boyle 2014a). Dubbed the 'Ambassadors', and said to have knocked on 15 000 doors, they carried two documents with them. First, a fact sheet on the deal from the 'Communications and Royal Affairs Department' – now headed by Vladimir Mogale; and second, a 'community consultation process form', asking whether the Bapo should 'continue with' or 'leave this equity transaction'. The fact sheet was strong on the 'details' and 'benefits of the deal' but provided no information about the possible downsides and risks. Moreover, it was subsequently reported that the Ambassadors 'knew little about the transaction and focused instead on the infrastructural needs of the community' during their house-calls (Boyle 2014a). The Office of the *Kgosi* claimed that 99 per cent of the completed 'consultation process forms' had been in favour of pressing ahead.

On 29 July 2014, a *kgotha kgothe* – or general meeting – was convened in the Segwaelane Village Community Hall, to secure the requisite community resolution that would enable the Traditional Council to enter into a binding agreement with Lonmin. The hall was filled to its capacity of 400, with 200 to 300 more following proceedings outside. Villagers, observers, journalists, lawyers and others crammed together to hear the meeting open with prayers and a sermon – 'The Storm is Over' (Proverbs 10: 25–32) – and a welcome from *Rangwane*. Then the Master of Ceremonies, Neo Moerane, and Lehlohonolo Nthontho started presenting the terms and benefits of the deal. Two hours of questions and answers followed. A representative from Nedbank, which had been tasked with producing the valuation, spoke in strong support, brandishing a copy of the 50-page report. But Nthontho declined requests from the floor to see it, or the great bundle of other documents that made up the agreement. As *Rangwane* bought the meeting to a close, community members signed the resolution and filled in the voting slips, which required their names and identity numbers. The reported tally was 779 in favour and 51 against. The Bapo chief was notable throughout by his absence.

Early the following morning, Lonmin CEO Ben Magara signed the deal with *Rangwane* and two other community representatives. Immediately, a 'regulatory release' was issued to the London Stock Exchange (where Lonmin was listed) and the Minister of Mineral Resources put out a statement 'welcoming the agreement'. According to Lonmin's regulatory release, there were three major elements to the agreement. First, the Bapo would waive their statutory right to receive royalties in exchange for a R564 million lump sum, which would be used to buy shares in the parent company – later valued at 2.25 per cent of Lonmin's issued equity. Second, the Bapo would receive a 'deferred royalty payment' of R20 million, for five consecutive years to be used for its 'administration costs'; a new 'community development trust' would be funded with a minimum of R5 million annually; and Bapo companies would be given preferential opportunities to bid for an estimated R200 million-worth of Lonmin tenders, for an 8-month period. Finally, however, the Bapo would agree to a ten-year embargo on the sale of their Lonmin shares, which could also not be used as collateral during that decade. They would also transfer their 7.5 per cent stake in the neighbouring Pandora joint venture to Lonmin and lease the surface area of their mineral-bearing farms to Lonmin at no extra cost, decisively ending some 45-years of rentier landlordism.

Such were the known details of the agreement, but much remained outside the public domain. There was no information about how the valuation had been reached, nor precisely how the different elements of the deal would be managed. Mining analysts canvassed by the *Mail & Guardian* questioned the wisdom of surrendering a guaranteed royalty stream for more risky dividend payments in a depressed platinum market (Steyn 2014). The Office of the *Kgosi* wasted little time in setting up a new Bapo-ba-Mogale Investments Company. This realised the *Rangwane* faction's ambition to escape the D-account system and control Bapo funds Nthontho was appointed as CEO of the investment company. For its part, Lonmin's new BEE partner bought the mining multinational a precious 2.25 per cent closer to realising its empowerment target and the agreement was approved at a general meeting of its shareholders in London.

But no sooner had the Lonmin shareholders cast their deciding vote in August 2014, than the political ground on which the whole transaction had been founded would again start to shift and crack, revealing the fault lines that still ran deep beneath. In September 2014, two community groups – 'the Liaison Committee of the Bapo-ba-Mogale Community' and *Serodumo Sa Rona* – gave notice of their intention to apply for a judicial review of the July agreement (Greve 2015). It was, they said, unlawful on a number of counts. The July *kgotha kgothe* had neither been representative of the community at large – only 1.9 per cent of the 40 000-strong tribe had actually voted – nor had the procedure followed customary processes of decision-making. Moreover, although the resolution implied that those present had made an informed decision, none of the detail of the transaction had been circulated. But the most significant charge concerned the question of whether *Rangwane* and the other two community members who had signed the agreement had in fact the authority to do so.

It transpired that the membership of the new Traditional Council was only published in the provincial gazette on 8 August 2014 – a full week after the transaction had been signed off. The community groups argued that the wording of the MEC's letter clearly restricted *Rangwane's* temporary powers to routine administration. The question of *locus standi* had thus again emerged to challenge the objectives and actions of the *Rangwane* faction, and once more it was the provincial government that, through its negligence or otherwise, had contributed to the problem.

In August 2014, Abbey Mafate, a newly elected member of the Traditional Council was suspended without pay and called to a disciplinary hearing by the GRC. The letter was issued by *Rangwane*, 'on behalf of *Kgosi* Mogale', and listed a number of charges, including participation in 'illegal meetings' with a grouping in Wonderkop village, which 'destabilizes traditional authority governance' (Malindi 2016). A colleague on the Traditional Council, Tshepo Maakane, was suspended in a similar manner on charges that included insulting the chief. Both Mafate and Maakane had, from an early stage, been vocal in their criticism of the impending conversion deal, writing to the premier, the local police and the Office of the *Kgosi* in an effort to stop the July *kgotha kgothe* from happening altogether. Their argument had been that the Traditional Council did not have the legal authority to call the meeting, as it had not yet been gazetted.

Seen from this perspective, the charges against Mafate looked like an attempt to silence dissenting voices within the Traditional Council (compare Mnwana and Pickering and Motala in this volume). Mafate and Maakane took the case to court; the judge found the councillors' suspension 'irrational and procedurally unfair', and ordered their reinstatement. However, it has since been reported that, on arriving at a Traditional Council meeting, Mafate and Maakane were handed letters placing them on 'special leave' (Bloom 2016).

In the wake of the July 2014 agreements, Lonmin's own head of business development admitted that the equity swap was not the strongest element of the deal; rather, the 'real prize' was the R200 million in business opportunities afforded by the 18 months preferential procurement window with Lonmin (Steyn 2014). To this end, Lonmin gave Bapo Investments a start-up sum of R40 million in two tranches over 2015 and 2016 to help it tender for, and manage, its supply contracts. But *Rangwane* accused Lonmin of continuing with a 'divide and rule strategy' in its dealings with the Bapo. The key issue was that a R120 million bussing contract and a R100 million protective equipment contract had been awarded to other suppliers. It also emerged that Bapo Investments was being sued for R30 million for failing to pay an ore-transport contractor (Timse 2016). The PP reported in 2016 that Bapo Investments was deep in debt, despite having borrowed R100 million from the Public Investment Corporation, and an undisclosed sum from First National Bank (Tau 2016).

The Bapo Investments CEO was accused of being unaccountable to the community and unleashing political violence against his opponents (Bloom 2016; Boyle

2016b). In July 2016, a crowd of 150 people, led by the 'Ambassadors' – the unemployed Bapo youth first mobilised to secure consent for the 2014 deal – stormed the Madibeng FM radio station, forcing it to cancel a planned interview with critics of Nthontho (R2K 2016). The presenter of the show subsequently received death threats. In September, five Bapo activists were attacked at a community meeting convened to discuss Nthontho's removal, again by the Ambassadors. After being briefly arrested, the alleged assailant was reportedly seated among members of the Traditional Council when the two suspended councillors, Mafate and Maakane, attempted to resume their positions in October.

## CONCLUSION

This chapter shows that the question of chiefly succession and legitimate community representation has been at the heart of Bapo-Lonmin conflicts since 1994. As I argue elsewhere (Capps and Mnwana 2015), legal struggles that involve the identification of collective entitlements to land and resources, can lead to new kinds of political divisions as branches of chieftaincies, and groups within communities, compete to be beneficiaries. For long periods, the Bapo were without a functioning and legally recognised administrative authority, in large part due to the internecine conflicts within its ruling elite. This at times worked in the interests of both the mining company and elements within the provincial government, which was entrusted with the fiduciary control of its finances through the D-account system, from which large amounts of money disappeared.

The situation was further compounded by uncertainties in the new legislation governing traditional authorities, and by the haphazard manner of its implementation. A consequence was frequent litigation around the question of the legal standing of different parties claiming to act on behalf of the Bapo in commercial transactions and court proceedings. The mounting pressures to see through the royalty-to-equity conversion – and hence reconstitute the Bapo as a shareholder in Lonmin – also helped to shape the political process. Lonmin was keen to get a legally recognised traditional authority in place. The provincial government, after a period in which dysfunctionality in Bapo may have suited some of its officers, also become committed to the 'reconstitution' of the royal family. This temporarily reduced debilitating political competition, and secured a stable foundation on which to build a new traditional council.

The authority of the *Rangwane* and Traditional Council was not, however, fully accepted. As in other cases in this book, mining resources exacerbated tensions between chiefs and community. This may in part have been rooted in continuing struggles between different factions of the tribal elite. It was also the result of mismanagement of Bapo Investments, the vehicle that had recently been set up to control their income independent of the provincial government. One of the charges levelled against the suspended councillor Abbey Mafate was his alleged involvement in 'illegal' village meetings aimed at 'destabilising' the (new) traditional authority. Other village-level groups also felt that infighting within the Bapo elite had paralysed service delivery and undermined governance structures. They have also taken up a role pursuing claims over the mineral-rich land that is currently registered to the tribe. New resources have exacerbated divisions in this and similar groupings, defined as traditional communities, where chiefs and traditional councils have become intermediaries, but have not been able control or effectively redistribute resources.

NOTES

1   The MARTISA project at SWOP is funded by the Ford Foundation (Grant No. 0120–6086), whose financial support is gratefully acknowledged. Stanley Malindi was co-author of a longer working paper (Capps and Malindi 2017) on which this chapter is based. This details the division of labour between us and provides full academic referencing for the archival and oral sources used in the chapter, which, for the sake of brevity, have been kept to a minimum. I provide a footnote at the beginning of each chapter section to indicate where they can be found in the working paper. In addition to Stanley's assistance and insight, I would like to acknowledge the support of Kally Forrest, Thantaswa Lupuwana, Geoff Budlender, Brendan Boyle, Henk Smith, Wilmien Wicomb, Gregory Maxaulane, Sonwabile Mnwana, Katlego Ramantsima and Andrew Bowman at various points in this research, as well as the residents of the Bapo-ba-Mogale traditional authority area for their engagement and information. Many thanks also to William Beinart for his extensive help with transforming the longer working paper into this book chapter. All errors, naturally, remain my own.
2   Unless otherwise indicated, full references to the primary sources used in this section of chapter can be found in Capps and Malindi (2017: 5–12).
3   Pretoria National Archives (PNA). BAO series, file 52/1093/15/2.
4   This administrator was Abel Dlamini, whose tenure is discussed further below.
5   Unless otherwise indicated, full references to the primary sources used in this section of chapter can be found in Capps and Malindi (2017: 13–19).
6   Mogale v Maakane and Others (1106/2010) [2010] ZANWHC 18 (29 July 2010) para 29 ('*Mogale*').
7   The Traditional Authority of the Bapo ba Mogale Community v Kenoshi and Others 3187610 [2010] ZAGPPHC para 53.1 ('*Traditional Authority of Bapo be Mogale*', referring to Sithole AJ 2008, the Bapo ba Mogale Traditional Authority v Mogale and Others, North West High Court (Mafikeng) Case No. 800/2008.
8   The Bapo ba Mogale Traditional Authority v Mogale and Others, 800/2008 [2008] ZANWHC ('*Bapo ba Mogale*').

9   Unless otherwise indicated, full references to the primary sources used in this and the following chapter section can be found in Capps and Malindi (2017: 20–27).
10  M. Thlape, MEC for Local Government and Traditional Affairs to *Kgosi* B.E. Mogale, 'Re: Bapo ba Mogale Community Administration: Section 10 of the North West Traditional Leadership Act No. 2 of 2005', 24 March 2014 (cited in Capps and Malindi 2017: 22).

REFERENCES

Benchmarks. 2012. 'Policy Gap 7: Lonmin 2003–2012'. The Benchmarks Foundation. http://www.bench-marks.org.za/press/lonmin_report_print.pdf

Bloom, Kevin. 2016. 'What's Mine is Mine: How the Bapo ba Mogale Got Robbed of R800 Million'. *Daily Maverick*, 26 October. https://www.dailymaverick.co.za/article/2016-10-26-whats-mine-is-mine-how-the-bapo-ba-mogale-got-robbed-of-r800-million/

Bowman, Andrew. 2016. 'Dilemmas of Distribution: Financialisation, Boom and Bust in the Post-Apartheid Platinum Industry'. SWOP Working Paper 7. Society, Work and Politics Institute, University of the Witwatersrand, Johannesburg.

Boyle, Brendan. 2014a. 'Lonmin: Wealth Still Far Off'. *Business Day*, 14 April.

Boyle, Brendan. 2014b. 'On the Record with Hugh Eiser and Brenda Boyle'. *South African Crime Quarterly* 49 (September): 65–70. https://doi.org/10.17159/2413-3108/2014/v0i49a784

Boyle, Brendan. 2016a. 'Bapo Chief and Marikana's Missing Millions'. *City Press*, 25 July.

Boyle, Brendan. 2016b. 'Bapo Traditional Council Tries to Defy Court'. http://www.custom-contested.co.za/bapo-traditional-council-tries-defy-court/

Capps, Gavin. 2012a. 'A Bourgeois Reform with Social Justice? The Contradictions of the Mineral Development Bill and Black Economic Empowerment in the South African Platinum Mining Industry'. *Review of African Political Economy* 39, no. 132: 315–333.

Capps, Gavin. 2012b. 'Victim of its Own Success? The Platinum Mining Industry and the Apartheid Mineral Property System in South Africa's Political Transition'. *Review of African Political Economy* 39, no. 131: 63–84.

Capps, Gavin and Malindi, Stanley. 2017. 'Dealing with the Tribe: The Politics of the Bapo/Lonmin Royalty-to-Equity Conversion'. SWOP Working Paper 8. Society, Work and Politics Institute, University of the Witwatersrand, Johannesburg.

Capps, Gavin and Sonwabile Mnwana. 2015. 'Claims from Below: Platinum and the Politics of Land in the Bakgatla Traditional Authority Area'. *Review of African Political Economy* 42, no. 146: 606–624.

Claassens, Aninka. 2008. 'Power, Accountability and Apartheid Borders: The Impact of Recent Law on Struggles over Land Rights'. In *Land, Power & Custom: Controversies Generated by South Africa's Communal Land Rights Act*, edited by Aninka Classens and Ben Cousins, 262–292. Cape Town: UCT Press.

Claassens, Aninka and Boitumelo Matlala. 2014. 'Platinum, Poverty and Princes in Post-Apartheid South Africa: New Laws, Old Repertoires'. In *New South African Review 4*, edited by Gilbert Khadiagala, Prishani Naidoo, Devan Pillay and Roger Southall, 113–135. Johannesburg: Wits University Press.

Comaroff, John L. 1974. 'Chiefship in a South African Homeland: A Case Study of the Tshidi Chiefdom of Bophuthatswana'. *Journal of Southern African Studies* 1, no. 1: 36–51.

De Souza, Monica. 2014. 'Justice and Legitimacy Hindered by Uncertainty: The Legal Status of Traditional Councils in North West Province'. *South African Crime Quarterly* 49: 41–56.

Forrest, Kally. 2015. 'Marikana Commission: Unearthing the Truth or Burying It?' SWOP Working Paper No. 5. Society, Work and Development Institute (SWOP), University of the Witwatersrand, Johannesburg.

Greve, Natalie. 2015. 'Community Members Challenge Legality of R564m Lonmin BEE Deal'. *Creamer Media's Mining Weekly*, 17 March.

Jara, Mazibuko. 2011. 'Traditional Councils Perpetuate Apartheid Tribal Schema'. *De Rebus* (July): 32–34.

Khunou, Freddy. 2014a. 'A Path of Legitimization Patterns of the Royal Family of the Bapo-ba-Mogale Community: Setting the Record Straight'. Unpublished paper, Law Faculty, University of the North West, Mahikeng.

Khunou, Freddy. 2014b. 'Presenters Guide/Research Manual'. Subsidiary Document of Khunou (2014a), above. Unpublished paper, Law Faculty, University of the North West, Mahikeng.

Khunou, Freddy. 2014c. 'Research Project Executive Summary'. Subsidiary Document of Khunou (2014a), above. Unpublished paper, Law Faculty, University of the North West, Mahikeng.

Malindi, Stanley. 2016. 'Continuity or Rupture? The Shaping of the Rural Political Order through Contestations of Land, Community, and Mining in the Bapo ba Mogale Traditional Authority Area'. MA thesis, University of the Witwatersrand.

Manson, Andrew. 2013. 'Mining and "Traditional Communities" in South Africa's "Platinum Belt": Contestations over Land, Leadership and Assets in North-West Province c. 1996–2012'. *Journal of Southern African Studies* 39, no. 2: 409–423.

Manson, Andrew and Bernard Mbenga. 2003. '"The Richest Tribe in Africa": Platinum-Mining and the Bafokeng in South Africa's North West Province, 1965–1999'. *Journal of Southern African Studies* 29, no. 1: 25–47.

PP (Public Protector). 2016. 'Public Protector Thuli Madonsela Updates Bapo-ba-Mogale on Her Investigation into Alleged Looting of their Resources'. Office of the Public Protector, 29 July. http://www.gov.za/speeches/public-protector-thuli-madonsela-updates-bapo-ba-mogale-her-investigation-alleged-looting

PP (Public Protector). 2017. 'Report of the Public Protector in Terms of Section 182(1)(b) of the Constitution of the Republic of South Africa, 1996 and Section 8(1) of the Public Protector Act of 23 of 1994: Allegations of Maladministration in the Bapo ba Mogale Administration'. Office of the Public Protector.

R2K (Right2Know Campaign). 2016. 'R2K Alarmed at Threats to Madibeng FM Staff'. Statement released by the Right to Know Campaign. http://www.r2k.org.za/2016/07/23/r2k-alarmed-at-threats-to-madibeng-fm-staff/

Steyn, Lisa (Right2Know Campaign). 2012. 'Lonmin Unlucky in Love'. *Mail & Guardian*, 7 to 13 December.

Steyn, Lisa. 2014. 'Lonmin Inks New Deal with Bapo'. *Mail & Guardian*, 8 August. https://mg.co.za/article/2014-08-08-lonmin-inks-new-deal-with-bapo

Stone, Setumo. 2013a. 'Details Vague, but North West's Investment of "Surplus" Defended'. *Business Day*, 26 November.

Stone, Setumo. 2013b. 'Lonmin May Boost Community's Stake'. *Business Day*, 3 December.

Stone, Setumo. 2013c. 'Mining Royalties Fail to Reach North West Communities'. *Business Day*, 4 October.

Stone, Setumo. 2013d. 'Not Feasible to Completely Freeze Controversial D-Account, Says Premier'. *Business Day,* 26 September.
Stone, Setumo. 2014a. 'D-Account Was Never Probed'. *Business Day,* 19 August.
Stone, Setumo. 2014b. 'Wider Probe into Mining Royalty Funds'. *Business Day,* 25 July.
Swart, Heidi. 2012a. 'Bapo Community Wants Lonmin Rights Back'. *Mail & Guardian,* 23 November. http://mg.co.za/article/2012-11-23-00-bapo-community-wants-lonmin-rights-back
Swart, Heidi. 2012b. 'Platinum Wealth Holds no Shine for People Left in the Dust'. *Mail & Guardian,* 29 June. http://mg.co.za/article/2012-06-28-platinum-wealth-holds-no-shine-for-people-left-living-in-the-dust
Tau, Poloko. 2016. 'How Bapo's R616m was Blown'. *City Press,* 9 October.
Timse, Tabelo. 2016. 'Lonmin's "Bapo Deal" in Crisis'. *Mail & Guardian,* 19 October.

CHAPTER

5

# Mining, Graves and Dispossession in Mpumalanga

Dineo Skosana

At Tweefontein Colliery Complex, 25 km south-west of Witbank in Mpumalanga province, lie graves that will be impacted by multinational commodities and mining company Glencore PLC (Glencore) open-cast coal mine expansion plan. The Tweefontein farm, and several other farms such as Boschmansfontein and Klipplaat, are sites of formal and informal cemeteries with graves that belong to former migrant labourers and labour tenants from South Africa and Mozambique. The change of Glencore's mining method from underground to open-cast mining disturbs about a thousand graves, which are legally protected by the National Heritage Resources Act, Act 25 of 1999 (NHRA). The negotiations about the grave relocations began with the affected families in 2011, but the relocations commenced in 2012, before these were concluded. This ignited a dispute between the mine and the owners of the graves.

South Africa's Mineral and Petroleum Resources Development Act, Act 28 of 2002 (MPRDA) gives particularly strong rights over land to those who are licensed by the state to mine (see Capps, Beinart in this volume). While contradictions between mining legislation and the heritage law provide a context to the contestations over graves, this chapter explains why grave relocations are sensitive from the perspective of the owners of the graves. I draw on interviews to argue that ancestral remains are mediators of life and death for the living. They are evidence of a history that is entangled with narratives of land dispossession, restoration and contested forms of evidence in the current political dispensation. Graves validate belonging for those whose status was historically disregarded. I first present a description of the grave relocation process and then explore the idea of graves as a body of evidence in the post-apartheid era.

To explain why graves are subject to contestations, my interviews delved into the families' experiences of the removal of their ancestral graves and the reburial of their remains. My questions probed, amongst other things, ideas and issues related to consultation, access to information and awareness of legal cultural rights. I also intended to evaluate inconsistencies and irregularities in the application of legal provisions in the NHRA and MPRDA. I conducted 14 interviews with the families whose graves were relocated by Glencore. It was imperative to first understand why the deceased were buried on the Tweefontein farm. The use of oral history allowed me to gather information about the historical background of the surviving family members and to establish a connection to the deceased.

A signed relocation agreement with heritage consultants Professional Grave Solutions (PGS) enabled the process of selective sampling so that only families who were affected by the relocations were identified and interviewed. All the families were pleased to share their experience with me and echoed the general sentiment that the mining company violated their rights. I continually had to remind the family representatives that I was not a legal practitioner, a journalist or a government employee. Nonetheless, the families gauged the interviews as an opportunity to begin to advance concerns they could not raise with the mine. Many graves initially located on the Tweefontein farm were of former labour tenants and migrant labourers whose families now live around Witbank and Ogies. In this chapter, I focus on the graves of the former labour tenants and not the migrant labourers. Seventy-seven of the graves covered in this chapter date back to the 1950s and 1960s, while some date back to the 1920s and 1930s. These are remains of women, men and children who died from various causes including short- and long-term illnesses, as well as accidents.

## DIGGING THE DEAD FOR COAL

All the interviewed families recalled being approached by the mine's consultant, *Baba* Shorty Mgcina, a local old man employed to facilitate the negotiations. When asked how he was appointed as a consultant, *Baba* Mgcina recounted:

... Mr Leeds, I was his driver, said to me, Shorty, you'll be retiring in the next few months ... me and the mining committee are thinking of giving you a job. The coal seam underground is running out. Workers under Glencore mine will soon be out of jobs. We are now going to mine using the open-cast method. So, we would like you as a local person born here to be the person of contact for the relocations of graves project because you know almost everybody.[1]

To give a description of his responsibility in the project, *Baba* Shorty Mgcina said 'the important role that I play is to identify people. I look for the owners of the graves. They take me to their graves. People say yes, we know these graves. I work through referrals.' The Tweefontein grave relocations were publicised through local newspapers, as well as the radio. The meetings between Glencore and the affected families began in 2011 and were intensified in 2013. In 2015, during a meeting with representatives of Glencore and PGS, a company representative advised me to 'put your research interviews on hold, in order not to disturb the mine's negotiation process.'

At first, the mine conducted consultations with groups of affected families. This gave families the chance to discuss with each other their legal rights and to pool ideas about adequate compensation for the relocations of their graves. After realising the effects of group dynamics, the PGS consultants decided to conduct private family consultations. Families see this as a divide-and-rule strategy. During his interview, Peter Mokalapa, a family representative, described his first encounter with the mine's consultant: 'There was a radio announcement that if you have graves on these cemeteries be informed that they will be relocated. They then came to the houses of the people who responded.'[2] The house visits accelerated the negotiations as most families were made to believe that they could not challenge the mine's decision to relocate their graves. Mokalapa further explained the mine's strategy when he said, 'They would tell you that you refusing the relocations slows down the process as some families have already agreed. In fact, they used dividing tactics on us. We should have been united on this issue.' A Mathibela family representative, Jimmy Mavimbela, mentioned an additional critical reason for not refusing to relocate when he said, 'The thing is, when the mine tells you that they want to relocate your graves, you already know that they have money and can afford good lawyers. You agree to everything because hiring a lawyer is very costly. So, you just go along with the mine's instructions.'[3]

All the affected families echoed the sentiment that the PGS consultants failed to facilitate a dialogue about the relocations during their visits. Instead, the consultants conveyed Glencore's decision to relocate the families' ancestral graves. The consensus among the families that I interviewed is that they were simply informed about the grave relocations and that this was not a negotiated process. For instance, the mine issued its scheduled dates for relocations after each visit. The proposed date was often on a weekday, which meant that some family representatives could not attend because they had to be at work. This complemented Glencore's rule that not more than two people per family be allowed to attend the relocation and reburial process. Most of the families stated that the graveyard was already fenced when they went to exhume their loved ones. In an interview, Abel Mtshweni recounted his experience on the day: 'As visitors, we had to get permission from the gate. You are kitted in safety boots, glasses, helmet and a vest, just like someone who is going into an underground mine, not graves.'[4]

Glencore granted permission to family representatives to bring a priest from their church denomination. However, on each family's scheduled day for relocation the mine provided inadequate transportation for family members to travel to the new gravesite. This meant that only one member per family could oversee the process. Families who wished to be accompanied by their relatives had to organise their own transport and this was always a financial challenge. The mine's failure to provide sufficient transportation was a major concern for the families because in most instances it meant that the family representatives, who were sometimes younger, or lacked knowledge related to customs performed during relocations, were not part of the process. Concerned about the mine's travel arrangements Peter Mokalapa disclosed during an interview that

> ... at the gate, few people are permitted. I understand that because when you are many you might not be able to control the people, but there should at least have been transport for people to get to the reburial cemetery, because we don't know every ritual that ought to be performed and there are elders who know all these. Now that we left them, it means things did not go accordingly. The mine did not follow our protocol. They did not even allow us to bring a priest. They brought their own priest.[5]

Although the presence of a priest hired by the mine worried some families, not everyone was concerned about this. For instance, Jimmy Mavimbela offered a different perspective when he said, 'No, it's no longer *intoyabafundisi* [a priest related matter], it is a cultural thing because we slaughter. The family must be there to see where the remains are relocated. A snuff [crushed tobacco] is needed when communicating with your ancestors. When you get home, you slaughter and drink traditional beer. Relocations are more of a cultural thing – different from normal burials.'⁶

All the families mentioned that the dead must be spoken to during the relocation process. They are informed prior to being moved about the disturbance of their place of rest and assured that they will be rested at another site. This is done to ensure that the spirit of the deceased does not linger and torment the living.

The Mathibela and Mabhena are the only families who challenged the mine when agreements related to the relocations could not be reached. These families have the most graves on the affected cemetery – 11 and 35 respectively – and used these numbers as leverage during their negotiations with the mine. The representatives from both families whom I interviewed are relatively educated and to some extent informed about their legal rights. Amon Mathibela owns various local stores in Kwa-Mhlanga, whilst Dan Mabhena is the son of Chief Mabhena whose chieftaincy is based in the former Kwa-Ndebele homeland. Both families are well regarded in their communities and have strong business connections.

Recalling the negotiations Amon Mathibela recounted:

> They sent this Boer man to conduct the negotiations. If you ask my wife, she will tell you that I sent Henk off. He was here, seated, and I told him to leave because this is my house. I said, 'You are not here to tell me what you are going to do with my graves'. I told him that if I want, I can delay this process for three to five years. 'I am not stranded for money. If you come to my house, you negotiate with me otherwise, get out!' He never came back. They sent Shorty Mgcina, instead. They had to negotiate.⁷

Dan Mabhena explained that the mine wanted to directly negotiate with his father in the hope that he would sign the agreement for the relocations.

> I told the mine that they can relocate the graves provided they will take care of the families because we are the beneficiaries of that place. The mine had to consider opening job opportunities. We gave them an endless list with our demands. When they realised that these demands were hefty, they began giving people money – bribing those with similar surnames to sign on our behalf. As we speak, we do not know what happened to our graves and who signed for the relocations. It's something I still need to take up.⁸

To further clarify why there were contestations, Amon Mathibela gave a similar rationale to Dan Mabhena when he said, 'Our culture says that you cannot be a Skosana and want to appease ancestors from Mathibela. That's what the mine intended to do. They wanted to slaughter a cow and call all the affected families to feast on it. That is unacceptable!'[9]

Although the Mathibela family were eventually able to reach an agreement with the mining company, the Mabhena, whose ancestral graves belonged to former labour tenants who lived on the farm for over 50 years, could not come to an amicable understanding. This is because the company could not agree to their terms related to compensation for the Tweefontein farm for which they have launched a land claim. Mathibela mentioned that their family's land claim was initiated by his uncle in the first call for claims in 1998, and that they do not have documentation to verify their claim because of the then land claim system. Like all the interviewed families, they contended that the standard R1 500 wake fee, determined by the mine together with the consultants, was inadequate compensation for the number of years their families lived on the farms on which the mines are situated and for the relocations of their homes that took place, mostly in the 1970s and 1980s, when mining began to expand.

For most families, there was no consultation or negotiation with regards to an adequate compensation. All the families except the Mathibela and the Mabhena felt compelled to accept this compensation fee because Glencore did not want to negotiate. Thus, the Mathibela are the only family that was compensated R9 000 per grave. Explaining how their family representative could negotiate R99 000 for their 11 graves, Mathibela recounted:

> I had already erected tombstones for my father and some of the elders. I said to them that I will not agree to have my graves relocated in the manner that you usually do. So, I went to home affairs in Witbank. I asked them to disclose how much I should be compensated per grave? They said, there is no specific fee. The agreement is essentially between me and the mine. So, I said to them, how much will the mine make from the piece of land that my eleven ancestral graves occupy? The home affairs department then said, the matter is not within their jurisdiction. So, I delayed the process. Three weeks after, the mine came to me with an offer of R9 000 per grave plus transport and other services. They said they will erect tombstones for the graves which already had tombs and my choice of headstones. We had an agreement.[10]

Glencore honoured their agreement with the Mathibelas, but this was not the case for all the families. Families were concerned that graves with headstones were not replaced. They identified these as graves where their loved ones were buried with permanent headstones inscribed with the date of birth and death of the deceased. Only a few were modern marble headstones. The company failed to honour its verbal and written agreements even though some families had clearly indicated on the relocation forms that they would like headstones to be erected on their graves.

Failure to document agreements is one of the major problems in this process. Families whose graves are less than 60 years old did not have copies of their relocation agreements and were not aware that these could be accessed online or at the local municipality. Moreover, there are no legal systems to verify completed documents. Thus, any person can sign an agreement as the rightful representative. Shorty Mgcina, during my interview with him, revealed the repercussions of this when he mentioned that, on a few occasions, people falsely claimed for financial gain that certain graves held the remains of their ancestors. He also disclosed instances where there have been generational tensions, with younger family members perceiving the elderly as being susceptible to signing agreements they didn't understand. The tensions were mostly sparked by the R1 500 compensation, which the younger generation considered inadequate in respect of land that they argued belongs to their ancestors. The families tied their demands for higher compensation to ideas about ownership. Some of the families who have graves claimed ownership of the sites of the graves in the sense that they either historically owned the land and were removed without compensation for the commencement of mining activities, or that the deceased family members worked the land as labour tenants.

Both the young and old family representatives expressed concerns with the actual relocation process. According to the NHRA, section 36, graves are categorised in terms of location and age: those inside and outside of a formal cemetery, and those graves that are newer or older than 60 years. To exhume archaeological graves (those over 100 years old), those of victims of conflict, of royal or traditional leaders, or any grave or burial ground older than 60 years situated outside a formal cemetery, a permit must be obtained from the South African Heritage Resources Agency. Graves that are less than 60 years old and inside a formal cemetery require permission from the Health Department and/or a local municipality to relocate. The oldest grave recorded in interviews was from 1906 and 8 of the 4 families knew of graves that dated back to the 1950s or earlier. But there were no adequate general procedures for different categories of graves in relation to the families.

In other respects, the mining company and its representatives improvised throughout the process with each family. For example, while some family representatives reported arriving at graves that had already been opened with the remains exposed, some families could witness the exhumations. All families had the opportunity to witness the removal of the remains of their family members from the ground. Those who owned old graves recalled finding degraded skeletal remains, which blended with the soil. With the assistance of an undertaker hired by the mining company, the remains were placed in black plastic bags.

None of the families were pleased with the provision of black refuse plastic bags for the removal of their remains. The Mathibela family was particularly vocal about this to the mine. Their representative recounted lashing out: 'This is not acceptable! A black plastic bag is for rubbish. It is the same even when I go to a shop and you use a black plastic bag for me, I don't accept it. I did not accept the bags. These people are too important for me to be placed in a *dust bin* bag. Something you throw away? Never! These people must be respected.'[11]

Moreover, all the families were opposed to the provision of small coffins for the reburials. They rationalised this as disrespect for their ancestors and disregard of their cultural beliefs. The Mathibelas are the only family who demanded nine adult coffins and two child coffins, whilst other families felt compelled to accept the small coffins. Families revealed that they were not consulted about the coffin sizes, the desired type, or the quality. Jimmy Mavimbela explained: 'We would have chosen our own coffins because we buried our people initially in the coffins we liked and picked for them as a family.'[12] Families also complained that the remains from different families were transported together to reduce costs. This is considered disrespectful because they held the view that the spirits of the deceased should not be combined. The coalescing of the spirits is believed to confuse ancestors and may be a bad omen in the long term.

Most families received the R1 500 compensation fee only after the reburial. This made it more difficult to purchase the necessary items and groceries needed to conduct traditional rituals before the relocations. This creates spiritual instability, they all explained. The families incurred the cost of the items and traditional ceremonies that were necessary for themselves and for their ancestors' wellbeing. Not only was I able to identify problems related to spiritual security, it was also evident that some representatives and their families needed counselling.

Although grave relocations are gradually becoming a common phenomenon in South Africa and globally, all the families expressed this as being their first experience and consequently, a shocking and emotionally draining process. Evelyn Nyathi, for instance, recalled: 'I found clothes on my remains. Sibongile, my daughter, was wearing a little dress and a little jersey with flowers. God did well because there were contestations over that grave. Anna had been saying it's their grave. Her sibling's grave. So, when we got there, we found Sibongile's clothes which she wore when she drowned.'[13]

Esther Mtshweni, whom I interviewed with her son, said 'I saw my mother when I was asleep, and she said she needs traditional mats. You know a dream is strange. I knew that my mother had died. But I spoke to her as we are speaking. My husband had not yet mentioned that the graves will be relocated in April. So, when the date came, I took the mat my mother mentioned on a dream and placed it on the box.'[14]

Many families also recalled the traumatic experience of seeing remains for the first time. Although some had not met the deceased, they were told stories about them by an older member of their family. This gave life and meaning to the deceased to the point where the living developed a physical and spiritual connection. The general sentiment expressed by the families was that Glencore treated their remains like objects that stood in the way of production and profit making.

## LAND AND ATTACHMENT IN SOUTH AFRICA

Not only did colonialism and apartheid rule through sweeping discriminatory policies and practices premised on constructions of racial difference, segregation and coercion were sustained through systemic land expropriation and legislation. Conquest resulted in widespread appropriation of land, which largely became divided into farms privately held by whites. For those African people on the farms, Abie Dithlake (1997: 220) writes that, 'as a result of systemic land dispossession, Africans were forced into changing and fluctuating productive relationships with the land. They moved through land ownership, sharecropping, and labour tenancy to total landlessness.' Solomon Plaatje (1995: 13) witnessed this process after the passing of the Natives Land Act of 1913 and wrote that, 'awakening on Friday morning, June 20, 1913, the South African native found himself, not actually a slave, but a pariah in the land of his birth'. Historians agree that this piece of legislation demonstrated an intensified goal to inhibit the growth of the African peasantry. Some land was reserved for African communities, which became the basis of the migrant labour system, which Harold Wolpe (1972: 444) labelled as 'the new basis for cheap labour'.

I want to re-establish a connection between dispossession and the way in which colonialism and apartheid are understood as systems that divested people of citizenship (James 2013; Nkambule 2012). By doing so, I can argue that graves are a form of evidence that validates citizenship in the post-apartheid South Africa (James 2009). Land dispossession was the withdrawal of the status of belonging, rights and responsibilities attached to being a citizen of the country. As mentioned above, fluctuating ties to land were introduced through labour tenancy and the migrant labour system. Labour tenancy regulations were more clearly defined in the 1913 and 1936 Acts as well as legislation in 1964 that envisaged the gradual abolition of tenancy. Nevertheless, some African families could establish themselves on white-owned farms, especially on farms that had absentee landowners (Dithlake 1997).

This applies to the farm Tweefontein, which featured in my interviews. When asked why they buried at Tweefontein, Esther Mtshweni recalled, 'My uncle used to stay there. This was also before the mine was operating. It was farms then. They were farm labourers.' Ranaka Motaung who lost her child in 1987, also indicated that her father - who is also buried in Tweefontein - was a labour tenant.[15] The position changed for these families when mining expanded in the 1970s. Some families were removed without prior arrangement for resettlement; this was at the height of apartheid.

Other descendants of the deceased whose graves were on Tweefontein and neighbouring farms were moved in the early 1990s to the then informal settlement in Hlalanikahle (Witbank). The Mathibela family was relocated to Ogies. The criteria for the provision of resettlement houses is not clear. It seems the mine provided alternative housing in the newly developed, Phola Park (Ogies) for those who worked for the mine but did not provide housing for those who were not employed in the mine. During his interview, an old man, John Mnguni recalled, 'We grew up on that farm. My parents stayed there. Then I moved to Phola when they removed us. My parents were no longer alive... they were farm labourers on the mielie-meal plantation.'[16] An interview with Mgcina also indicated that some family members who had graves on these farms returned to homes that were outside South Africa, mainly in Mozambique. The idea of home could be fluid. Some connected home with their birthplace, where the umbilical cord falls and is buried usually by the cattle kraal. The umbilical cord marked the place where the living would one day be buried. It maintained a physical and spiritual connection between labour tenants and migrants to home but many homes were reconstituted during the period of land dispossession (Plaatje 1995). Often, people's social relationships were disrupted, and sometimes completely broken during movement or resettlement. Some labour tenants were buried on the farms, while some were buried in their place of birth. Rebekah Lee and Megan Vaughan (2008: 365), writing more generally, ask:

> how would the dead be ensured safe passage into the afterlife, if not buried at 'home' under the watchful eyes of the living? And how would the community attain ritual and spiritual closure without the assurances brought on by

the ceremonial treatment of the body of the deceased? ... Throughout southern Africa, the migrant labour system imposed a necessary mathematics of distance upon the delicate calibrations of social and kinship relations.

Thus, in the space of disconnectedness, African families were motivated to create burial societies, as well as mortuaries to ensure that their deceased reach home timeously to receive traditional burials (Lee 2011a). Lee (2011b: 228) argues that 'the fear of death was expressed not so much in any anxiety associated with the premature ending of one's life, but rather in the possibility that death could happen "far away" or "far from home"'. Hence, modes of dealing with death away from home were invented to ensure that distance and disconnect were bridged in death, and that belonging was re-established. The coercive nature of apartheid was also important. In other words, families that voluntarily moved for various reasons may have found ways of managing this connection with graves. But it is the coercive elements of the apartheid era that played some role in sensitising and politicising the connection with graves.

## GRAVES AS EVIDENCE IN LAND RESTITUTION

Although the Tweefontein graves belong to former labour tenants and migrant labourers, some of whom were not from South Africa, and whose owners could not be located as a result, my analysis of graves as a form of evidence is only applied to those labour tenants who were originally born in South Africa and are by law in the post-apartheid era permitted to claim land.

The colonial ghost that embodies, amongst other things, a moment of disruption, appropriation and assimilation, compels 'post-colonial' societies to revisit the past in order to 'validate present attitudes'. According to David Lowenthal (1985: 40): 'The past validates the present in two distinct ways: by preserving and by restoration'. How then, does a ruptured society regain what was lost, if 'colonial modes of evidence' are tainted, and the dispossessed 'oral transmission accumulates actual alterations unconsciously, continually readjusting the past to fit the present?', asks Lowenthal (1985: 41). Put simply, how does the state validate land dispossession in the current land restitution programme, when documentation of removal was never issued? This is a thorny issue in the current political landscape in South Africa. My findings do not provide solutions but offer an insight into an alternative form of evidence in the current restitution programme.

The conceptual framework of Zoë Crossland (2009), an anthropologist who explores evidential practices on human remains, is important for my argument. Her work examines the remains of a popular and notorious nineteenth-century convicted Australian bushranger and gang leader, Edward 'Ned' Kelly, whose remains were found 130 years after they went missing following his execution in the old Melbourne Gaol. Crossland investigates Kelly's remains to show how an interpretation of these as evidence requires a complex fusion of disciplines, namely: criminology, anthropology, medicine and heritage studies. In her work, she draws from the nineteenth-century evidential paradigm in anthropology, which was informed by Sigmund Freud's work. Crossland establishes four different evidentiary conceptions of the dead body: 'The reading of bodily symptoms to diagnose interior states and faculties; the body as evidence of individual identity – that is, as identical with the person who is understood to inhabit it; the body as evidence of the past, including as symbol of nation, ethnicity or other larger group, identity, or position; and lastly, the body as evidence of crime' (Crossland 2009: 71).

These different ways of interpreting the dead body were developed by different disciplines from which, for example, physicians who explored diseases during dissections in the eighteenth century concluded that the dead body is a site for understanding the living. In another body of work developed by anthropologists, the body was theorised as an evidence of identity – an approach that was popular in the nineteenth century, for documenting colonial subjects, and for the regulation of criminal bodies. Crossland's (2009: 74) idea of the body as evidence of the past is useful to my work. For her, the corpse 'refers not only to a body but also to a collection of facts or objects, as in a corpus of material, evidence, or knowledge'. This means that dead bodies are not only evidence in forensics – for example, in post-mortems or, if buried, to exhume for further examination.

Dead bodies and graves have agency in other ways as a repository of memory and a connection with ancestors that have potential to act. Accordingly, I want to go back to Evelyn Nyathi's account during the interviews. She recollected, 'I found clothes from my remains. Sibongile my daughter was wearing a little dress and a little jersey with flowers. God did well because there were contestations over that grave. Anna had been saying it's their grave. Their sibling's grave. So, when we got there – we found Sibongile's clothes which she wore when she drowned'.[17] In line with Crossland's theory, Evelyn's daughter's remains resolved a contestation over ownership, by speaking beyond the grave, challenging those who claimed the deceased was theirs. By doing so, Sibongile's remains become active agents within a network of complex relations that involves more than one claimant over ownership.

In the larger scheme of things, the interviewed families articulated the same view that graves are evidence of their past. Some of the families launched claims to land in the first round of calls by the Department of Rural Development and Land

Reform, in 1998. For example, Dan Mabhena, who belong to a chiefly lineage, was adamant that the Tweefontein farm that is currently mined, is theirs. The family mentioned the presence of graves on the farm as proof. The Mabhena representative recounted in an interview:

> We wanted a meeting. We were five representatives, including the Ntuli. We said to them [the mining company] that they can relocate the graves provided they will take care of our families because we are the beneficiaries of that place. For that, the mine must consider us. For that, the mine must consider opening job opportunities. We gave them an endless list with our demands. When they realised that these demands were hefty, they decided to bribe people and some of the people who were relocated in the area have nowhere to go. So, we have not met with Glencore.[18]

When asked what the Mabhena's relationship was with the Ntuli, he explained, 'We lived alongside the Ntuli, and the Skosana. That's why there are at least 55 graves there'. However, if graves are a form of evidence, alongside other forms of evidence presented in the land claims courts and in restitution claims, what are the limitations of this evidence in contemporary South Africa?

First, let us establish that land is 'a key source in mobilising political power, including through electoral politics' (Moyo, Tsikata and Yakham 2015: 16). Therefore, the authors observe that land reform can be a critical site of electoral struggles when domestic class, race and ethnic power structures are unevenly pitched in relation to unequal land distribution. Land reform formed a part of the African National Congress's (ANC) election campaign discourse, prior to 1994. At the time, there were high hopes that land restitution would not only redress the injustices experienced by black South Africans who had been dispossessed of land rights but also contribute to the objectives of tenure security, land distribution and rural development that underpinned the new democracy's wider land reform ambitions (Walker et al. 2010).

After its election to power in 1994, the ANC passed several pieces of legislation to begin to compensate those who were dispossessed during colonial and apartheid South Africa: policies were developed around restitution and redistribution programmes. By 2005, the acting director general of the Department of Land Affairs (DLA) reported to parliament that 79 969 investigations into the claims made by 1998 had been launched (Walker et al. 2010). Although most land restitution claims have been settled, there is a general sentiment amongst scholars that South Africa's land redistribution is a failure (Leysho 2009; Walker 2008; Claassens and

Cousins 2008). This failure is attributed to a wide range of problems including the market-driven land reform system; the lack of post-settlement support; the politicisation of Communal Property Associations (CPAs); the absence of support for small-scale black farmers; the incompetence of the officials; and tensions between communities and chiefs who launch claims on their behalf (Hall 2009; Lahiff 2009).

Noteworthy in these accounts are the exclusionary effects of mineral legislation and its contribution to the failure of land reform in post-apartheid South Africa. The Minerals Act 50 of 1991 was passed to safeguard the interest of mining companies and a conservative white minority who wanted to maintain the status quo (Harshe 1993). The legal agreements entered between 1991 and the new MPRDA (2002) are still binding to date. Parts of the mineral-rich land in South Africa cannot be redistributed because the land was legally leased for exploration or mining by the previous regimes. In addition, there is inadequate research that explores mine-induced removals. This complex relationship between mineral law and land reform is overlooked in scholarly accounts.

The historians and communities seeking to make sense of past events at this point turn to archival sources. However, scholars have begun to problematise the forms of evidence generated by existing archives (Hamilton et al. 2002; Lalu 2009). The consensus is that existing archives must be engaged with caution because, like the political climate in which they were constructed, they embody colonial and apartheid power relations and biases that sought to sustain particular narratives and a discourse of dominance (Lalu 2009: 32). It nevertheless is the case that archives do sometimes contain evidence of which families were established as tenants on particular farms. Such evidence can arise in a number of contexts including court cases, legal disputes and forced removals in which the state played a part.

Historically, communities were not issued with land tenure deeds on farms. The archival records of tenancy are very uneven. As a result, many rely partly on oral evidence, or on their knowledge of grave sites, in order to establish their residence on farms as tenants in the current political dispensation. These are also important in finding evidence for the number of grave sites on farms in the context of grave relocations where private farm owners deny access to the owners of graves. This was articulated by communities in seven provinces when I monitored the Restitution of the Land Rights Bill. Deborah James (2009) also records denial of access by former labour tenants for grave visits on privately owned farms.

In Crossland's work the dead body and its place of rest are evidential of the past for the living. The grave reveals 'an identity and a history of violence enacted on it' (Crossland 2009: 76). Read in numbers, the graves display ancestral history and social relationships. Usually, family members were not buried far from one another.

Most of the 11 Mathibela graves, for example, are placed in close proximity to each other. In this informal cemetery are some graves with Zulu or Pedi surnames, which illustrates that the deceased may have moved in search for work and unlike the Mathibela, may not have established familial networks. In pointing to these past events and processes, the body as evidence demands that attention be paid to the lives and identity of the deceased.

## CONCLUSION

I established from my interviews at least three points of contestations over graves and their remains. Firstly, the families were not satisfied with the actual relocation process. Their reasons included: inadequate transport provisions; the presence of a priest hired by the mine for some relocations; the process of gathering, removal and reburial of their remains; the use of black plastic bags for the remains; the provision of standard small coffins for young and adult remains; and the unfulfilled promise of providing tombstones. All of these illustrated to the families the urgency to relocate material things that stand in Glencore's way of generating profit, as well as a complete disregard of the families' beliefs.

The second concern was the provision of the R1 500 compensation fee (wake fee). The families complained that this amount was inadequate for the disturbance of their ancestral remains. The fundamental concern was that the amount could not purchase the items necessary for the performance of rituals that ensure harmony between the dead and the living. They all suggested that the success and misfortune in the lives of the living are attributed to ancestors and that there is always an ongoing conversation between themselves and the dead. Depending on how serious or urgent the extent issue was, the family might perform rituals either at their home or by visiting a grave. For example, some families mentioned grave site visits for issues such as pre-lobola negotiations, illness, recurring deaths in the family, misfortune, failure to conceive or to secure employment. This demonstrates that graves played a significant role in providing spiritual security.

Thirdly, and tied to the second concern, was an argument that the mine should not pay only the wake fee of R1 500 for graves that lie on land that is claimed by families. This raised questions about what constitutes fair compensation for intangible connections to graves and the land? Debates over the ownership of the Tweefontein farm remain unresolved. Glencore argued during preliminary interviews in this study that the farm belongs to the company. Even if this is not the case, the mining permit allows the mine to have access to the minerals. This is problematic in a country mired in the process of land restitution. I have shown here that families recognise that graves and oral memories are the only form of evidence they have in order to validate their claim of ownership, their history, belonging and identity. Some families have made land claims under the Restitution Act and make claims in a general sense that they have a connection with the sites of graves or the area that was their home. Recently, the precedence of the MPRDA was challenged in the Maledu court judgment, which gave the recognition of the informal land rights of communities who live in areas affected by mining.

I drew from a theoretical framework that emphasises that the dead body provides evidential traces. The dead body and grave sites validate identity in criminology as well as in anthropology and allow forensic research. In this argument, bodies and grave sites validate belonging and citizenship. This is because land dispossession in colonial and apartheid South Africa was an act of confiscating the status of belonging. Therefore, in a context where oral evidence can be altered and colonial archives are now turned to with scepticism for telling the story of dispossession from the appropriator's view, graves become an indication of belonging. They help to construct a history of family ties in as much as they reflect involuntary movement and estranged social networks.

NOTES

1   Shorty Mgcina, interviewed by Dineo Skosana, Phola Park, Ogies, 13 May 2015.
2   Peter Mokalapa, member of group interviewed by Dineo Skosana, Vorsman, Witbank, 28 April 2016.
3   Jimmy Mavimbela and Mrs Esther Mtshweni, interviewed by Dineo Skosana, Kwaguqa, Witbank, 20 May 2016.
4   Abel Mtshweni, interviewed by Dineo Skosana, Phola Park, Ogies, 11 June 2016.
5   Mokalapa, interview.
6   Mavimbela, interview.
7   Amon Mathibela, interviewed by Dineo Skosana, eKangala, 11 June 2016.
8   Dan Mabhena, interviewed by Dineo Skosana, Witbank, 20 August 2016.
9   Mathibela, interview.
10  Mathibela, interview.
11  Mathibela, interview.
12  Mavimbela, interview.
13  Evelyn Nyathi, member of group interviewed by Dineo Skosana, Vorsman, Witbank, 28 April 2016.
14  Mrs Esther Mtshweni, interview.
15  Ranaka Motaung, interviewed by Dineo Skosana, Hlalanikahle, 20 August 2016
16  John Mnguni, interviewed by Dineo Skosana, Phola Park, Ogies, 28 April 2016.
17  Nyathi, interview.
18  Mabhena, interview.

## REFERENCES

Claassens, Aninka and Ben Cousins, eds. 2008. *Land, Power and Custom: Controversies Generated by South Africa's Communal Land Rights Act*. Cape Town: UCT Press.

Crossland, Zoë. 2009. 'Of Clues and Signs: The Dead Body and Its Evidential Traces'. *American Anthropologist* 111, no. 1: 69–80.

Dithlake, Abie. 1997. 'Labour Tenancy and the Politics of Land Reform in South Africa'. In *No More Tears: Struggles for Land in Mpumalanga, South Africa*, edited by Richard Levin and Daniel Weiner, 219–225. Trenton: Africa World Press.

Hall, Ruth. 2009. 'Land Reform: How and for Whom? Land Demand, Targeting and Acquisition'. In *Another Countryside: Policy Options for Land and Agrarian Reform in South Africa*, edited by Ruth Hall, 62–91. Bellville: The Institute for Poverty, Land and Agrarian Studies (PLAAS).

Hamilton, Carolyn, Verne Harris, Michèle Pickover, Graeme Reid, Razia Saleh and Jane Taylor, eds. 2002. *Refiguring the Archive*. Dordrecht: Kluwer.

Harshe, Rajan. 1993. 'Understanding Transition towards Post-Apartheid South Africa'. *Economic and Political Weekly*, 18 September. https://www.epw.in/journal/1993/38/perspectives/understanding-transition-towards-post-apartheid-south-africa.html

James, Deborah. 2009. Burial Sites, Informal Rights and Lost Kingdoms: The Contesting of Land Claims in Mpumalanga, South Africa'. *Africa* 79: 228–251.

James, Deborah. 2013. 'Citizenship and Land in South Africa: From Rights to Responsibilities'. *Critique of Anthropology* 33 no. 1: 26–46.

Lahiff, Edward. 2009. 'With What Land Rights? Tenure Arrangements and Support'. In *Another Countryside: Policy Options for Land and Agrarian Reform in South Africa*, edited by Ruth Hall, 93–117. Bellville: The Institute for Poverty, Land and Agrarian Studies (PLAAS).

Lalu, Premesh. 2009. *The Deaths of Hintsa: Post-Apartheid South Africa and the Shape of Recurring Pasts*. Cape Town: HSRC Press.

Lee, Rebekah. 2011a. *African Women and Apartheid: Migration and Settlement in Urban South Africa*. London: Tauris Academic Studies.

Lee, Rebekah. 2011b. 'Death "on the Move": Funerals, Entrepreneurs and the Rural–Urban Nexus in South Africa'. *Africa* 81, no. 2: 226–247.

Lee, Rebekah and Megan Vaughan. 2008. 'Death and Dying in the History of Africa since 1800'. *Journal of African History* 49, no. 3: 341–359.

Leyshon, Donald John. 2009. 'Land Reform, Restitution and Entitlement in Post-Apartheid South Africa'. *Journal of Southern African Studies* 35, no. 3: 755–768.

Lowenthal, David. 1985. *The Past is a Foreign Country*. Cambridge: Cambridge University Press.

Moyo, Sam, Dzodzi Tsikata and Diop Yakham, eds. 2015. *Land in the Struggles for Citizenship in Africa*. Dakar: Council for the Development of Social Science Research in Africa (Codesria).

Nkambule, Sipho. 2012. 'Citizenship as a Tool of Social Inclusion and Exclusion in Post-Apartheid South Africa'. *Journal of Community Positive Practices* 2: 170–185.

Plaatje, Solomon T. 1995. *Native Life in South Africa*. Johannesburg: Ravan Press.

Walker, Cherryl. 2008. *Landmarked: Land Claims and Land Restitution in South Africa*. Johannesburg: Jacana Media.

Walker, Cheryl, Anna Bohlin, Ruth Hall and Thembela Kepe, eds. 2010. *Land, Memory, Reconstruction and Justice: Perspectives on Land Claims in South Africa*. Pietermaritzburg: University of KwaZulu-Natal Press

Wolpe, Harold. 1972. 'Capitalism and Cheap Labour Power: From Segregation to Apartheid'. *Economy and Society* 1, no. 4: 425–456.

CHAPTER

6

# The Abuse of Interdicts by Traditional Leaders in South Africa

Joanna Pickering and Ayesha Motala

The Constitutional Court's judgment in *Pilane* (2013) struck down a set of interdicts obtained by a senior traditional leader prohibiting meetings of certain members of Motlhabe village, one of the communities or settlements falling within the area of the Bakgatla-ba-Kgafela traditional council in North West Province, ostensibly on the strength of his customary law powers as a traditional leader.[1] The *Pilane* judgment held that the use of interdicts by traditional leaders to ban meetings or gatherings of dissenters violates the latter's constitutional rights to freedom of expression, association and assembly.[2]

The judgment was received as a major legal victory not only for the Bakgatla-ba-Kgafela traditional community but also for traditional community members across South Africa, vindicating their constitutional freedoms and customary rights in the face of the increasing abuse of chiefly power (Mnwana 2014: 27 and in this volume). However, the judgment was all but ignored by many traditional leaders and local courts. Interdicts and other court orders continued to be sought and obtained by traditional leaders to silence and restrain their critics, rather than engage in meaningful dialogue or use customary dispute resolution forums.

This chapter gives an overview of recent examples of the use of interdicts and other restrictive legal tactics by traditional leaders across several rural communities of the North West, Limpopo and Mpumalanga provinces against their own community members, seemingly in order to assert their claims to authority and in the process stifling debate and dissenting voices that challenge their authority.

Recourse to formal legal measures to validate versions of customary law that directly violate fundamental constitutional freedoms is a significant development considering the emphasis in the 1996 Constitution on striving for parity between common law and customary law. This is demonstrated, for example, by the recognition in the Constitution that the Bill of Rights 'does not deny the existence of any other rights or freedoms that are recognised or conferred by... customary law... to the extent that they are consistent with the Bill' and by the courts' constitutional obligation to 'apply customary law when that law is applicable' (sections 39(3) and 211(3)). Moreover, as will be shown by the examples set out below, recourse to formal legal procedures often conflicts with pre-existing customary dispute resolution mechanisms that aim to build community consensus or at least social equilibrium.

The contours of change have been shaped not only by court processes but also the changing legislative and political framework. The persistence of traditional leaders in asserting centralised authority through formal legal measures is also reflected in current and proposed legislation. For example, the Traditional Leadership and Governance Framework Act, Act 41 of 2003 (TLGFA), enacted to regulate the institution of traditional leadership, purports to promote transparency and constitutionality within traditional governance systems. However, despite these goals, it arguably resurrected apartheid structures, keeping in place traditional leaders appointed under apartheid, and continued to recognise tribal authorities of the previous dispensation (now called 'traditional councils') if they met certain conditions (LARC 2015: 2017). Moreover, there has been no effective transformation of these traditional structures. Most untransformed traditional authorities are continuing to operate, making important decisions ostensibly on behalf of their communities (see Duda and Ubink in this volume).

The powers of traditional leaders have thus been progressively strengthened through legislation and practice based in part on their historical authority in the Bantustan era as well as their own political organisation locally and nationally. In some areas the capacity of rural communities to hold them to account may have ebbed. In such a context, constitutional jurisprudence emphasising participatory governance tends to be ignored. This chapter discusses particular local struggles that illustrate the emergence of patterns of contestation over customary law and practice. The evidence discussed provides a window into differing interpretations of customary law and how these are mobilised through formal legal channels (see Budlender, Fay, Chaskalson in this volume). In particular, this chapter examines several judgments delivered since *Pilane*. These cases raise three key issues.

Firstly, they tend to demonstrate an interpretation of traditional authority that is contested by ordinary community members, who argue that it conflicts with customary practices on the ground. In this way, the cases show that both historical interpretations of customary law as well as the frontiers between customary law and formal legal rules and processes remain unsettled. Secondly, they point to the difficulty of enforcing Constitutional Court judgments that favour freedom of association and freedom of speech in the contexts examined. Lastly, they reveal that the national and local legal framework governing traditional leadership has also contributed to the manner in which the powers and functions are interpreted and applied. The discussion raises questions regarding the apparent disjuncture between legislative developments and constitutional jurisprudence. There follows a discussion of the seminal judgment, *Pilane*, and a subsequent section discusses three examples of interdicts granted by local courts.

## BACKGROUND TO THE *PILANE* JUDGMENT

The Bakgatla-ba-Kgafela is a 'traditional community' made up of 32 villages located in the Pilanesberg area of North West Province, under the leadership of *Kgosi* (chief) Nyalala Pilane (see Mnwana in this volume). It should be noted that the term 'traditional community' is derived from the TLGFA, which replaces the word 'tribe' with 'traditional community' and retains the disputed tribal boundaries created in terms of the 1951 Bantu Authorities Act. While the Traditional Council has some powers in terms of the TLGFA, there is also a democratic local government structure, and not all who live in the area see themselves as subjects of the Traditional Council. The Bakgatla in the North West are affiliated with the Bakgatla in Mochudi, Botswana. The paramount chief in Botswana, then Chief Linchwe II, appointed Pilane as *kgosi* of the Moruleng traditional community in North West Province on 6 April 1996.[3] The appointment was subsequently recognised by the premier of the province.

*Kgosi* Pilane has faced mounting resistance to his leadership, primarily due to his lack of transparency and accountability in mining and other corporate deals, and allegations of corruption against him (see Mnwana in this volume). In fact, a grassroots community organisation, the Concerned Bakgatla Anti-Corruption Organisation, worked tirelessly and with few resources to have the chief brought before the Regional Magistrate's Court at Mogwase, where he was convicted on more than 40 counts of fraud. However, he was later acquitted by the North West High Court though the judgment acknowledged that 'much criticism can be leveled against the manner in which

[Nyalala Pilane] as the person in charge of the tribes' money, administered it ... There is great suspicion that funds may have been misappropriated in the process.'[4]

The Commission of Inquiry into Traditional Claims and Disputes within the North West Province, in particular those of the Bakgatla-ba-Kgafela (previously known as the Maluleke Commission, thereafter the Baloyi Commission) unearthed evidence of millions of rands of mining revenue that is missing through dubious deals by *Kgosi* Pilane, his council and associates (Bloom and Wales-Smith 2018).

Furthermore, *Kgosi* Pilane is no stranger to using intimidating legal tactics, especially interdicts, to scare off critics. Under South African law, an interdict is essentially an order made by a court, in favour of the applicant (who brings the interdict application), prohibiting another person or persons (known as the respondent or respondents) from performing certain acts. An interdict is generally first granted on an interim basis. Later, a further court hearing is held, at which time the court decides whether to make the interdict final (in other words, permanent).

For an interim interdict to be granted, an applicant is required to show, amongst other things, that he or she has a 'well-grounded apprehension of irreparable harm' if the interdict is not granted and that he or she has no other satisfactory remedy.[5] When it comes to a final interdict, the applicant must prove that such harm has actually been committed or is reasonably apprehended. Again, it must be shown that no other satisfactory remedy exists.

In 2008 and again in 2011 (prior to the *Pilane* judgment), *Kgosi* Pilane successfully interdicted a group of disgruntled residents, led by David Pheto, from holding their own community meetings to mobilise against him. Amongst other complaints, the group felt that *Kgosi* Pilane was co-opting the community into endorsing dubious mining transactions. The North West High Court held that Pheto and others, not being members of the 'royal family', did not have *locus standi* to call meetings or represent any group of community members within Bakgatla-ba-Kgafela. In the 2011 judgment (*Pilane*, 2011), the Court held that Pheto and the rest of the group were 'doing everything within their means to unseat and undermine the authority' of *Kgosi* Pilane and the Traditional Council and that their behaviour bordered on 'vexatious'. The Court accordingly ordered a punitive costs order against Pheto and the other respondents to the interdict.[6]

## THE *PILANE* JUDGMENTS

The villagers of Motlhabe village had for years been angered by the alleged mismanagement of the affairs of the Bakgatla-ba-Kgafela at the hands of *Kgosi* Pilane and the Traditional Council, including the misallocation and abuse of resources derived from platinum mining on Bakgatla-ba-Kgafela land to the benefit of those loyal to the *kgosi* and Traditional Council. In addition to these grievances, there was a leadership dispute between Mmuthi Pilane and the officially recognised headman (locally called *kgosana*) of Motlhabe, Tlhabane Pilane. Complaints about the *kgosana* included him not being the correct leader in terms of customary law and failing to attend to governance matters in the village.

Things reached boiling point when in July 2009 members of the Motlhabe village, led by activists Mmuthi Pilane and Reuben Dintwe, attempted to secede from the Bakgatla-ba-Kgafela traditional community. A letter was addressed to the Traditional Council announcing the intention to become an 'Independent Tribe' that would no longer fall under the jurisdiction of the Traditional Council. The attempted secession was abandoned after the Traditional Council threatened to take the secessionists to court.

When Mmuthi Pilane and Reuben Dintwe called a meeting to discuss once again the issue of secession in January 2010, they received a call from the police informing them that they would be arrested should the meeting proceed. They decided to cancel the meeting.[7] However, acting on the erroneous belief that the meeting would in fact go ahead, *Kgosi* Pilane and the Traditional Council launched an urgent application in the North West High Court. There they successfully obtained a series of interdicts on disquietingly broad terms, interdicting Mmuthi Pilane and Dintwe from, among other things, proceeding with the meeting to discuss secession, organising or proceeding with any meeting purporting to be a meeting of the traditional community or the Motlhabe Tribal Authority, holding themselves out to be a traditional community or traditional authority of any kind and taking any steps which would have a 'distracting or reducing or belittling effect on the status, role and function' of the *kgosi* and the Traditional Council.

On the return date to make the interdicts final, the North West High Court confirmed three of the interdicts, which prohibited Mmuthi Pilane, Dintwe and any others 'acting through them or in collaboration with them', from:

1. Organising or proceeding with any meeting purporting to be a meeting of the Traditional Community or Tribal Authority without authorisation from the statutorily recognised Traditional Council;
2. Taking any steps contrary to statutes regarding traditional leadership or the customs of the traditional community;
3. Pretending or holding themselves out as a traditional authority of whatever kind.[8]

Both the North West High Court and the Supreme Court of Appeal denied leave to appeal. With assistance from the Legal Resources Centre, Mmuthi Pilane and Reuben Dintwe (the applicants) approached the Constitutional Court to have the interdicts set aside, contending that the interdicts limited their constitutional rights to freedom of expression, assembly and association.[9]

*Kgosi* Pilane and the Traditional Council (the respondents in the Constitutional Court hearing) argued that the High Court had correctly granted the interdicts because they, and they alone, were recognised structures in terms of custom, and in terms of the TLGFA and its provincial version – namely, the North West Traditional Leadership Governance Act. Thus, no other formation was able lawfully to convene meetings 'under the guise of an officially recognised traditional leadership structure'. The respondents argued that in terms of customary law only the *kgosi* could convene a meeting of the traditional community to discuss governance issues and only he was permitted to convene a 'people's assembly', or a *kgotha kgothe* (as such meetings are known locally). Additionally, the respondents submitted that, by attempting to secede and meet as the 'Motlhabe Tribal Authority', this demonstrated a persistent intention by the applicants to disobey the respondents' authority.[10]

The majority judgment of the Constitutional Court pointed out, in relation to the legislative recognition of the respondents, that since the law does not expressly restrict the existence of customary leadership that has not been legally recognised, the position was far from clear.[11] The Court went on to state that the meeting's agenda clearly included a discussion about lawful methods of secession: that pointed to a clear distinction between the applicants and the respondents. In the circumstances, it would be difficult to show how the applicants' actions could be understood as an attempt to steal the identity, authority or powers of the respondents, when the very terms of the meeting concerned their desire to disassociate themselves from the respondents. Moreover, the Court noted that the mere use of a particular name did not necessarily imply that the applicants wanted to assume the respondents' authority. In any event, the applicants were only alerted to the respondents' objection to using the name 'Motlhabe Tribal Authority' during High Court proceedings.[12]

In considering the interdicts, the Court made some general comments regarding interdicts in customary leadership disputes. The Court emphasised the constitutional recognition of customary law and its evolution as an independent, living body of law in keeping with the changing lives of the people whom it governs. The Court also emphasised the importance of the applicants' rights to freedom of expression, including the freedom to express views critical of existing traditional leadership, stating that 'in the absence of more convincing argument from the respondents in relation to their own rights against which the applicants' interests are to be balanced, one is hard-pressed to find in the respondents' favour.' The Court remarked that the exercise of these rights would not 'result in chaos and disorder'; on the contrary, they would strengthen the country's democracy and its institutions.[13]

The Court noted:

> The restraint on the applicants' rights is disquieting, considering the underlying dissonance within the Traditional Community and the applicants' numerous unsuccessful attempts to have this resolved. The respondents' litigious record also portrays a lack of restraint on the part of the Traditional Community's official leadership in employing legal devices to deal with challenges that should more appropriately be dealt with through engagement. This could be seen as an attempt to silence criticism and secessionist agitation and, if so, would not be a situation that the law tolerates.

Furthermore, the Court commented that the leadership dispute cried out 'for meaningful dialogue between the parties, undertaken with open minds and in good faith'.[14] In so doing, the Court delivered a clear message that the use of courts to silence dissenting voices was inappropriate, especially in a constitutional democracy where robust engagement should be favoured over litigation wherever possible, and given the numerous attempts by Pilane and Dintwe to resolve the situation through engagement.

Consequently, the second and third interdicts were unanimously reversed due to their 'over-breadth'.[15] The first interdict against organising or proceeding with any meeting purporting to be a meeting of the Traditional Community, was also reversed by a majority of eight out of the ten justices who heard the case.

In their dissenting judgment, Chief Justice Mogoeng and Justice Nkabinde held that traditional leadership should be approached with the necessary understanding and sensitivity in order to preserve it and that threats to traditional leadership should not be taken lightly. It was held that a special status is required in order to convene a *kgotha kgothe*: such meetings are convened by a leader who has the power to do so and, accordingly, has the power to restrain an 'imposter' (anyone other than those authorities empowered to call such meetings) from calling a meeting.[16] The justices thus agreed with the High Court judgment that the applicants could not give themselves symbols of state to proclaim a legitimacy they did not have.

This minority judgment held that, despite the applicants' claims to the contrary, they had in fact attempted to convene a *Kgotha Kgothe*, and by doing so, had attempted to usurp the powers of *Kgosi* Pilane and were undermining and threatening his position. The minority judgment held that the respondents were thus entitled to approach the High Court to resist the usurpation of their rights by the applicants who were not authorised in terms of customary law and statute to convene the meeting. The two dissenting justices did not agree with the majority judgment's setting aside of the first interdict, arguing that this would provide 'an avenue for undermining legitimate traditional structures, leadership and governance and the erosion of the rule of law'.[17]

The implication of the minority judgment was that only those recognised by law as traditional leaders had the authority to call meetings, at least on any topic relating to the business of the Traditional Council and that the applicants' constitutional rights to freedom of association and freedom of expression were trumped by the need to maintain order in the officially recognised 'traditional community'. The minority judgment appears to mirror the reasoning advanced by traditional leaders and accepted in the local courts when seeking to interdict community members from gathering or protesting, namely a position that attributes a special status to traditional leaders as the ultimate decision-makers in a given community, which appears at odds with the idea of participatory and multilevel governance emphasised by the majority judgment. As set out in the examples below, this position is often in contrast to the claimed customary practices on the ground (see Budlender, Duda and Ubink in this volume).

The majority judgment was received as a legal victory not only for many members of the Bakgatla-ba-Kgafela traditional community but also for traditional community members across South Africa, vindicating their constitutional freedoms in the face of the increasing abuse of chiefly power. The judgment confirmed the importance of democratic participation not only as a constitutional right but also under customary law and made it clear that traditional leaders could not, in an attempt to quell criticism, suppress the constitutional rights of traditional community members to freedom of association and expression.

Moreover, the *Pilane* judgment further confirmed a growing body of constitutional jurisprudence relating to living customary law. Given the historical manipulation of customary law and traditional leadership in the apartheid period, it was crucial to bring traditional leadership in line with principles of the new constitutional dispensation and to re-emphasise the concept of living customary law within the national legal framework. Accordingly, the Constitutional Court recognised that the institution of customary law is protected as a 'living' body of law, subject to the Constitution (see Budlender and Fay in this volume).

Section 211 of the Constitution recognises the 'institution, status and role' of traditional leadership, but makes such recognition subject to the Constitution. The

Constitutional Court has thus emphasised 'living' customary law rather than 'official' customary law. Whereas living law refers to the law 'actually observed by the people who created it', official customary law is 'a body of rules created by the state, traditional authorities and legal profession.' (Bennet 2008: 138). Furthermore, the Constitutional Court has emphasised the participatory aspects of customary practice and traditional leadership. In the *Bhe* (2005) judgment, the Court pointed out the historical manipulation of customary law and traditional leadership by apartheid authorities and held as follows: 'The positive aspects of customary law have long been neglected. The inherent flexibility of the system is but one of its constructive facets. Customary law places much store in consensus-seeking and naturally provides for family and clan meetings which offer excellent opportunities for the prevention and resolution of disputes and disagreements.'[18]

Over a series of judgments the Constitutional Court warned of the dangers of adopting an autocratic interpretation of customary law inherited from colonialism and apartheid at face value and instead asserted the need for an examination of the changing 'living law' which existed, and exists, in practice on the ground (Claassens and Budlender 2016). These judgments have strongly criticised restrictions imposed on the rights and freedoms of rural people in the interests of authoritarian interpretations of chiefly power.

## GA-CHOKOE, MOHLALA AND MAHLAKE CASES

Despite this case law, and the *Pilane* (2013) judgment in particular, similar interdicts continue to be granted by local courts, as illustrated by the Ga-Chokoe and Mohlala examples. Ga-Chokoe is one of 42 villages making up the Mapela traditional community, located about 30 km north of Mokopane in Limpopo in the former Lebowa homeland. The community surrounds Anglo American Platinum's Mogalakwena mine, the largest open-cast platinum mine in the world. Mapela is the site of ongoing community contestation to traditional leadership as well as sharp community divisions as a result of disputes related to mining developments.

In December 2015, an application for an interim interdict against a member of the Ga-Chokoe village was brought to the Mahwelereng Magistrate Court in the district of Morolong in Limpopo Province in the context of a long-running traditional leadership dispute. At the village level, local traditional leaders are referred to as headmen or headwomen (*ntona* or *mmantona* respectively, in Sepedi). Each village has one headman, who, together with his or her cabinet or council, administers village affairs and is responsible for holding regular meetings with the village and taking any village concerns or issues to the chief of the traditional community. In Ga-Chokoe community members interviewed considered the headman a particularly important customary institution, given that it is only at village level that most people are able to participate directly in decision-making processes.[19]

The appointment of headmen and acting headmen in Limpopo is regulated by the Limpopo Traditional Leadership and Institutions Act, 2005 (section 12(1)(a); section 12(2); 15(1)(a)). This statute is meant to complement the national legislation relating to traditional leadership institutions, enacted to deal with issues specific to the province. The appointment occurs in two stages. Firstly, the royal family concerned must identify a headman in terms of customary law of the traditional community concerned and then notify the premier of this appointment. Secondly, the premier must then recognise the new headman by notice in the government gazette and by issuing a certificate of recognition to the person so recognised unless there is evidence or an allegation that the identification of the new headman did not occur in terms of the relevant customary law.

In interviews, village members claimed that the custom of the Ga-Chokoe village is that the successor to the headman should traditionally be appointed from the children of the first spouse of the previous headman. However, in this case, upon the death of the headman of the Ga-Chokoe village, it was decided that none of the children of his first wife was mature enough to be appointed. Accordingly, another village member, Emily Chokoe, was appointed as headwoman. However, when she ceased engaging with the community's elders on issues relating to her governance, including engagements with mining companies, despite having undertaken to govern in close partnership with her elders, the community's elders decided to remove her as acting headwoman and instead appointed another person to act in this position, namely Albert Chokoe. So began a long-running leadership dispute, which culminated in a legal dispute between the two villagers, each claiming to be the rightful acting headman.[20]

In December 2015, Emily Chokoe approached the court on an urgent basis for an order interdicting Albert Chokoe, as well as a colleague of his (seemingly on the sole basis that he was Albert Chokoe's employee) and 'any other agent associated with them' from holding public gatherings. An interim (that is to say, temporary) interdict was granted by the local Magistrate's Court. According to interviews with villagers, the interim interdict had a chilling effect on the usual meetings and engagements conducted within the village. For example, after the interim interdict was granted, the royal family elders decided to hold a meeting with the community to discuss the headmanship dispute. The police arrested Albert Chokoe on contempt of court charges, merely on the accusation that he had attended the meeting, although in reality he had not been present.[21] Bi-weekly meetings of community elders held to discuss community issues were also prevented from happening, for fear of being arrested for contempt of the interdicts.

The imposition of an interdict in these circumstances would appear to be in direct conflict with the Constitutional Court jurisprudence discussed above, in particular the *Pilane* judgment of 2013, which confirms the inherent nature of customary law as participatory rather than exclusionary. Further, the *Pilane* judgment makes it clear that, in the case of a bona fide dispute, robust engagement and meaningful dialogue should be favoured over litigation, as this serves to strengthen democratic practices, achieves greater accountability and openness, and respects rural citizens' fundamental rights of freedom of association, freedom of opinion and freedom to make political choices. Legal tactics such as interdicts, on the other hand, serve to criminalise debate and dissent, especially given the unequal balance of power of the parties involved.

Moreover, the interdicts in this matter bear a striking resemblance to those set out by the Constitutional Court in the *Pilane* matter. Their effect on the respondents' rights is similarly disquieting, especially given the existence of an ongoing bona fide headmanship dispute. The facts in the Ga-Chokoe matter, like *Pilane*, seemed to cry out for meaningful dialogue between the parties. But the existing dispute resolution mechanisms in terms of the customary law of Ga-Chokoe were ignored in favour of a restrictive legal remedy. In terms of the custom of the village, disputes are traditionally discussed and resolved via local forums, starting at the village level, rather than through the courts.[22] While members of the community attempted to resolve the issue through community meetings, this process was hampered by the interdict, as illustrated by the fact that Albert Chokoe was arrested for allegedly participating in one such meeting, and by the cancellation of community meetings out of fear for being held in contempt of the interdict.

Albert Chokoe was able to obtain pro bono legal assistance from the lawyers of Richard Spoor to oppose the interim interdict being made final (that is to say, permanent). His counsel argued that the interdict should not be confirmed, since, apart from the dire implications of an interdict on his constitutional rights to association and free speech and the fact that it went against the precedent set in the *Pilane* judgment, Emily Chokoe had in any event failed to establish the necessary technical requirements for securing a final interdict.

Ultimately, the Magistrate's Court found in Albert Chokoe's favour and refused to confirm the interdict. Although the judgment did not expressly rely directly on *Pilane* or other Constitutional Court authority, it did recognise the fundamental point that 'if the interdict is finally granted it will have the effect of preventing the respondents from attending Kgoro ya Moshate (the royal compound) at Ga-Chokwe where important customary issues are discussed'.[23] The magistrate, as in the case of the Constitutional Court in *Pilane*, acknowledged the importance of protecting vital customary institutions as well as recognising the Constitution.

It is worth noting that successfully opposing the interdict may well have been impossible without the intervention of legal representatives. In most instances, this is not an option for community members faced with legal intimidation by a traditional leader or community representative. Cases like this one can usually only be pursued where pro bono support is obtained and this is only available from a relatively narrow group of legal support agencies. Moreover, the very real threat of punitive costs orders (discussed in further detail below) further deters or prevents community members from opposing legal action taken against them.

The Limpopo case of *Mohlala* (2014) grew out of a traditional leadership dispute between Chief Billy Mampuru, the traditional leader of the Bapedi ba Mamone, and Mathume Mohlala, the traditional leader of the Batlokwa-ba-Mogodumo.[24] Historically, the Bapedi had settled on the western side of the Makabjane River, and the Batlokwa on the eastern side of that same river, with the Batlokwa functioning separately. However, Chief Mampuru attempted to assert his authority as the legitimate traditional leader over both villages.

Chief Mampuru applied to the Magistrate's Court in Nebo for an interdict against Mohlala to prevent Mohlala (and others) from calling any meetings and to prohibit Mohlala from discharging his duties as chief. Mampuru argued that he was the legitimate chief of both villages within his area of jurisdiction including Vergelegen village where Mohlala allegedly resided. Mampuru argued that Mohlala did not fulfil the criteria to be recognised as a chief. Mampuru also pleaded prejudice on the part of his community because Mohlala was alleged to be disturbing development and inviting outsiders to control Vergelegen village as he was claiming to be the chief. Furthermore, Mampuru alleged that Mohlala was pretending to be *kgosi* and that his conduct would cause 'bloodshed unnecessarily'. Mampuru also alleged, in establishing the grounds for the interdict, that 'the respondents' actions are unlawful and that an interdict is required to stop the respondents from continuing with their unlawful conduct and to infringe upon my rights to administer a conventional community as I was still installed as a Chief'.[25] In answer to the allegations, Mohlala stated that the communities were entirely separate and they did not owe allegiance to any other traditional leader under customary law, including Mampuru who was the traditional leader only of the Bapedi ba Mamone. Furthermore, Mohlala denied that the Batlokwa traditional community fell under the jurisdiction of Mampuru in terms of living customary law and that this jurisdiction had been imposed by apartheid authorities. Mohlala also clarified his residential area as Hooggelegen and denied that he was pretending to be *kgosi* of Vergelegen. Moreover, Mohlala claimed that he exercised his authority as traditional leader in accordance with customs and traditions. While Mohlala's arguments were based primarily on customary law, Mampuru relied on his certificate of appointment as chief of the Bapedi ba Mamone which was issued in terms of the Black Administration Act of 1927, and a notice confirming his area of jurisdiction in terms of the Bantu Authorities Act of 1951 that was issued in a government gazette dated 7 February 1969.

In 2017, Mampuru again applied for an urgent interdict against Mohlala and others on similar terms, citing the same notices issued in terms of homeland legislation and alleging, amongst other factors, that Mohlala was falsely holding himself out to be the traditional leader in the area, calling meetings to address community members which confused and divided the community. In attempting to establish the urgency of the interdict, Mampuru alleged that Mohlala was unlawfully allocating stands to people on land reserved for development. The matter was struck off the roll during March 2017 for want of urgency.

This case illustrates the additional elements of the legal and social processes involved when chiefs apply for interdicts. Chief Mampuru approached the court for relief based on powers given to him by apartheid laws. In specific areas, the validity and status of such homeland legislation has been rescinded but the position is not always clear and reference is made to this older legislation as well as authority entrenched in the Bantustans.

Tensions between Speaker Mahlake, a resident of Ga-Joseph village in Mpumalanga, and the traditional leader of the area, Chief Mashego, go back to 2010, with the chief claiming that Mahlake wanted to displace him. Mahlake had attempted to form a farmers' organisation with farmers from neighbouring communities to address social needs, such as food security and job creation. According to Mahlake, Chief Mashego suspected him of conspiring to topple his chieftaincy and to have a new chief appointed, ostensibly based on the fact that Mahlake and others formed the Bakone Royal Council. Letters addressed from the Bakone Royal Council to Chief Mashego and to the House of Traditional Leaders during 2012 gave notification of the formation of the Council, whose main mission, as stated, was to establish and sustain Bakone cultural heritage and showcase Bakone traditional activities.

In the *Mahlake* (2016) case,[26] the Magistrate's Court in Bushbuckridge, Mpumalanga, granted an interdict in favour of the Moreipuso Traditional Council against Mahlake, restraining him and anyone acting upon his instructions from holding a Heritage Day celebration meeting at Wales, a neighbouring area. The interdict also prohibited him from coming anywhere near Wales on that particular day without the council's permission. One of the grounds relied upon by the Traditional Council was that the meeting would cause bloodshed between members of the community and those attending the meeting.

According to the founding affidavit put forth by a member of the executive committee of the Traditional Council, the youth of Wales were mobilising against the Bakone Royal Council meeting to be held on 24 September 2016. The meeting of another royal council from outside the village was viewed by the youth as an act of aggression and a hostile takeover, and they were ready to protect the village with their lives. Although the meeting on 24 September 2016 was intended to be a celebration, with international delegates attending, the court held in favour of the Traditional Council, also ordering the sheriff to take any necessary action should Mahlake or anyone else acting on his instructions fail to comply with the order. This case presents an interesting dimension to the potential overreach of interdicts in limiting the right in the Constitution (section 31(1)(a) and (b)) to enjoy culture and form cultural associations.

## *LOCUS STANDI*: ONLY THE CHIEF MAY BE HEARD?

While traditional leaders frequently resort to legal strategies to reproduce their own power, community members are often denied the possibility to do the same. A common legal tactic employed by traditional leaders is to argue that community members lack the necessary *locus standi* (legal standing) to bring or defend litigation, or to call public gatherings or community meetings.

This argument was used during the apartheid era and has been reproduced in democratic South Africa. For example, in 1956, Jacob Pilane filed a petition accusing Chief Tidimane Pilane of failing to account for the use of imposed taxes. The judgment of the Transvaal Supreme Court centred on the argument that 'the chief had no responsibility to account to anyone of his individual subjects' about the tribal accounts and that Jacob did not have standing to file a court application against the chief (Mnwana in this volume). A costs order was made against Jacob, and when he was unable to pay, Tidimane confiscated his cattle and agricultural tools. Jacob and his family were also harassed. The same approach has been adopted when it comes to the authority to call community meetings. In *Pilane* (2011), the Court held, somewhat confusingly, that 'whilst everybody and anybody has the right to call a meeting and enjoys freedom of association, nobody is allowed to call a meeting for and on behalf of an entity...whilst he or she does not have the necessary *locus standi* to do so'.

In the judgment of the North West High Court in *Pilane* (2010), later overturned by the Constitutional Court, Judge Landman held, in respect of the respondents' secession attempt and the manner in which the meeting was called, that:

> It is abundantly clear that in a constitutional dispensation no person or body of persons may create or reproduce structures otherwise than in terms of and in accordance with the constitutional processes contained within the Constitution which is the supreme law ... I adopt it and express it thus: Any action by a parallel but unsanctioned structure that is neither recognised by the law or custom, seeking to perform and assume functions which are clearly the exclusive preserve of such recognised authorities, ought to incur the wrath of the law.[27]

This approach conflicts starkly with the jurisprudence of the Constitutional Court, which emphasises the protection of the rights to freedom of expression, association, assembly and other rights guaranteed in the Constitution.

As Aninka Claassens and Boitumelo Matlala (2014: 118) write:

> Key to the current conflicts is an interpretation of customary law that holds that only officially recognised traditional leaders have authority and *locus standi* in issues pertaining to land and mineral rights. Traditional leaders argue, and courts uphold, that only they, and officially constituted and recognised 'traditional councils', have the right to call meetings, to access information and to represent people living within the tribal jurisdictions delineated during apartheid. On this basis interdicts are routinely granted to stop community meetings that seek to get to the bottom of, and discuss remedies for, abuse of power. Concerned citizens seeking to crack open the opaque web of laws, regulations and multibillion mining deals are shut out and shut down, in some instances with punitive costs orders awarded against them for their troubles.

Apart from their effects on freedom of association, interdicts can also have devastating financial and personal effects on those they are granted against. Even when obtaining victories in the courts, community members still suffer the day-to-day consequences for standing up to locally powerful traditional leaders. Mmuthi Pilane, despite being the successful applicant in the *Pilane* matter, has not been safe from continued attempts to silence him. In mid-2016, he was arrested under peculiar circumstances on a charge of kidnapping and was later released on conditions that he might not hold or attend community meetings in the Bakgatla area (Claassens 2016). This clearly contradicted the spirit and logic of the *Pilane* judgment.

David Pheto's experience provides another example of the potentially calamitous effects of interdicts. After the punitive cost order was granted in *Pilane* (2011), Pheto lost his livelihood. The Court ordered Pheto alone to pay the costs. Pheto's equipment at his legal practice was attached, as was the equipment in the butchery in Moruleng that he operated with his siblings (Mnwana 2014). Both businesses had to shut down. In addition, Pheto and other leaders had to pay the attorneys' legal fees from their own pockets. Pheto was effectively silenced.

The abuse of court processes by traditional leaders not only significantly limits rural citizens' fundamental rights of freedom of assembly, expression and association, but it also risks eroding existing customary institutions that seek to promote participatory and democratic decision-making and robust engagement. This is all the more concerning in light of the legislative context, which appears to strengthen the rights of traditional leaders and weaken those of ordinary rural citizens to hold their leaders accountable and to demand transparency.

## TRADITIONAL LEADERSHIP: NEW LEGISLATION

Colonial and apartheid renditions of customary law and chiefly power significantly shaped the interpretation and application of customary law prior to South Africa's transition to democracy. Seeking to manipulate traditional leaders for their own gains, apartheid lawmakers facilitated an approach to customary law that, in general, gave centralised decision-making power to traditional structures, while ignoring aspects of customary law based on participatory governance. Despite pronouncements from the Constitutional Court to the contrary, this mythology of all-encompassing chiefly power is at risk of being further concretised in legislation and policy. As discussed above, while the TLGFA purports to promote transparency and constitutionality within traditional governance systems, it resurrects apartheid structures and continues to recognise traditional councils that are similar to the tribal authorities of the previous dispensation. These make important decisions ostensibly on behalf of their communities.

Moreover, the TLGFA (section 20) provides for various roles and functions that may be allocated to traditional leaders and traditional councils, including land administration, administration of justice and management of natural resources. These roles and functions may be devolved by national or provincial government through legislation or other measures. Ambiguous provincial provisions can be seen to contribute to the misuse and misinterpretation of such legislation. An example is the North West Traditional Leadership and Governance Act, 2 of 2005 (sections 18(2) and (3)). These provisions stipulate that a *kgosi* shall enjoy the status, rights and privileges conferred upon *kgosi* by the customs and traditions applicable within the traditional community, and shall be entitled to loyalty, respect, support and obedience of any member of the traditional community in the lawful execution of functions. The Limpopo Traditional Leadership and Institutions Act 6 of 2005 (section 18) also fails to provide clear guidelines on the roles and functions of traditional leadership, using broad terms to describe them, such as promoting the interests of the traditional community.

The TLGFA also provides, more generally, that a traditional council shall '[administer] the affairs of the traditional community in accordance with customs and tradition'. This is not clearly defined and in practice these broad provisions have been used to hamper community participation in decision-making processes and are interpreted as granting broad powers to traditional councils, even when they are not explicitly devolved. A prime example is the R600 million missing from the Bapo-ba-Mogale community trust account, which according to the report by the Public Protector (2017), is attributed to the maladministration of the account by the North West Department of Local Government and Traditional Affairs, and the Bapo Traditional Administration (see Capps in this volume).

In Mapela, Limpopo, a scandal erupted over a traditional leader signing a R175 million settlement agreement with Anglo American Platinum without consulting with the community. He claimed to have been authorised by the Traditional Council to negotiate the deal despite no traditional council elections having taken place in Limpopo. Elections for the 40 per cent component of traditional councils are required in terms of the TLGFA. Limpopo's failure to hold those elections points to the ambiguous status of the Traditional Council based on its lack of statutory legal standing (Jewett 2016). This presents a further complication to the legality of the agreement. A mechanism for reconstitution exists in an amendment to the TLGFA, the Traditional Leadership and Governance Framework Amendment Act 2 of 2019, that was signed into law, effective from 28 November 2019. It provides an extended time frame of two years for traditional councils to reconstitute.

The Traditional and Khoi-San Leadership Act 3 of 2019, which will replace the TLGFA once it comes into effect, similarly provides in section 25 that a department within the national or provincial sphere of government 'may, through legislative or other measures provide a role for a kingship or queenship council, principal traditional council, traditional council, Khoi-San council, traditional sub-council and traditional and Khoi-San leaders in respect of any functional area of such department: Provided that such a role may not include any decision-making power'.

Section 24 allows kingship, queenship or traditional councils to enter into partnerships and agreements with municipalities, government departments and any other persons or institutions. The original clause failed to include any direct requirement for community consultation. Due to pressure from civil society and rural communities, it was initially amended to require that any partnership or agreement entered into is subject to prior consultation with the relevant community *represented by such council* (clause 24(3)(c), emphasis added). This effectively retained extensive decision-making power for the councils, who act on behalf of the community.

Amendments subsequently required a partnership or agreement to also be subject to a decision in support taken by a majority of the community members present at a prior consultation. However, the partnership or agreement requires written confirmation of the council's support for it but does not include a requirement for similar community consent. The framing of this legislation suggests strong support by government for expanding the power of chiefs and traditional councils. The Traditional and Khoi-San Leadership Act was eventually passed by both Houses of Parliament during early 2019 and the president signed it into law in November 2019, despite demands having been made by civil society and rural community organisations that the Bill be scrapped (Mabasa 2019; Mokgoroane 2019).

It is clear from the cases cited in this chapter that some traditional leaders have tried to assume more far-reaching power over the people settled in their areas and are using old and new laws to validate that power – even if it violates rights protected in the Constitution, as affirmed in *Pilane* and other judgments. While some challenges have been successful, it is disconcerting that interdicts with broad terms are being granted to traditional leaders, despite there being dispute resolution mechanisms available through customary law that can be applied.

## CONCLUSION

This chapter has set out to illustrate how the Constitutional Court's groundbreaking judgment in *Pilane* cut across a tendency in lower courts to reinforce the authority of traditional leaders. It seemed to herald a new era for the interpretation of chiefly power in democratic South Africa. But in subsequent years there was growing evidence that it was being ignored or overlooked by traditional leaders and local courts. The Traditional and Khoi-San Leadership Act may reinforce disregard of the Constitutional Court decision.

Interdicts and other court orders continue to be sought and obtained by traditional leaders. In this regard, it is vital that the *Pilane* judgment be brought to the judiciary's attention to ensure the protection of constitutional and customary rights when those rights are threatened by traditional leaders. The courts can play a role in mediating conflicts between chiefs and community members where this is not possible in customary forums, and where appropriate. However, as long as the frontiers between customary law and formal legal rules and processes remain unsettled, and as long as there remains a disjuncture between the Constitutional Court jurisprudence and local political realities, enforcing the principles laid down in *Pilane* is likely to remain a challenge.

NOTES

1. Our thanks to Phiwe Ndinisa, who assisted with some of the original research.
2. Pilane and Another v Pilane and Another [2013] (4) BCLR 431 (CC) ('*Pilane* 2013').
3. Pilane and Another v Pheto and Others (582/2011) [2011] ZAWHC 63, 30 September 2011 ('*Pilane* 2011'), para 8.
4. S v Pilane and Another (CA 59/2009) [2010] ZANWHC 20 ('*Pilane* 2010'), paras 89–90.
5. Setlogelo v Setlogelo 1914 AD 221.
6. *Pilane*, 2011, para 55.
7. *Pilane*, 2013, para 10.
8. Pilane and Another v Pilane and Another (263/2010) [2011] ZANWHC 80, para 36.
9. *Pilane* 2013, para 16.
10. *Pilane* 2013, paras 24, 26.
11. *Pilane* 2013, para 44.
12. *Pilane* 2013, paras 56, 58.
13. *Pilane* 2013, paras 34, 70, 69.
14. *Pilane* 2013, paras 71, 72.
15. *Pilane* 2013, para 80.
16. *Pilane* 2013, paras 78–79, 103–105.
17. *Pilane* 2013, paras 14–119.
18. Bhe and Others v Magistrate Khayelitsha and Others [2005] (1) SA 580 (CC) ('*Bhe* 2005'), para 45.
19. V.C., J.P. and A.C. Interviewed by Joanna Pickering and Phiwe Ndinisa, Ga-Chokoe village, Mapela, Limpopo Province, 7 April 2017 (V.C., JP., AC interview).
20. Chokwe v Chokwe and Another Case No 710/2015, Magistrates' Court in the District Mogalakwena, held at Mahwelereng ('*Chokwe*, 2015'). Respondent's Heads of Arguments, 5 April 2016 and unreported judgment, 14 July 2016.
21. *Chokwe*, 2015, Respondent's Heads of Argument, paras 18, 21.
22. VC. JP., AC. interview.
23. *Chokwe*, 2015.
24. Mohlala v Mampuru (A141/2014) (GNP) ('*Mohlala*, 2014'), (unreported), includes Founding affidavit of Mampuru Billy Mampuru, 24 April 2013, case no. 116/13.
25. *Mohlala* 2014, Founding affidavit.

26 Moreipuso Traditional Council v Speaker Mahlake, Case number 648/16, Magistrate's Court for the District of Bushbuckridge.
27 *Pilane*, 2010.


REFERENCES

Bennet, Thomas. W. 2008. '"Official" vs "Living" Customary Law: Dilemmas of Description and Recognition'. In *Land, Power & Custom: Controversies Generated by South Africa's Communal Land Rights Act*, edited by Aninka Claassens and Ben Cousins, 138–153. Cape Town: UCT Press.
Bloom, Kevin and Sasha Wales-Smith. 2018. 'Stealing the Crust: How Bakgatla Ba Kgafela Were Robbed of Their Inheritance'. *Daily Maverick*, 1 February. https://www.dailymaverick.co.za/article/2018-02-01-stealing-the-crust-how-the-baktatla-ba-kgafela-were-robbed-of-their-inheritance/#gsc.tab=0
Claassens, Aninka. 2016. 'Hope for Battle-Weary Mining Community'. *Business Day*, 20 July. http://www.pressreader.com/south-africa/business-day/20160720/281792808376776)
Claassens, Aninka and Geoff Budlender. 2016. 'Transformative Constitutionalism and Customary Law'. *Constitutional Court Review* 6: 75–105.
Claassens, Aninka and Boitumelo Matlala. 2014. 'Platinum, Poverty and Princes in Post-Apartheid South Africa: New Laws, Old Repertoires'. In *New South African Review 4: A Fragile Democracy – Twenty Years On*, edited by Gilbert Khadiagala, Prishani Naidoo, Devan Pillay and Roger Southall, 113–135. Johannesburg: Wits University Press.
Jewett, Tamara. 2016. 'Mining, Land, and Community in Communal Areas III: Community Governance'. *Helen Suzman Foundation*. https://hsf.org.za/publications/hsf-briefs/mining-land-and-community-in-communal-areas-iii-community-governance.
LARC (Land and Accountability Research Centre). '2015. Submission on the Traditional and Khoi-San Leadership Bill of 2015'; submission on the Traditional Leadership and Governance Framework Amendment Bill, 2017. http://www.larc.uct.ac.za
Mabasa, Nkateko. 2019. 'People Take the Fight against Traditional Leaders to President Ramaphosa'. *Daily Maverick*, 5 June. www.dailymaverick.co.za/2019-06-05
Mnwana, Sonwabile. 2014. 'Chief's Justice?' *South African Crime Quarterly* 49: 21–29.
Mokgoroane, Letlhogonolo. 2019. 'The "Bantustan Bills" Remain Disastrously Flawed'. *Mail & Guardian*, 5 June. www.mg.co.za/article/2019-06-05
Public Protector of South Africa. 2017. 'Report on an Investigation into Alleged Improper Prejudice Suffered by Bapo Ba Mogale Community as a Result of Maladministration by the Former Bapo Ba Mogale Administration and the Department of Local Government and Traditional Affairs in the Management of the Bapo Ba Mogale D-account'. Report number 5 of 2017/2018. Pretoria: Office of the Public Protector.

CHAPTER

7

# Resisting the Imposition of *Ubukhosi*: Contested Authority-Making in the Former Ciskei

Thiyane Duda and Janine Ubink

South Africa forms the arena of a protracted '"fight for *ubukhosi*" – a struggle by chiefs for the recognition of the institution of chieftainship and of chiefly power' (Mager and Velelo 2018: 15). With the transition to democracy, as part of the political negotiations, *iinkosi* succeeded in ensuring that traditional leadership was recognised in the 1996 Constitution 'according to customary law' (Southall and Kropiwnicki 2003; Oomen 2005; Ntsebeza 2011).[1] Though constrained by the Constitution, their influence on the government has increased considerably, particularly through the vehicle of the Congress of Traditional Leaders of South Africa (CONTRALESA).

The fight for *ubukhosi* is pursued at both central and local levels. We have decided to use largely the isiXhosa terms because we wish to make the point that the English words, 'king', 'chief' and 'headman', do not adequately capture the descriptions of various levels of the traditional leadership hierarchy, *inkosana* (headman or headwoman), *inkosi* (senior traditional leader), *ikumkani* (king). We should recognise that these terms are changing, and this is the usage now promoted by the provincial government and the Department of Cooperative Governance and Traditional Affairs, but they are also found in many rural communities in the Eastern Cape and in this sense we are seeking to decolonise the language used to refer to the institution of traditional leadership. Regarding the central government, the legislative arena has been fundamental. Parliament has drafted a slew of proposals aiming to formalise and centralise the power of senior traditional leaders. The Traditional Leadership and Governance Framework Act of 2003 (TLGFA) recognised traditional leadership within apartheid-era boundaries, but simultaneously tried to make traditional authority somewhat more democratic by introducing the requirement that 40 per cent of the members of traditional councils should be elected and one-third women. Section 25(2a) of TLGFA mandated the establishment of a Commission on Traditional Leadership Disputes and Claims to investigate and resolve all traditional leadership disputes in the country, as well as traditional authority boundary disputes and the establishment, disestablishment, merging or division of 'tribes'.

The traditional council membership requirements have, however, been ignored in many provinces and the government has not taken action against defaulting councils. And the Commission on Traditional Leadership Disputes and Claims proved unequipped to deal with the high number of claims and unable to 'cleanse [traditional authority] of its apartheid accretions and deformities' (Peires 2014: 15; Buthelezi and Skosana 2018). Many of its decisions have been and currently are being challenged in court. Our case study of the amaHlathi community is a case in point. Laws and bills following the TLGFA, including the Communal Land Rights Act of 2004 (struck down by the Constitutional Court in 2010), the Traditional Courts Bill of 2017, and the Traditional and Khoi-San Leadership Act (Act 3 of 2019), were less concerned with transforming traditional leadership to fit into the new democratic dispensation, than to entrench a form of chieftainship carried over from apartheid (Delius 2019b). The legislation has been severely criticised: for bolstering the powers of traditional leaders while ignoring participatory features and multi-level decision-making; for compromising democracy and rural people's citizenship rights; and for contravening the 'fundamentally democratic conception of customary law' set out by the Constitutional Court, which holds that '[customary] law comes from practice and practice comes from the people' (Claassens and Budlender 2013: 80; Claassens 2011; Ntsebeza 2011; Mnisi Weeks 2012). They have led to a strong rural-based protest movement, the 'Stop the Bantustan Bills Campaign'.

Resisting the imposition of *ubukhosi* has been particularly focused in the former Bantustans (homelands), where *iinkosi* have continued to strive for reconstruction of their status and for expansion of their powers in and over local communities. Many people support traditional leadership. They see it as part of their cultural identity, as an answer to their need to belong, and to be different (Mager and Velelo 2018: 14). They may also see them as viable and accessible local agents in a context of ineffective elected local government institutions. These people are not challenging accountable traditional leadership, but resist the undue allocation to traditional leaders of broad powers that are customarily not theirs. There are, however, also areas where people regard traditional authority as an institution imposed on their communities against their wishes. The former Ciskei area of the Eastern Cape is an area where the extension of the role and powers of *iinkosi* was resisted in the apartheid era when Tribal Authorities were imposed. This period was characterised by many forced removals, land dispossessions and betterment schemes, which resulted in communities made up of people from diverse origins, without shared leadership structures. The imposition of *iinkosi* and *iinkosana* on these communities met with resistance over a long period (Westaway 1997; Manona 1997; Southall and Kropiwnicki 2003; Mager and Velelo 2018).

This chapter analyses two case studies in the former Ciskei with little history of traditional leadership institutions, where attempts by *iinkosi* and their followers to expand their influence and power over rural villages have been met with popular resistance. The first case study centres on the amaHlathi community where a protracted struggle has been fought regarding the legitimacy of the institution of senior traditional leadership. The other case study concerns Keiskammahoek South, which features a struggle over who has the power to appoint village heads – royal families or local communities – and whether village heads' accountability lies downward to the community or upward to *iinkosi*.

Both amaHlathi and Keiskammahoek were settled by a mixture of those identifying as amaMfengu and amaXhosa. This chapter investigates how communities, *iinkosi* and government officials represent the history of *ubukhosi* in the case study areas. How does the messy history of movement, settlement and (re-)making of communities and authority structures in the former Ciskei relate to the deployment of tradition for claim-making? As the history of these localities does not match the crude understanding that every community had a *inkosi* in the pre-colonial and colonial era, how do the new laws impact on these local claims? Anne Mager and Phiko Velelo (2018: 17) point to 'the challenge ... to try and make sense of the maladies of a complex and multi-layered past and the ways this past influences the present'. While they place this challenge on the desk of scholars, a similar conundrum faces courts, traditional leadership commissions and government officials. This chapter shows that chiefs and government officials display not so much an 'inability to accept the complexities of a layered past', but rather a deliberate obliviousness to those complexities in order to further the fight for *ubukhosi* with an invented past.

This chapter results from the involvement of one of the authors, Thiyane Duda, as a researcher in the Amahlathi case study area since 2015. He was brought into contact with the community by the Legal Resources Centre (LRC), to help with research and to assist in taking statements in the preparation for a court case. The LRC was operating as counsel for the AmaHlathi Crisis Committee (ACC) in a case against the senior traditional leader. In 2016, when his involvement as a researcher for the court case ended, the authors initiated a research project on the fight for *ubukhosi* and local resistance against it. They jointly conducted in-depth interviews between December 2016 and May 2017 with respondents from both case study areas as well as from other localities. Interviewees included senior traditional leaders, headmen, headwomen and their councillors, as well as villagers, members of the local crisis committees, South African National Civic Organisation (SANCO) leaders, non-governmental organisation (NGO) members, ward councillors and lawyers. While the authors thus entered the field through one of the two opposing sides contesting the leadership structure of amaHlathi, they have engaged with both sides, via interviews as well as court documents.

## *UBUKHOSI* IN THE CISKEI

Among the amaXhosa, positions of *ubukhosi* are deeply rooted. In pre-colonial times there were checks and balances on the authority of *iinkosi*: chiefs needed the support of the 'clan-section heads'; people could move away from *iinkosi* that were unpopular; and unpopular incumbents could be dismissed and replaced by a rival (Peires 1982). In the second and third decade of the nineteenth century, the great upheavals and population movements resulting from the *mfecane* changed these conditions. Population pressure increased, land became scarce and rivalry between *iinkosi* of the same polity was curtailed. This shifted the balance of power away from councillors and commoners towards *iinkosi* in the last decades of the pre-colonial period, although *iinkosi* among the amaXhosa still usually needed support from their councillors for important decisions (Peires 1982).

The area that became the Ciskei was formally annexed to the Cape Colony in 1847, but it took another 50 years to fully impose colonial rule. British colonial rule attempted to introduce some areas of private property and elected representatives for African people, with the aim of breaking the power of *iinkosi*. The Cape Colony ruled through headmen, generally selected by the men in the villages, subject to the magistrate's approval. The power of *iinkosi* was simultaneously curtailed, particularly their judicial responsibilities (Wotshela 1994; Mager 1999). Through the Glen Grey Act of 1894, the administration introduced councils (*iBunga*) whose members were elected by men with individual tenure to land (Mager 1999). However, policy changed as segregation became entrenched in the early decades of the twentieth century. In 1927 the Native Administration Act initiated the restoration of *ubukhosi* and the government of Africans through native law and custom. Despite this gradual retribalisation, the Native Affairs Department in the former Ciskei districts continued to work extensively with the elected headmen (Mager 1999: 105–107; Ntsebeza 2011: 78).

In 1951, however, the National Party government introduced the Bantu Authorities Act as the pillar of its apartheid system in the rural areas that were largely occupied by African people. This Act founded the Bantustan system meant to deflect demands for African enfranchisement and national citizenship (Southall and Kropiwnicki 2003: 54). It 'shifted the official administrative focus from headmen and provided for the establishment of so-called Tribal Authorities (TAs) which in many cases were associated with the chiefdoms which once existed in the former Ciskei' (Manona 1997: 49). D.M. Groenewald (1980: 88) points out that whereas in some places this Act legalised structures that were still in existence, in the Ciskei it 'amounted to a purposeful reconstruction of something which had to a large extent been destroyed.' It turned *iinkosi* into state functionaries with executive tasks, with headmen as their subordinates. Tribal Authority leaders were identified through genealogical research but in areas where highly diverse communities had settled, which did not have a common ethnically defined leader, the law provided for the creation of elected Community Authorities instead of Tribal Authorities. This was the case in several communities with a large number of people identifying as Mfengu such as in Tsitsikama (Deliwe 1997) and Keiskammahoek (Manona 1997).

The executive tasks of *iinkosi* in the Bantustans, their increased powers of arrest, search and seizure, and their augmented scope for misappropriation all eroded legitimacy of these positions in the eyes of their people. This, plus their payment by the government, made *iinkosi* more dependent on the South African state and Bantustan ruling parties for their authority as well as for their material well-being (Southall and Kropiwnicki 2003: 55–56; Charton 1980: 179). Clan-section heads lost much of their leverage over *iinkosi*. *Iinkosi* councils were increasingly made up of their dependents, offering fewer checks and balances for the interests of commoners (Manona 1997: 58).

The Ciskei was granted internal self-government in 1972 (Charton and Renton kaTywakadi 1980: 123), with a legislature consisting of elected members as well as *iinkosi*. To the extent that people identified with pre-colonial categories these were largely Rharhabe amaXhosa and amaMfengu. The ancestors of the latter largely originated in areas taken over by the Zulu kingdom during the *mfecane*, and fled to Xhosa country around 1818 to 1828. The name amaMfengu derives from the verb *ukumfenguza*, which means 'to wander about seeking service' (Peires 1982: 88). It was later corrupted into 'Fingo' by Europeans. Some became fully absorbed in southern Nguni communities, others lived semi-autonomously in a client-patron relationship with *iinkosi*. The colonial government played on the grievances of amaMfengu over the servitude and exactions demanded of them by the amaXhosa to draw them into an anti-Xhosa alliance. Some amaMfengu groups collaborated with the colonial government in frontier wars, for which they were rewarded with large portions of amaXhosa land (Peires 1989).

Ethnic tensions persisted in the twentieth century not only because of this nineteenth-century legacy but also because some amaMfengu were absorbed into missions, acquired better education and held the majority of professional salaried positions and headmanships (Jackson 1975: 30; Peires 1989: 398). In 1973, in the first election for the government of the Ciskei there was strong rivalry between the mainly amaMfengu supporters of Justice Mabandla (later Ciskei National Party (CNP)) and the mainly amaXhosa supporters of Lennox Sebe (later Ciskei National Independence Party (CNIP)). After the latter group won with a small margin – probably due to governmental interference in the elections (Peires 1989: 399; Charton and Renton kaTywakadi 1980: 130) – the new government led by Chief Minister Sebe set about reducing the power of amaMfengu.

As at that time a disproportionate number of recognised chiefs were amaMfengu, and as *iinkosi* outnumbered elected members in the 1973 Ciskei legislature (Southall and Kropiwnicki 2003: 55), getting control of *ubukhosi* was an important strategy of the new Ciskei government. The South African government's consolidation of the Ciskei, undertaken to create geo-political unity, led to the addition of white-owned farmlands and an influx of persons displaced from areas that were newly designated as white. These changes allowed for the creation of new positions of *ubukhosi* each with a territory and a following. In addition, the Ciskei government converted all Community Authorities into TAs, which similarly allowed for the creation of positions of *ubukhosi*. After the 1973 elections, eight new Rharhabe and one position of *ubukhosi* were created, all of which went to Sebe supporters (Peires 1989: 400). This turned Sebe's narrow majority into a comfortable margin and put the CNP out of reach of power, which caused the swift defection of a number of its members to the CNIP. After the elections of 1978, the Ciskei became a de facto one-party state (Manona 1985: 72, 80; Peires 1989: 401–402).

The TAs in this period of Ciskei self-government (1968–1994) were 'largely reduced to vehicles for [ruling party] C.N.I.P. programmes, fund-raising ventures, and directives' (Manona 1985: 83). While employed with a wide range of duties for the Ciskei government, they were given hardly any guidance from the government on how to go about their tasks, nor were they given the independence or financial means to respond to concerns and needs of their communities. They became largely identified with the interest of the Ciskei state, and due to their limited local legitimacy had to rely heavily on penalties and coercive measures.

As *iinkosi* increasingly operated as state functionaries, resistance against apartheid included frequent and violent rebellion against TAs, *iinkosi* and *iinkosana* (Southall and Kropiwnicki 2003: 56–57; Ntsebeza 2011: 79). While in some areas of the Eastern Cape these actions may mainly have signalled an opposition against the Bantustan version of *ubukhosi* or specific *iinkosi* (Mager and Velelo 2018: 164–165), in several areas of the Ciskei, residents' associations were specifically set up 'to combat Sebe's attempts to impose tribal authorities upon areas where they had not existed previously' (Southall and Kropiwnicki 2003: 56). In March 1990, following the military coup in neighbouring Transkei, the Ciskei Defence Force, led by Brigadier Gqozo, toppled Ciskei's Chief Minister Sebe. Gqozo became the new head of state and identified with the African National Congress (ANC) at that time. He emphasised that the people were to determine their own faith in democratic political structures, and promised the dismantling of the unpopular TA system. Shortly thereafter, he announced that all headmen had to resign.

While Gqozo retained *iinkosi*, he also encouraged the formation of residents' associations made up of elected representatives. This was taken up so eagerly by the population that soon the whole system of *ubukhosi* was on the brink of collapse, and Gqozo started to fear the associations' popularity and their support from militant youth. In a swift reversal, the administration abolished residents' associations and tried to re-introduce headmen. Many communities refused to elect new headmen or violently attacked them and their followers. Gqozo's regime collapsed in 1993 and was replaced by a caretaker administration until the democratic elections of April 1994 (Mager and Velelo 2018: 165; Manona 1997: 61–65; Southall and Kropiwnicki 2003: 57–58).

After the first provincial and local elections in 1994 and 1995, the ANC tried to centralise power and impose its authority and, as a corollary, to contain the powers and aspirations of *iinkosi*. Lungisile Ntsebeza (2011: 84–85) writes: 'In those early days of democracy, the provincial government of the EC was arguably the most radical on the issue of the chiefs. It was in the EC, especially in the Ciskei, that tribal authorities were wiped out and replaced by residents' associations.' The new Constitution, however, provided for provincial houses of traditional leaders and conflicts arose around the composition, functions and finances of this body in the Eastern Cape. *Iinkosi* also tried to retain a role in rural governance, development projects and service provisioning.

After a first few radical years, the Eastern Cape ANC political leadership started to realise that their antagonising of *iinkosi* was strengthening the United Democratic Movement (UDM) (Ntsebeza 2011: 85). This opposition party, founded in 1997, was led by Bantu Holomisa, last leader of the Transkei, who had initially joined the ANC. He had substantial backing, particularly in the former Transkei, and actively courted traditional leaders. The presumption that *iinkosi* were rural 'vote-brokers' led to ANC delegates visiting important and strategic traditional leaders during which 'it is probable that concerns were addressed, and promises were made' (Southall and Kropiwnicki 2003: 66–67; Peires 2000: 111). Salaries of *iinkosi* and headmen were raised and some *iinkosi* were awarded a place on the ANC list for the provincial legislature.

Roger Southall and Zosa De Sas Kropiwnicki (2003: 67–77) concluded that *iinkosi* of the Eastern Cape had been largely contained by the ANC, with the authority of *iinkosi* mainly depending on the state, just as during apartheid. The rebellious behaviour of *iinkosi*, aligning themselves with opposition party UDM, triggered the ANC into some pragmatic concessions, increasing salaries and confirming the local status of *iinkosi*. They argued that the ANC did not devolve significant powers to them. However, Jeff Peires (2000: 113) concluded around the same time that 'the long-term prospects for the traditional leaders in the Eastern Cape remain very good. They have maintained their traditional legitimacy, as well as their incontrovertible physical presence in each and every administrative area.' In hindsight, the pragmatic concessions could be seen as the start of a rapprochement between ANC government and *iinkosi*, at the national as well as provincial level.

## THE BATTLE OVER CHIEFTAINCY IN AMAHLATHI COMMUNITY

AmaHlathi traditional community, located about 15 km north of King William's Town is the scene of a protracted dispute over senior traditional leadership. The settlement of amaHlathi was probably established in 1853 and consisted of a mixed population of amaMfengu (Jackson 1975: 30; Wilson et al. 1952: 1). According to William Hammond-Tooke (1958: 125–128), after the promulgation of the 1951 Bantu Authorities Act, there were attempts to establish a TA over the amaHlathi, composed of the locations Donnington, Tyusha, Ezeleni, Upper Ezeleni and Kwelerana, which would bear the title '*Igunya laphantsi kwaMahlathi*' (the Authority below the forests). This suggests the origins of the name amaHlathi, which community members now use interchangeably with the name Ezeleni (after a local church). At that time, there had been no central *ubukhosi* of the area, only headmen whose position was unrelated to any royal descent. The community proved unable to agree on a *inkosi* chief and Melville Myoli was elected as chief headman instead (Hammond-Tooke 1958: 125–128). Interviews in amaHlathi community in 2016–17 suggest that agreeing on one *inkosi* to represent the community was still difficult.

While historical documents make clear that amaHlathi registered as a Community Authority instead of a Tribal Authority in 1957, both Hammond-Tooke (1958) and local community members (in interviews) ignore this distinction and speak of Tribal Authority instead. A.O. Jackson (1975: 31) is altogether unable to make the distinction as he classifies 'Amahlathi-Fingo' as a 'Tribal or Community Authority' without *inkosi*. In interviews community members also described a history of headmen without *ubukhosi*, such as in Nkangeni: 'Before the imposition of the chief the villages had headmen. A *sibondana* also known as a *ibhodi* (petty-headman) governed at the sub-village level, while a *sibonda* (headman) governed at village level. Above the village level there was a Tribal Authority, which was governed by the chief headman as there was no chief … The Chief Headman was elected in a general meeting by the community.'[2]

AmaHlathi Community Authority was disestablished and amaHlathi TA established in 1982 when Sebe appointed Nontsapha Maqoma (Nonesi) as *inkosi*. According to community members, this was not her real name. They claimed that Sebe found her in Mdantsane in East London and gave her the name Nonesi and the surname Maqoma with the intention of passing her off as of royal descent. Nonesi was the name of a princess of amaTshawe, a royal clan of amaXhosa to which the woman was only related by marriage.[3] With the imposition of Nonesi the Sebe regime also replaced amaMfengu headmen with amaTshawe headmen.[4] Nonesi had an intermittent reign over amaHlathi until her death in 2000.[5] After the fall of Sebe and Gqozo in the early 1990s, Nonesi had no effective presence in the amaHlathi community, and under the influence of SANCO the community changed its headmen system of governance to chairpersons elected in each village and sub-village for five-year terms.[6] This ran parallel to the elected local government system.

In 2006, Nonesi's son, Luvuyo Maqoma was officially recognised by the government as the senior traditional leader of amaHlathi traditional community, something most villagers only started noticing when he began allocating land and tried to convince chairpersons to become his *iinkosana* (headmen) – arguing that they would receive a salary as *iinkosana* that they were not receiving as chairpersons. When villages refused to select an *iinkosana*, Luvuyo started to appoint them himself, from among the amaTshawe clan.[7]

Luvuyo Maqoma was mainly supported by newcomers, labour tenants, by some identifying as amaXhosa and young people who see his leadership as an opportunity for economic gain. His claim to the senior traditional leadership of amaHlathi divided the community between the people supporting the elected chairpersons and those supporting the new *iinkosana*. People no longer attended each other's funerals and ceremonies. Both sides attempted to block the other's access to government services and development projects. Ward councillors found it challenging to work in such a divided community. It was reported that Maqoma tried to prevent the award of a land restitution claim by one of the villages unless he was involved. The anti-Maqoma group feared he would get power over their land, and that he was diverting development funds to himself and a few followers.[8]

In 2010 they made representations to *Kumkani* (King) Sandile of the amaRharhabe branch of amaXhosa, the provincial legislature and the provincial House of Traditional Leaders. Eventually they were referred to the Eastern Cape Provincial Committee of the Commission on Traditional Leadership Disputes and Claims, where the group lodged a claim as the ACC for the disestablishment of the senior traditional leadership of amaHlathi traditional community.

At a hearing convened by the Commission in March 2013 the ACC argued that the amaHlathi villages had never had *ubukhosi* and that it was contrary to their custom for one to be imposed on them. Maqoma and his supporters countered the claim with three arguments. First, that the amaHlathi land belonged to *Kumkani* Ngqika of amaRharhabe and was occupied by the amaXhosa groups amaNdlambe and amaNtinde. Second, that Luvuyo Maqoma is a descendant of *Kumkani* Ngqika and that his traditional leadership was confirmed by the Rharhabe house. Third, that the amaHlathi community had accepted both Nonesi (the regent mother) and her son, as they had purchased Nonesi an *umnweba* (a traditional leadership robe) and organised Luvuyo's initiation into manhood. The ACC had a very different view of things. In their opinion, the amaHlathi had settled on unoccupied land awarded to them by the British for fighting on their side during some of the frontier wars; the amaHlathi community never had an *inkosi*; Luvuyo Maqoma did not hail from a royal family, nor was he recognised by *ubukumnkani* (kingship) of amaRharabe; and neither he or his mother were ever recognised by the community – under Sebe's volatile and repressive rule, the community had no choice but to pay for Nonesi's robe and Luvuyo's initiation.[9]

The Commission conducted field research on the matter and concluded in its 2012 report that 'all available sources on the area trace chieftainship only as far back as 1982 during the period of Sebe'.[10] It also noted that Luvuyo's father and grandfather were never *iinkosi*. While the field report backed up the ACC's claim, the Commission's final report recommended *against* the disestablishment of the senior traditional leadership arguing that 'AmaHlathi is an integral part of the land of Ngqika from whom [Luvuyo] Maqoma descends'.[11] The Commission provided no historical evidence for this claim. Its decision contradicted not only its own field research, but also the finding of the Commission on Restitution of Land Rights, finalised only one year earlier, that overwhelming historical, oral and archival evidence made it clear that Luvuyo Maqoma is not *inkosi* of amaHlathi.¹² Interviews furthermore demonstrated that Maqoma's own recounting of the history had several conflicting elements and diverged substantially from the history enunciated by the elder he himself had referred us to, in order to confirm his version and prove his *ubukhosi*.¹³ In a conversation with a community member, two members of the Commission later admitted that the amaHlathi recommendation was changed by the premier of the eastern Cape.¹⁴ The commissioners relayed that the premier had followed the Commission's recommendation in only one of ten recent cases, and advised the ACC to appeal. But in October 2013, citing the Commission's recommendation, Premier Kiviet dismissed the ACC's claim and confirmed Luvuyo Maqoma as the senior traditional leader of amaHlathi traditional community.¹⁵

In 2016, the ACC applied to the High Court for review of the decision. In the case, the ACC argued the Commission had erred in the application of its mandate, which was simply to consider and apply customary law and the customs of the relevant traditional community when considering a dispute or claim, as set out in section 25(3) of the TLGFA. They reasoned that the imposition of a senior traditional leader on them – one that was intermittent, ineffective and not recognised as legitimate by the community – did not extinguish or alter their customary law. They furthermore argued that 'how we came to be on the land is not an issue before the commission and is irrelevant to the issue in dispute'.¹⁶ To be on the safe side they did, however, bring in an expert witness, Professor Jeff Peires, who stated that while the land in question was originally occupied by amaXhosa, it was never ruled by the Ngqika house of amaRharhabe from whom Luvuyo claims descent.

In her March 2017 affidavit explaining the grounds for her decision, former Premier Kiviet again focused on landownership as the source of traditional authority. She stated that the community of amaHlathi never abolished the senior traditional leadership that reigned on the land prior to the amaHlathi settling on it, as they never defeated the previous occupants of the land. Instead, by settling on the land, the people of amaHlathi 'subjected themselves to the reign of those customary leadership structures that predated their settlement'.¹⁷ But a new premier, Phumulo Masualle, was elected at that moment and distanced himself from the decision. He stated that he would not oppose the relief sought by the applicants and in May 2017, all state respondents bar Maqoma withdrew from the case, leaving him as the only respondent. In June 2017, the Bhisho High Court heard the review application unopposed, set aside the former premier's decision and granted a court order for the disestablishment of the senior traditional leadership over the residents of amaHlathi.

This decision notwithstanding, in March 2018, residents of amaHlathi who were present at a public hearing at the *komkhulu* (great place) of amaRharhabe on the

Traditional Leadership and Governance Framework Amendment Bill, found those associated with the *komkhulu* of amaRharhabe still referring to Maqoma as the senior traditional leader of amaHlathi. Questioned by the residents, the spokesperson of the *ikomkhulu* of amaRharhabe said the Eastern Cape Department of Local Government and Traditional Affairs had not informed them that the senior traditional leadership of amaHlathi has been disestablished. AmaHlathi residents later learned that the department had defied the court order and reinstated Luvuyo as the senior traditional leader of amaHlathi on the basis of a court application made by Maqoma for the rescission of the court order. In April 2018, the ACC's attorney wrote to the Member of Executive Council (MEC) of Local Government and Traditional Affairs, demanding the implementation of the court order and pointing out that the application for rescission does not suspend the court order. While the rescission application is still pending in court, Maqoma and his *iinkosana* have formally been removed from the office by the government of the Eastern Cape (see Pickering and Motala, and Chaskalson in this volume for the difficulty of enforcing court decisions).[18]

Evidence presented during the different stages of the dispute displays that amaHlathi does not have a history of senior traditional leadership. The oral record and historical evidence show that attempts to create a hereditary *ubukhosi* of amaMfengu over amaHlathi in the 1950s failed as the community could not agree on *inkosi*. The evidence that there was no *bukhosi* over amaHlathi until 1982 is consistent. *Ubukhosi* of amaXhosa was created and imposed on amaHlathi by President Sebe for his own political reasons.

Despite this evidence, the Eastern Cape government focused only on how the amaHlathi acquired the land. Reminiscent of Sebe's actions, contemporary Eastern Cape government officials and traditional leaders are holding on to, and thereby rekindling, the historical rivalry between amaMfengu and amaXhosa, which was not evident in the community. Premier Kiviet rested her decision largely on this division and the historical fact that amaMfengu people fought on the side of the British. She accepted the tenuous, constructed connection linking Luvuyo Maqoma to *iinkosi* of the early nineteenth century, and his son Maqoma, whom she supposed had authority over this land before it was settled by amaHlathi ancestors.

Premier Kiviet's decision was rooted in a conception of traditional authority invented by the apartheid state, which linked traditional authority to bounded pieces of land. This ignores the historical evidence that 'space and place are dynamic and, like social relations, are constantly contested and restlessly remade' (Mager 1999: 6). Mager describes the Ciskei as a shifting political construction in which powerful players, including colonial agents, were able to impose 'space-specific meanings'. Such processes of remapping and reconfiguring space occurred as much before as after conquest, and certainly during the *mfecane*.

This framing of traditional leadership derived from land rather than people, and from claims over land that attempted to overturn nearly two hundred years of amaHlathi settlement. This approach differs from customary ideas that traditional leaders get their legitimacy from the people, as captured in the isiXhosa idiom '*inkosi yinkosi ngabantu*' (*inkosi* is *inkosi* through the people), which is also found in many other southern African languages. The community's articulation of its leadership structure reflects this conception of custom, as it insists on determining its own leadership structure, in line with its history and contemporary practice. This is also in line with the Constitutional Court's conception of customary law, as articulated in its jurisprudence, that custom flows from practice and practice flows from the people (see Budlender and Fay in this volume).

Luvuyo Maqoma claimed senior traditional leadership in 2004 after the TLGFA was enacted. Clearly the new law and increasing ANC support for traditional leadership provided some of the impetus. Premier Kiviet's power to determine chieftaincy disputes stemmed from another legal change. The 2010 amendment of the TLGFA transferred final decisions of disputes from a commission consisting of experts on customary law and traditional leadership to the premiers. This amendment opened traditional leadership disputes to political interference and recreated the top-down colonial model where decisions about *ubukhosi* were imposed by the government. The courts currently seem to be the only arena where communities may get a fair decision. For communities, however, accessing courts requires substantial community organisation as well as assistance from legal aid centres. And even when communities win in court, this case shows they do not necessarily have the support of the state.

## THE TLGFA AND THE BATTLE OVER HEADMEN IN KEISKAMMAHOEK SOUTH

Like many areas of South Africa, Keiskammahoek has a history of changing occupation. In the eighteenth century, the Khoekhoe pastoralists who inhabited the area were ousted by amaXhosa who expanded from their territory east of the Great Kei River. By 1853, after their defeat in the War of Mlanjeni, many amaXhosa were expelled by British colonial forces and the area was added to the Cape Colony as a Royal Reserve. The colonial government allowed groups of amaMfengu to settle on the conquered lands – as well as a small number of Europeans – to create a buffer 'in order to separate the colonists from the warlike Xhosa' (Mills and Wilson 1952: 3). The government recognised village headmen, who were chosen by the people but had to be approved by the colonial state. In 1952, the *Keiskammahoek Rural Survey* published the results of several years of multidisciplinary research in the area of Keiskammahoek plus 15 villages (locations), each led by a headman. While people from other groups had moved into the area, the amaMfengu still formed about three quarters of the population of the district (Wilson et al. 1952: 1).

Government involvement in headmen elections increased in the 1950s and 1960s as officials wanted to ensure the installation of headmen who supported betterment (Westaway 1997: 20–25). Betterment programmes brought in increasing numbers of people who were not amaMfengu, particularly amaXhosa (Manona 1980). In the villages with communal land tenure, headmen's control over land 'gave them some of the attributes of chiefs' (Wilson et al. 1952: 27) and the office was mainly seen as hereditary, although any heir needed to be confirmed by the villagers and formally appointed by the Native Commissioner. In villages with freehold and quitrent title, headmen were much less powerful as they could not allocate fields, and the hereditary element was much less stressed in the selection of new headmen. People referred to their headmen as *inkosi* (chiefs), but addressed them as *isibonda* (headmen) or by their clan name (Wilson et al. 1952: 22–38). Chris de Wet (1997: 13) says that 'although the Mfengu settlers had brought their values and customs with them... the villages had never been traditional settlements'. The area of Keiskammahoek did not possess leadership structures above the village level.

For Keiskammahoek South, the location of our case study, the apartheid government created a Community Authority in 1966, recognising that a Tribal Authority could not be established in these circumstances (Manona 1997: 53). As noted, the Sebe government had a strong incentive to create new positions of *ubukhosi* and as a result, in 1979 he introduced a *inkosi* in the area to act as the head of the Ngqika (Keiskammahoek South) Tribal Authority, including seven villages, with its Great House in the village of Burnshill. According to Ashley Westaway (1997: 16) the TA structures in Keiskammahoek had very little bearing on daily life in the locations. Cecil Manona (1997: 54), however, says that the Ngqika TA influenced the selection of headmen, although the magistrate retained a final say. The people also lost their influence on the nomination of TA councillors, and participation of villagers in local administration declined heavily. This disjuncture between leaders and villagers, combined with the TA's limited financial resources, its dependence on the central government, and the perception of widespread corruption of the TA, severely damaged the trust of people in the *inkosi* and their headmen. In Keiskammahoek South, opposition to Ciskei rule was strong in the 1980s and included resistance against the imposition of unpopular headmen (Manona 1997: 57–61). When Brigadier Gqozo, having abolished headmen, reintroduced them in 1991, those in Keiskammahoek met with serious resistance, including the burning down of the house of the Burnshill headman. According to Manona (1997: 64–65), a residents' association was formed and the TA was by then virtually non-existent.

In the early twenty-first century struggles re-emerged over the right of communities to elect or select their own village heads. These are generally traced back to the introduction of the TLGFA and the Eastern Cape Traditional Leadership and Governance Act (2005), which were followed by ANC statements that *iinkosana* could be brought back. *Iinkosi* and traditional councils argued that these laws gave them the power to select headmen in villages that used to select their own headmen or that have, since the early 1990s, had a different system of elected village leadership in the form of civics. These new headmen, they furthermore claim, should hail from *ebukhosini* (the royal family). They ignore sections 11 and 18 of the Eastern Cape Traditional Leadership and Governance Act, which says that the identification of headmen should be done 'with due regard to applicable customary law' and that the person selected needs to 'qualif[y] in terms of customary law'. In the words of a local activist: 'Traditional leaders use law, but they only refer to those parts of the Framework Act that empower them. They say nothing about accountability or the power of the community.'[19]

The royalisation argument is facilitated by the use of the term '*inkosana*' in the Eastern Cape Governance Act to refer to headmen. This term means son of an *inkosi* in isiXhosa, and traditional councils argue that it stipulates that headmen positions have to be filled with members from *ebukhosini*. Legally there is no basis for such argument, as the Governance Act defines *inkosana* as 'a headman or headwoman of a traditional community as defined in section 1 of the Framework Act', and the Framework Act defines headmanship as 'the position held by a headman or headwoman'. Nevertheless, the use in the provincial Act of this term seems to imply a hereditary position. A local activist states: '*Inkosana*, that is a strange construction. Do you realize what the implications are? It is a false construction. *Inkosana* means prince, male child of a chief. With this term they change headmen into princes. Through a linguistic construction.'[20]

Similar struggles over 'the royalisation of village leadership' are occurring in other areas of the Eastern Cape (Ncapayi 2015; Ncapayi and Ntsebeza 2015; Wicomb 2015). One widely reported dispute concerns Cala Reserve, situated in the former Transkei district of Xhalanga. This resembles the conflict in Keiskammahoek, in the sense that it is an area with high numbers of amaMfengu settlers with a long history of selecting their own village leaders. This case has been elaborately documented by Fani Ncapayi (2017). To summarise his work, in Cala Reserve, anticipating the upcoming retirement of headman Fani, the community selected the retiring headman's right-hand man, Gideon Sitwayi, as his successor. The KwaGcina Traditional Council (KTC) refused to accept Sitwayi, and selected a new headman, a taxi owner who had mostly been based in Cape Town, and who claimed to hail from the local family of *ubukhosi*. When the community questioned the right of the KTC to make this choice, the KTC argued that the election of headmen by communities 'has stopped since the new law [the Governance Act], which instructs that the royal family elects the headman' (Ncapayi 2017: 6). They said that the community could only object to their choice if there was evidence that the nominee was a criminal or a rapist. Nkosi Gecelo added: 'Whether you like it or not, it is the royal family that decides on the headman'.[21]

The Cala Reserve Planning Committee contacted the Eastern Cape Department of Local Government and Traditional Affairs and the premier of the province. When that proved fruitless, the dispute was taken first to the Magistrate's Court and on appeal to the High Court in Bhisho. At the latter court, they argued that the *ubukhosi* did not consider the customary law of the area in replacing the headman, according to section 18 of the Eastern Cape Governance Act. The expert witness, Lungisile Ntsebeza, stated that for more than a hundred years until the present, communities in Xhalanga district, including Cala Reserve, have elected their own headmen. Appellants – which besides *inkosi* and the KTC also include the Eastern Cape premier and the MEC for Local Government and Traditional Affairs – argued that the *ubukhosi* did take into account existing customary practice in identifying the new headman as he is a member of the royal family. They thus equated the customary law regarding selection of headmen with following the lines of genealogical *ubukhosi*. Lawyers appearing for the provincial authorities furthermore argued that the laws did not require the popular views of the community to be taken into account, nor envisage community consultation.

The judge concluded that 'the practice of electing headmen in the Xhalanga district is part of the customary law of the Xhalanga community'.[22] He furthermore pointed to the fact that both the Framework Act and the Eastern Cape Governance Act (section 3, 2) state that the institution of traditional leadership must be transformed 'so that democratic governance and the values of an open and democratic society may be promoted'. The court's interpretation of section 18 followed this requirement but the judgment did not resolve this dispute. In 2013 two elections for the position were held with different candidates elected. The headman elected in the process run by *inkosi*, Yelelo, was recognised by the state under former Premier Kievit, but community members planned to go to court again.

As in the case of Cala Reserve, Keiskammahoek South does not have a history of *ubukhosi*. Although the TA appointed by Sebe did survive the transition to democracy, it meant very little for most people in the area and had limited practical impact on their lives. They governed their villages through elected village heads and civics. Respondents report that they were not consulted about the TLGFA and that many people did not want to be a traditional community with a traditional council. Although the Act allows communities to choose, they were not given the opportunity to say they did not want to be a traditional community. Many villages boycotted the elections for (the 40 per cent elected) traditional councillors, which led to extremely low voter turnout – estimated at two per cent by one interviewee, with even less in neighbouring Rabula.[23]

The issue with the Eastern Cape Governance Act is thus not only who gets to select a village head and from which family, but also the subordination of village heads to *iinkosi*, and the increasing authority of *iinkosi* over village affairs. A community leader explained: 'The *inkosana* works according to the law and custom of the royal family, but we want someone that would listen to the people. If that person does not listen to the people, then they should be removed.' A second added: 'If the position of *inkosana* is for a life time, that would be dangerous ... We also don't want someone who will say the chiefs own all the land.'[24] The local struggle to maintain their elected village heads is thus also in opposition to the introduction of upwardly accountable instead of downwardly accountable leaders and to the expansion of the authority of *ubukhosi* in their villages.

The attempts at royalisation of village leadership demonstrates the impetus of the fight for *ubukhosi* by *iinkosi*. They invoke legislation to alter custom and increase their power over rural people. Policies and actions – as well as inaction – of the Eastern Cape administration strengthen and support political strategies of *iinkosi*. This impacts on the character of traditional communities and leads to the centralisation of local power in the hands of senior traditional leaders. In this, both *iinkosi* and government ride roughshod over the 'complexities of the layered past' (Mager and Velelo 2018: 12) of the people of Keiskammahoek South. They propagate a simplistic vision of rural life in the former Bantustans, in which every rural community is regarded as a traditional community, where a senior traditional leader calls the shots. For Keiskammahoek South this means reverting to a history that never was.

With the exception of the decade after Sebe imposed the Nqgika Tribal Authority in 1979, the villagers in Keiskammahoek South have selected their own village leaders since their arrival in the 1850s. *Iinkosi* and the government choose to equate customary law with whatever the *ubukhosi* (royal house). This ignores questions regarding the legitimacy of that particular *ubukhosi*, the extent of popular support for a specific *inkosi*, and any moves towards greater democratic rights that the people of these communities have made since the demise of apartheid. This is not confined to the Eastern Cape, as is clear from Peter Delius (2019b) who laments the comprehensive failure to incorporate the need to secure and sustain popular support for *iinkosi* – according to him a vital aspect of pre-colonial *ubukhosi* – into post-colonial reform of the institution.

## CONCLUSION: LAWS, HISTORIES AND TRADITIONAL AUTHORITY

Post-1994 laws entrench a form of traditional leadership that was fixed in the apartheid era where authority flows from above and from control over specific areas rather than followers. A process is in train that strongly centralises the power of senior traditional leaders while disregarding lower levels of decision-making and popular participation and support.

These laws continue to link traditional leadership to the boundaries of apartheid's Tribal Authorities. The amaHlathi case shows, however, that when these boundaries do not align with powerful *iinkosi*, the provincial government and *iinkosi* redirect the debate to the question of which groups were the original rulers before colonial conquest. They leapfrog colonialism and apartheid and revert to an argument about occupation patterns just before conquest. This freezes traditional authority as it is imagined nearly two centuries ago. Yet the period before conquest was one where space and place were heavily contested; configurations of power and authority were constantly in flux (Delius 2019b; Mager 1999).

The history of amaMfengu communities complicates and disrupts the grand historical narrative of land dispossession, in which colonialism and apartheid entailed the dispossession of land from the indigenous populations by the invading colonisers. In our two case studies, we illustrate a concerted effort by traditional authorities and the provincial government to assert the power and authority of amaXhosa traditional leaders in areas where amaXhosa groupings were conquered and displaced by colonial power in the mid-nineteenth century. In these cases, however, people identifying as amaMfengu occupied the land. Their settlements often became mixed, including those identifying with various amaXhosa groups. Current attempts at establishing Xhosa authority and control over land have emphasised largely dormant historical tensions between amaMfengu and amaXhosa over amaMfengu people siding with the British during the frontier wars.

Delius (2019b) sees such claims to indigeneity as a wider process in South Africa. Local power holders attempt to erase and rewrite colonial and apartheid-era history, with a disregard for the descendants of people who have lived in these areas since then. Both *iinkosi* and the government claim that their assertions are in line with tradition, but the settlement of the former Ciskei was messy and layered; *ubukhosi* was fragmented and largely dormant until Sebe imposed amaXhosa as *iinkosi* under the apartheid TA system. These cases thus challenge the notion of amaXhosa overlordship. They rather display highly contested leadership positions from the period of the Bantustans when traditional authority became increasingly uncoupled from popular support.

Both case studies draw attention to the Eastern Cape government's support for a model of traditional authority that empowers senior traditional leaders and *ubukhosi*, even in contexts where local communities strongly contest this model, arguing that it contravenes their custom as well as their democratic rights. By imposing a one-size-fits-all model of traditional leadership, where every traditional community must have a senior traditional leader and those leaders possess the power to designate village heads without participation of the community, *iinkosi* and the Eastern Cape government propagate a narrowly delineated notion of traditional leadership. The original Bantu Authorities Act allowed for a diversity of models – Tribal or Community Authorities – as well as for locally elected leadership at village level. The Eastern Cape government, especially under Premier Kiviet (2009–2014) seemed to habitually side with senior traditional leadership, paying no attention to accountability of or checks and balances on *iinkosi*, nor to the democratic rights of the constituents. Premier Phumulo Masualle (2014–2019) distanced himself from some decisions of his predecessor. It remains to be seen what approach the new administration, in office since May 2019, will take.

In the Cala Reserve Case, the court concluded that a system that granted rural people fewer democratic rights in respect of the identification and appointment of headmen than under homeland rule contravened both the Framework Act and the Eastern Cape Governance Act in the stipulation that traditional leadership needs to be brought in accordance with the dictates of democracy, but the provincial government proceded to act in ways that disregarded that ruling. Whereas the Framework Act gives communities the right to self-identify as traditional communities or not, in practice this option is ignored. With its support for headmen selected by the *ubukhosi*, the government is furthermore replacing leaders with downwards accountability for ones who are only accountable upwards. This is particularly relevant as in this area local government is reported in interviews as weak and ineffective.

New laws are an important tool in this struggle. They 'effectively "retribalise" the countryside and minimise rural democracy',[25] and perpetuate the disjuncture between the regulation of South Africa's former Bantustans and the rest of the country. The strong alliance between provincial government and traditional leaders means that communities usually approach officials to no avail, even when they are well organised with evidence that supports their claims. Courts may offer better opportunities, but require community organisation and legal assistance against this alliance of *iinkosi* and government.

The two case-studies discussed in this chapter do not stand alone. The now-deceased amaXhosa king, Mpendulo Zwelonke Sigcawu, attempted to impose Xhosa senior traditional leaders over various Eastern Cape amaMfengu traditional communities, who have a long history of living under their own authority structures, with the aim of gaining control over their land (Ngcukana 2017). Speaking of South Africa as a whole, Delius (2019a: 8–9) sees 'growing ethnic mobilization and conflict at local levels with long submerged identities being resuscitated by individuals and groups in pursuit of office' and emphasises how such processes 'have also contributed to a growing emphasis on and debate about which groups are "indigenous" and/or were the original rulers'. Imposing *iinkosi* against popular wishes and strengthening their control over (sub-)village communities are deeply political moves. This chapter shows how *iinkosi* and government officials freely interpret history and tradition to further the fight for *ubukhosi*.

NOTES

1 We use the terms *inkosi or iinkosi* to refer to a traditional leader or traditional leaders. We also do not use 'the' in front of the term because the 'i' in '*inkosi*' translates to 'the' in English.
2 Villagers in Nkangeni, interviewed by Thiyane Duda and Janine Ubink, 2 December 2016 (Nkangeni interview). Cf. interviews in Mbaxa, Jafta/Kwelerhana, Gubevu and Nothenga, cited below.
3 Nkangeni interview; villagers in Gubevu, interviewed by Thiyane Duda and Janine Ubink, 4 December 2016; chairperson of Nothenga village, 6 December 2016 (Nthonga interview).
4 Cwengcwe affidavit and resolution, Claimant Research for Cwengcwe Community Land Claim – Final Report, 15 January 2012, annexure C.
5 Claimant Research Cwengcwe Claim Report, Applicants Founding Affidavit, para 33.
6 Villagers in Nkangeni, interviewed by Thiyane Duda and Janine Ubink, 2 December 2016; villagers in Mbaxa, interviewed by Thiyane Duda and Janine Ubink, 3 December 2016; villagers in Jafta/Kwelerhana, interviewed by Thiyane Duda and Janine Ubink, 3 December 2016; Nothenga interview.
7 Villagers in Gubevu, interviewed by Thiyane Duda and Janine Ubink, 4 December 2016.
8 Villagers in Mbaxa, interviewed by Thiyane Duda and Janine Ubink, 3 December 2016; former ward councillor Amahlathi municipality, interviewed by Thiyane Duda and Janine Ubink, 4 December 2016; villager in Cwengcwe, interviewed by Thiyane Duda and Janine Ubink, 8 December 2016.
9 Recommendation on the Traditional Leadership Claim of AmaHlathi Traditional Council by AmaHlathi Community Council represented by B. Kiva against Luvuyo Maqoma, 2013.

10   Field report of the Eastern Cape Provincial Committee of the Commission on Traditional Leadership Disputes and Claims for the AmaHlathi senior traditional leadership dispute, 6 August 2012.
11   Eastern Cape Provincial Committee, Recommendation on the Traditional Leadership Claim of AmaHlathi Traditional Council by AmaHlathi Community Council represented by B. Kiva against Luvuyo Maqoma, 2013.
12   Commission on Restitution of Land Rights' Final Research Report on the Cwengcwe Community Land Claim, page 18, para 15.4.
13   Chief, *iinkosana* and secretaries, AmaHlathi Traditional Council, interviewed by Thiyane Duda and Janine Ubink, 6 December 2016; elder in Gubevu, interviewed by Thiyane Duda and Janine Ubink, 7 December 2016.
14   AmaHlathi Community Council Member, interviewed by Thiyane Duda and Janine Ubink, King William's Town, 8 December 2016.
15   Office of the Premier, Eastern Cape, Decision on Traditional Leadership claim on AmaHlathi Traditional Council by B. Kiva claimant against Luvuyo Maqoma (respondent), 10 October 2013.
16   Founding affidavit in Mnikeli Elliot Kiva v Premier of the Eastern Cape Province and five others, case no 662/15, EC High Court Bhisho, para 33 (hereafter *Kiva*).
17   *Kiva*, 'Reasons for the decision', submitted by Noxolo Kiviet.
18   Michael Bishop, Legal Resources Centre, counsel for AmaHlathi Action Committee, interviewed by Thiyane Duda and Janine Ubink, Cape Town, 18 July 2019.
19   Representative of Ntinga Ntaba kaNdoda, NGO based in Keiskammahoek, interviewed by Thiyane Duda and Janine Ubink, Cata, 30 May 2017 (Ntinga Ntaba kaNdoda interview).
20   Ntinga Ntaba kaNdoda interview.
21   Cf. Premier of the Eastern Cape and Others v Ntamo and Others (169/14) [2015] ZAECBHC 14; 2015 (6) SA 400 (ECB); [2015] 4 All SA 107 (ECB) (18 August 2015) (hereafter *Ntamo*), para 12.
22   *Ntamo*, paras 48–49.
23   Ntinga Ntaba kaNdoda interview.
24   SANCO chair and two SANCO members, interviewed by Thiyane Duda and Janine Ubink, Ngqumeya, 30 May 2017 (SANCO interview).
25   Ntinga Ntaba kaNdoda interview; SANCO interview.

REFERENCES

Buthelezi, Mbongiseni and Dineo Skosana. 2018. 'The Salience of Chiefs in Postapartheid South Africa: Reflections on the Nhlapo Commission'. In *The Politics of Custom: Chiefship, Capital, and the State in Contemporary Africa*, edited by John L. Comaroff and Jean Comaroff, 110–133. Chicago: University of Chicago Press.

Charton, Nancy. 1980. 'The Legislature'. In *Ciskei: Economics and Politics of Dependence in a South African Homeland*, edited by Nancy Charton, 149–184. London: Routledge.

Charton, Nancy and Gordon Renton kaTywakadi. 1980. 'Ciskeian Political Parties'. In *Ciskei: Economics and Politics of Dependence in a South African Homeland*, edited by Nancy Charton, 122–148. London: Routledge.

Claassens, Aninka. 2011. 'Contested Power and Apartheid Tribal Boundaries: The Implications of "Living Customary Law" for Indigenous Accountability Mechanisms'. *Acta Juridica* 2011, no 1: 174–209.

Claassens, Aninka and Geoff Budlender. 2013. ' Transformative Constitutionalism and Customary Law'. *Constitutional Court Review* 6: 75–104.

Delius, Peter. 2019a. 'Mistaking Form for Substance: The Disjuncture between Pre-Colonial Dynamics and Post-Colonial Policies in Relation to the Role of Chiefs'. Paper presented at the conference 'Citizenship and Accountability' 17–18 June 2019, Bonavero Institute of Human Rights, University of Oxford.

Delius, Peter. 2019b. 'Mistaking Form for Substance: Reflections on the Key Dynamics of Pre-Colonial Polities and Their Implications for the Role of Chiefs in Contemporary South Africa'. In *Traditional Leaders in a Democracy: Resources, Respect and Resistance*, edited by Mbongiseni Buthelezi, Dineo Skosana and Beth Vale, 24–49. Johannesburg: MISTRA.

Deliwe, Dumisani. 1997. 'Forced Removal and Land Restitution in South Africa: A Case Study of the Mfengu in Tsitsikama'. In *From Reserve to Region: Apartheid and Social Change in the Keiskammahoek District of (Former) Ciskei, 1950 to 1990*, edited by Chris de Wet and Michael G. Whisson, 267–296. Grahamstown: Institute for Social and Economic Research, Rhodes University.

De Wet, Chris. 1997. 'Historical Background – Keiskammahoek up to 1950'. In *From Reserve to Region: Apartheid and Social Change in the Keiskammahoek District of (Former) Ciskei, 1950 to 1990*, edited by Chris de Wet, and Michael G. Whisson, 1–15. Grahamstown: Institute for Social and Economic Research, Rhodes University.

Groenewald, D.M. 1980. 'The Administrative System in the Ciskei'. In *Ciskei: Economics and Politics of Dependence in a South African Homeland*, edited by Nancy Charton, 82–96. London: Routledge.

Hammond-Tooke, William D. 1958. *The Tribes of King William's Town District*. No. 41. Pretoria: Government Printer.

Jackson, A.O. 1975. *The Ethnic Composition of the Ciskei and Transkei*. Pretoria: Department of Bantu Administration and Development, Ethnological Publications, No. 53.

Mager, Anne K. 1999. *Gender and the Making of a South African Bantustan: A Social History of the Ciskei, 1945–1959*. Oxford: James Currey.

Mager, Anne K. and Phiko Jeffrey Velelo. 2018. *The House of Tshatshu. Power, Politics and Chiefs North-West of the Great Kei River c. 1818–2018*. Cape Town: UCT Press.

Manona, Cecil. 1980. 'Ethnic Relations in the Ciskei'. In *Ciskei: Economics and Politics of Dependence in a South African Homeland*, edited by Nancy Charton, 97–121. London: Routledge.

Manona, Cecil. 1985. 'Local Government'. In *Rural Development in South Africa: A Case-Study of the Amatola Basin in the Ciskei*, edited by Chris de Wet and Simon Bekker, 69–89. Grahamstown: Institute of Social and Economic Research, Rhodes University.

Manona, Cecil. 1997. 'The Collapse of the "Tribal Authority" System and the Rise of Civic Associations'. In *From Reserve to Region: Apartheid and Social Change in the Keiskammahoek District of (Former) Ciskei, 1950 to 1990*, edited by Chris de Wet and Michael G. Whisson, 49–68. Grahamstown: Institute for Social and Economic Research, Rhodes University.

Mills, M.E. Elton and Monica Hunter Wilson. 1952. *Keiskammahoek Rural Survey: Land Tenure*. Vol. 4. Pietermaritzburg: Shuter and Shooter.

Mnisi Weeks, Sindiso. 2012. 'Regulating Vernacular Dispute Resolution Forums: Controversy Concerning the Process, Substance and Implications of South Africa's Traditional Courts Bill.' *Oxford University Commonwealth Law Journal* 12, no. 1: 133–155.

Ncapayi, Fani. 2015. 'Whether You Like it or Not, it is the Royal Family That Will Decide on Headman Here'. Provincial seminar on 'The Meaning of Democracy in Post-1994 Rural South Africa', East London, 26–27 August 2015.

Nacapayi, Fani. 2017. 'Emerging Rural Struggles against Unelected Traditional Leaders and the Role of the Courts: Lessons from Rural Villages of the Eastern Cape'. Unpublished paper.

Ncapayi, Fani and Lungisile Ntsebeza. 2015. 'The Re-emergence of Rural Resistance and the Role of Organic Intellectuals with Specific Reference to the Xhalanga District in the Eastern Cape'. Unpublished paper.

Ngcukana, Lubalalo. 2017. 'Tribal Tensions Brew an Eastern Cape Land War.' *City Press*, 12 March.

Ntsebeza, Lungisile. 2011. 'Traditional Authorities and Democracy: Are we back to Apartheid?' In *The Fate of the Eastern Cape: History, Politics and Social Policy*, edited by Greg Ruiters, 75–92. Pietermaritzburg: University of KwaZulu-Natal Press, 75–92.

Oomen, Barbara M. 2005. *Chiefs in South Africa: Law, Power and Culture in the Post-Apartheid Era*. Oxford: James Currey.

Peires, Jeff B. 1982. *The House of Phalo: A History of the Xhosa People in the Days of Their Independence*. Berkeley: University of California Press.

Peires, Jeff B. 1989. 'Ethnicity and Pseudo-Ethnicity in the Ciskei'. In *The Creation of Tribalism in Southern Africa*, edited by Leroy Vail, 390–410. Berkeley: University of California Press.

Peires, Jeff. B. 2000. 'Traditional Leaders in Purgatory Local Government in Tsolo, Qumbu and Port St Johns, 1990–2000'. *African Studies* 59, no. 1: 97–114.

Peires, Jeff B. 2014. 'History versus Customary Law: Commission on Traditional Leadership: Disputes and Claims'. *South African Crime Quarterly* 49, no. 1: 7–20.

Southall, Roger and Zosa De Sas Kropiwnicki. 2003. 'Containing the Chiefs: The ANC and Traditional Leaders in the Eastern Cape, South Africa'. *Canadian Journal of African Studies* 37: 48–82.

Westaway, Ashley. 1997. 'Headmanship, Land Tenure and Betterment Planning in Keiskammahoek, c. 1920 - 1980'. In *From Reserve to Region: Apartheid and Social Change in the Keiskammahoek District of (Former) Ciskei, 1950 to 1990*, edited by Chris de Wet and Michael G. Whisson, 16–48. Grahamstown: Institute for Social and Economic Research, Rhodes University.

Wicomb, Wilmien. 2015. 'Victory for Democracy in Rural Eastern Cape'. *Ground Up*, 19 August.

Wilson, Monica, Selma Kaplan, Theresa Maki and Edith Walton. 1952. *Keiskammahoek Rural Survey. Social Structure*, Vol. 3. Pietermaritzburg: Shuter and Shooter.

Wotshela, Luvuyo. 1994. 'Transformation in Late Colonial Ngqika Society: A Political, Economic and Social History of African Communities in the District of Stutterheim (Eastern Cape), c.1870–1910'. MA thesis, Rhodes University.

CHAPTER

# 8

# Black Landlords, Their Tenants and the Native Administration Act of 1927

Khumisho Moguerane

This chapter explores the long history of African reserves, chiefs and landholding in the Tswana-speaking areas of the northern Cape. These left a deep legacy that shapes rural society to the present. After the South African War (1899–1902), British rule gradually created two judicial and property jurisdictions in the countryside: a sphere of representative political institutions and private property for those classified as 'white' and one of chieftaincy and common property in the 'black' reserves. The untold story of territorial segregation is of a colonial government that failed fully to achieve these ends despite the coercive powers at its disposal. The reason for this failure, I argue, was that the commons were not 'free', but rather intricate and essentially hierarchical moral economies. We need to analyse the changing balance of power in these 'communal tenure' areas in order to understand the outcomes in respect of land and political authority. Mahmood Mamdani (1996: 23) argues that colonialism in the reserves produced a decentralised despotism in rural South Africa, as 'the authority of the chief fused in a single person all moments of power: judicial, legislative, executive, and administrative.' I identify a different process that involved, to a greater extent, the refashioning of citizenship and relations on the land from below.

The dilemma, as state bureaucrats recognised, was how to ensure that Europeans' social reproduction sustained itself where their population would never overtake that of existing African societies. The way forward was to delineate and fix reserves for the exclusive occupation of the 'black' population. These had to be territories on which the colonial government had the jurisdiction to control the movement of people and allocate land. In Natal, for instance, the wars of conquest had brought existing polities to their knees, and turned them into 'locations', entirely the property of the Crown, governed through headmen the British appointed.

This was not the case everywhere, especially not into the hinterlands of Bechuanaland, where literacy and Christianity had strengthened chiefly institutions. Chiefs held large farms as private property along the border of the Molopo Reserves. Chiefs collected tribute and other rents from the mixed peoples who had settled on these 'private locations'. They also held some private property in the reserves. For the most part however, the pattern of landholding in the reserves was an ambiguous negotiation. According to 'custom' and oral tradition, land was 'free', but in practice, tenantry on the land was mediated by chiefly rule. Commoners accepted 'placement' on the wards that senior chiefs controlled as an extension of the paramount chief's 'gift'. In return, they assisted chiefs to plough their lands (*pacha*) and find water for animals.

At this time, European settlers rented some of these same lands from chiefly landlords. Their rents were often paid in infrastructural developments like dams, boreholes, windmills, fences, cottages, stables and orchards. Indeed, this was a frontier of mixed skin colouring and *métissage*. Beyond the reserves and chiefs' private lands, on 'white'-owned farmlands, there was a range of other landholding arrangements – not least sharecropping by largely 'black' tenants. Social relationships were negotiated across these fluid zones.

This chapter describes how British and Cape colonialism ultimately gained control of the reserves of British Bechuanaland. I argue that the outcome of these contestations over authority in these reserves established a template for a relationship between property and political citizenship that became a bedrock for new conceptions of identity in these reserves. These relied less on loyalty to a 'tribal' chief and more on affiliation to a hybrid institution that coupled an increasingly symbolic 'tribal' bureaucracy under chiefs to the ever-growing, indispensable government bureaucracy of the Native Commissioner.

As a result the 'white' Native Commissioner, and not a 'black' chief, applied 'customary law' to scenarios as diverse as marriage and inheritance. In each district, people from various reserves observed, but also shaped, these laws and regulations.

They claimed rights and privileges in the reserves through the office of the Native Commissioner as 'subjects' of chieftaincies that were not in the reserves, a great distance away, and even fictional. The making of race and segregation in early twentieth-century South Africa illuminates how ordinary people themselves embraced racial difference. This was less a calculation of interest and more a moral response to the very dilemmas of existence that colonial rule precipitated. A shift in the arrangements of political citizenship, and its boundaries of skin colouring, reflected a new synthesis of self-identification that underpinned ethical negotiations in a changing colonial setting of rights and resources.

Furthermore, the principle that facilitated this institution was not primarily colonial legislation. The Natives Land Act of 1913, as this chapter describes, failed dismally to attenuate chiefly power and loosen property relations from chieftaincy. Popular struggle from below achieved these ends. Historians have described conflicts between Barolong chiefs of various lineages in the Molopo Reserve, especially between the Rapulana and Tshidi (Ramoroka 2009; Starfield 2008). However, they have not considered how ordinary householders took advantage of these conflicts to strip chiefs of power and to lobby the support of the colonial government against chiefs. This chapter focuses on these contestations and their role in reconfiguring the relationship between chieftaincy and property. Echoing studies of other African contexts over the long term, I emphasise the significance of the homestead as a central institution in shaping rural strategies and identities (Vansina 1990). Such struggles from below helped to turn territories controlled by chiefs, where access to land was unequal, into areas dominated by forms of homestead-based tenure, which were commons.

Moreover, this chapter describes how ordinary people, mostly men, came to acquire land (a site to erect a homestead, fields and access to grazing lands) freely such that the experience of property on these commons was effectively 'private property'. The homestead head enjoyed autonomy on the property, letting and selling as he wished, constrained only by the intimate hierarchies of family life and a grid of moral expectations, rather than external institutions of governance. Chieftaincy can coincide with a range of property relations and, under the changing circumstances of moral life, proves remarkably malleable. Ultimately, what successfully opened up these reserves was popular struggle and a 'privatisation from below' that effectively turned territories of unequal access to land in Bechuanaland into commons where family land rights were nevertheless very strong (Beinart, Delius and Hay 2017). The pattern of landholding that emerged shaped the Native Administration Act of 1927.

## CHIEFTAINCY AND LANDHOLDING IN BECHUANALAND

John Iliffe (2007) observes that in a history of slow, struggling, often unsuccessful state formation in Africa at least until the second half of the second millennium, southern Africa was a striking exception. 'Hereditary chieftainship, the homestead as social unit and the ideological predominance of cattle became shared cultural characteristics of South Africa's Bantu-speaking people who', he argues, 'had few of the stateless societies so common elsewhere on the continent' (Iliffe 2007: 103). When the first Europeans crossed the Orange River, guided by 'brown people' in the late 1770s, the Barolong kingdom was one of the strongest southernmost societies that had become prominent after 1600, and was trading as far as Delagoa Bay (Legassick 2016).

The Barolong were part of a diffuse political geography of chiefdoms, village associations and other institutions of political authority on the highveld (Landau 2010). People could and did survive, away from or along the margins of chiefdoms and state-like institutions, but the institution of chieftaincy already had a long, deeply entrenched history along and across the Orange River. The wars and famines of the 1820s and 1830s in the interior caused mass displacement of people and political instability, but on the heels of this devastation, young men were learning to read and write and accumulating resources by exploiting new trade routes to the north. They became evangelists and teachers, and gathered followers through the twin institutions of school and church (Volz 2011). These 'ecclesiastical statehoods' flourished well into the early twentieth century.

From the late eighteen century, these polities flourished, swelling their populations by incorporating European and other migrants into a fluid and heterogenous mix (Legassick 2010; Landau 2010). By the nineteenth century, the 'Bechuana' referred to the political sphere on the highveld, north of the Orange River towards and across the Molopo River, of people who shared similar dialects and cultural practices. Protestantism and literacy encouraged cultural projects that coupled a shared language, history and cultural heritage to territorial states and divine destiny (Hastings 2001). By then, the interpretation of the *morafe* – the unit of political citizenship – was fast narrowing towards a uniform composition of a 'tribe' living under a centralised chieftaincy, like the 'Bamongoato' under Khama, the 'Bakoena' under Bathoen, or the 'Barolong' under Montsioa, and so on. Along the Molopo River, conflicts over land came to a head in the 1870s and early 1880s, as independent Boer republics established themselves on lands occupied mainly by amorphous lineages of Barolong, who were themselves competing for territory.

Britain annexed Bechuanaland in 1885, ending the frontier wars, demarcating and protecting the boundaries of the new reserves it established in British Bechuanaland (Shillington 1985). This was a rushed and reluctant colonisation (Robinson and Gallagher 1983). The imperial government wished to intervene as little as possible in the region, including in the existing pattern of settlement. Along the Molopo River, it established the reserves and allocated one to each of the contending lineages of Barolong that it recognised. Whoever was living on territory that had become part of a reserve became, with or without their consent, or perhaps even their knowledge, subjects of the ruling clan in each reserve. The Land Commission of 1886 had 'purposely refrained from defining boundaries between the tribes or sections of tribes considering the reserves to be available for all natives no matter of what nationality'.[1] Yet, chiefs remained somewhat disgruntled that some of their old lands were a part of others' reserves and these discontents festered into later decades.

Britain diverted from its standard practice of formal annexation elsewhere in southern Africa. The reserves of British Bechuanaland were 'tribal property', not Crown lands. They belonged to African themselves, and Britain agreed not to interfere with how chiefs governed themselves in the reserves. The reserves were, according to this negotiated settlement of 1885, autonomous entities. They were free from direct government control. Homestead heads paid hut tax from 1892, but there was no formal amendment to the terms of the negotiated settlement. In fact, when Britain ceded British Bechuanaland to the Cape Colony in 1895, it agreed that the terms of colonisation in 1885 would continue unchanged.[2]

In each reserve, chiefly bureaucracies created emblems and other paraphernalia that symbolised their 'national' peculiarity. Educated Barolong like James Molebaloa were well versed in and produced 'histories' of the Barolong chiefdoms according to 'tribes' or 'nations' of the three main Barolong lineages recognised by Britain in Bechuanaland – the Ratshidi, the Ratlou and the Rapulana.[3] Chiefs relied on this understanding of identity when allocating 'placement' on the land. These differences, although not always significant, were central to the practices of citizenship in their reserves. Nevertheless, personal relations like marriage muted these differences significantly. So did the broader new encapsulation of 'Bechuana', which coexisted alongside narrower identifications according to clans, lineages, regional ties and other collations. The emerging traditions of 'Sechuana' along the northern frontier reflected intriguing cultural syncretism, including adaptations in the practices of landholding. These changes encouraged debates about which ways of life were 'tradition' and lent those men and women their personhood (*botho*). While the government's understanding was that any reserve was home to all 'nationalities', for chiefs and ordinary people, settlement was subject to the routines of citizenship that assimilated newcomers into the *morafe*.

Reserves' populations had hierarchies of difference, amongst which distinctions between 'foreign' and 'native' were central. This distinction was a matter of degree, typically contested, but always central to negotiating the terms of tenancy that secured belonging to the *morafe*, as a community of 'persons' (*batho*). This was the backdrop to tenancy in these polities, which mediated citizenship through the fluid categories of 'newcomer' or 'native'. The latest arrivals paid the highest rents. As they streamed into the new British territory, many white settlers leased lands from Barolong chiefs. They paid rents in cash and some made infrastructural improvements. Some of them married, or lived with, Barolong women. These tenants made themselves subject to the cultural prescriptions of 'placement'. The 'natives', mainly dark-skinned residents, paid tribute and contributed their rents through labour. The records of the chiefly bureaucracy in the Molopo Reserve from the 1880s to the 1930s contain not a single incident where one or more people rejected chieftaincy as an institution but brim with contestation over the limits and configuration of chiefly rule. There were also flashpoints between chiefs themselves.

These conflicts sharpened in the Molopo Reserve towards the tail end of a long and serious drought with important consequences for the pattern of race and segregation in this part of South Africa. The drought started a few years after the South African War but was most severe from 1910 to 1913. Not even Silas Molema, a senior and enterprising Barolong chief, could feed his family through the winter and spring of 1912. For four months, his nephew, Reverend Joshua Moshoela, sent grain by rail from Klerksdorp, in the Orange Free State, to Mafikeng.[4] Chiefs were severely cash strapped. The reserves already had too many people for the productive land available, but the reserves' boundaries were immovable. Land shortages elsewhere meant people could not readily leave except to take tenancies on white-owned farms. Conflicts emerged over the boundaries set by the Land Commission for British Bechuanaland in 1886 (Shillington 1985: 174).

The Cape government and the Union government after 1910 wished to do away with the 'special conditions' of colonisation under which chiefs could decide who lived there, whatever their skin pigmentation, and how they were to hold land. From 1902, the Cape government had tried to bring these reserves under the Native Locations Act of 1884, as Crown lands belonging to the government. Chiefs insisted that the terms of their negotiations with Britain at the time of annexation still stood. As that drama unfolded through the highest courts of the land from 1902 to 1913, the same group of actors were involved in boundary disputes.

In 1912, chiefs in Mafikeng proceeded to the Supreme Court to challenge the Union government's attempt to appropriate the Molopo Reserve. The Native Affairs Department had insisted that all 'whites' leasing property in the reserves must pay their rents into the Cape's treasury, and not to chiefly landlords. In the meantime, regent and paramount chief, Lekoko Marumoloa (Montsioa) was unwilling to allow either the resident magistrate or the Native Affairs Department to interfere in internal disputes. Unlike Badirile Montsioa whom he succeeded, Lekoko Marumoloa was entirely unwilling to let the court of the resident magistrate intervene, even when its decision was in his favour, aware that intervention of any sort by the colonial government undermined the reserve's political and territorial autonomy.

## RIETFONTEIN BOUNDARY DISPUTE

Rietfontein was one in a cluster of boundary disputes between Barolong chiefs in the 1910s. It deserves special consideration because it coincided with the litigation contesting the colonial government's jurisdiction in these northern reserves. Rietfontein is also an example of the inconsistency of British policy on the ground in Bechuanaland. It demonstrates the web of variegated arrangements of British colonisation in southern Africa, where every case was, potentially, an exception to an imprecise, often haphazard, set of policies. Settler governments, on the other hand, wanted permanent, practicable solutions towards social order. They wished to manage the demographic and political challenges of territorial segregation according to skin colour in a single framework.

In 1912, Lekoko Marumoloa communicated to the Native Affairs Department, through the attorney Spencer Minchin, that he had the independent jurisdiction to govern and intervene in the allocation of land at Rietfontein.[5] This settlement, at the eastern edge of the Molopo Reserve, adjoined the Transvaal Province, and a fence separated the two provinces of the Cape and Transvaal. According to Z.K. Matthews' account in 1945:

> About 1874, some of the Rapulana crossed the Transvaal boundary and moved over into Tshidi territory, to Lotlhakane (Rietfontein) in the Cape, where they settled, it is said, with the permission of Chief Montshiwa [Montsioa], who was then at Sehuba, not far from Lotlhakane. For a few years the Rapulana and the Tshidi lived together in peace in this land of their forefathers, but about 1880 Montshiwa became dissatisfied with the attitude of the

Rapulana who apparently refused to acknowledge that they were subject to his jurisdiction, although they lived within what he regarded as his territory. Montshiwa accordingly made an attack on the Rapulana and drove them out of Lotlhakane across the Transvaal boundary to Polfontein where the main body of the Rapulana had remained. At Polfontein a counter-attack was organised. With the help of the Ratlou under Moshwete and some European freebooters the Rapulana returned to attack Montshiwa and eventually they succeeded in dislodging him from Dithakong (Sehuba). Hard pressed, he withdrew to Mafikeng... Eventually in 1882 the parties agree to a settlement of the dispute. Under this settlement Montshiwa lost to the Transvaal much territory which he had formerly claimed as his own. The land obtained by the Whites under this treaty was named Goshen.[6]

As far as the Tshidi nobility was concerned, Rietfontein was a ward of the Rapulana under their rule, not only because they were earlier colonisers of the land, and therefore its chiefs, but also because the Land Commission of 1886 had allocated Montsioa territorial jurisdiction across the entire reserve. The Rapulana, on the contrary, believed that the land belonged to the Rapulana chief, Machabi, and was theirs as spoil because they had won the war against Montsioa. Moreover, as far as the Rapulana were concerned, Rietfontein was an independent domain, whose autonomy had received unambiguous confirmation from a ruling by the former Resident Magistrate and Civil Commissioner of the Mafeking District, C.G.H. Bell, in 1898.

In 1912, the Secretary of Native Affairs, Edward Dower, hoped to enforce the authority of the Department with respect to this dispute as well as the status of the Barolong chiefs.[7] When conflict arose as to whether Paul Montsioa, the Tshidi sub-chief at Rietfontein, had authority to allocate and use lands that were also claimed by the Rapulana camp, his response remained measured, instructing Lekoko 'to deliver up possession of the lands in question'.[8] The Department was not directly contesting Lekoko Marumoloa's claim that he had jurisdiction to act in Rietfontein. Rather it was directing him towards an interpretation of that power as limited, as no more than maintaining law and order. Immediately after drawing in the harvest, in early summer, Paul Montsioa 'again started ploughing the lands which he held within the area.' When the Superintendent of Natives, H.J. Frost, called on his house, his family told him he was at the cattle post.[9] The Tshidi chiefs were effectively ignoring the government.

Frost had to deal with the immediate causes of the dispute over land. He was an observer of indigenous societies at a time when the Department of Native Affairs still encouraged officials to take a deep interest in ethnographic details. Frost was aware that people settled on the land in layers, like sediments, and allowed time to establish their roots as indigenous. People could reconstitute their 'origins' in different times, genealogies and places through oral repertoires of their 'origins'. Hence, it was bureaucratically expedient to adjudicate cases not based on contested histories of the past, which were not consistent, but on the precedent set by a ruling of a colonial court or commission. In light of his interpretation of Bell's 1898 ruling, Frost reversed the Native Affairs Department's earlier recommendation and as a result the Department now dismissed the Rapulana's claim over these particular lands in Rietfontein.[10]

Lekoko Marumoloa's response was not, however, entirely celebratory. He wrote to the Resident Magistrate in Mafikeng, N.C. Welsh: 'I hope now rest and peace will be restored'.[11] But he was determined to interpret the dispute as a 'Barolong' matter, and therefore as subject to the personal jurisdiction of their traditional authority. He wanted Welsh to understand that peace at Rietfontein would come not because of the Native Affairs Department's intervention, but when the Barolong themselves had resolved the conflict. Similarly, the Rapulana did not accept the government's decision.

The bumper harvest in the autumn of 1913 was the first substantial yield of many years but it only heightened the conflict about who owned the fields. In May, Frost and the new Resident Magistrate, R.C. Lloyd, made their way to Rietfontein after householders complained 'concerning the treatment received by them from Headman Paul Montsioa in connection with the lands out there'.[12] It seems that the Rapulana took advantage of the change of guard in the magistrate's office to press their case. Moreover, evidence of evictions elsewhere in the reserve and the swelling number of people who presented their claims suggests a more pervasive moment of dispossession of lands by chiefs. Some of the Tshidi chiefs were targeting placement holders whose rents were not forthcoming and replacing them with new tenants.

On 29 May 1913, 'a large number of Natives' gathered at Rietfontein to make representations to the resident magistrate and the superintendent of natives. Lloyd recorded the proceedings and, working through an interpreter and transcriber, took extensive notes. The Rapulana claims were based on their original conquest, their subsequent inheritance and the rights they had acquired. They presented detailed genealogies, insisted that Paul was taking lands from them and that 'Paul is not our chief'. Lloyd stated that whatever the historical claims, the Land Commission of 1886 'purposely refrained from defining boundaries between tribes or section[s] of tribes considering the reserves available for all natives no matter of what nationality'.[13] He studied Sidney Shippard's report of 1886 and realised that Shippard had both recognised Rietfontein as a miniature independent reserve within the Molopo Reserve, and had given the Tshidi paramount full territorial jurisdiction and right to collect tribute from the householders there. The Native Affairs Department retained the Land Commission's principle of allowing paramount chiefs' full territorial jurisdiction in each reserve. It dismissed the Rapulana's claim.

## THE MOLOPO RESERVE, TENANCY AND THE NATIVES LAND ACT OF 1913

Evidence of evictions in other parts of the reserve suggests that those in Rietfontein were not concerned merely with political objectives. The threat of eviction pressured 'placement' holders to support chiefs through hard times. The prolific writer, journalist, politician and one of the founders of the South African Native National Congress (SANNC), Solomon Plaatje, had been trying over many months to borrow money from Joshua Molema and Lekoko Marumoloa and had failed. He was living in Kimberley at the time, but like other educated Bechuana in the cities, he was attempting to maintain some roots in the countryside. At the beginning of May 1913, weeks before the gathering above, he received notice of his eviction from his 'placement' by Maduo Mcoa.[14]

Plaatje was due to have met the Minister of Native Affairs, J.W. Sauer as a member of the SANNC's delegation to the Union government to represent chiefs, but he did not go. He was both without money and aggrieved that the very chiefs he was representing had dispossessed him of his lands. He wrote to Silas Molema that 'as I had no means to go our affairs were not represented' and proceeded to describe his eviction as a tale of 'such sorrows as the wrenching of heart of finance that I find myself in'.

> Maduo [Ncoa] has given away my field and the site of my house to Mr Ephraim Molema and he says he is confiscating my house on his lands. Ncoa has spoken before Chief Joshua Molema and the late Mrs Palo Molema and the sons of Mmona that he has given me fields on his farm (*fa a mpeile tshimo*), how can he renege just like that.

Chiefs were not the only ones evicting people and expelling them from the reserve. A few months before this, on 24 January 1913, the Native Affairs Department had communicated to Paramount Chief Lekoko Marumoloa that it considered whites who had contracts in the Molopo reserve 'squatters' and was extracting them.

Five days later, the Supreme Court of Appeal reserved judgment in the litigation between the Barolong chiefs and the Union government. The Minster of Native Affairs, Sauer, understood that the court had ruled in favour of the chiefs. After a decade of litigation between chiefs of the Molopo Reserve and the colonial and Union governments, the Supreme Court ruled that the government had no legal right to intervene in these reserves without an Act of parliament. His 'anti-squatting' laws in these reserves were therefore not valid.

This outcome of the litigation shaped the Department's decision towards the Natives Land Act of 1913 (Moguerane 2016). As a national measure the legislation was a cornerstone of the Union government's project of segregation. It was typical of the British policy of reservation elsewhere to settle Africans according to neat 'tribal' enclaves under a salaried headman appointed by the government. The legislation, however, also emerged specifically out of the 'special conditions' of colonisation in colonial Bechuanaland, which prevented the colonial government from intervening in the governance of these reserves, which were not Crown lands. The Natives Land Act of 1913 allowed the government to incorporate these autonomous reserves of former British Bechuanaland into the 'Schedule of Native Areas'.

The legislation demarcated and fixed the boundaries of such scheduled areas, which included all existing reserves, and installed the governor general as owner and therefore principal landlord of these scheduled territories. It included anti-squatting legislation that prohibited any person not classified as white from occupying land outside scheduled areas unless employed by 'white' landowners. Only people categorised 'black' could reside in and buy property in the scheduled areas. These areas became a domain of 'native administration' under the jurisdiction of a salaried headman and a Native Commissioner. The point was to cut down the capillaries of hereditary power through which subjects paid rents according to hierarchies of lineage, gender and generation that locked out those unwilling or unable to pay from settling in jurisdictions of 'traditional' authority.

The Secretary of Native Affairs, Edward Dower, explained to Lekoko Marumoloa that the intention of the colonial government was to ensure that reserves survived as realms of custom, in this instance 'Sechuana'. Chiefs were arguing that the pattern of landholding in the reserves, where rents allowed them a significant margin of private accumulation, was 'Sechuana' and that it did not undermine the 'customary' imperative that 'Lekoko owns the land in the Reserve [and] holds it for the people'.[15]

Shortly after his eviction, Plaatje travelled through the districts of the Orange Free State, the Cape and the Transvaal to document the consequences of the Natives Land Act of 1913 on white-owned farms (Plaatje 2007). Overnight, sharecroppers had to pack up their belongings and drive their stock from the lands they had worked for years, through the winter's chill, with nowhere to go. Some set off to the Molopo Reserves where evictions – of all 'whites' by the Native Affairs Department, and of vulnerable 'blacks' by chiefs – were happening at the same time. Plaatje travelled to England as a member of the SANNC's delegation to lobby the British government to nullify the promulgation of the Natives Land Act of 1913. The idea of a 'Schedule of Native Areas', he wrote, made no sense, because how could 'natives', or anyone for that matter, buy lands in the reserves, which were absolutely *not* common areas, but jurisdictions where people settled and lived according to the peculiar prescriptions of their own 'clans' (Plaatje 2007: 23). In his understanding, these reserves were not open to the African sharecroppers evicted from what became 'white' farmland as the colonial government intended, but neither were they property for anyone, including chiefs, to dispose of as if they were freehold property – an instance that his own eviction from the Molopo Reserve represented.

Plaatje explains that the only way landholding in these areas could be that of common areas, was if they became landscapes of private property, which required that the 'clan' disband or cease to exist. Otherwise, those 'who had grown up among white people', meaning those whose sensibility was not congruent to the reciprocal practices of clan life on the land, should have the right, like whites, to purchase land outside these areas. Cultural sensibility, not skin pigmentation, should be the basis for territorial segregation.

> What are these Scheduled Native Areas? They are the native locations which were reserved for the exclusive use of certain native clans. They are inalienable and cannot be bought or sold, yet the Act says that in these 'Scheduled Native Areas', natives only may buy land. The areas being inalienable, not even members of the clans, for whose benefit the locations are held in trust, can buy land therein. The areas could only be sold if the whole clan rebelled; in that case the location would be confiscated. But as long as the clans of the location remain loyal to the government, nobody can buy land within these areas – let alone a native outsider who had grown up among white people and done all his farming on white man's land (Plaatje 2007: 23).

This paradox – that the route towards the making of the commons was privatisation of land – is made very clear in Plaatje's now-classic *Native Life in South Africa*. Allowing for the privatisation of the reserves, in practice, even if not necessarily through titling, was the answer if these jurisdictions of 'custom' were to absorb additional black people. However, as Plaatje describes, 'exclud[ing] the arid tracts of Bechuanaland', locations had 'been granted on such a small scale that each of them got so overcrowded that much of the population had to go out and settle on the farms of white farmers through lack of space in the locations' (Plaatje 2007: 24.) The impediments to territorial segregation according to skin colouring were not unique to Bechuanaland. Elsewhere they were worse.

The Natives Land Act of 1913 ejected whites from the reserves, except traders and some village dwellers. It intended to settle only 'black' peoples in the reserves, but in agropastoralist societies where chieftaincy remained resilient, enduring understandings of 'placement' meant earlier settlers of the land, especially chiefs, could extract rents from newcomers. There was no possibility of commons where chiefly rule, which educated Africans like Plaatje still embraced, remained strong and relatively autonomous from the colonial government. The colonial government's attempt to create commons from above, he suggested, could only mean 'rebellion'. What would be the point, not to mention the political cost, of expelling sharecroppers from white farmlands if the reserves remained closed to them? In fact, the government policed skin colouring in the reserves, but still allowed 'black' sharecroppers to drift back to white farmlands.

The Natives Land Act of 1913 meant the Molopo Reserve became Crown land. Nevertheless, the government was a long way from accomplishing its designs. Chiefs remained powerful. At the end of June 1913 about 200 people gathered at Rietfontein, including the paramount Lekoko Marumoloa and local chiefs. Frost had called the meeting. He stated that he 'had not come to address ... the Rietfontein question in general but only to verify the statement as to the allocation of lands'. He proceeded to the lands in question to map the positions of at least 55 'holders' in the contested lands.[16] A few weeks later, Lekoko Marumoloa presented the Tshidi chiefs' own narrative of the history of Rietfontein, informing Lloyd that 'this is a civil matter between my people and according to the power vested in me by the Government, I have the exclusive jurisdiction to decide the matter at my "Kgotla"'. Lekoko also wrote that officials 'would like to see the native people split up and the power of the Chief broken that they may have great and glorious name that they have destroyed us'.[17]

The government decided in 1915 that it had the authority to settle the Rietfontein dispute. The Rapulana wanted the resident magistrate to 'make a division of the Molopo Reserve', so they could establish themselves on their own land.[18] It appears they invited the rector of the Anglican Church, Reverend George Robinson to establish a church in Rietfontein. When Frost requested Lekoko Marumoloa to indicate a suitable spot, he refused, on the grounds that this was 'merely a pretext to stamp their authority at Rietfontein'. A Rapulana man responded: 'Where on earth have you ever seen a people hindered to worship their God by those in authority, asking that instead of worshipping God they must be worshipped? Those in power do not want us to build a church house, they want us to worship on trees.'[19]

In February 1917, the government recognised both Paul Montsioa and George Motuba, representing the Rapulana, as headmen on its payroll. Paul was paid £12 per annum, twice the amount of George's stipend. In April, Silas Molema, whose son-in-law Bakolopang Montsioa had succeeded Lekoko Marumoloa as chief of the Tshidi Barolong, asked the resident magistrate to clarify the position of Paul Montsioa at Rietfontein: 'If we continue to quarrel within ourselves about the question of precedence and jurisdiction we shall never be a nation.'[20]

In fact, as far as the question of landholding and chiefly power was concerned, the government's failure was not only at Rietfontein. Chiefs tried to remain gatekeepers even as the population of the reserves swelled. As Silas Molema put it before the Beaumont (Natives Land) Commission in 1916: 'We are now more in number than when the reserve was made' and are 'multiplying every year'. As a consequence, '[We] can only receive some of our people who went to work in the mines and on the farms, but those who went away a long time ago I could not receive back because the land is only big enough for us' (Starfield 2008: 146). Furthermore, the promulgation of the Natives Land Act of 1913 had meant a haemorrhage of 'white' cash rents from the Molopo Reserve. The consequence, contrary to what the legislation had intended, was not to attenuate transactions of rents in the reserve, but in fact to thicken and ramify them. There was not enough land to go around, but the political tradition of absorbing new settlers into the landscape, and nativising them through rents continued.

Black newcomers became the new cash cows to replace European tenants. Silas Molema decided to construct a dam on one of his properties, Madibespruit, in the reserve – an undertaking that 'white' tenants would previously have been expected to handle. In the process, he became indebted to Stephanus van Jaarsveld, one of his tenants on his private property, Vryhof, outside the reserve, who undertook the work.[21] Molema thus leased Madibespruit from 1919 to a group of 'Fingoes and Xosas'. As people who had agreed to be 'governed by the Rules and Customs of the Barolong Nation', in the words of the contract, they performed all the labour commoners in the polity rendered to chiefs under customary law, but also much more. In addition to paying hut tax of 12 shillings, they paid an annual contribution of 3 shillings to the Barolong National Fund, and 'any special levy made by the Paramount Chief' and ploughing his field 'with their ploughs and fields', the Fingoes and Xosas aforementioned agree and bind themselves to plough each season one garden of, and for the benefit of Silas Tawana Molema, being a plot of arable land measuring 900 × 400 wherever indicated by the said Silas Molema, and they further bind themselves to cultivate and sow with their own seed, reap and thrash the crop of the said garden at their own expense and deliver the produce to the said Silas Molema... reside and plough on the premises, and to graze their stock thereon, provided they undertake as they hereby do, to effect improvements on the same building houses, making dams and sinking wells.[22]

At the same time, Molema continued to make placements of families on his land on less onerous terms.

## COURT DECISIONS, THE NATIVE ADMINISTRATION ACT AND THE MAKING OF THE COMMONS

When landholders made collective claims for land, as the Rapulana were doing at Rietfontein, their narratives of the past were not consistent, and opposing claimants presented their own version of history. The colonial government tried to rely on the courts to establish precedents, but the colonial court's decisions, just like those of the paramount chief, did not derive from historical 'truth'. The political tradition that absorbed waves of settlement on the land legitimated different computations of rental duties and rights. It was not only that the colonial government had limited powers in these northern reserves. The customs of landholding were ambiguous and intricate, and so open to contestation that decision-making from above, by government or chiefs, could not necessarily sway practice. Moreover, like all rules of practice, 'custom' is never prescriptive. It is often like a road map resting open on a table, but hardly used, because people follow the 'beaten tracks' of experience and improvisation to navigate changing circumstances (Bourdieu 1980: 35; see Budlender and Fay in this volume). The Natives Land Act of 1913 had installed the colonial government as the 'supreme landlord' of the 'Scheduled Areas', but could not break the violent deadlock over land in the small settlement of Rietfontein, Eventually, the Tshidi nobility chose the legal route that had earlier brought dividends and took the matter to court.[23]

The Supreme Court's decision, delivered in December 1920, was that 'the Chief's jurisdiction is personal and not territorial' (see Duda and Ubink in this volume). This had enormous implications for the Tshidi chiefs and potentially more widely.

According to the ruling, 'the chief cannot exercise jurisdiction over any particular area (such as the Molopo Reserve) but only over the natives belonging to his own tribe'.[24] Chiefs had the right to rule only those that accepted them based on their own interpretation of ancestry. The Rapulana, who identified as subjects of chiefs in the Transvaal, became kings over their own wards, but so, potentially, were the amaMfengu and amaXhosa on Madibespruit. So was every homestead head who had been 'nativised' as a newcomer on the land through the myriad transactions of rents and status that stretched across the reserve. They could claim to have a chief elsewhere, although some still insisted being 'naturalised Barolong'.[25] This had not been the practice in the Molopo Reserve, or other reserves of former Bechuanaland, but legally speaking such territories could become a free for all after the Supreme Court ruling because it cast doubt on the authority of established chiefs. The court's judgment was not standard practice of 'native administration', but it benefited the Rapulana's view that they were 'cutting themselves away' from the Tshidi paramountcy in Mafikeng.

These events of the early 1920s coincided with pressure on the Department towards 're-establishing its effectiveness' (Dubow 1989: 89). It increasingly sought to monopolise every sphere of government that had to do with 'native affairs', and therefore resented the establishment in 1920 of the Native Affairs Commission, under Dr C.T. Loram. This commission emerged from the promulgation of the Native Affairs Act in 1920 to support 'indirect statutory forms of black political representation, as the basis of a moderate segregation solution' (Dubow 1989: 44). The Native Affairs Commission sat in Mafikeng on 6 and 7 April 1923, hearing representations from 'Lotlamoreng [Badirile's successor], other Chiefs, Counsellors, Headmen and a large number of natives'.[26]

It is significant that the records of this meeting were later attached to the files of the implementation of the Native Administration Act of 1927, which extended the authority of the Department such that by 1928 'it was potentially more powerful than it had ever been' (Dubow 1989: 87). F.S Malan, deputy prime minister and in charge of the Native Affairs Department, had met the same people in Mafikeng shortly before this, and most likely dispatched the Natives Affairs Commission to hear representations. At the top of the complaints by 'Lotlamoreng's supporters' was

> that legislation should be passed to overrule the decision of the Appellate Division of the Supreme Court... in as much as:– (a) personal instead of territorial jurisdiction in the case of Chiefs is not in accord with either Native custom or European practice, is subversive of discipline, leads to difficulty in the management of Reserves and creates friction, (b) the Natives object to the reserves being under the Locations Act, 1884, as this means (i) that

the final allocation of land is taken out of the Chief's hands and put into the hands of the Magistrates or other Government officials, and (ii) that the existing allocations will be disturbed.[27]

They reiterated that the government was guilty of a breach of faith in disregarding the terms of annexation, diminishing the rights of the chiefs and claiming to own the land.

The spirit of these objections is, most strikingly, against the objectives that the Natives Land Act of 1913 had sought to achieve. Apart from 'blackening' these northern reserves, it had clearly failed. Rather, the legal transformation of former British Bechuanaland into 'locations' emerged, almost unexpectedly, with the popular rebellion at Rietfontein. This pressure from below ultimately loosened chiefly power. From the 1920s, the office of the paramount chief in the reserve became considerably weaker, but as an institution of rule, chieftaincy thrived. The resident magistrate, who before could do little to quell contestations over land, now had the confidence of the people to resolve such conflicts.

The shift in power dynamics between chiefs and commoners in the Molopo Reserve was not lost on Loram and the Native Affairs Commission. As soon as he returned to Pretoria, he wrote to the resident magistrate in Mafikeng, A.J.R. Wilmot, to ask for his opinion on 'a matter I am investigating in which we are both interested viz. the position of the courts of the native Chiefs'.[28] Wilmot's response was an exhaustive description of 'native administration' in the territories of his jurisdiction, which he felt remained weak. He recommended that there should be courts of appeal for chiefly judgments, 'in the first instance to the court of the Magistrate and thence to the Supreme Court'.[29] In addition, 'Natives should have the option of taking their cases direct to the Magistrate courts in the event of either party objecting to the chief'. He thought in civil cases, the chiefs' jurisdiction should not exceed debt or damage of £50, and that they should not hear criminal cases where the fine would be more than £10.

Wilmot wanted chiefly power to weaken even further and that of the officials on the ground to be strengthened. Once this was accomplished, then 'chiefs should be given jurisdiction over Natives of all tribes residing within their territory, which should be defined and proclaimed' because, as matters stood, 'natives, residing in the stadt, who are not of the Chief's tribe, can with impunity disregard the rule to the detriment of good order'.[30] Nevertheless, the response of the Department to the 'representations' people had made to the Native Affairs Commission was: 'There can be no question of reversing by legislation' the decision of the court.[31] 'Having regard to the progress in civilisation of a larger number of Native people, and to the weakening of the tribal tie owing to modern conditions of industrialisation, locomotion and education, any question as to the jurisdiction of Native Chiefs would be little likely to commend itself to general acceptance among the Natives.'

Chiefs could continue to allocate lands, the Secretary for Native Affairs continued, but 'the final allocation of land should be in the hands of an impartial officer' who would have the 'power to rectify abuse'. The Department denied that there were ever any 'special conditions' of annexation under British rule. As far as the sensitive matter of 'foreigners' was concerned, the Department relied on Shippard's decision as president of the Land Commission in 1886 to 'purposely refrain from defining any boundaries between tribes or sections of a tribe' such that reserves were available for 'all natives no matter what their nationality might be'. It also concluded that 'difficulties in the management of reserves are not likely to arise if the advice of the Government Officials appointed in the interest of the Natives is sought'.

The situation in Bechuanaland presented the Department with a successful template to open up the reserves to settlement. The solution was not at this stage a policy of 'indirect rule', where a government-appointed chief allocated lands under communal tenure. Chieftaincy was to operate as an institution of direct rule, for people who had no attachment to the 'clan system' that Plaatje described, and wished to carry on with their independent business on the land without the reciprocal obligations that citizenship in the reserves entailed. Incomers were fast becoming the majority in these reserves, under the jurisdiction of the 'white' Native Commissioner or resident magistrate, who had the final authority over their right to enter reserves and hold their land.

All who wished to dissociate themselves from reciprocal obligations that mediated chiefly and patriarchal power in the reserves could legally do so. The entity of 'the government', embodied by colonial officials on the ground, as the sole recipient of taxes for large parts of the population, had become the custodian of the infrastructure of personhood. Not only were officials the centre and apex of transactions of rents, they also tried to control demographic pressure. The only way to settle black peoples into the reserves was to transform white government officials on the ground into paramount chiefs. They – and not the chiefs – would have territorial jurisdiction over the reserves, which in a nutshell, was the spirit of the Native Administration Act of 1927.

The 1927 Act made the Native Affairs Department through the governor general, the 'Supreme Chief of all natives' and allowed this 'Chief' to make and alter laws in the reserves by proclamation rather than a parliamentary process. The Native Affairs Department did not consider this legislation as particularly novel but as the application of proven practical measures and principles drawn from different provinces. While Saul Dubow (1989) sees the 1927 Act as a radical departure, in many respects it followed processes already apparent on the ground in Bechuanaland. The self-made local historian and observer, James Molebaloa (1936) thought that there was little new. He had earlier laid out his objections to the proposed Native Affairs Administration Bill of 1917, which the government did not then pass, but which intended simply to 'take over' from the Natives Land Act of 1913 as a 'scheme for the creation of common native areas' in the reserves.

With respect to the 1917 Bill, Molebaloa (1936) explained that the government would put an end to the administration of justice through the courts, 'shutting the doors of the Supreme Court in the faces of the Native litigants', and instead confer powers upon Native Commissioners. For him, the 'Native Reserves in Bechuanaland are tribal property, set apart for the exclusive use and occupation of the Barolong tribes, and to turn them into a cosmopolitan native area ... is equal to the confiscation of freehold farms ... and a distinct violation of the Annexation Act of 1895'. This would constitute a radical transformation that would 'disorganise the tribal management'. Plaatje had made a similar point that territorial segregation made it impossible to maintain political geographies for 'the exclusive use of native clans'. The Department was facilitating a process of unravelling just such 'tribal' allegiances' and fashioning new routes of political citizenship through its own control over access to land.

In the Molopo Reserves, chiefs, as Silas Molema explained to the Beaumont Commission in 1916, had been gatekeepers. By the 1920s, ordinary people were increasingly appropriating land from below, even letting it to others. In the 1930s and 1940s, the court of the paramount chief, Letlamoreng Montsioa, who succeeded Bakolopang Montsioa, heard contestations over land that reveal continuing migration into the Molopo Reserve, despite the paramount chief's injunction that his sub-chiefs 'must not place foreigners on the lands of the Barolong'.[32] People were placing themselves on the land without anyone's permission and resisted eviction. In the 1940s, Isaac Schapera counted that only 21 of 84 different wards in Mafikeng were Barolong settlements. The composition of people in most wards was a mix of Hlubi, Thembu or Sotho, who spoke different languages (Starfield 2008: 148). They were all 'black', squeezed together on properties that were diminishing in size. The large majority had no attachment to the local chief.

In the Molopo Reserves of Bechuanaland, part of the impetus to dissolve chiefly authority had come from below. Chief and their supporters, like James Molebaloa, felt chiefly power had completely frayed. They lamented the loss of ways of the past, before their reserves became a 'dumping ground for the overflowing black population of the industrial centres, some of whom do not tend to make the best of citizens'

(Molebaloa 1936). For men like Molema, Plaatje, Molebaloa and Lekoko Marumoloa, manhood meant secure roots in the countryside, where one knew and was known by others along a hierarchy of gender and generation, in ways that confirmed and amplified personal esteem. One's neighbours could not just be anybody, but persons (*batho*) who shared a consensus around the moral requirements of personhood, and not merely putting the plough to the ground, but demonstrating respect for social hierarchy.

For a young man to be ready for adulthood, and qualify for a placement of his own, attachment to a 'Barolong' or 'Bechuana' community of belonging had been necessary. Now they had to share it with 'black' peoples from elsewhere. There was a new conversation about hierarchy and the limits of hereditary power as chieftaincy was reconfigured and the government took on a more central role. The hereditary chiefs lost much of their control of the reserve but some continued to realise their ideals as agricultural producers, tilling the land with their own hands. From the early 1930s, the archive of the Molemas, and other members of these erstwhile black landlords, fill up with the humdrum news of harvests, purchases of seedlings for yellow peach and naartjies, trouble with locust invasions, and so on.[33] Letlamoreng Montsioa, a former mine worker with little interest in education, championed a yeoman peasantry and set himself up as a model farmer. Their own tenure was sufficiently secure for investment. These territories became part of apartheid's Bantustans. Mafikeng became the capital of Bophuthatswana.

There is little agrarian production in Mafikeng today, but even now, householders' investment in their property on 'tribal lands' is enormous, and takes the form of fashionable homes. There are no rents, no obligation to chiefly households, but also no title deeds. Across South Africa, settlements on former reserves or Bantustan territories share this feature. The commons are de facto private holdings. Where people are letting property, they do so without asking anyone for permission, and pocket the profits. Yet, this informal privatisation did not corrugate an enduring moral habitus. A home of one's own remains a central requirement for personhood in these areas.

NOTES

1   University of the Witwatersrand Historical Papers (UWHP), Silas T. Molema and Solomon T. Plaatje Papers (Molema Papers) (1874–1932), A979Bc3.2, R.C. Lloyd to E. Barrett, 23 May 1913. Emphasis in original.
2   UWHP, Molema Papers A979Ba29, S. Shippard to L. Montsioa, August 1895.
3   UWHP, Molema Papers A979Aa2.56, J.Molebaloa to S.T. Molema, 4 May 1914.
4   UWHP, Molema Papers A979Aa1, J. Moshoela to S.T. Molema, 25 June, 2 and 17 July, 9 August, 2 September, 2 and 16 October 1912.

5   UWHP, Molema Papers A979Bd1, H. Frost to L. Montsioa, 2 January 1913.
6   Pretoria, University of South Africa Library, Fort Hare Papers, Z.K. Matthews, ZKM_A2_42_Part 2.
7   UWHP, Molema Papers A979Bd1, H. Frost to E. Welsh (quoting communication from E. Dower), 22 January 1912.
8   UWHP, Molema Papers A979Bd1, E. Barrett to E. Welsh, 14 October 1912.
9   UWHP, Molema Papers A979Bd1, H. Frost to E. Welsh, 25 November 1912.
10  UWHP, Molema Papers A979Bd1, E.Barrett to E. Welsh 11 March 1913.
11  UWHP, Molema Papers A979Bd1, L. Montsioa to E.C. Welsh, 13 March 1913.
12  UWHP, Molema Papers A979Bd1, H. Frost to L. Montsioa, 23 May 1913. Emphasis in original.
13  UWHP, Molema Papers A070Bd1, R.C. Lloyd to E. Barrett, 23 July 1913.
14  UWHP, Molema Papers A979d30, S. Plaatje to S.T. Molema, 12 May 1913.
15  Cape Town Archives (CTA) File CSC 2/1/1/717, Illiquid Causes 1913 Volume 21, 244–254, Chiefs representations to commission of inquiry in Lekoko Montsioa vs the Minister of the Interior and the Divisional Council of Mafeking.
16  UWHP, Molema Papers A979Bc3.2, H. Frost to R. Lloyd, 2 July 1913.
17  UWHP, Molema Papers A979Bc3.2, L. Montsioa to R. Lloyd, 2 July 1913 and L. Montsioa to G. Weavind, 18 January 1914.
18  UWHP, Molema Papers A979Bd1, S.J. Molema for Lekoko to G. Weavind, 8 January 1915.
19  UWHP, Molema Papers A979Bd1, S.J. Molema for Lekoko to H. Frost, 12 April 1915.
20  UWHP, Molema Papers A979Bc3.2, S.T. Molema to R. Lloyd, 20 April 1917.
21  UWHP, Molema Papers A979Aa3, S. Minchin to S.T. Molema, 4 July 1914.
22  UWHP, Molema Papers A979Aa3.5.15, Agreement, S.T. Molema with 'Fingoes and Xosas', 24 March 1919.
23  UWHP, Molema Papers A979Bd1, S. Minchin to S.T. Molema, 24 October 1917.
24  UWHP, Molema Papers A979Be3, A.M. Wilmot to Chiefs and Headmen, 23 December 1920.
25  UWHP, Molema Papers A979Aa3, E. Mabusela to S.T. Molema, 4 February 1927.
26  CTA, 1 MFK 9 File 2/6/2, Native Administration Act, No. 38 of 1927 (1923–1931), Representations to Native Affairs Commission.
27  CTA, 1 MFK 9, File 2/6/2, Native Administration Act, No. 38 of 1927 (1923–1931), Representations to Native Affairs Commission.
28  CTA, 1 MFK 9, File 2/6/2, Native Administration Act, No. 38 of 1927 (1923–1931), C. Loram to J. Wilmot, 20 April 1923.
29  CTA, 1 MFK 9, File 2/6/2, Native Administration Act, No. 38 of 1927 (1923–1931), J. Wilmot to C. Loram, 5 May 1923.
30  CTA, 1 MFK 9, File 2/6/2, Native Administration Act, No. 38 of 1927 (1923–1931), J. Wilmot to C. Loram, 5 May 1923.
31  CTA, 1 MFK 9, File 2/6/2, Native Administration Act, No. 38 of 1927 (1923–1931), Secretary for Native Affairs to J. Wilmot, 22 May 1923.
32  School of Oriental and African Studies (SOAS), GB 102 MS 380268, Molema, Silas Modiri, South African Political Activist Papers (1941–1966), notes on cases at the kgotla.'
33  These records are in the personal archive of Sebopioa Molema, at Signal Hill, Mafikeng.

REFERENCES

Beinart, William, Peter Delius and Michelle Hay. 2017. *Rights to Land: A Guide to Tenure Upgrading and Restitution in South Africa*. Johannesburg: Jacana Media.

Bourdieu, Pierre. 1980. *The Logic of Practice*. Stanford: Stanford University Press.

Dubow, Saul. 1989. *Racial Segregation and the Origins of Apartheid in South Africa, 1919–36*. Basingstoke: Macmillan.

Hastings, Adrian. 2001. *The Construction of Nationhood: Ethnicity, Religion and Nationalism*. Cambridge: Cambridge University Press.

Iliffe, John. 2007. *Africans, the History of a Continent*, 2$^{nd}$ edition. Cambridge: Cambridge University Press.

Landau, Paul. 2010. *Popular Politics in the History of South Africa, 1400–1948*. Cambridge: Cambridge University Press.

Legassick, Martin. 2010. *The Politics of a South African Frontier: The Griqua, the Sotho-Tswana and the Missionaries*. Basel: Basler Afrika Bibliographien.

Legassick, Martin. 2016. *Hidden Histories of Gordonia: Land Dispossession and Resistance in the Northern Cape, 1800–1990*. Johannesburg: Wits University Press.

Mamdani, Mahmood. 1996. *Citizen and Subject: Contemporary Africa and the Legacy of Late Colonialism*. Princeton: Princeton University Press.

Moguerane, Khumisho. 2016. 'Black Landlords, Their Tenants and the Natives Land Act of 1913'. *Journal of Southern African Studies* 42, no. 2: 243–266.

Molebaloa, James. 1936. *The Barolong and Native Affairs Administration Bill, Native Affairs and Amacqumukwebe Tribe*. Self-published.

Plaatje, Solomon.Tshekisho. 2007. *Native Life in South Africa*, first published 1916. Johannesburg: Picador Africa.

Ramoroka, Malose. 2009. 'The History of the Barolong in the District of Mafikeng: A Study in the Intra-Batswana Ethnicity and Political Culture from 1852 to 1950'. PhD diss., University of Zululand.

Robinson, Ronald and John Gallagher (with Alison Denny). 1983. *Africa and the Victorians: The Official Mind of Imperialism*. London: Palgrave Macmillan.

Shillington, Kevin. 1985. *The Colonisation of the Southern Tswana, 1870–1900*. Johannesburg: Ravan Press.

Starfield, Jane. 2008. 'Dr S. Modiri Molema (1891–1965): The Making of an Historian'. PhD diss., University of the Witwatersrand.

Vansina, Jan. 1990. *Paths in the Rainforests: Towards a History of Political Tradition in Equatorial Africa*. Madison: University of Wisconsin Press.

Volz, Stephen. 2011. *African Teachers on the Colonial Frontier: Tswana Evangelists and their Communities during the Nineteenth Century* New York: Peter Lang.

CHAPTER
# 9

## Customary Law and Landownership in the Eastern Cape

Rosalie Kingwill

In memorable terms, Tania Li (2010: 408) makes a fundamental point about land:

> Land is solid. It is fixed in place. You cannot roll it up like a mat and take it away. It is invested with meanings, identities, and attachments, and it provides the basis for the muddy, grounded practices from which most of the world's population continues to derive an agrarian livelihood. Making it liquid, turning it into a fully-fledged commodity that flows without boundaries, is a giant step. Hence, it is not surprising that there are efforts to keep it solid, to stop the flow, and to insist on the fixity of land and – by extension – of the people attached to land.

Freehold title has been imbued with the idea of 'ownership' of land in Western civil and common law systems in the twentieth and twenty-first centuries. Title or ownership of land is the very epitome – symbolically and materially – of land with 'liquid' qualities as implied in the quote above. What happens when people resist the shift to liquidity that commodifies relationships to the land? What if other values inform holding land? What are these other values? Allowing landownership to flow without boundaries shifts the subject-object relationship of people-to-land from people belonging to land to land belonging to people (Peters 1998: 360). Land that belongs to people can be disposed of; at least that is the rationale if not the obligation.

In this chapter I look at the interface between these states of 'solid' and 'liquid' by analysing evidence of local customary practices that come into play in two case studies in the Eastern Cape. In both cases land is held in freehold title that is effectively maintained as patrimonial property in families. Despite the legal conversion to title that should in theory encourage individualisation and alienability, the land is in most cases regarded as a family entitlement that is inalienable. These two states of allowing or obstructing 'the flow' of land are usually constructed as a binary, with individual and communal or collective tenure opposed to each another. Closer examination reveals a more complex picture, with implications for the interpretation of customary law, and in particular, 'living customary law'. Oversimplification tends to depict the two states as a choice between two routes with clear consequences. In reality, the shift from one state to the other is neither unilinear nor clear-cut, and the outcomes may be variable. The findings suggest that there is a continuum between ideas about ownership that do not conform to dualistic or essentialist interpretations of the common law or customary law.

I demonstrate my argument by showing that Africans who acquired land in freehold title in the mid-nineteenth century devised ways of managing the mutable qualities of landownership by strengthening the control over familial bonds in relation to their fixed plots of land. The land became the link between generations of family members. Parting with it would be tantamount to social annihilation. To market-oriented economists, this amounts to a contradiction in terms. In a capitalist context, private ownership emphasises the fungible properties of land so that capital investment and productive potential can be realised. Actual or potential sale of land is a critical element in this approach. Switching ownership and control of land from solid to liquid or the reverse involve trade-offs. Either way there are social costs and benefits. Blocking or unplugging the boundedness of ownership recalibrates historic claims and the value of land.

Historic claims to land dispossessed in the past have come to the forefront in recent times. Li's distinction between land as fixed or fluid informs her argument (2010) concerning alienability of land and how this articulates with the concept of 'indigeneity'. The latter puts emphasis on the strength of prior claims in contexts where dispossession is a threat. Li attempts to de-essentialise the concept of indigeneity by suggesting that, as an idea, it has developed as a *defensive* vehicle to counter a new wave of dispossession amidst a surge of global capitalism threatening rural people's access to land in Asia, Africa and South America.

Indigeneity as an idea helps to raise the visibility of historic claims to land by groups of people who feel the need to amplify their political voice, usually minorities. As majorities, Africans do not tend to self-identify by the term 'indigenous', but they do share a similar perception or experience of vulnerability to external threats to land. In Africa the idea of indigeneity may be compared with customary law as a source of distinction and collective identity.

Customary law is frequently invoked in the debates about how to address security of tenure in South Africa's land reform programme. In spite of its stated priority in policy, tenure reform has been riddled with tensions. The urgency of legal reform, and the surge of concern about the reassertion of chiefly power and traditional authority have focused attention on the importance of customary law for protecting rights to land. The emphasis on protection or defence has resulted in policy and academic scholarship disproportionately focused on the role of law and legal institutions, almost always at the level of community. The focus on the collective as the social unit that controls – and now potentially or actually holds the land – has diverted attention from the small-scale processes of property formation in and between families, and how these shape power and authority in their wider communities.

## TENURE AS A VEHICLE FOR SOCIAL DISTRIBUTION OF LAND?

Contrary to much of the literature on customary law as a redistributive vehicle or a 'right to culture', Li's argument looks at the underlying logic of mechanisms often labelled in terms of 'indigeneity', which in Africa could be transposed to autochthony or customary law. Her argument dispels the myths of cultural essentialism in debates about preservation of customary landholding. Drawing mainly from concrete examples in Asia, Li suggests that a re-interpretation of indigeneity presupposes culturally distinct formations of landholding that are 'collective and inalienable' – a notion assumed to be 'naturally present among indigenous people' (Li 2010: 385). She argues that this label has been conjured up for vulnerable people who are assumed to need protection from market forces by advocacy groups and others (whom she labels 'governors' or 'would-be governors'), much as colonial governments had done before (Li 2010: 386, 399, 403).

Li is sceptical about the attribution of cultural difference or 'alterity' to groups whose rights are threatened, with its emphasis on 'the unique vulnerability and the special virtue of the group to be protected and their intrinsic attachment to their land' (Li 2010: 386). She argues that this discourse of alterity, which she dubs 'the communal fix', overlooks the dynamics of dispossession from below, since the assumption misconstructs processes of dispossession as being necessarily or solely imposed from above, arising from the perception that capitalism appears as 'an external force against which indigenous people and their allies stand united' (Li 2010: 385). She is concerned that 'building walls' around communities based on interpretations of indigeneity as a permanent attachment of a group of people to a fixed area of land can be a form of incarceration, placing them within the confines of new barriers.

Li's article drew wide responses from researchers who endorsed the need for a better understanding of the microprocesses of dispossession, which are obfuscated when communities are represented as victims of capitalism intruding only from outside. While some agreed wholeheartedly, others defended a more nuanced position, arguing that some forms of collectivity may represent redistributive relationships that go beyond managing dispossession alone. Pauline Peters (in Li 2010: 404) pointed out that in Africa colonial governments had mainly relied on indirect rule for which they created 'units of [ethnic] authority to govern indigenous peoples, thus overriding their preoccupations about exposure to the market'. The pattern of recognising chiefly governance and traditional authorities indelibly shaped the trajectory of customary law and 'communal' tenure in Africa to the present.

Peters has argued prolifically over the past two decades that despite the cover of communalism, there is increasing evidence from all over Africa of pervasive and intensified conflict and competition over land revealed in processes of exclusion, deepening social divisions and class formation (Peters 1998, 2002, 2004, 2013). She notes that revisionist scholarship of the 1980s and 1990s emphasised qualities of flexibility, negotiability and contingency in African customary law that ensured equitable access to land. She suggests that these ideas have contributed to a new misconception of customary law as inherently redistributive and able to withstand the most acute dispossessory effects of capitalism. With increasing social differentiation, customary law can mask inequality. Though she accepts that the revisionist literature successfully challenged visions of customary law as backward and resistant to change, or that lack of title was a disincentive for investment and modernisation, Peters (2004: 270–71) suggests that the time has come to face more squarely the complex face of customary tenure amidst mounting evidence of growing social inequality.

Li (2010: 386, 408) grapples with people's efforts to stave off capitalism's dispossessory effects. Striking back, however, involves complex and diverse responses, which, as Li argues are 'polymorphous'. In some cases, people have voluntarily entered into market relationships that have resulted in dispossession. Others pursue ideas of indigeneity to stave off dispossession, which in Africa flow alongside the rising tide of customary law. These ideas tend to go hand in hand with collectivism and identification with a community. More latterly, the concept of 'new customary law' has emerged under the influence of 'neo-liberalisation of customary tenure' revealed in new class dynamics and inequality (Chimhowu 2019: 897). These can be messy encounters, since capitalism does not follow a unilinear pattern but represents a set of ambivalent and often contradictory forces, 'each with its own history of violence, law, hope, and struggle' (Li 2010: 400).

## THE AMBIGUITIES OF TITLE

Debates have raged for at least a century regarding the pros and cons of systematic titling as a vehicle for economic advancement, resurfacing in the 2000s in response to increasing competition and corporate interests in investment in agribusiness (Boone 2019; German and Braga 2019). Antara Haldar and Joseph Stiglitz (2013: 51, 59) conclude that a reason for title not taking root in some African contexts is because it has been inadequately grounded in the social context and the cognitive framework of the agents. This analysis rings true, though in the Eastern Cape examples that I examine, there can be no disputing the fact that individual titling took root among the titleholders. However, it became enmeshed in the cultural understandings and identities as well as social consciousness and organisation of the families with title. In so doing, they overturned the conventional legal and regulatory processes of the state. I conclude that the problem must be interrogated using cognitive frameworks that do not construct identity and culture in opposition to the operation of title. In other words, the 'customary' can manifest in many ways.

The idea that social norms are embedded only in property relations described in terms of customary law overlooks the fact that rules governing transmission of title (disguised in statute) are also normative. Who in the family is regarded as having rights of succession? This is a question of cultural practice transmuted to law or custom. A number of examples of historic and current practices involving black ownership with title are emerging in South Africa (see Moguerane and Capps in this volume). In the Eastern Cape cases discussed here, customary kinship ties are maintained over statutory rules to control property relations and transmission. This puts brakes on processes of alienation by any individual named as an heir or owner.

## A SHIFT TO THE 'HYBRID'?

A new tendency in the literature departs from the stereotypes of communal and individual tenure as opposites, using the prism of hybrid governance. Deborah

James (2007) discusses new forms of collective ownership, while I have focused on tenure systems that combine customary social organisation with family governance of land held with title (Kingwill 2014, 2017). Discussion of hybrid governance shifts the spotlight from the units that hold the land – such as individual or collectivities – to the units of administration. 'Co-production' of public administration by state, citizens and other civil or private institutions is another way of seeing emergent modes of governance implying that citizens, corporates or civil society organisation participate in governance, but usually with the state in the dominant position (Sorrentino, Sicilia and Howlett 2018). This is a useful lens for understanding highly localised systems of management in customary or local tenure contexts such as African freehold, though with a reversal of the roles, with the state playing the minor role. The limited reach of the state means that local actors virtually replace state authority. For example, in informal settlements community organisations are often the effective governors, and over time hybrid governance may emerge where local and state actors agree to a division of functions (Barry and Kingwill 2020).

These new forms of authority meld with pre-existing, differentiated, gendered and often hierarchical property relations and emergent systems of local land governance. In the case of individual title, the holding and control of land reverts to kinship structures, resulting in tenure institutions that its adherents call 'family property'. In communal property associations (CPAs), which are also registered in title (albeit collective ownership) access to, and control of land are similarly mediated by customary social institutions. Despite the overlay of democratic governance, these processes nevertheless tend to cleave along pre-existing lines of differentiation, for example ethnic identities or prior claims, as well as differential wealth and status in and between families. When prior relationships, for example, between 'first-comers' and 'newcomers' or 'outsiders', or putative owners and tenants, these relationships can be fraught and become submerged in intractable contests.

The strengthening of community claims may emphasise inclusive mechanisms to draw the poor and landless members of kinship groups into claimant groups, cutting across lines of class. James (2007) argues, however, that there were continued lines of division among dominant and less dominant groups, and that differentiation frequently corresponded with kinship and ethnic ties.

In these examples, it is moot to argue whether rights are privatised as collective or individual property. They defy stereotypical description in these terms and challenge the conventional construction of customary or communal tenure. The ambivalence of privately owned property, whether by a collective or family (meaning kin group), is revealed by struggles and contests that are timely reminders of the inadequacies of tenure reforms that are conceptualised in dualist terms.

The struggle to conceptualise property relations rooted in land also mirrors discourses involving moveable property, such as cattle, where commercial production and social reproduction are intertwined. Donna Hornby and Ben Cousins (2019) use the example of cattle as signifiers of differentiation and commercialisation of property relations in CPAs but also their solidifying role in social reproduction.

Urban contexts provide fruitful lenses for examining these issues. Firstly, pre-existing social relations are not left behind in the rural areas when people move to towns and cities, though they change and adapt. This has implications for recording or registering tenure. Secondly the urbanisation rate in Africa and South Africa has escalated exponentially, and with it, policies that encourage formalisation, with mixed results. While initial registration of rights in surveyed townships is considerably easier than in rural areas, where pre-existing rights are embedded in complex social and spatial relations, the initial registration is but a small step in the process of maintaining title over time. Updating records is frequently ignored, particularly when rights devolve through the family and sales are often unregistered (Kingwill 2014, 2017; Abubakari, Richter and Zevenbergen 2019). In general, formalisation seldom keeps up with rates of occupation and migration to urban areas. The state's land administration lacks the means by which to recognise tenure in informal settlements since there is a presumption of 'illegality'. Tenure is flimsily confirmed via anti-eviction laws. This encourages community forms of control over access to land as well as recognition and management thereof. These examples provide a window into how customary or local practices interface with weak managerial capacity in the state, producing hybrid local governance that follows a different logic from that of the formal cadastre (Barry and Kingwill 2020).

Penetrating these complexities requires deconstruction of ownership. In its formal meaning, ownership comprises a composite construct of a subject's rights, restrictions and responsibilities in relation to a property object. It is an abstraction of how land relations are modelled in a formal registration system (Abubakari, Richter and Zevenbergen 2019), where identified rights holders are matched with delineated property objects. In customary, neo-customary or hybrid models, there tend to be multiple subjects with variable and differentiated rights and overlapping and multiple property objects. Thus, you find both bundles of rights holders and bundles of property objects, rather than the simple dictum of a 'bundle of rights'. This suggests an imperative to redefine property in terms of relations between people concerning objects rather than between subjects and objects. Clearly the national property register is not constituted to recognise these configurations.

## SEARCHING FOR POLICY

Official land reform programmes involve changes in distribution, occupation and ownership of land, but also involve confirming existing rights, perhaps through new instruments. As illustrated by chapters in this book (Fay and Beinart), experts with various backgrounds, including anthropologists, historians and lawyers, as well as facilitators and activists, are frequently called upon to provide evidence or opinions regarding the historic claims or recommendations for tenure when redistribution, restitution or tenure projects are initiated or rights disputed. In their capacity as academic researchers, consultants, policy advisers or expert witnesses in judicial proceedings, experts provide interpretations of historic claims based on their own research as well as the perspectives of claimant families and communities. They offer opinions and proposals regarding tenure policy; some have been directly involved in policymaking, a role that has fluctuated over time. They may also adopt the role of agents of change by actively lobbying various constituencies and advocating for new policy or policy adjustments regarding land tenure.

There are a great many contingencies involved when experts are called in. Methodologies, ideologies and disciplines differ. There has been limited conscious reflection on the influence of such inputs; this edited collection makes a start. Before the formal land reform programme emerged from the post-apartheid constitutional era, a major focus among activists, academics and lawyers, many of them white, was on struggles against forced removals and the imposition of apartheid in the countryside. These threw up networks of land committees, including many non-governmental organisations (NGOs) affiliated to the National Land Committee (NLC). I have worn many of the caps described above over the past three decades and have been active in lobbies regarding tenure policies. I first became involved with land issues in the 1980s and for a 15-year period was an employee and later board member of the NLC-affiliated Border Rural Committee (BRC).

Land activists working with communities threatened with forced removal prioritised defending the rights and claims of people who faced overwhelming threats. These communities had organised themselves into political groupings and the emphasis was on collective identities defending their rights against threats of removal of entire villages as well as incorporation into Bantustans. The focus on forced removals, including legal cases, was part of the anti-apartheid resistance, where details of land tenure were secondary to the human rights dimensions of forcible resettlement. Tenure tended to be oversimplified, as forced removals became indelibly associated with community struggle, which suppressed the longer-term implications of differentiation. In Mgwali, for example, a settlement with title long threatened with forced removal, conflicts emerged on its reprieve. Landholders had differentiated rights based on 'first-comers' who had been awarded distinctive quitrent rights and those without title, including extended family members and influxes of tenants and so-called squatters evicted from white-owned farmland. The hierarchical organisation of these rights was thrown into contestation when land and tenure reform policies were introduced, since non-titleholders were thereupon granted rights that questioned the superior claims of the quitrenters. These and many other similar contestations have proved to be irresolvable in terms of the present legal framework.

A pre-Constitution law, the Upgrading of Land Tenure Rights Act 112 of 1991 (ULTRA), was supposed to resolve some of these problems by upgrading so-called lower-order rights, such as quitrent, to freehold ownership, but it has simply magnified the divisions. It was these seemingly intractable complications that drew me to research on African landholding systems in the Eastern Cape. African communities and individuals who owned land with title registered in the Deeds Office were the very communities, known in the apartheid era as 'black spots', that were among the key targets of forced removal, since they often owned land outside the homelands. Activists and reformers who were involved in these struggles in the countryside were thus often exposed to varied forms of tenure and land administration outside the core areas of the Bantustans.

Other reformist measures by the National Party government during the dying days of apartheid included the Abolition of Racially Based Land Measures Act 108 of 1991, the Advisory Commission on Land Allocation (ACLA) (later Commission on Land Allocation) and the Distribution and Transfer of Certain Land Act 119 of 1993. Along with ULTRA, these combined the ideas of distribution of state land to victims of racially motivated removals with the upgrade or 'transfer' of rights. The NLC, its affiliates and communities with which they worked were partially drawn into these processes, though they objected to the ALCA's narrow terms of reference and interpretation of land reform.

The emphasis shifted as apartheid crumbled and activists began reorienting their understandings of land struggles and tenure reform to accommodate far broader objectives for land reform. After the formal transition to democracy in 1994, the scope opened up for activists to contribute to policy interventions. The Constitution paved the way for a new paradigm and a suite of rights-based tenure laws were passed between 1994 and 1998. Attempts to develop new legislation governing customary forms of tenure were informed by notions of collective or communal tenure with democratic community governance and an emphasis on retention of the commons. The rules were often expressed in local constitutions that grew out of community organisations that developed during the apartheid-era struggles, becoming a mirror of what would become the post-apartheid constitutionalisation of law (see Weinberg in this volume).

The CPA Act was the model for a new form of collective property with democratic community governance for redistributed land or land restored in terms of the Restitution of Land Rights Act, 22 of 1994. Individual registration of existing rights in rural areas was not emphasised in early policies, but extant individual titles remained protected. Approaches to the configuration of local community-level structures and powers of governance shifted substantially across the sequence of policymaking. Statutory community entities based on democratic norms were increasingly overshadowed by tribalist notions of governance concretised in traditional authorities in rural 'communal' areas. This resulted in much contestation, as this volume attests. An unresolved uncertainty in policy concerns the question of registration of individual rights, new or existing. Formalisation of individual rights through title was actively encouraged for urban tenure. In addition, the old reformist pre-Constitution laws remained on the statute books, coexisting but not harmonised with the new, resulting in sometimes contradictory assumptions and administrative procedures for each.

In my advocacy and policy work in recent years I have argued that a missing element in attempts to reconstruct coherent paths to tenure reform has been the reconfiguration of state land administration institutions. An exercise in overarching institutional integration would need to grapple with harmonising the contradictory tendencies between pre- and post-Constitution policies and laws and be more aligned with the realities on the ground. The CPA model, for example, has laid bare many of the tensions and contradictions in current legal frameworks, including unresolved dilemmas when land is transferred in group or individual title.

## TENSIONS AND CONTRADICTIONS IN THE TRANSFER MODEL

Despite different emphases on, and forms of, transfer of rights via the Deeds Registry, the transfer model was a common thread in pre- and post-constitutionalism. It inspired my interest and research in historic forms of title like quitrent and freehold among some groups of Africans as well as certification of occupational rights. Quitrent tenure was widespread in parts of the former Ciskei and southern Transkei, while freehold was more limited. Quitrent was an aspect of official policy in the nineteenth century but stopped being implemented in the 1920s. The system of occupational rights known as permission to occupy (PTO) emerged to accommodate community members without title (extended kin or newcomers) on the land reserved for commonage.

Working from the Eastern Cape, I had come to see the significance of older forms of individual title issued mainly to the amaMfengu whose chiefships and clanships had been disrupted during their diaspora. Quitrent was adaptable and lent itself to civil administrative control and intervention. This in turn limited the power of chiefs and elevated colonial-appointed headmen as intermediaries. Like freehold, quitrent entailed registration of title in the Deeds Registry, but with conditions constraining inheritance and subdivision. Various qualifications became woven into systems of 'native administration' on recommendations of the Native Affairs Department, such as a patriarchal interpretation of customary inheritance that was inscribed in the Native Administration Act 38 of 1927. The rules for African title provided for the transfer of property held in title to 'heirs' defined in terms of male primogeniture. Prior to colonial governance traditional land tenure had, by definition, no proprietary rights. By allowing the passage of land to the eldest son of the family, customary law was twisted way beyond its logic, and was consequently mostly evaded. Evidence from my research shows that families did not adhere to the concept of an individual heir, since it contradicts the notion of patrimonial property held in family descent groups whereby property passes intergenerationally without transfer to heirs.

In the official system of registration, proprietary rights are confirmed by naming identified individuals on the title deed on transfer. The concept and execution of 'transfer' of land through sale or inheritance reveals the tensions between customary concepts of property and the common law. Customary practices tend to suppress appropriation that would give individuals powers of alienation on transfer. Thus, policy goals with the double-edged objectives of confirming both customary practices and systems of transfer seem to be in fundamental tension. Families with title found a way of maintaining both, but since this requires breaking the law by avoiding transfer to heirs (or even to buyers), the contradictions in law remain.

The premise of my argument, drawn from the evidence of African freeholders, is that concepts of individual and communal ownership do not capture the realities of tenure relationships. The case studies discussed below suggest that practices of devolution reveal the logic of property ownership and should be the first unit of analysis.

In its current configuration, the transfer model misses family affiliation and also glosses other lines of social differentiation in families or communal property institutions. Differentiation can be either ascribed or achieved (Berry 1993). Ascribed attributes are birth and biological identity, while attained attributes are gained through education, class positions or material assets. People had multiple social identities and were members of multiple social groups (Berry 1993). These multiplex relationships resulted in particular configurations of human-land relationships.

Moreover, 'land, labour and capital are combined differently in different processes of production and exchange' (Berry 1993: 166). These differential social relations all play a crucial role in land tenure in the societies under discussion. The implications for South Africa are that while communities' common struggle as black people against apartheid and land dispossession united them politically, this did not mean tenure was seen in inherently egalitarian terms.

During the struggles against apartheid, social differentiation was secondary to the main struggle against racial injustice. There was a recognition of differentiation by gender, but seldom in the context of broader social processes. The emergence of extra-legal systems of tenure and the concept of 'living customary law' are testament to the lack of fit between the realities of social relations on the ground and current legal frameworks.

## AMBIGUITY AND DIVERSITY

The process of claiming and restoring land in terms of the Restitution of Land Rights Act 22 of 1994 threw up the problem of how to define the social unit claiming the land in stark relief. Who is claiming? How do claimants' kinship relations affect the outcome of the claim in terms of access rights? What legal entity or entities will hold the land? Who decides? The difficulties of concretising the social composition of the claimant groups have been compounded by ubiquitous tenancy arrangements that sparked tensions between owners and tenants among many claimant communities.

Gavin Capps (2010) analysed collectivised privately owned land, which he calls a 'tribal-title-trust regime', along the platinum belt. I wish to discuss a comparable theme from cases of individual title that arose in the Cape Colony at an earlier period when colonial ideas about the 'civilising effect' of private property rights were at their height, and the boundaries between race, class and culture more fluid. The field research sites highlight the challenges faced by individual landowning families who acquired land in freehold title. They clung to their titles over successive generations in an environment that became increasingly hostile to African ownership. Freeholders were set apart in many ways, including a status of superiority associated with '*notenga*' (those who bought), but were not immune from the overriding concerns of the white South African ruling classes with race. They were exposed to the blunt edges of 'native administration', segregation and apartheid, as well as the turbulence of forced removals and the imposition of Bantustans.

The field sites are Fingo Village, a township in the town of Makhanda (Grahamstown) and Rabula, a rural locality in the former Ciskei. Rabula comprises smallholder hamlets and resettlement villages in the district of Keiskammahoek. The land in question was acquired in freehold in terms of Sir George Grey's policies that allowed for voluntary purchase of land by Africans. Evidence shows that they paid prices considerably higher than white settlers paid (Du Toit, 1954: 27627–8), signifying a level of wealth by the buyers at the outset. The first titleholders in Fingo Village also acquired freehold title in the 1950s in terms of Grey's regulations. They did not purchase the land but were granted the titles on recommendation of the city authorities, which were attempting to clean up the informal settlement that housed the bulk of the workforce by formalising the land into surveyed plots in ownership. They were generally poor, and some families lost their land over time. Surviving titleholders maintain that Queen Victoria gave them the titles as her signature appears on the original deeds.

The policy permitting purchase was an aspect of Cape liberalism in the mid-nineteenth century that favoured assimilation of 'civilised values' among segments of Cape African society who were receptive to it. African people were permitted to purchase private land in the Cape until the imposition of the Native Trust and Land Act of 1936. But policy had already turned towards separate African reserves in the wake of the mineral revolution. Rural Africans' access to privately owned land contracted rapidly with the onset of formal segregation and their settlements were placed under segregated authority.

In the early twenty-first century, the descendants of these early bearers of title, who self-identify as members of family units (which translate into descent groups) continue to trace their relationship to the land that their forebears acquired by title in the nineteenth century. They refer to their land as 'family property'. Title has continued to devolve through successive generations to the present. They did not entirely escape the potential for dispossession through the conversion of land to a 'liquid' asset. Many of the original titleholders lost their land through indebtedness and foreclosure, leading to later generations' avoidance of offering land as security for loans. Those who survived the ravages of forced removals held on to title. Nor did freeholders escape from the racialised geography of Bantustans and urban ghettoes. As was the case of other black settlements (tellingly called 'locations'), they were governed by 'native administrators' in various guises and in Rabula through African intermediaries.

## DRILLING DOWN TO THE FAMILY

The adaptation of Western-style ideas of ownership to African norms and values was not as radical as it is often assumed. African ideas about landholding absorbed the shift to fixity of land without involving fundamental changes to customary social relationships. Social relations under title continued to be shaped by patterns of unilinear descent, which emphasised the primary role of a common ancestor. The common ancestor in the case of the freeholders was the 'first man' in the family to acquire the title. He was known as *ukhokho* (great-grandfather) and all subsequent claims were traced from his name (as the adopted surname) in patrilineal sequence. He became the family name-bearer of the landowning lineage. Most freeholders prefer to retain the ancestral name on the title deed as a representation of the patrimony, rather than the name of a contemporary 'owner' who may have powers of alienation.

The concept of individual ownership and inheritance was not novel in African society but was restricted to moveable property (predominantly cattle). When landownership became a fixed under title, the land was considered inalienable social property, and transfers of cattle continued to mediate social relationships. There was no major conceptual leap to apply traditional patterns of property holding to private landownership, save for the problem that the land was not divisible like herds of cattle and their offspring. The solution was for the family to cohere around the fixed property that became the stabilising fulcrum around which familial relationships revolved.

Sale of land did occur, resulting in irrecoverable losses of land through debt and foreclosure, often understood as a form of dispossession. Unlike cattle and herds that could multiply and replenish, land could not be replenished or redeemed when it was sold or lost through indebtedness. A study of some of the property transactions among the first generation of owners in Rabula shows that there was buying and selling of land. Some fathers bought additional properties for their sons in Rabula when land was still available. However, families who had lost land had experienced it as trauma, which led to precautions against mortgaging and the development of tighter social controls over both family and land.

By the close of the nineteenth century there was no more available land left to acquire in Rabula, which added to the logic of retention. Sons could no longer access their own land and a pattern emerged of families coalescing around the family properties that began to sprout multiple homesteads. In conditions of declining returns from agrarian production (which delinked land and production) land increasingly came to represent social security in a world of growing uncertainty and was thus not used as a means to realise the asset through sale. Families were educating their children and sending them off to work, keeping the family property as an anchor for holding together tight family networks. In both the rural and urban sites, properties remained owner-occupied despite younger generations spreading out to live nearer places of employment, mainly in larger urban areas nearby.

Rabula freeholders have rarely resorted to sub-division unless to resolve intractable family conflicts. This tendency may be contrasted with the peasantries of Europe, which in some cases resorted to 'endless divisibility' by dividing up properties between children (Ladurie 1979: 62–63). In Rabula, owners opted instead to consolidate customary concepts of extended families around properties. In some senses this response was closer to the English model of non-divisibility, which, however, resulted in primogeniture and individual inheritance in contrast to the African model in my examples.

In Fingo Village, the properties were large (1 000 m$^{2)}$ by comparison with current township plots about one-fifth of that size. These have also not been subdivided, but instead developed rows of tenant houses known as 'flats'. Some wealthier family members live on properties elsewhere in Makhanda but maintain strong links to, and controls over, the 'family property'.

Tenancies developed in both sites. In Fingo village they had clearly subordinate rights and were known as tenants. In Rabula tenants and some offspring began to move onto the commonage and became labelled squatters. They were later moved to resettlement villages within Rabula by the South African Native Trust. This set the stage for lasting conflict over the rights to the commonage between the titled *notenga* and those who settled without title. The distinctions have blurred with ongoing social assimilation, and some members of titled smallholder families moved by choice to the serviced resettlement villages. Titleholders, however, retain a distinctive status and strongly defend their claims.

The relatively large smallholdings of the rural freehold villagers allowed for the expansion of families to accommodate multiple generations on the same site. The owners co-opted the unilineal features of descent with the accent on tracing kinship relationships from the common antecedent, or *ukhokho*. This form of social organisation regulates devolution across time through the family linked to the 'first man', that is, the lineage, rather than through individuals. It can be contrasted with the potentially corporatised Western-oriented nuclear family, which has become centred on conjugality and not a descent group, with individual powers of proprietorship, testation and alienation.

Descent-based groups link members intergenerationally in perpetuity through the genius of a unilinear descent pattern that replicates seamlessly across generations without producing independent familial structures. The pattern is generated by members tracing their kin through one gender: it can be male or female. In these Eastern Cape instances, the pattern is of patrilineal descent, through the male line. Descent groups assign statuses, rights and duties, which are highly gendered, and these are reproduced through various formalities and ceremonial events. Although unilineal societies define membership in terms of agnatic kin in patrilineal societies, or uterine kin in matrilineal societies, they also maintain a range of important relations with other relatives defined outside of the descent group. Thus, for example, in patrilineal contexts, daughters maintain close links with their mothers and mothers' kin and may also inherit moveable property from their mothers. Family members do not have single identities, but the focus here is on the implications of kinship for the passage of immovable property. In the case studies access is usually associated with agnatic kinship.

Landowning descent groups were considerably strengthened by becoming property-holding entities in the context of title. Descent groups in lineal relationships can sustain property over time and, in theory, in perpetuity, in contrast to relationships that spread out like branches of a tree from both parents that attach inheritance rights to particular individuals. The model protects sisters of the lineage but provides little by way of lasting rights for wives who are not members of the descent group (Kingwill 2014; Peters 2019; German and Braga 2019). When applied to landownership, the descent group has the advantage of owning separately from its individual members, which could be abstracted as a juristic identity. This construct is a bit like private trusts in statutory law, where members are not liable for the fate of the trust as a whole.

This model does not go without challenge, particularly from wives who are increasingly pushing for more autonomy and pressuring for conjugal rights of inheritance. Some of their struggles have borne fruit in the Constitutional Court judgment, *Bhe* (2005) that resulted in a change of the law making the Intestate Succession Act 81 of 1987 (with amendments) applicable to all South Africans, a move away from customary succession.[1] A recent Constitutional Court judgment, *A S* (2020), has ordered that community of property must be retrospectively applied to black marriages contracted in terms of the Native Administration Act of 1927 that had forbidden it.[2] African male elders had at the time strongly and successfully lobbied against its incorporation in law as the concept was regarded as a threat to patriarchal property relations and anathema to patrilineal succession. These renewed legal challenges may signal more lasting changes to how kinship is traced in 'living customary law'. One noticeable trend is the incidence of women not marrying and applying for their own plots in their family names (Moguerane 2018; Kingwill 2014). This is one way of resolving the tension. There is no longer a clear-cut distinction between common law and customary law models of ownership and inheritance.

The tensions can be seen in struggles by those who seek to retain 'family property' within families and those who struggle for individual control. Conjugal ties are being strengthened for purposes of property control, and the patrimonial estate is no longer the only model, inducing great tension between the genders. Where the family construct is concretised in the Intestate Succession Act, the conjugal couple is the primary bearer of the property relationship and family relations are traced through the mother and father who have equal weight, as relationships are traced bilaterally. Family membership is bounded within a very small circle of members (parents and children) regarded as eligible for succession. This tight definition of family signified a shift from more extended relationships in earlier versions of the law. This model allows for concentration of property in individual hands without gender distinctions.

When property is tied up in descent groups, on the other hand, relationships are traced unilineally and the replication of this structure depends on highly gendered distinctions. However, all siblings, brothers and sisters, claim rights through their ties of common descent. Thus, daughters (also identified as unmarried sisters), like their brothers, have claims. Wives have affinity through marriage and not consanguinity, but a wife is not member of the descent group into which she marries. The descent group is the principal bearer of property in contrast to the conjugal couple (cf. Peters 2019). A shift to inheritance of land by individuals would result in changing patterns away from descent group control and potentially empower wives but disinherit some members of the family, particularly siblings.

The mechanism that emerged to protect family property from these challenges was the reimagination of the traditional concept of custodianship. Individuals are chosen to manage the family property, known as the 'responsible person', sometimes referred to as *umgcini ekhaya* from the verb *ugcina*, to 'look after', meaning a keeper or guardian. *Umeli*, which means representative (of the family) is also gaining common use in urban contexts. This idea is at odds with an 'heir', in isiXhosa, *indlalifa*. Custodianship is closer to the traditional concept of *indlunkulu*, the head of the family who has delegated responsibilities of caretakership of the whole family. In the past this position was always a man, but this is changing. In Fingo Village custodians appointed to manage the property are increasingly women. Men were reported to be a potential weak link in the familial chain in their propensity to be become indebted to local moneylenders and selling the property. The world of officialdom and legalese confuses the role of custodian with the owner. City officials are motivated to identify owners to ensure that service debts are paid by the registered owner. There are strong social sanctions by family and community members against those who threaten the sanctity of family property. Attempts by family members to sell in Fingo Village routinely results in acrimonious family conflicts.

Some scholars have observed strikingly similar dynamics and patterns among titleholders in Kenya and Zimbabwe and have labelled it 'descent ideology' (Berry

1993; Cheater 1987; Haugerud 1989; Mackenzie 1989, 1993). Other scholars show the importance of kinship in matrilineal societies and warn that new inheritance laws have the potential to disinherit female siblings (Peters 2019; German and Braga 2019)

## SOCIAL DIFFERENTIATION

The delinking of landownership and production meant that landownership did not leverage increased production, but it did provide freeholders in Rabula with social anchorage as a basis for upward social mobility. Second-and third-generation families invested in the education of their children, resulting in a significant number being employed in the civil service. Many entered teaching and other professions.

The broad pattern confirms Sara Berry's (1989, 1993) analysis that there is a relative lack of investment in productive capacity of the land, and more emphasis on investment in social relations and networks. Concentration and commercialisation occur within customary systems but largely without dispossession through reliance on social networks for labour and access to resources, including state resources (Berry 1993). My examples confirm the broad thesis that relationships do not 'close' over private property, nor result in dispossession of members. But it implies some brake on class formation.

Peters (2004) argues for a sharper focus on the implications of social differentiation. My interviews show differentiation within families, between generations, genders and wealth. Status by virtue of birth is less important than in the past, while personal attributes and 'achieved status', such as trustworthiness (*thembekileyo*), education and individual wealth have become more important. Family cohesion and inclusivity are based on social affiliation and maintaining social organisation and control, not on principles of creating egalitarian relationships. Inclusive strategies are not necessarily equalising (Berry 1989). There are conflicts and struggles over land and novel solutions are found to mediate them, but often continue to sustain a broad pattern of descent ideology. Small adaptations become regularised over time, a phenomenon Sally Falk Moore (1978: 39, 47–48) calls 'situational adjustment'. An example is for women in Rabula and Fingo Village to retain their family name in order to strengthen their legitimate rights of access and authority as sisters and secure the rights of their children.

As mentioned, some men and women do strain to get out of the obligations of family property and gain more independent rights in order to use property as a basis for accumulation. In Fingo Village, one woman wanted to use the family home as a

B&B, and in another case, siblings wanted to start a tavern. Both faced opposition from their families. A woman in Rabula formally surveyed a plot within the family property, built a bungalow, and registered it in her name directly against the wishes of the wider family. She retained the family name and passed it on to her children. Another female sibling similarly retained the family name, passed it to her children and was set to become the family custodian of the family property in Rabula.

These examples point to changes in gender relationships and greater individuation of property relationships but without fundamentally changing kinship relationships. As families are increasingly stretched geographically, they also invest in homes elsewhere, leaving family homes controlled by their closest kin. There is thus an element of continuity in these adaptations, or what Peters calls 'systematicity' (1997: 138).

## CONCLUSION

This chapter is concerned with the variables that come into play in the construction of property and demythologises the idea of 'the customary' as inherent in social or collective ownership. Debates about land tenure reform tend to oversimply the social composition of collective and individual units of ownership and to represent them as a binary, which the evidence does not support. Property relations are relative and contingent.

The portrayal of gender discrimination in terms of 'women's rights' in African customary systems of landholding is also limiting, as it ignores the way rights pass through families intergenerationally and include daughters or sisters, albeit it at some disadvantage. Customary family units are not automatic harbingers of female dispossession, while many Western family forms have potentially dispossessory effects (see for example, Claassens and Mnisi 2009). Male patriarchal powers were indeed strengthened in official renditions of customary law, which can be seen, for example, in the conversion of roles of custodianship to claims of inheritance under the guise of male primogeniture.

The evidence confirms the importance attached to kinship and descent in property relations (Peters 2019). Political economy and kinship are not mutually exclusive concerns of research, and indeed the building blocks of familial relationships are an essential ingredient of political economy, and key signifiers of gendered power relations. This does not mean that family is neutral ground. It is always a site of struggle around property and power relations (Peters 1997).

The evidence also questions the conceptual distinction conventionally drawn between 'inclusivity' and 'exclusivity' as indications of a rigid contrast between social versus asset-forming property. In the examples provided, family membership is defined as inclusive of all categories of family members regarded as kin, who are not named or quantified. Kinship relationships are, however, sufficiently exclusionary to prevent the passage of family property out of the descent group. These exclusionary tendencies do not necessarily result in exclusive control over access to land by individuals (Berry 1993; Okoth-Ogendo 1989: 11).

The argument formed around the cases suggests that it takes more than individual title to create 'economic' individuals, even more so when families are not arranged in family structures with individual proprietorship and rights of inheritance. The evidence suggests that title does not necessarily invoke progressive or even capitalist transformation, though it does potentially allow more control at the localised level of family. The freeholders in the study show how titleholders use their titles as a means of securing a *social asset* through family ownership, seemingly at the cost of the expansion of productive capacities and relations. Larger questions arise as to how these practices impact on ideas about rights-bearing individuals in a constitutional democracy.

This chapter has raised several questions as to how we think about property in the context of dispossession. Those like Hernando de Soto (2000) who argue in favour of leveraging capital from land through title disregard the reality that to do so requires the right and capacity to alienate it, which means loosening tenure to make it *less secure*. This challenges the argument in favour of title to increase security of tenure. Title does seem to strengthen tenure security against a range of possible threats to dispossession by the state and developers in the cases discussed. However, it does so by defending ownership as patrimonial property that constrains alienation. To many economists this contradicts the purpose of title.

Finally, the chapter contributes to the long-debated scholarship regarding the usefulness of the concepts of 'informal' versus 'formal' institutions. It strongly supports recent arguments that these are artificially constructed opposites that should be understood as metaphors rather than concrete reality, which is a multidimensional but interconnected continuum of forms. (Guha-Khasnobis, Kanbur and Ostrom 2007).

NOTES

1   Bhe and Others v Khayelitsha Magistrate and Others 2005 (1) SA 580 (CC) (*Bhe* 2005).
2   A S and Another v G S and Another 2020 (3) SA 365 (CC) (*AS* 2020).

REFERENCES

Abubakari, Zaid, Christine Richter and Jaap Zevenbergen. 2019. 'Plural Inheritance Laws, Practices and Emergent Types of Property: Implications for Updating the Land Register'. *Sustainability* 11, no. 21: 60–87.
Barry, Michael and Rosalie Kingwill. 2020. 'Evaluating the Community Land Records System in Monwabisi Park Informal Settlement in the Context of Hybrid Governance and Organisational Culture'. *Land* 9, no. 4. https://www.mdpi.com/2073-445X/9/4/124/htm
Berry, Sara. 1989. 'Social Institutions and Access to Resources'. *Africa* 59, no. 1: 41–55.
Berry, Sara. 1993. *No Condition is Permanent*. Madison: University of Wisconsin Press.
Boone, Catherine. 2019. 'Legal Empowerment of the Poor through Property Rights Reform: Tensions and Trade-Offs of Land Registration and Titling in Sub-Saharan Africa'. *The Journal of Development Studies* 55, no. 3: 384–400.
Capps, Gavin. 2010. 'Tribal-Landed Property: The Political Economy of the BaFokeng Chieftaincy, South Africa, 1837–1994'. PhD diss., London School of Economics and Political Science.
Cheater, Angela. 1987. 'Fighting over Property: The Articulation of Dominant and Subordinate Legal Systems Governing the Inheritance of Immovable Property among Blacks in Zimbabwe'. *Africa* 57, no. 2: 173–195.
Chimhowu, Admos. 2019. 'The "New" African Customary Land Tenure: Characteristic, Features and Policy Implications of a New Paradigm'. *Land Use Policy* 81: 897–903.
Claassens, Aninka and Sindiso Mnisi. 2009. 'Rural Women Redefining Land Rights in the Context of Living Customary law'. *South African Journal of Human Rights* 25, no. 3: 491–516.
De Soto, Hernando. 2000. *The Mystery of Capital: Why Capitalism Triumphs in the West and Fails Everywhere Else*. New York: Basic Books.
Du Toit, Anthonie. 1954. 'The Cape Frontier. A Study of Native Policy with Reference to the Years 1849–1866'. In *Archives Year Book for South African History*, v. 1. Pretoria: Government Printer.
German, Laura and Carla Braga. 2019. 'Decentering Emergent Truths on Tenure Security: Genealogy of a Global Knowledge Regime'. Paper presented at the XVII Biennial IASC Conference, 'In Defense of the Commons: Challenges, Innovation, and Action,' Lima, Peru, 2 July 2019.
Guha-Khasnobis, Basudeb, Ravi Kanbur and Elinor Ostrom. 2007. 'Beyond Formality and Informality'. In *Linking the Formal and Informal Economy: Concepts and Policies*, edited by Basudeb Guha-Khasnobis, Ravi Kanbur and Elinor Ostrom, 1–18. WIDER Studies in Development Economics. Oxford: Oxford University Press.
Haldar, Antara and Joseph Stiglitz. 2013. 'Analyzing Legal Formality and Informality: Lessons from Land-Titling and Microfinance Programs'. In *Law and Economics with Chinese Characteristics: Institutions for Promoting Development in the Twenty-First Century*, edited by David Kennedy and Joseph Stiglitz. Oxford: Oxford University Press. Oxford Scholarship Online, doi: 10.1093/acprof:oso/9780199698547.003.0004
Haugerud, Angela. 1989. 'Land Tenure and Agrarian Change in Kenya'. *Africa* 59, no. 1: 61–90.
Hornby Donna and Ben Cousins. 2019. '"Reproducing the Social": Contradictory Interconnections between Land, Cattle Production and Household Relations in the Besters Land Reform Project, South Africa'. *Anthropology Southern Africa* 42, no. 3: 202–216.
James, Deborah. 2007. *Gaining Ground? 'Rights' and 'Property' in South African Land Reform*. Johannesburg: Wits University Press.

Kingwill, Rosalie. 2014. 'The Map is Not the Territory: Law and Custom in "African Freehold": A South African Case Study'. PhD diss., University of the Western Cape.

Kingwill, Rosalie. 2017. 'An Inconvenient Truth: Land Title in Social Context – A South African Perspective'. In *Land, Law and Governance: African Perspectives on Land Tenure and Title,* edited by Hanri Mostert, Leon C.A. Verstappen and Jaap Zevenbergen. Cape Town: Juta.

Ladurie, E. le Roy. 1979. 'Family Structures and Inheritance Customs in Sixteenth-Century France'. In *Family and Inheritance: Rural Society in Western Europe 1200–1800,* edited by Jack Goody, Joan Thirsk and Edward P. Thompson, 37–70. Cambridge: Cambridge University Press.

Li, Tania. 2010. 'Indigeneity, Capitalism and the Management of Dispossession'. *Current Anthropology* 51, no. 3: 385–414.

Mackenzie, Fiona. 1989. 'Land and Territory: The Interface between Two Systems of Land Tenure, Murang'a District, Kenya'. *Africa* 59, no. 1: 91–109.

Mackenzie, Fiona. 1993. '"A Piece of Land Never Shrinks": Reconceptualising Land Tenure in a Smallholding District, Kenya'. In *Land in African Agrarian Systems,* edited by Thomas J. Bassett and Donald Crummey, 194–221. Madison: University of Wisconsin Press.

Moguerane, Khumisho. 2018. 'A Home of One's Own: Women and Home Ownership in the Borderlands of Post-Apartheid South Africa and Lesotho'. *Canadian Journal of African Studies* 52, no. 2: 139–157.

Moore, Sally Falk. 1978. *Law as Process: An Anthropological Approach* (2000 ed., reprinted with International African Institute). Oxford: James Currey.

Okoth-Ogendo, Hastings W.O. 1989, 'Some Issues of Theory in the Study of Tenure Relations in African Agriculture'. *Africa* 59, no. 1: 6–12.

Peters, Pauline. 1997. 'Introduction: Revisiting the Puzzle of Matriliny in South-Central Africa'. *Critique of Anthropology* 17, no. 2: 125–146.

Peters, Pauline. 1998. 'The Erosion of the Commons and the Emergence of Property: Problems for Social Analysis'. In *Property in Economic Context,* edited by Robert Hunt and Antonio Gilman, 351–378. Lanham, MD: University Press of America.

Peters, Pauline. 2002. 'The Limits of Negotiability: Security, Equity and Class Formation in Africa's Land Systems'. In *Negotiating Property in Africa,* edited by Christine Juul and Christian Lund, 45–66. Portsmouth: Heinemann.

Peters, Pauline. 2004. 'Inequality and Social Conflict over Land in Africa'. *Journal of Agrarian Change* 4, no. 3: 269–314.

Peters, Pauline. 2013. 'Land Appropriation, Surplus People and a Battle over Visions of Agrarian futures in Africa'. *The Journal of Peasant Studies* 40, no. 3: 537–562.

Peters, Pauline. 2019. 'Revisiting the Social Bedrock of Kinship and Descent in the Anthropology of Africa'. In *A Companion to the Anthropology of Africa,* edited by Roy Grinker, Stephen Lukemann, Christopher Steiner and Euclides Gonçalves, 33–62. Oxford: John Wiley & Sons.

Sorrentino, Maddalena, Mariafrancesca Sicilia and Michael Howlett. 2018. 'Understanding Co-production as a New Public Governance Tool'. *Policy and Society* 37, no. 3: 277–293.

CHAPTER

# 10

# A History of Communal Property Associations in South Africa

Tara Weinberg

In 1996, two years after Nelson Mandela's African National Congress (ANC) government came to power in South Africa, workshops were being held all over the country to discuss how land reform could benefit groups who were dispossessed of their land rights under colonialism, segregation and apartheid.[1] One of these workshops took place in the Dithakwaneng Community, near the town of Vryburg in the North West Province. The workshop was run by the Association for Community and Rural Advancement (AnCRA) with the assistance of several non-governmental organisations (NGOs) in the Surplus People Project (SPP) network, including the Transvaal Rural Action Committee (TRAC) and the Association for Rural Advancement (AFRA). During the 1980s, these organisations played a key role in helping people in rural areas defend themselves against the apartheid government's forced removals. After 1994, black South Africans who were dispossessed of land as a result of racial discrimination could lodge a claim through the Land Restitution Act. Participants at the Dithakwaneng workshop were the victims of forced removals. In 1996 they became land claimants who were workshopping new forms of property holding that would let them manage land as groups. In particular, they were debating collective land holding entities called communal property associations (CPAs).

At the Dithakwaneng workshop, a facilitator from AnCRA, Peter Mokomele, encouraged the participants to grapple with ideas about land law. He elaborated that they should think about 'rules governing societies (unwritten codes and how we have come to follow them)'. Mokomele asked claimants to write down some rules they were aware of, and what happened if people violated these rules. The participants studied how the newly minted South African Constitution of 1996 was put together and discussed 'how they [constitutions] hold us together in society'.[2] The idea was to come up with a constitution for the CPA that would help bring the community of Dithakwaneng land claimants together. Disputes arose at the workshop between local organising committees (for land security, schools and water) and traditional leaders, whom many land claimants associated with the corrupt Bantustan government of Bophuthatswana. Mokomele asked participants to think about how to write a constitution that would promote democratic leadership in their community, while acknowledging the fissures.

Meanwhile, across the country in Driefontein, Mpumalanga, another land transfer was taking place. The Council Board, a committee elected by the community of Driefontein, had signed a document to acknowledge that a new piece of land would be transferred to the community. Outside the office, people cheered and ululated. The title deed would be held by the Masihambisane Community Trust for the benefit of the Driefontein community to use for housing, farming, grazing or other purposes they desired. The Driefontein residents were the descendants of black farmers who had bought Driefontein in 1912 via a 'syndicate' or company of land buyers. In the early 1980s, the government earmarked Driefontein for removal. Mr Yende, 'a man who called himself a chief' agreed to the government's plan and anticipated that he would receive a house in the area to which residents would be relocated in exchange for his cooperation in the removal.[3] The Driefontein residents overthrew Yende's leadership committee and elected the Council Board in its place. The Board led an ultimately successful battle against forced removals. Yet, in the years between 1912 and 1995, Driefontein had become so crowded that it was difficult for residents to exercise their land rights. People who had not been dispossessed, but whose fortunes had declined under apartheid, could apply for land under the land redistribution programme. As in Dithakwaneng, the residents of Driefontein needed to develop a legal entity that could take transfer of this land.

This chapter discusses the history of communal property institutions in South Africa, especially the emergence of CPAs. It traces how communities, land activists and lawyers forged new juristic entities for holding property collectively, in part through struggles against forced removals 'from below'. It focuses particularly on the former Transvaal province (today the provinces of Gauteng, Mpumalanga, Limpopo and North West). This part of the country had a high number of black-owned farms – including Dithakwaneng and Driefontein – located in areas that the apartheid government had set aside for white ownership and therefore earmarked for removal. Through a combination of archival work generated by NGOs over this period and oral history interviews with land claimants, activists, lawyers and government officials, this chapter addresses how ideas of collective forms of property ownership came about legally, politically and socially.

Workshops like the one at Dithakwaneng, together with broader evidence, provide insight into how black land claimants were carving out alternatives to the reified and limiting conceptualisations of property entrenched during the apartheid period. Under colonialism and apartheid, South Africa's legal system played a significant role in constraining black people's ability to hold land. It served to buttress the eviction of black South Africans from their land. This meant that for most of the twentieth century, 'lawfare' (Comaroff and Comaroff 2006) became an ineffective instrument for black South Africans to make claims on land. In this context, black South Africans often filtered their land claims through chiefs, some of whom were accountable to those that supported them, while others were not (Hornby 2017; Beinart, Delius and Hay 2017).

However, by the late 1980s, the language of official law, which seemed accessible only to a minority of educated black South Africans for most of the twentieth century, had become a key language of poor and working-class black people. The law had become a vehicle not only for defending their interests but also articulating visions for a more just law of property. As the apartheid government started to negotiate with communities over land, lawyers, NGO workers and community activists workshopped legal entities through which land claimants could receive, hold and manage land as groups. They posited communal property institutions as key alternatives to private property or to control by traditional leaders, especially in places where land claimants felt traditional leaders had been complicit in their removal, or attempted removal.

In 1994, after the ANC government came to power, the Land Restitution Act and its accompanying restitution programme provided an explicit means through which individuals or groups dispossessed of land could claim it back. In 1996, the CPA Act was passed, providing a mechanism that would allow people to hold property as a group. In implementing CPAs, land claimants engaged with the complex dynamics of property ownership, including property's propensity to include some while excluding others. In this chapter, I discuss how claimants foregrounded the importance of both official and social recognition of their land rights. They also raised the question of how individual title deeds could be balanced with family members' rights to land. As Christian Lund (2016: 1201) notes, 'struggles over property and citizenship are as much about the scope and constitution of political authority as they are about access to resources and membership of a political community'. The story of how CPAs were made is therefore as much about land claimants' visions for social and political community as it is about property. While CPAs and community trusts have their roots in the rural political activism of the late-apartheid period, they also draw on older traditions of political practice and thought around buying and managing land as a group. This chapter offers a history of collective forms of landownership that has received limited attention in debates about land reform.

By 2019, 1 573 CPAs had been established across South Africa (Department of Rural Development and Land Reform 2019).[4] They have generally failed to live up to claimants' hopes for security of land tenure, economic prosperity and recognition of local or customary property rights (Cousins and Hornby 2017; Parliament of the Republic of South Africa 2017; Office of the Presidency 2019). The Department of Rural Development and Land Reform (DRDLR) has offered CPAs little support in the way of finance, capacity and land administration. There have been numerous disputes among CPA members. Traditional leaders have attacked CPAs, arguing that these institutions usurp their customary powers over land (see Duda and Ubink in this volume). They have also sought to capture CPAs. Yet despite these problems, CPAs are compelling institutions. As one of the few options available for land claimants to hold land collectively, they offer insight into the struggles over and ideas about property articulated by black South Africans in the 1980s and 1990s.

## BATTLES AGAINST LAND DISPOSSESSION: BUILDING PROPERTY FROM STRUGGLE

During the apartheid era (1948–1990), white landowners and the South African government removed at least 3.5 million people from the land where they had been owners, tenants and farmworkers (SPP 1983). The great majority were resettled in ethnically designated areas called Bantustans, which came to comprise only about 13 per cent of the country's surface area. The largest category of people removed – 1.7 million – were those living on farms (SPP 1983). This included farm tenants, who had retained some access to land on the white-owned farms. Their rights were gradually diminished in legislation from the Native Land Act of 1913 onwards. This Act did not immediately stop purchase by Africans but they were increasingly required to do through groups that identified with 'tribes' (Mulaudzi and Schirmer 2007; Feinberg 2015). Purchase largely ended after the Native Trust and Land Act (1936), which also established the rule that any group of more than six black people who had cooperated to purchase land had to constitute themselves as a tribe under a chief; in order to retain the land they had bought, identification with a chief and ethnic identity became increasingly necessary.

Africans struggled with the upending of material and social worlds that accompanied displacement: many lost their homes, cattle, farmland and other assets. Many ended up in settlements located within homeland boundaries that were dense in population yet far removed from urban employment and services. Over 614 000 people were removed from 'black spots' – areas of African ownership within districts designated as white (Winkler 1992). The government saw the increase in the size of the Bantustans as a quid pro quo. But, while whites could purchase the formerly black-owned farms, much of the land in the Bantustans was already settled. Moreover, some of those moved found themselves located in areas administered by tribal authorities at a time when black South Africans as a whole were increasingly engaged in civil disobedience and protest, including rural associations opposed to incumbent chiefs (Murray and O'Regan 1990).

The Dithakwaneng residents, for example, were forcibly removed from their farms in 1973. Like Driefontein, their land was considered a 'black spot'. In 1973 bulldozers and tractors arrived to demolish their houses and residents were moved initially into the Bantustan of Bophuthatswana set aside for people designated to be ethnically and linguistically Tswana. At that point, some residents of Dithakwaneng were still making a living off farming the land, but they were in the minority. Owing to the way in which their land access had been undercut over the years, most Dithakwaneng residents relied on a mix of farming and wage work (as farmworkers, domestic workers or mine workers). In Dithakwaneng, the chief, Modiakoma Mahura, helped resist the forced removals. But when the group was removed to Bophuthatswana, they were put under the jurisdiction of other chiefs whom they did not recognise. In the late 1980s, after hearing that land activists were taking up cases of forced removals in other parts of the Transvaal, Mahura and other residents enlisted the help of attorneys in Johannesburg to record the details of their eviction and look into forms of redress.

As the case of Dithakwaneng illustrates, land dispossession was not an event but a process. Within the areas reserved for Africans that became Bantustans, white administrators relied on the notion of communal land as 'traditionally African' and, although there were regional differences, attempted to codify land tenure in an increasingly national system (Cross 1991: 77). In the Bantustans, chiefs, headmen and government officials had the powers to allocate land rights (but not title deeds) through the permission to occupy (PTO) system (Beinart, Delius and Hay 2017). Hence under apartheid South Africa's property system took on a racialised division: chiefs and communal areas for black people; individual title deeds for whites. As Rosalie Kingwill (2014: 23) argues, the two systems of land tenure reified customary land tenure *and* individual title deeds, belying the complex, messy and more diverse history and reality of land occupation on the ground.

Some chiefs played an important role in struggles against forced removals, such as in Dithakwaneng before the eviction. In certain places, traditional leaders received grassroots support for their functions in land affairs. For example, in Ekuthuleni in KwaZulu-Natal traditional leaders ratified land allocations that had been decided upon at other levels of the group or community (Alcock and Hornby 2004). In Ekuthuleni, land claimants forming a CPA desired a form of property holding that would allow traditional leaders to make key decisions about land (Hornby 2017). But there are other places where chiefs exercised their authority in unaccountable ways (Beinart, Delius and Hay 2017: 15–16). Both here and in areas outside the Bantustans, rural people organised themselves in ways *not* acknowledged, recognised or supported by the apartheid government's model of chiefly power and its dominant system of property.

As noted, in the 1980s, anti-eviction organisations drew in lawyers and activists who had cut their teeth working with public interest law initiatives such as the Legal Resources Centre (LRC) and the Black Sash (Burton 2015). Organisations like the Black Sash worked with lawyers to find loopholes in the law that might offer at least temporary reprieve from eviction (Burton 2015: 86). Geoff Budlender was engaged in these strategies as a lawyer for the LRC during this period. He recalls: 'The law wasn't only unhelpful. It was fundamentally against us. The Black Administration Act was decisive (Section 5 stated that "the Governor General may order the removal of any tribe or portion thereof or any Native from any place to any other place within the Union")'. Budlender added that he 'couldn't figure out what to do. So I tempered my arrogance as a lawyer and learned from fieldworkers and from the clients. So in Driefontein we litigated on pensions and the right to hold gatherings [not on land issues]. We tried to keep the other side busy and engaged, as this would allow time for people to mobilise.'[5]

During the 1980s and 1990s, groups like Dithakwaneng were able to mobilise more openly. Many of them had been displaced as communities and conceived their claims and political organisation collectively. When it became clear in the early 1990s that land restitution would become a reality, lawyers, land activists and claimants turned their attention towards the kind of property holdings that would facilitate community ownership of land. CPAs seemed an especially good fit for contexts like Dithakwaneng, where residents had originally bought land as a collective. They allowed full ownership of land through a title deed that was assigned to the community. The CPA Act offered the opportunity for people to shape official property arrangements into alignment with local land tenure systems rather than rely on rigid apartheid-era structures, such as allocation by civil servants and chiefs.

There were various indirect antecedents to the forms of collective organisation that claimants established under CPAs and community trusts. These included committees established in earlier years for land purchase, religious-based groups, farmers' associations and anti-eviction committees. In Driefontein and neighbouring Daggakraal, there was a long history of landownership committees. When black farmers bought land there in 1912, they did so with the assistance of Pixley ka Isaka Seme's syndicate, the Native Farmers' Association (NFA). Seme was a prominent lawyer and one of the founders of the ANC. The NFA's board, which would govern the affairs of the landowning syndicate, was made up of black directors. The NFA's Articles of Association, written by Seme, set out in detail the procedures for how the syndicate would run, including nomination of board members, annual meetings, the quorum needed to make decisions and how the company's shares would be distributed.[6] In meetings with land buyers, Seme advocated individual title deeds or 'divided shares'. As more black farmers arrived to buy land through Seme's scheme, further land committees emerged. The Daggakraal Natives Committee contested Seme's vision, requesting 'undivided shares' and more accountability by the board of directors.[7]

In most land-buying syndicates, including Driefontein, residents developed committees as well as norms for how land tenure and leadership processes should unfold. In the 1980s, the Driefontein Council board of directors coordinated resistance to forced removals. It also dealt with property disputes, managed requests for land or residential sites, and assisted with access to pensions and unemployment benefits.[8] The board comprised a mixture of landowners (like Saul and Beauty Mkhize) and tenants (such as ANC activist Zebulon Ndlagamandla), cutting across class and gender divisions. Driefontein organisers included stalwart activists and youth. The Driefontein board had established a set of rules to bind their community long before the existence of CPA constitutions. They referred to these rules in isiZulu as *imithetho eyisisekelo*, translated as 'foundation rules'.[9] The Driefontein 'foundation rules' acknowledged every resident's access to communal grazing areas and mills, and sought to regulate affairs between families, such as landowners and tenants, or newcomers and long-time residents. Driefontein landowner Catherine Madlala, who has lived in the area for half a century, relates that residents developed rules for tenants' land use over the years, as issues arose. One of these rules was that tenants, who paid for use of a portion of a landowner's plot, were allowed to build only with mud, as this was considered less permanent than brick. They were also not allowed to keep cattle, as space was limited.[10] However, Madlala acknowledges that these rules were regularly broken, often with the consent of the landowners or the Council board. Nevertheless, the rules were fundamental to the way that the community was organised and resisted forced removals.

Tessa Cousins and Donna Hornby (2017) describe the 1990s as a time of constitutional fervour in the land reform sector. Activist lawyers were involved in exciting legal innovations as they built the new South African Constitution (Klug 2000). In this context, people in Driefontein and elsewhere built on their struggles against forced removals to adapt their earlier rules and incorporate them into their new trust boards or CPA constitutions. Land claimants were attuned to the changing political context. CPA workshops became a space for reformulating relationships with both official law and the government; claimants were keen that the government should solicit their advice to facilitate solutions that would best suit their needs. Land claimants' framing of their demands upon the state post-1994 suggest that they believed they were entitled to the participatory process that democracy portends. The workshops became key spaces in which land reform policy and land tenure law were debated (James 2007; Walker 2008).

## CREATING A VISION FOR PROPERTY THROUGH CPAS

In this section I discuss two interconnected aspects of the vision for property law that land claimants articulated through CPA workshops: first, the importance of both social and legal recognition of their land rights; second, the challenges of balancing individual title deeds with family rights to land.

AFRA, formed in Natal in 1979, brought together lawyers, academics, progressive church leaders and liberal activists. Among the key figures were Peter Brown, John Aitchison, Ilan Lax, Cherryl Walker and Jean Ngubane (Sato 2012). AFRA conducted research in rural Natal, collecting evidence on evictions of black landowners, labour tenants and farmworkers. They engaged the services of lawyers to stall or prevent evictions, and also supported people who were under threat of eviction in their efforts to mobilise. In the early 1980s several more land-focused organisations emerged, taking up AFRA's model of action research, advocacy, litigation and solidarity-building, including: the Grahamstown Rural Committee in the Eastern Cape, AnCRA and the TRAC. These organisations were closely linked to the SPP, a Cape Town-based research centre that sought to publicise and support struggles against forced removals.

In 1983, AFRA and the SPP convened a workshop to bring communities affected by removal together with lawyers and NGO workers. At the workshop, participants discussed how legal forms of struggle could work as part of a broader strategy (Sato 2012). The format for the workshop set the foundation for the workshops that were to follow, including CPA workshops. The workshop began with storytelling and case studies, inputs on various topics, and then a question and answer session where communities from different parts of the country compared their situations and strategies.

The Black Sash, a liberal anti-apartheid organisation of mostly white women, founded TRAC in 1983 and initially employed Aninka Claassens, Marj Brown, Joanne Yawitch and Lydia Kompe (Burton 2015: 93). TRAC worked together with the LRC to orchestrate litigation that might stall evictions, support local organising efforts against forced removals and create a media storm about removals. Between 1983 and 1988, there were intense struggles against forced removals all over the Transvaal. In his interview Budlender recalled: 'I had a steady flow of people coming to me from communities where they had been removed, as well as under threat of removal. Our work must have spread by word of mouth. That's how Saul Mkhize [from Driefontein] found me.' In 1985, the provincial land NGOs came together to form the National Land Committee (NLC) that would play a very influential role in developing policy and law for the ANC's first Department of Land Affairs.

In 1989, the apartheid government began to move away from its Bantustan consolidation model. It also transferred some land with title deeds to individual black smallholders. In 1990, the government established the Advisory Committee on Land Allocations to consult with communities who had lost land. By this point, a few communities had successfully won legal battles to have land returned to them. For example, the courts ratified the rights of the Mogopa community in the North West to reoccupy their land.[11]

Geoff Budlender and Johan Latsky wrote an influential paper in 1991, based on a land workshop held in Houwhoek, Western Cape, setting set out the laws that had led to racial discrimination in the land sector. They emphasised the importance of consultation with black communities in developing new laws that would be sensitive to both existing and new land rights (Budlender and Latsky 1991). One week after the unbanning of the ANC in 1990, lawyers, TRAC and other land NGOs met with the ANC Land Committee to discuss future land law and policy. Derek Hanekom, the ANC government's first minister of Land Affairs in 1994, remarks, 'Soon after 1991, before legislation was in place, we were trying to work things out via the committees and groups that already existed. We knew there couldn't just be one piece of legislation. People say we were idealistic and maybe we were. But we were workshopping the way forward. Civil society was at the heart of constructing our new land reform system.'[12]

These collective efforts led to the passing of the Provision of Certain Land for Settlement Act (1993), which allowed the transitional government to redistribute land titles to claimants via trusts. Hanekom recalled that the SPP and NLC networks played a key role in developing land policy and law for the new democratic government. He established a 'tenure reform core group', which comprised academics, land activists and fieldworkers: 'In 1994 I brought people on board who were connected to the grassroots [land struggles]. People like Aninka Claassens, Geoff Budlender, Ben Cousins, Lydia Kompe and Sithe Gumbi.'[13] In 1994, Hanekom's department steered through the Restitution of Land Rights Act. Claassens described how activists and lawyers who had been involved in anti-eviction work had to consider not only how to secure new land but to protect land rights once land had been redistributed. This led to the series of workshops and Claassens notes that many claimants in the south-eastern Transvaal wanted group-based land tenure systems. Lawyers were brought in to devise communal property institutions that would best suit claimants' needs.[14]

Drafting the CPA Act between 1994 and 1996 brought up challenges that hit at the heart of land problems in South Africa, including how to recognise a range of local and customary land tenure forms, how to be specific enough to hold those in power accountable, and how to right the wrongs of the past in the context of a property system that seemed inherently unequal. CPA drafters often came up against the limits of the law. Budlender, by then director general of Land Affairs, notes that they considered undivided shares (where every member of a community has equal access rights to land) to be impractical from an administrative point of view and 'we did not consider overhauling the property system entirely ... we did have lengthy discussions with the deeds office about how to register land rights. But it was all still premised on an ownership model.'[15] Individual title deeds remained a persuasive concept in South Africa's transition period. Catherine Cross argues that in a context where the legal recognition of property was limited to title deeds as it was in South Africa, it was difficult to rally support for other, more local kinds of land tenure systems (Cross 1991). Cross advocated for CPAs to be absorbed into the Deeds Office, which because of South Africa's rigid cadastral system, would require the specific demarcating of the outer boundaries of each piece of land.

Lawyer Richard Rosenthal was instrumental in developing forms of community trusts that land claimant groups could use to acquire and manage land. However, Rosenthal warned that trusts lacked accountability because if community members had problems with the trustees they needed to take a case to court and request the intervention of the Master of Trusts. This was too expensive and cumbersome for most rural communities. The legal team, including Henk Smith and Kobus Pienaar of the LRC, developed the idea of a CPA, as an alternative to a trust. Budlender explained in an interview that there was vigorous debate regarding how specific the Act should be: 'Rosenthal wanted very detailed rules to cover all eventualities. I thought a light touch with limited details was more practical. The problem is, if you have rules in the law, you will soon arrive at a situation where an entity does something illegal.' The final Act reflects Budlender's approach, leaving it to each community to develop more specific provisions in their CPA constitution. Budlender reflects that 'in the end neither was practical as we [DLA] lacked the resources to manage CPAs. Running even a light touch entity is complicated and expensive. In companies, they have resources put to manage that. In this kind of entity, it was a somewhat idealistic exercise, given our lack of capacity.'

Proponents of CPAs were brainstorming ways to distinguish post-1994 landholding from the forms of tenure devised for black people by the apartheid regime. The draft policy framework on CPAs considered various forms of communal property institutions including cooperatives, unit trusts, share block schemes, South African Development Trust (SADT) land and tribal trusts within South Africa, *kibbutzim* in Israel, and *Ujaama* in Tanzania.[16] The CPI teams decided that SADT land and tribal trusts (which made chiefs trustees) should be discarded, as they were apartheid-era property forms that perpetuated a bifurcated land tenure system between black and white people, as well as entrenching chiefs' power.

Sithe Gumbi, land scholar and practitioner, and former registrar of CPAs in the DRDLR, says there has been debate about trusts as opposed to CPAs since their inception in the early 1990s. Gumbi believes CPAs are a better vehicle for controlling conflict in land reform communities, because, unlike trusts, they incorporate oversight mechanisms from the DRDLR. In Gumbi's view, trusts allowed for abuses of power by local elites, such as traditional leaders. While at AFRA, Gumbi had worked with land claimant groups who felt that traditional leaders had 'sold them out'. CPAs could develop a form of landholding that kept traditional leaders' role on land in check.[17]

CPAs were thus devised to provide land claimants with official legal recognition of their land rights as groups – in the form of title deeds in the name of the CPA. However, social recognition of land rights was also an essential part of the creation and maintenance of this property form (Verdery 2003; Lund 2016). Mokomele emphasised the importance highlighted in workshops on developing CPAs from the ground up: 'As a facilitator, I cannot pronounce my own vision on the community'.

Instead he would guide land claimants by saying, 'the name CPA is new. But in terms of rules, it's something you've always been doing. We want to embed the rules in established tradition. For example, when a person arrives in the village there is a process they must follow to acquire land.'[18]

When working for AnCRA, Mokomele ran CPA workshops using a participatory rural appraisal approach, which drew on practices and funding from Germany. The first workshop would involve discussing the history of the community, such as memories of relationships that people had and how decisions about land were taken. This included mapping out rights and relationships to land, which acted as a social verification of the land claimants. At the next workshop they would devise a 'shopping list' for what they wanted to do with the land: they would brainstorm a vision for the new land and community. He says this process was time-consuming, as in some situations, 'it had been 20 years or more since people were together. People would say, "We used to live this way but how do we want to live now, given the experiences we've had."'[19]

Hornby (2017) explains how she and her colleagues from AFRA engaged with land claimants in Ekuthuleni, KwaZulu-Natal in 1997 through a process that also foregrounded social understanding of land tenure. Residents in Ekuthuleni were seeking registration of their existing land rights (this was not a restitution claim) and AFRA had been called in by the Department of Land Affairs to assist. AFRA fieldworkers began by walking around Ekuthuleni land with community leaders – in this case chiefs and headmen – asking who used which land for what purpose. They drew up a preliminary map of the area, marking all the layers of land rights (many of which were overlapping, such as shared grazing, or footpaths across residential areas). Over the next few months, various residents came to look at the map, talk to the AFRA team and make amendments. AFRA fieldworkers then took the map to every household in Ekuthuleni to get their input. What emerged was a map representing a collective social understanding of land rights in Ekuthuleni. They eventually decided that a CPA would be the closest fit to their tenure practices, although it was by no means perfect.

After the implementation of CPAs from 1996, a number of problems emerged. One of these was the tension between CPA committees and traditional leaders – particularly those chiefs who had been appointed by the apartheid government and lacked local support. Mokomele believes that people held 'traumas about traditional leaders and their roles in removals. So during our workshops these were also issues we would bring up before we can talk about the land plan.'[20] Hanekom acknowledges that during his stint as minister of Land Affairs he was reticent to criticise abuse of power by traditional leaders, especially around election times when his party relied on them to mobilise the rural vote. He notes that 'whether that's the reality or the perceived reality is another thing, but a lot of us in ANC believed it to be real'.[21] This situation became even more complicated during Gumbi's time as CPA registrar between 2006 and 2013. When Gugile Nkwinti became minister of DRDLR in 2009, he put pressure on Gumbi and other officials to favour trusts over CPAs and to avoid establishing CPAs in places where traditional leaders existed. Gumbi noted that based on his work in AFRA (as a fieldworker from 1990 to 1996), he feared that traditional leaders would wrest control of land via trusts and this would be a problem in areas where traditional leaders were complicit in forced removals.[22]

Regardless of this pressure, Gumbi tried to remain even-handed in his treatment of CPAs and traditional leaders. One example where these pressures came to a head was with the Bakgatla-ba-Kgafela CPA in North West Province where the Bakgatla Traditional Council, particularly Chief Nyalala Pilane, entered into business agreements with mining companies, ostensibly on behalf of their broader communities – but have siphoned off the royalties for themselves (see Mnwana and Pickering and Motala in this volume). Around 2008, Lulu Xingwana, then minister of Agriculture and Land Affairs, instructed Gumbi to deregister the provisional Bakgatla CPA even though Gumbi argued that the CPA was the option that the community democratically selected. Due to the stand he took, Gumbi faced intimidation and pressure from individual traditional leaders and the Congress of Traditional Leaders. He had to have security escort him from his car in the parking lot to his office door.

Another major challenge was that CPAs required substantial human and material resources on the part of the government. Since 1994, land reform matters have made up only one per cent of South Africa's national budget. One of the CPA drafters, Kobus Pienaar, used the analogy of a car with no one to service it. Mokomele remarked in an interview that in situations where people had been scattered during removals, and then came together to claim land, sometimes 'the only thing you have in common is the land. Everything else is different. So you can't be surprised if there's conflict. In certain communities especially you can see how apartheid divided people.' He referred to Schmidtsdrift in the Northern Cape, where the Group Areas Act had separated people into the category of 'Griquas' and 'Tswanas.' Mokomele reflected: 'There could be two brothers, one classified "Griqua" and one "Tswana native". These guys had constituted one community and didn't see themselves as different but apartheid did. And so their kids did too, when they reunited decades later. How do you rebuild that old community for those who remember past bonds or build a new one with the youngsters?'

In these situations of mistrust, constitutions were particularly tricky to devise. Even when there was goodwill, hidden dynamics would emerge. For instance, some people felt they had a right to lead in perpetuity as they had sacrificed a great deal in the struggle against apartheid. Mokomele said he would warn people: '"You are gonna fight." They'd say "No, we won't!" I said, "But just in case let's put some rules and regulations down." We'd hammer out the constitution when people were still relaxed.'[23]

Land activist and TRAC organiser Lydia Kompe believes CPAs made the most sense in areas where residents had been bound together by a common struggle against forced removals, such as Driefontein. She says: 'We had Driefontein in mind when we set up CPAs. Here was a community that had been organised for many years. They went from pillar to post until they reached a reprieve from removal. All this struggle brought them together.' Kompe believes that Driefontein residents had spent many years adapting and practising norms – for governance and land tenure – that made sense for the dynamics in their community. She argues that their CPA drew from the earlier Council board, 'now legalised': 'you know at *kgotlas* we don't write things down. Someone came up with this idea of a constitution for CPAs and trusts, to write these agreements down. Every committee I worked with had its own agreement and rules. That's why when we drew up the CPA Act, we thought, okay, we already have these sort of constitutions.'[24]

Budlender notes: 'All we knew were communities who had resisted forced removal or who had been removed. That was our universe'; ideally they needed more time and research. In many land reform situations, the focus is on the moment of 'contract' (Dua 2019) – when legislation comes into being or a title deed is transferred into the name of a communal property institution. But this moment of legal ratification reflects pre-existing negotiations and power relations. Kompe and Mokomele imply that CPAs had a better chance of succeeding in places where residents had built practices and relationships of trust that preceded ownership. Official recognition of land rights is intimately tied up with social recognition.

Deborah James (2000) and Cherryl Walker (2008) argue that land restitution as a concept in mainstream discourse homogenises the history of land struggles in South Africa and that lawyers, activists and the new state were part of this process. But the evidence I have offered in this chapter shows that CPAs were not imposed in an entirely top-down fashion. Dispossessed communities and black landowners helped to forge the ideas that went into CPAs, drawing on their struggles against forced removals in the 1980s. Their priorities were reflected in the legal formalisation of CPAs, which to some degree incorporated social recognition of their land rights.

## INDIVIDUAL RIGHTS AND FAMILY RIGHTS

One of the challenges that CPA creators and members faced from the outset was how to balance individual rights, family rights and the ownership powers of the CPA (see Beinart in this volume). Many land claimant groups agreed that, considering how many overlapping land rights existed between and within households, individual title deeds would be restrictive. In her work on quitrent landholders in the Eastern Cape province, Rosalie Kingwill (2014 and in this volume) has noted that families often avoided renewing the name on their title deeds, as it was more beneficial to have the deed in the name of a dead relative. A living relative could sell off the land without consulting the family; a dead one could stand in for the broader family tree, making it harder for individual members to transact land without consultation. But although titles held by individuals would not fit the realities of most land claimants, they also realised that by transferring title to a CPA, the rights of households and individuals within those households would be elided (Hornby 2017).

Land activists responsible for the CPA property model in the early and mid-1990s – especially in NGOs – emphasised an egalitarian distribution of wealth. A consultation group brought together by the DLA in 1994 to draft a policy framework on communal ownership argued that CPAs could balance the 'broad public interest' of land reform with the 'narrower private interest of the community concerned, and its individual members'. The CPA Act also envisioned the inclusion of all those with an interest in the land – such as labour tenants – within the boundaries of the claimant community.[25] Neither the CPA Act of 1996 nor the Interim Protection of Informal Land Rights Act of 1996 offered much assurance to individuals within the group. The CPA Act considered the CPA 'community' to mean 'a group of persons, which wishes to have its rights to or in particular property determined by shared rules under a written constitution' (section 1 (iv)). The CPA Act required that 'a member may not be excluded from access to or use of any part of the association's property which has been allocated for such member's exclusive or the communal use except in accordance with the procedures set out in the constitution' (section 9 (1)(d)). However, the drafters envisaged that CPA constitutions would devise rules that were sensitive to each specific community.[26] The CPA constitutions were to be imbued with the values being articulated in South Africa's broader Constitution-making process, including (as the NLC put it) 'non-racism, non-sexism, integrity, transparency, accountability and gender equality'.

When CPAs actually came into existence, workshops were held to discuss tensions between community and family rights.[27] Claimants would draw up maps of their land and whose rights would be exercised where. But when they tried to implement these maps, they found little recourse in the law to help them. In order to counteract the marginalisation of household rights, AFRA organised a piece of participatory theatre. Participants were asked to imagine that a CPA already existed. Who were all the role-players involved? What did they have rights to? What happened if rights clashed? How would they balance the CPA's powers to allocate land with those of traditional leaders? Did listing as CPA members entitle them to land rights? By workshopping these and related questions, residents of Ekuthuleni tried to translate their local land tenure dynamics into the vessel of a CPA. They decided the best mechanism would be a registry of rights within the CPA that could be overseen by the DLA. However, this plan fell through when it became clear the DLA did not have the capacity to oversee such a registry. And so, there was a disjuncture between social and legal recognition, as well as individual and group rights. This is a conundrum that remains unsettled.

Women in particular found it difficult to assert their rights to land within the family, and within the broader CPA. In many claimant communities, women fought for membership in their own names as well as for positions of leadership on CPA committees. Kompe recounts how rural women's committees from all over the country came together to form the National Movement of Rural Women in 1990, to push for recognition: 'We were fighting not only apartheid but also men who used "culture" as the argument that no women should own land'.[28] In Driefontein, women, who had been excluded from leadership in the early 1980s, fought their way onto the Council board and then the Masihambisane Trust. Beauty Mkhize, Jane Vilakazi, Catherine Madlala and others would come together at night and strategise how to intervene in meetings. They argued that they were the ones on the front line when the bulldozers approached, as men were often away working in the cities. They too were the guardians of farming on their plots. They united with youth who had also often been excluded. By the early 1990s, they were at the forefront of decision-making about land in Driefontein. This gender equality came about through struggles and melded with the making of communal property institutions. But it remained challenging to implement in CPAs.

Most CPA workshops involved a mapping process, when participants were drawing up the boundaries of their community, literally and figuratively. In a workshop for the Putfontein CPA in Ramatlabama in the North West Province in 1996, most of the participants were the descendants of the original nineteenth-century purchasers.[29] The participants decided that some people would be excluded from the reconstructed Putfontein 'community' – in this instance, labour tenants who had worked for the purchasers and would only be given grazing rights. The Putfontein group's decisions about the role of labour tenants reveals friction between the expectations held by some of the Putfontein land claimants and the inclusive model that activists had in mind for CPAs – in which also those in need of land and not only those seeking restitution should benefit from the process. Claimants came up against activists who argued CPAs should play a role in correcting the wrongs of South Africa's exclusionary property system as a whole.

Similar dynamics emerged elsewhere between historic land purchasers and their tenants (Hornby 2015; James 2000). So long as people were engaged in struggles against forced removals, they came together and stuck together.[30] As a TRAC pamphlet warned in 1989, 'It is important to look beyond the romantic stories of rural struggles to the conflicts, divisions and inequalities in rural society. This is not a never-never job for after the revolution.' Hornby (2015: 53) argues that it was difficult to resolve the 'contradiction between social reproduction and economic accumulation'; differentiation among land claimants manifested when the group considered not only how to hold land but also how to manage enterprises on the land.

Conflicts bubbled to the surface between different kinds of land rights holders. In Driefontein residents partially resolved these tensions by looking to histories of struggle. The descendants of the land purchasers had individual plots. Once the eviction was stayed and the possibility emerged of getting new land, purchasers started evicting tenants. However, some intervened, including purchasers and said, 'The tenants were part of the struggle against eviction — you cannot now evict them'.[31] As land transfers became imminent through South Africa's land reform process, landowners asserted their historical rights to 'ownership' while labour tenants had argued that their *struggles* had given them rights to land (Hornby 2015). But without social recognition or capacity within the CPA Registrar's Office, it was difficult to enforce tenants' rights or to purchase additional land for them.

All forms of property involve mechanisms of inclusion and exclusion (Verdery 2003). But title deeds in South Africa have a particularly strong habit of 'cutting the network' (Strathern 1996) of relationships developed through social ties and common struggles. When putting the title deed in the name of a CPA, attempts were sometimes made to slice off the network around the edges, leading to exclusion. Activists in Driefontein tried to deal with the disputes between land purchasers and tenants to broaden the 'network' and shape a form of property holding that was theoretically more inclusive than a replication of the older ownership rights. CPAs had to grapple with these tensions with uncertain outcomes. Some of the burden of creating a more equal society was in a sense placed on poorer rural families.

## CONCLUSION

During the 1980s and 1990s people involved in struggles against eviction in the rural areas sought out new forms of organisation and property holding that differed both from those available in the Bantustans and also from individual privately owned smallholdings. CPAs emerged from the interaction between land claimants, lawyers and activists. Organisations such as AFRA, AnCRA and TRAC ran workshops in which land claimants debated and practised legal repertoires of claim-making. Together they workshopped strategies to shield people against evictions and articulate ideas about a national land tenure system that would govern how land would be transferred in a democratic South Africa. Their views drew on their varied experiences and their immediate practices as landholders – as well as arguments about redressing inequality in a democratic South Africa.

During the implementation of land reform, the intensive workshops that occurred in places like Dithakwaneng and Ekuthuleni gradually fell away (Cousins and Hornby 2017). The process of establishing a CPA increasingly involved limited engagement before land transfer and cut and paste constitutions. CPA members struggled to hold committees accountable and to make decisions about land use. Government officials found it difficult to understand tensions within CPAs and often assumed that traditional leaders held power over land. CPA members were in turn frustrated about the lack of support and sometimes thought that restitution and the CPA process failed to account for social recognition and tenure realities. The history of CPAs suggests that contemporary South African property law, which has roots in colonial and apartheid systems that undermined African society and bolstered white authority, continues to pay insufficient attention to local forms of knowledge and legitimacy about property. More investment in and acknowledgement of the networks that comprise property forms like CPAs is critical if South Africa is to create a more equal property system and society.

NOTES

1   Thanks to the Social Sciences Research Council, the Race, Law & History Program, African Studies Centre, Department of Afroamerican and African Studies, and the Department of History at University of Michigan, Rosalie Kingwill, William Beinart, Laura Phillips, Aninka Claassens, Sithe Gumbi, Derek Peterson, Rebecca Scott and Sam Erman.
2   University of the Witwatersrand Historical Papers (UWHP), National Land Committee (NLC) archive K.7.3 AG3246, Association for Community and Rural Advancement (AnCRA), Case Study of Dithakwaneng Community, 1999.

3   Beauty Mkhize, interviewed by Tara Weinberg, Cape Town, 21 February 2019 (Mkhize interview).
4   Community trusts are harder to quantify as they are registered with the Master of the High Court, and trusts for the purpose of land reform are not distinguished from other trusts.
5   Geoff Budlender, interviewed by Tara Weinberg, Cape Town, 30 May 2019 (Budlender interview).
6   Pretoria, National Archives, NTS 3439 56/308, National Farmers' Association Articles of Association, 18 October 1912.
7   Pretoria, National Archives, NTS 3440 56/308 Daggakraal Natives Memorandum to his Worship the Native Commissioner for Wakkerstroom, 1920.
8   Jane Vilakazi, interviewed by Tara Weinberg, Driefontein, 24 November 2018.
9   Aninka Claassens, interviewed by Tara Weinberg, Cape Town, 25 June 2018 (Claassens interview).
10  Catherine Madlala, interviewed by Tara Weinberg, Driefontein, 25 February 2019 (Madlala interview).
11  UWHP, Transvaal Rural Action Committee (TRAC) archive 3 pub AG2375, manuscript entitled '*Umhlaba*: Rural Struggles in the Transvaal in the 80s', November 1989. See also Lydia Kompe, interviewed by Tara Weinberg, Polokwane, 18 November 2018 and Matlala, 13 September 2019 (Kompe interview).
12  Derek Hanekom, interviewed by Tara Weinberg, Johannesburg, 22 September 2019 (Hanekom interview).
13  Hanekom interview.
14  Claassens interview.
15  Budlender interview.
16  UWHP, TRAC archive 11 cpa AG2735, Richard Rosenthal Consultancy, Draft Policy Framework for Legislative Proposals on Communal Ownership, 20 July 1994.
17  Sithe Gumbi, interviewed by Tara Weinberg, via Skype, 24 January 2020 (Gumbi interview).
18  Peter Mokomele, interviewed by Tara Weinberg, Johannesburg, 23 August 2019 (Mokomele interview).
19  Mokomele interview.
20  Mokomele interview.
21  Mokomele interview; Hanekom interview.
22  Gumbi interview.
23  Mokomele interview.
24  Kompe interview.
25  UWHP, NLC archive 1.1 AG3246, National Land Committee Work Programmes: Work plans 1991–1995.
26  Gumbi interview.
27  David Mayson and Rick de Satge, interviewed by Tara Weinberg, Cape Town, 21 February 2019.
28  Kompe interview.
29  UWHP, TRAC archive 11 cpa AG2735, Report of CPA Workshop Proceedings in Putfontein, 1998.
30  Claassens interview; Donna Hornby, interviewed by Tara Weinberg, via Skype, 26 June 2018.
31  Mkhize interview.

## REFERENCES

Alcock, Rauri and Donna Hornby. 2004. 'Traditional Land Matters: A Look into Land Administration in Tribal Areas in KwaZulu-Natal'. Pietermaritzburg: Occasional Paper for the Legal Entity Assessment Project (LEAP).

Beinart, William, Peter Delius and Michelle Hay. 2017. *Rights to Land: A Guide to Tenure Upgrading and Restitution in South Africa*. Johannesburg: Jacana Media.

Budlender, Geoff and Johan Latsky. 1991. 'Unravelling Rights to Land to Agricultural Activities in Rural Race Zones'. *South African Journal of Human Rights* 24: 155–177.

Burton, Mary. 2015. *The Black Sash: Women for Justice and Peace*. Johannesburg: Jacana Media.

Comaroff, John and Jean Comaroff. 2006. *Law and Disorder in the Postcolony*. Chicago: University of Chicago Press.

Cousins, Tessa and Donna Hornby. 2017. 'Leaping the Fissures: Bridging the Gap between Paper and Real Practice in Setting up Common Property Institutions in Land Reform in South Africa'. In *Untitled: Securing Land Tenure in Urban and Rural South Africa*, edited by Donna Hornby, Rosalie Kingwill, Lauren Royston and Ben Cousins, 320–360. Pietermaritzburg: University of KwaZulu-Natal Press.

Cross, Catherine. 1991. 'Landholding Systems in African Rural Areas'. In *A Harvest of Discontent*, edited by Mike de Klerk, 63–98. Cape Town: IDASA.

Department of Rural Development and Land Reform. 2019. 'CPA Annual Report 2018–2019'. drdlr.gov.za/sites.

Dua, Jatin. 2019. *Captured at Sea: Piracy and Protection in the Indian Ocean*. Oakland: University of California Press.

Feinberg, Harvey. 2015. *Our Land, Our Life, Our Future: Black South African Challenges to Territorial Segregation, 1913–1948*. Pretoria: Unisa Press.

Hornby, Donna. 2015. 'Cattle, Commercialisation and Land Reform: Dynamics of Social Reproduction and Accumulation in Besters, KwaZulu-Natal'. PhD diss., University of the Western Cape.

Hornby, Donna. 2017. 'Becoming Visible on the Grid: Attempts to Secure Tenure at Ekuthuleni'. In *Untitled: Securing Land Tenure in Urban and Rural South Africa*, edited by Donna Hornby, Rosalie Kingwill, Lauren Royston and Ben Cousins, 94–131. Pietermaritzburg: University of KwaZulu-Natal Press.

James, Deborah. 2000. 'Hill of Thorns: Custom, Knowledge and the Reclaiming of a Lost Land in the New South Africa'. *Development and Change* 31, no. 3: 629–649.

James, Deborah. 2007. *Gaining Ground: 'Rights' and 'Property' in South African Land Reform*. New York: Routledge-Cavendish.

Kingwill, Rosalie. 2014. 'The Map is Not the Territory: Law and Custom in "African Freehold": A South African Case Study'. PhD diss., University of the Western Cape.

Klug, Heinz. 2000. *Constituting Democracy: Law, Globalism and South Africa's Political Reconstruction*. Cambridge: Cambridge University Press.

Lund, Christian. 2016. 'Rule and Rupture: State Formation through the Production of Property and Citizenship'. *Development and Change* 47, no. 6: 1199–1228.

Mulaudzi, Christopher and Stefan Schirmer. 2007. 'Land Struggles in the 20th Century'. In *Mpumalanga History and Heritage*, edited by Peter Delius, 351–392. Scottsville: University of KwaZulu-Natal Press.

Murray, Christina and Catherine O'Regan. 1990. *No Place to Rest: Forced Removals and the Law in South Africa*. Cape Town: Oxford University Press.

Office of the Presidency, Republic of South Africa. 2019. *Final Report of the Presidential Advisory Panel on Land Reform and Agriculture*.

Parliament of the Republic of South Africa. 2017. *Report of the High Level Panel on the Assessment of Key Legislation and the Acceleration of Fundamental Change*.

Sato, Chizuko. 2012. 'Casting a Voice for Rural Struggles during Apartheid: The Case of AFRA'. Institute of Developing Economies Discussion Paper No. 351, Japan External Trade Organisation.

Strathern, Marilyn. 1996. 'Cutting the Network'. *Journal of the Royal Anthropological Institute* 2, no. 3 (Sep): 517–535.

SPP (Surplus People Project). 1983. *Forced Removals in South Africa, Volume 1, General Overview*. Cape Town: Surplus People Project.

Verdery, Katherine. 2003. *The Vanishing Hectare: Property and Value in Postsocialist Transylvania*. Ithaca: Cornell University Press.

Walker, Cherryl. 2008. *Landmarked: Land Claims and Land Restitution in South Africa*. Johannesburg: Jacana.

Winkler, Harald. 1992. 'Direct Action to Restore Land'. *Work in Progress* 81: 26–27.

CHAPTER

# 11

## 'This is Business Land':
## The Hlolweni Land Claim, 1983–2016

Raphael Chaskalson

The 'land question' remains at the centre of South African political discourse. Land restitution has been an important strategy for addressing racially unequal ownership of land as well as forced removals in the apartheid era. This chapter focuses on the *Hlolweni* (2003) land claim, made by 883 families from three poor, rural communities in the Eastern Transkei (Mpondoland) – the villages of Mfolozi, Etyeni and Hlolweni. Starting in 1983, these families were forcefully removed from about 10 000 ha to make way for a sugar cane plantation and outgrower scheme. The families brought a restitution claim to the Eastern Cape office of the Land Claims Commission in 1995, which eventually came to court in 2009. By this time the Eastern Cape government, which controlled the land, had agreed to the claim but the claimants were opposed in court by three associations of black smallholder farmers who had been beneficiaries of the scheme. The claimants secured a favourable judgment in 2010.[1]

A historical study of this land claim is significant for two principal reasons. Firstly, it highlights important challenges in settling restitution claims on land in the former Bantustans (homelands), particularly when the chosen legal vehicle to hold the restituted land is a communal property association (CPA – see Weinberg in this volume). Secondly, the claim is significant from a broader historiographical point of view, in that it informs our understanding of how African 'communal tenure' has evolved over time. The central argument in this chapter is that wider economic and political forces affect how people perceive rights to a particular plot of land, and that these perceptions can change over time. The *Hlolweni* claim is an instructive case study because, during the period assessed here, three distinct understandings of how a piece of land may be used have evolved amongst the same group of people. This is an important argument, as much of the existing literature posits ideas of customary or communal tenure that are too static.

The question of who 'owns' land in the former homelands has been deeply contested historically. For much of the colonial and apartheid era, officials referred to the system of occupation in these areas as 'communal' or 'customary' tenure. Sydney H. Fazan, a Kenyan official writing on the Transkei during the 1940s, cites a number of magistrates claiming that codified systems of land administration were designed 'to copy Native custom' (Fazan 1944: 46–47). Land was considered 'the common property of the tribe, vested in the chief'. This argument implies a position of prominence for the chief in control over land transactions, and weak individual or household rights.

Scholars and activists have criticised this characterisation. Alastair Kerr (1953) argues that under African customary law, chiefs in South Africa had a largely administrative role in the allocation of sites to families and the regulation of grazing commons. This did not entail the right to alienate land already occupied, unless the occupants 'committed a serious crime' like witchcraft or 'disturbing the peace' (Kerr 1953: 13–15). Kerr also suggests that customary entitlements varied depending on the land's function. The wider community had rights to grazing commons, whilst individuals had strong rights to residential plots and arable fields (Kerr 1994). To emphasise the strength of these individual rights, Kerr explicitly uses the term 'ownership'. This marked a significant break with earlier South African jurisprudence, which suggested that there 'was no individual ownership of land in Native law' (Kerr 1953: 29–33).

Africanist scholars might object to Kerr's use of the term 'ownership'. For Sara Berry (1993: 106–107), narrow categories of communal or individual ownership obscure the fact that African tenure regimes have remained flexible over time, adapting to changing local circumstances (see Kingwill in this volume). Nevertheless, the key tenets of Kerr's argument have been influential in post-apartheid South Africa. For Ben Cousins and Aninka Claassens (2005: 250) traditional characterisations of communal tenure 'imply a common ownership of all resources of production, which is rarely the case'. They continue: 'Communities often restrict alienation of land to outsiders, and seek to maintain the identity, coherence and livelihood security of the group. In these systems, allocation of residential and arable land usually results in secure rights for individuals or families, with the household being the basic unit of production.'

They emphasise that rights to land and commonage have historically been 'nested' or 'layered' in nature. Although individual rights to residential and arable plots were recognised, people also had collective rights to other land like grazing commons and forest resources. Like Kerr, Claassens and Cousins (2008) stress the administrative role of chiefs and headmen. The Constitutional Court's subsequent jurisprudence emphasises that African customary law is 'living' – that is, based on mutually understood rules that evolve to meet the community's needs (see Budlender in this volume). In a recent survey of the court's jurisprudence, Claassens and Geoff Budlender (2016) use the concept of 'living law' to emphasise the strength of household rights and limitations on chiefly power. Given that African customary tenure has never been fully codified, and has been subject to many legislative interventions, understanding its evolution is a fundamentally historical question.

This recent scholarship emphasises the strength of household rights in areas under chiefly control. This chapter argues, however, that it is nevertheless too static an account of tenure relations in the former homelands. Berry's influential book *No Condition is Permanent* (1993: 15–16) stresses that 'agrarian change in Africa has been shaped by the way power, economy and culture have come together at particular times and places' and that tenure regimes adapt to local contexts. *Hlolweni* shows that three different understandings of rights to the same piece of land evolved over time, sometimes at the *expense* of household entitlements. These ideas were not necessarily imposed by a pliant chief, but came to be socially recognised – the essence of 'living law'. Thus, the central argument of this chapter is that Claassens and Cousins (2008) underplay the extent to which understandings of land rights can change, depending on economic and political circumstances. A related point is that people can have more than one understanding of land rights at the same time.

## THE POLITICS OF LAND AND DEVELOPMENTALISM DURING THE BANTUSTAN ERA

The 1951 Bantu Authorities Act conferred increasing power on tribal authorities in the former Transkei, of which Hlolweni was part (Southall 1982). The 1950s also saw the extension and consolidation of the homelands in pursuit of territorial segregation for the country as a whole. The bulk of new land purchased by the South

African government for the Bantustans was allocated to tribal authorities. The Transkei attained 'self-governing' status in 1963, followed by 'independence' in 1976 under Chief Kaiser Matanzima.

In the Transkei, tribal authorities became responsible for handling applications for plots of land. Recommendations would then be made to a magistrate who, in theory, would issue a permission to occupy (PTO) certificate to household heads. In parts of Mpondoland, these were not issued, as centralised state systems of land administration remained weak. Nevertheless, the conferring of greater power to transact land and resources onto Bantustan elites weakened the tenure security of rural people. Lungisile Ntsebeza (2006) documents an increasingly corrupt relationship between chiefs and the Transkei state. However, the interests of Bantustan governments and chiefs did not necessarily always align. Bophuthatswana leader Lucas Mangope supported Impala Platinum in a dispute with the Bafokeng Tribal Authority, who found themselves in a legal battle to accrue royalties from mining on tribal land. It was in Mangope's interest to maintain a good relationship with Impala: during the 1980s, tax from mining accounted for half of Bophuthatswana's government revenue (Capps 2016 and in this volume). In the Transkei too, some chiefs were undermined by the Bantustan government when it thought this necessary.

Although Matanzima was largely dependent on the South African state, he acquired important local powers and sought to impose a paternalistic vision of development onto the homeland's largely poor and rural population. In order to legitimise their nascent states, most homelands set up development agencies to promote industrial and agricultural employment within their borders. The Transkei Development Corporation (TDC) was established in 1976 and the Transkei Agricultural Corporation (TRACOR) in 1981. Much of the existing literature on homeland developmentalism stresses the economic irrationality and failure of these projects. Writing on the Transkei's Magwa Tea plantation, Thembela Kepe argues that homeland agricultural ventures 'were often less motivated by real concerns to reduce poverty, or by clear possibilities of economic success, but by complex political motives of the Apartheid government' (2005: 262).

At independence about 70 per cent of Transkei government revenues came from South African government grants. However, it is important to recognise that in spite of their political conservatism and economic dependence on South Africa, some in the homeland bureaucracies had ambitious visions of state-led development in the countryside. This caveat is not intended to legitimise the Bantustan project, or its authoritarian and corrupt attributes. Archie Nkonyeni (2012: 133), a former TDC board member who was appointed to the management of Magwa Tea in 1978, captures the nuance between apartheid politics and genuine developmental imperatives in the Transkei: 'It is true that the Apartheid government, for its own selfish desires, needed to create the façade of viable economies in the areas under the eye of Bantu Authorities. But this did not cancel the legitimate need for job creation in these areas, for the sole purpose of ensuring that people were not left helpless in the face of absolute poverty staring them in the face.'

The Transkei state viewed commercial agriculture as a key route to development (Nkuhlu 1989) and the North Pondoland Sugar (NPS) project fitted neatly into this vision. The sugar industry was highly developed in the neighbouring South African province of Natal, where companies were experimenting in the 1970s with smallholder outgrower initiatives in the homeland of KwaZulu. In 1976 Huletts Sugar reported positively on the feasibility of sugar production in Mpondoland. NPS was formed for this purpose with two equal shareholders – TRACOR and Magwa Tea.[2] The Transkei government also negotiated with South Africa to ensure that all produce could be milled in Natal, at C.G. Smith – the closest south coast sugar conglomerate. Management was outsourced to Lugg, Harrison and Associates, a Swaziland-based agricultural consultancy that also administered Magwa Tea. Keith Nicolson, a white farmer from Natal, was contracted as general manager. In 1983, he moved to the plantation site with his wife and children, where he remained for more than 20 years.[3]

Initially, the Transkei government sought the approval of the ImiZizi Tribal Authority, under whose jurisdiction the land of Hlolweni, Mfolozi and Etyeni villages fell. However, the chieftaincy had a far from smooth relationship with the homeland authorities and appeared to take community consent seriously. Stanford Mditshwa, the ImiZizi chief during the 1960s, had opposed the imposition of Bantu Authorities in meetings with Native Affairs officials.[4] His son Chalara, who succeeded him, opposed 'betterment' schemes during the 1970s. These included a soil conservation programme in the region later demarcated for sugar cane. The Transkei police detained him in 1978. Alfred Mlenzana,, who lived in the area demarcated for sugar, recalls that after Chalara was released in 1979, 'he stopped his resistance'.[5]

Following Chalara's release, two 'community meetings' about the project took place. Thokozile Nzimande recalls a meeting in Hlolweni in 1979, where agricultural officials told them that they would have to move. The Transkei Minister for Agriculture, Stella Sigcau (daughter of the Mpondo paramount chief and later African National Congress (ANC) cabinet member), was present. Nzimande recalled that the project was presented as a fait accompli and that people felt scared to object: 'If one raised voice, one risked arrest.' Similarly, Maqhwakuza Matha of Mfolozi remarked: 'This was the era of the Matanzimas and was an era of oppression. We would have been arrested if we had arranged protests against what was happening.'[6]

Another meeting took place on 17 September 1981 – more than a year after the cabinet memo approving the project. Claimants recall being offered two to three ha plots in exchange for moving, similar in size to smallholder schemes already operational in Natal.[7] It is doubtful that this meeting was well attended. Wilton Mvundla, who later became a beneficiary of the sugar outgrower scheme, first testified in the 2009 court case that the meeting was attended by 'about 200' and then later changed this to 500. Given that the outgrowers were opposing the claimants in court, he would have every reason to overstate community participation in the project to counter their narrative of not being consulted. Clearly, the project never achieved genuine consensus before operations began.

For the people living on the land, customary practices put great restraints on the removal of land rights without household consent. Lenford Gantsa and Maqhwakuza Matha's accounts emphasise the strength of household rights to homesteads and fields. 'The chief or headman was not allowed to take land allocated to a community member away,' Maqhwakuza claimed. Gantsa was more emphatic: 'To get land, you apply to the headman and it is allocated. But when the land is yours, it's yours. *Qha!*'[8] The claimants clearly believed that no chief or official could extinguish their household and common grazing rights. The Transkei government, by contrast, saw communal land as an asset they controlled, which could be used in a wider developmental vision. As the forced removals illustrate, the state believed that it had the right to alienate both homestead plots and grazing land, in spite of customary understandings of strong, layered rights to these areas.

The forced removals began at the end of 1983. Maqhwakuza Matha recalled: 'You would see a bulldozer coming, and then you knew it was time to go.'[9] In court documents and interviews, the claimants stated that they were only compensated for huts, and not for livestock or land rights. The most commonly offered figure for the compensation paid was R150. No transport for the removal of their belongings was offered and families were forced to settle on smaller plots in surrounding communities. During the first three years (1983–86), NPS ran as a commercial cane plantation managed by Nicolson and a small team of administrative staff. Some 3 000 ha were brought into cultivation and some 300 local African people were employed on a seasonal basis. Another 1 000 ha of timber was cultivated, partly as windbreaks and partly for harvesting.[10]

In 1986 NPS began a process of subdividing the rest of the land into plots of 10 to 11 ha. This was much larger than the 2 to 3 ha allegedly promised in the September 1981 meeting and that meant fewer outgrowers would get plots. Chris Dodson claimed that the 10 ha plot size was calculated to enable outgrowers to earn profits 'equivalent to wages paid to a truck driver in Durban – about R500 a month at the time'.[11] Of the roughly 1 000 families removed from the land, only 106 received plots. A further 200 plots were allocated to others. The key issue, as my interviews with claimants confirmed, was that most of those removed failed to get plots. They allege that the application process favoured wealthier people – 'teachers, nurses, government officials'.[12]

The application form for plots asked about levels of education, current employment and salary. Witnesses in the 2009 court case also allege that they were told to produce R500 as part of the application.[13] Mlenzana, a leader in the South African National Civic Organisation, aligned to the ANC, who was removed from Etyeni explained:

> People were invited to fill in forms to apply for a plot. They had to pay R500. Many people couldn't afford it. I applied but could not reach agreement on the basis on which plots should be allocated. I suggested that the plots should be two hectares per household. However, the reply was that it would not work if the plots were less than ten hectares. I then withdrew from the process. In the end, most of the plots went to teachers and nurses.

Nicolson denied charging money for plots but said he outsourced the allocation process to the chief's subordinates – 'maybe they wanted bribes'. He did, however, acknowledge that NPS wanted people who had 'proven skills'.[14]

NPS initially proved a relatively successful commercial venture. There is an incomplete list of tonnage figures in the court record: 4 072 tons were delivered to C.G. Smith in 1983/84 and 104 416 in 1994/95. Although yields per ha remained low by commercial standards, gross annual earnings reached R15 million in 1994.[15] 'At least half of that,' Nicolson claimed when interviewed in 2016, 'went back to the community in the form of smallholder earnings or labourers' wages. The farmers benefited, the taxis benefited – everyone benefited.' By 1992, the core estate was reduced to 500 ha and the venture was largely run on the basis of closely supervised smallholder plots of 10 to 11 ha. At this point NPS entered into a direct lease with the Transkei government, which would last 25 years and could be renewed.

As the venture gathered steam, however, tensions on the land increased. Those who were removed from the sugar zone had to settle on smaller plots in surrounding communities. These communities were not compensated for 'hosting' new arrivals and began to resent the presence of so many new families on the limited land available. The difficult of getting access to sugar plots led to continued disquiet. If the size of plot had been two ha and most of the removed families had been granted a plot, the project may well have won wider support. This plot size was common in the outgrower schemes in KwaZulu where the sugar companies generally worked with families already established on their own land. In Transkei, the government and project managers chose to use the old idea of an economic plot, because they wanted specialist growers and thought they had the political backing to do so. In fact, many of the successful plotholders had alternative incomes. It appears that a significant number of those displaced wanted to participate in sugar cultivation. This does not mean that they necessarily wanted to live on their old sites as well; all growers lived outside the scheme. For some, their conception of the land had clearly shifted in response to economic and political circumstances – both a forcible removal and, for a minority, an opportunity.

## THE *HLOLWENI* LAND CLAIM, 1995–2016

The Hlolweni, Mfolozi and Etyeni communities initially lodged separate claims soon after the Restitution of Land Rights Act was passed in 1994, but the Department of Land Affairs (DLA) subsequently amalgamated them into one. It was (and remains) common practice for the DLA to merge claims to ease the administrative burdens. For a decade after the *Hlolweni* claim was submitted in 1995, little progress was made. The land commissioner sought to reach an agreement between the various parties involved, but NPS and three associations of outgrowers opposed the claim. The claim was finally referred to the Land Claims Court in 2003, which could only hear the case on 16 May 2005. By this time, NPS was becoming unviable as a commercial venture. Chris Dodson, when interviewed, recalled that during the mid-1990s, the organised sugar industry stopped transport subsidies to outlying suppliers. NPS were on the outer peripheries of the sugar belt and soon felt the effects of dramatically increased costs. Tonnage reached a peak of 149 000 in 1996/97 but then declined steadily, totalling about 75 000 in 2003. Nicolson alleged acts of disruption by the claimants, including the burning of cane.[16]

Important changes in the ImiZizi chieftaincy added more complexity to an already volatile situation. It appears that key figures in the tribal authority were included in the outgrower scheme as a strategy of appeasement. Chief Chalara died soon after the project began in 1983, but his wife Harriet was allocated three plots. The chieftaincy passed onto their son Themba, who died in the 1990s without a son. By 2003 a regent, Jongamampondo Mditshwa, was acting. The Land Claims Court informed the ImiZizi Traditional Authority that they could apply for direct access to the case, given their interest in the land. Jongamampondo did not initially take up the offer, but later changed his position, filing an urgent application for direct access on 10 May 2005.[17] The traditional authority contended that it was custodian of the land under customary law.

The Communal Property Associations Act of 1996 created a new legal instrument to manage restituted or redistributed land placed in the control of communities (see Weinberg in this volume). After restitution, CPAs became owners of the land but were envisioned as inclusive, democratic associations with elected committees accountable to the wider community of members. Jongamampondo was worried that the land would be restituted to a CPA representing the claimants, which would compromise the traditional authority's control. His adviser Wiseman Bixi stated emphatically: 'You cannot have a CPA where there are traditional authorities – this is not the African way.'[18]

Jongamampondo's opposition took place in the context of important national political changes. The 2003 Traditional Leadership and Governance Framework Act (TLGFA) recognised pre-existing tribal authorities as traditional councils, provided that 40 per cent of members were elected and a third were women. Subsequently, the Communal Land Rights Act (11 of 2004) (CLARA) promised traditional councils greater authority over customary land within the old boundaries defined in the 1951 Bantu Authorities Act. In this context, it is not surprising the Jongamampondo became emboldened to demand greater control over the land, in opposition to the claimants' wishes.

Thus, by the time the *Hlolweni* case reached court in 2005, the claimants found themselves in a notably different institutional setting. Justice Moloto of the Land Claims Court refused the traditional authority's application for direct access, citing their failure to respond by the court's prescribed deadline in 2003. However, Jongamampondo immediately applied to the Supreme Court of Appeal for leave to appeal the ruling, which was granted. Although this court did not ultimately grant the traditional authority direct access, the hearing had to be postponed pending the outcome of their appeal. After the brief 2005 hearing, the state agreed to compensate the claimants financially, to the tune of R42 000 per household. The case about the land itself was postponed.

Meanwhile, in 2007, the DLA allowed the claimants' committee (who had represented the claimants in the 2005 hearing) to register provisionally as a CPA, pending the claim's final outcome. They named the provisional CPA Sinawo – 'we have the land' in isiXhosa. But Jongamampondo began to show public support to the outgrowers. In 2007, tensions boiled over and several hundred hectares of the estate were burned. The growers blamed the claimants, who denied responsibility, claiming that the fire was initially ignited as part of normal sugar harvesting processes. However, as the Eastern Cape Rural Development Agency reported, in the 2007/08 financial year, only 23 565 tons were harvested. By the following year, the sugar scheme had ceased to function.

## THE CLAIMANTS ASSERT 'COMMUNAL INDIGENOUS OWNERSHIP' IN COURT, 2009–2010

When the *Hlolweni* claim finally reached court, the only party left opposing the case were the growers. NPS, which no longer had the support of government, had withdrawn its opposition. Under the terms of the Restitution Act, the claimants had to show that they were forcibly removed from land under racially discriminatory legislation. Most restitution cases involved black claims to land that had been taken over by whites. In this case, both parties were black and this affected the nature of the case. It placed an onus on the claimants to show the strength of their previous land rights in relation to the Transkei government and the local chieftaincy. The majority of the court proceedings consisted of witness cross-examinations to establish the facts of the forced removal.

The initial dispossession was made under the Transkei Agricultural Development Act (1968) which allowed for state intervention to control land for conservation and development. It included many of the provisions of the Betterment Proclamation 116 of 1949, which enabled the Native Commissioner to declare soil conservation areas, demarcate distinct areas for residential, agricultural and grazing purposes and order the movement of settlements. Advocate Alan Dodson, leading the case for the claimants, emphasised that this was racially discriminatory legislation, as required under the 1994 Restitution Act. William Beinart, acting as expert witness, contended that betterment legislation was applied only to Africans and that white farmers would have been better compensated and consulted if the state wished to alienate agricultural land and settlements. The claimants also argued that legislation like the 1977 Public Security Act limited potential opposition to the project. The growers' counsel disputed the absence of consultation, but conceded that 'some measure of dispossession' took place.[19]

Having argued that the claimants were unjustly dispossessed and that racist legislation was applied, Dodson's next task was to explain the *nature* of their land rights. Here, the claimants attempted to define and assert well-established customary rights to land, within a novel legal framework provided by the jurisprudence of the Constitutional Court. The foundation of the argument came from the

*Richtersveld* case, heard by the Constitutional Court in 2003. This involved a community of Nama people in the Northern Cape who were dispossessed of land in the 1920s, to make way for diamond mining. After 1994, the ANC government granted sole mining rights to Alexkor, a company of which it was the sole shareholder. In a judgment with important legal implications, the Constitutional Court found: 'One of the components of the culture of the Richtersveld people was the customary rules relating to their entitlement to the use and occupation of this land. The primary rule was that the land belonged to the Richtersveld community as a whole and that its entire people were entitled to the reasonable occupation and use of the land and its resources.'[20]

The judgment emphasised the necessity of elevating this form of landholding to the same legal status as common-law ownership. Importantly, it referred to these land rights as both 'indigenous ownership' and 'indigenous title'. Dodson drew on this jurisprudence, asserting that the land rights of the claimants at the time of dispossession constituted 'communal indigenous ownership'.[21] Dodson emphasised the strength of household rights in this conception of ownership, and the inability of the chief or state to alienate land arbitrarily: 'Communal indigenous ownership is not something that simply operates at the level of leadership of the community, at the level of the chief or the level of the king. It is something that operates at all of the different levels. A marked feature of this is that it contemplates rights at the household level. These are very strong.'

As Beinart notes in this volume, this was not directly stated in the *Richtersveld* judgment, which restored land to an undifferentiated community of Nama/coloured people. This key difference was later borne out in Justice Bam's judgment in Hlolweni, handed down on 1 July 2010. It affirmed that the claimants 'enjoyed communal indigenous ownership' and that the Transkei state 'removed these rights'. Thus the community was 'entitled to restoration of the subject land, which will be transferred to a *communal entity or three communal entities* [my emphasis], whichever is determined to be the best option with the assistance of the Land Claims Commissioner.'[22]

By 'communal entity', Bam was clearly referring to a legal instrument representing the claimants that could manage the land. The claimants had already provisionally registered as a CPA and during court proceedings, the Department of Rural Development and Land Reform (DRDLR, formerly DLA) expressed a preference for restituting the land to a CPA. The DRDLR also committed R39 million to develop the land, conditional on an adequate business plan.

Fifteen years after submitting their claim, the claimants had won an important legal victory. The Transkei state's authoritarian developmental vision had reshaped tenure relations on 10 000 ha of land in Mpondoland for a couple of decades. Now another new conception of ownership was affirmed by the Land Claims Court. The claimants' assertion of 'communal indigenous ownership' was recognised in law to the exclusion of the traditional council, the growers and surrounding communities and ownership would now be in the form of a CPA, rather than customary tenure.

## 'BUSINESS LAND' AND BUREAUCRATIC STASIS, 2010–2016

Bam's ruling brought enormous relief and optimism to the claimants. This was short-lived. The Sinawo CPA only received confirmation of their permanent registration in March 2012 and, when research was conducted in 2016, still did not have a title deed. (A title deed was given over part of the land, about 5 000 ha, in 2019.) The 'development money' had not been paid and in 2016, the 10 000 ha lay unoccupied, used for grazing by surrounding communities with a limited amount of commercial forestry.

The DRDLR did not oppose the claimants in court, but was not able to resolve political problems that developed in the land reform process. The traditional authority, the CPA and the government all had different understandings of who has the rights to the land. Remarkably, all parties seem to agree that the land should *not* be resettled by households or smallholder farmers, but should be used for 'development' or 'business' purposes. This marks a shift away from the conception of land tenure put forward by both the claimants in court and the traditional authority in its appliction for direct access.

The claimants were particularly suspicious of the role of Zukile Pityi, head of the Eastern Cape Land Claims Commission, who allegedly promised them permanent registration for the CPA and a title deed for the land. They wished to restart sugar farming, to farm nuts and timber and to build a shopping centre.[23] They were only able to make a start on forestry. In August 2010, the DRDLR arranged for timber company Sappi to start a joint venture with the CPA. Sappi agreed to help rehabilitate neglected windbreaks that Nicolson and his workers planted, and to plant more timber. The agreement also included a commitment to train CPA members in tree-felling.

By October 2013, 140 ha of new timber had been planted and 40 ha of the original plantings had been harvested. At this stage, 100 workers were employed on the planation. In 2014, the company was managing 1 334 ha.[24] The CPA was paid nearly R4 000 for timber harvested in one month that year (Sappi 2014). This suggests that the plantation could become a significant generator of income but it used only a small proportion of the land. The CPA alleged that local people were using the area without their authority – for example, mining sand and selling it to building contractors. They could not get police intervention because they could not show that they owned the land.

In a brief interview the regent chief, Jongamampondo, gestured to the horizon and claimed, 'This is all my land'. His adviser Wiseman Bixi, interviewed a few days later, said: 'The government can't prop up a CPA on a traditional authority – that's like the South Africans propping up Renamo in Mozambique.' But when Jongamampondo was asked why those he claims as his followers had not resettled the land, he clarified: 'No, no. This is business land.' He then outlined remarkably similar plans to the CPA to develop the area – the construction of a shopping centre, a private hospital, macadamia nut farming and restarting the sugar plantation.

Jongamampondo has aggressively reasserted the claims of the traditional authority to the land, in spite of the court judgment. He has also entered into contracts on the land despite of the judgment conferring ownership rights to the CPA. At the time of research, the construction company Rumdel was paying the traditional authority to quarry on the land, close to where it straddles the R61 road. Two different companies – Sappi and Rumdel – conduct commercial operations within this area, entering into contractual agreements with different 'owners'.

Although the sugar outgrowers were only in operation for about 20 years, and were only lessees (not owners) of the 10 ha plots, they remained aggrieved at the loss of their rights and income. In 2015 the provincial premier held an unsuccessful meeting to try to resolve the position and insisted that five growers be included in the CPA.[25] The CPA believes the growers and Jongamampondo are collaborating and accuses them of vandalism of trees on their land.

The land claim has also become entangled with a succession dispute in the ImiZizi chieftaincy. The chieftaincy's recognised legitimate lineage came through Chalara, who died in the 1980s and his son Themba, who died in the 1990s. According to informants associated with the CPA, an open meeting was called by the ImiZizi Traditional Authority shortly after Themba's death. One of his nephews, Makhosini, who was working in Gauteng at the time, was chosen as the rightful heir. He returned to ImiZizi at some point in the early 2000s, only to find that the regent Jongamampondo claimed the chieftaincy in his own right.[26] The CPA has backed Makhosini. In 2016 he appeared to be supporting their claim to the land and was included on the CPA committee.

These interrelated conflicts have undeniably impacted on attempts to develop the land. Nicolson, in an interview, claimed that both the growers and claimants have approached him repeatedly to restart sugar cultivation:

> They say to me, '*Maqhasha* [employer], why don't you come and start sugar farming again?' I say, 'Guys, sort yourselves out and make peace. I won't come back until there is peace on the land and I have financial guarantees for my investments in tractors and seedlings.'

Nicolson's frustration speaks to more general problems plaguing restitution claims after they are finalised, particularly those that involve CPAs (see Capps, Motala and Pickering in this volume). Bam's judgment restituted the land to a specific group of people, not a loosely defined community like the *Richtersveld* claimants. This excluded the growers, but also surrounding communities that 'hosted' the claimants, some of which have indicated their unhappiness to Pityi.[27]

The *Hlolweni* impasse has also frustrated Pityi. Although he is 'all for the rule of law', the government's position was that no transfer could take place before the parties made peace. In his interview, Pityi claimed to be pushing for inclusion of Jongamampondo, the regent, as well as grower representatives, on the CPA:

> I understand that we need to comply with the judgment – but the people are not coming any closer to each other. I've had six meetings there. I've talked to the CPA and the traditional authority. I've told them, 'Look, guys, you have been living together. Before this claim came along, you accommodated each other, you stayed together, but when this claim came, it divided you. You killed each other, your families have fought.' I said to them, 'What makes you not want to come together now?' ... The last time I was there, I went there with the Deputy Land Claims Commissioner. We wanted to survey the land so that we can transfer title. But ... they are not agreeing.

Bam's judgment did not give the traditional authority any control over the land. But Pityi, backed by national policy under the Zuma government, said: 'The department's position is that CPAs are only suitable for areas where there are no chiefs – like farms.' This policy seems to be sustained despite a further judgment by the Constitutional Court in the *Bakgatla* case (2015, see Mnwana in this volume) that supported the formation of a CPA in North West Province without the inclusion of a chief. Pityi concluded that the CPA Act was a big mistake: 'This is a problem of our own making, and now we have to deal with it.' He acknowledged that the department had changed its position.

On their side, the CPA fear that once admitted to their committee, the regent and traditional council will try to control developments for their own advantage. The Sinawo CPA was ill-equipped to deal with these challenges. In 2016 it had 16 members, most of whom spoke no English and had limited literacy. They have few facilities and their adviser from the DRDLR, who had visited only a few times, was unresponsive to phone calls. It is unrealistic for them to provide a full business plan without sustained support. They do, however, appear to function democratically and minutes are kept.

Soon after the CPA Act was passed Kobus Pienaar (2000) argued that low levels of human capital, combined with the heightened risk of conflict with traditional leaders, meant that CPAs were unlikely to succeed without significant government or non-governmental organisation (NGO) help (see Weinberg in this volume). The CPA continues to believe in its exclusive rights to control the land, rooted in customary entitlements before the forced removal. But they now live elsewhere and have relinquished claims to settle the land. Jongamampondo appeared emboldened by government efforts to court traditional leaders and maintained – succession dispute aside – that the land is under ImiZizi Traditional Council. This claims to represent the whole ImiZizi population, who might argue they lost out indirectly when the sugar plantation was established. The former outgrowers also maintain that they have an interest in the land, under a form of tenure dissimilar to both of the main contending parties. Pityi perceived himself as arbiter of an intractable dispute.

It is striking, however, that since the claim was finalised in 2010, all the protagonists agreed that the land be reserved for 'business' or 'development'. This provides further support to the notion that 'the living law' on the land changes as local contexts evolve, a point that marks a significant break with Claassens and Cousins's argument. The central point of this chapter is that understandings of land rights have remained flexible over time. Yet, in proposing alternatives for customary land in the future, the land rights community is divided.

Currently, the most significant division concerns the extent to which different forms of land rights should be legally defined. Cousins (2008) cautions against stipulating rights to household and grazing land, partly because of the administrative limits, but also because definitions of rights in law necessarily restrict the extent to which customary law can evolve. For his approach to succeed, strong mediatory institutions, provided by the state, would need to exist on the ground to adjudicate potential disputes. The Land and Accountability Research Centre (LARC) at the University of Cape Town advocated an incremental upgrading of Interim Protection of Informal Land Rights Act (Act 31 of 1996) (IPILRA) rights in law, with a view to ultimately passing more permanent legislation: existing rights 'must be recorded in some form' so that people 'cannot have their land sold from under them' (Centre for Law and Society 2015: 5–6) This approach feeds into a wider literature on tenure reform elsewhere in Africa, which has increasingly emphasised a bottom-up, incrementalist approach to recording and upgrading of land rights (McAuslan 1999). There are also advocates of gradually upgrading of rights toward private, titled holdings (Beinart, Delius and Hay 2017).

The *Hlolweni* case suggests that policy must not fall into the trap of proposing a static idea of customary tenure. If we take the concept of living customary law seriously, allowances must be made for understandings of land rights to change in response to local contexts. A corollary of this is that household or common rights need not be perpetually sacrosanct, unless explicitly protected in law. In Hlolweni, most of the different interests involved seem to agree that the old family-based rights in the land that went under sugar have lapsed. The fact that the buildings of 883 claimant families have been dismantled, and that the old occupants have built elsewhere, is a factor in this. The CPA believes that it can own the land with a title and manage it as a business for collective benefit.

Thus legislation needs to balance stronger rights for vulnerable people with the need for tenure systems to remain flexible. Although Cousins' (2008) approach allows for flexibility, it does not offer explicit protection for households and relies heavily on the state's limited ability to mediate conflicts if the living law is disputed. LARC's bottom-up process of recording rights would certainly offer better legal recognition of people's rights, but may risk compromising flexibility in the long run. An alternative approach would be for new tenure legislation to regulate for a diverse range of scenarios in how people use land, thereby ensuring strong protections for vulnerable people in different circumstances. Developing this idea is an important research agenda for the future.

The ANC's approach to tenure reform has developed in contradictory directions. On the one hand, laws like IPILRA strengthened the ability of rural people to defend existing rights, whilst the CPA Act sought to democratise the management of land transferred to communities. These laws are unlikely to achieve their aims, given the reinvigoration of chiefly power in later legislation. The *Hlolweni* case shows that the ANC's uncertain approach to tenure reform has created a toxic situation, in which different actors claim ownership of the same piece of land. A court decision was not seen to resolve this (see Pickering and Motala in this volume). The potential for conflict in these situations is self-evident. When these contradictory approaches to tenure reform are considered in tandem with the state's poor record in supporting successful claimants, it is not surprising that the Sinawo CPA struggles to manage the land effectively. This case also calls into question the wisdom of reopening a wide range of new claims, as in the Resitution of Land Rights Amendment Act (2014), now suspended by the courts, when the old ones have not all been settled, and when the administrative capacity and clarity of policy to do so is lacking.

NOTES

1. Hlolweni, Mfolozie and Eyeteni Communities v North Pondoland Sugar [2003] LCC41/03 [Judgment 2010] ('*Hlolweni*').
2. *Hlolweni*, Index of Pleadings, Vol. 1, 65, 51, 73–85; see also Chris Dodson, interviewed by Raphael Chaskalson, Cape Town, 14 April 2016 (Hodson interview).
3. Keith Nicolson, interviewed by Raphael Chaskalson, Munster, 1 April 2016 (Nicolson interview).
4. Mthatha Archives (MTA), Minutes of Meeting of Imzimi Tribal Authority, 16 August 1962.
5. *Hlolweni*, Index of Pleadings, Vol. 2, 491; Alfred Mlenzana Pre-court statement.
6. *Hlolweni*, Thokozile Nzimande and Maqhwakuza Matha Pre-court statements.
7. *Hlolweni*, Transcription of court proceedings (Transcription), Vol. 1, 96.
8. Lenford Gantsa and five members of Sinawo CPA, interviewed by Raphael Chaskalson, Mfolozi, 23 March 2016 (Sinawo CPA interview).
9. *Hlolweni*, Transcription 61.
10. Nicolson interview.
11. Dodson interview.
12. Sinawo CPA interview.
13. *Hlolweni*, Index of Pleadings Vol. 2, 433–434; Sinawo CPA interview.
14. *Hlolweni*, Mlenzana Pre-court statement; Nicolson interview.
15. *Hlolweni*, Transcription, Vol. 2, 173.
16. Nicolson interview.
17. *Hlolweni*, Transcription, Vol. 1 96; Justice Moloto judgment, 26 May 2005, para 4.
18. Wiseman Bixi, interviewed by Raphael Chaskalson, Wild Coast Sun, 24 March 2016.
19. *Hlolweni*, Transcription, Vol. 1, 39–41; Vol 3, 298.
20. Alexkor Ltd and Another v Richtersveld Community and Others [2003] ZACC 18 Judgment, para 58. ('*Richtersveld*').
21. *Richtersveld,* para 49, 57; *Hlolweni*, Transcription, Vol. 3, 25.
22. *Hlolweni*, Justice Bam judgment, 1 July 2010, para 13–17.
23. Lenford Gantsa, interviewed by Raphael Chaskalson, Port Edward, 24 March 2016.
24. SAPPI and Sinawo CPA, Community Development Scheme Agreement, ratified 30 July 2014.
25. Zukile Pityi, interviewed by Raphael Chaskalson, East London, 30 March 2016 (Pityi interview); Sinawo CPA interview.
26. *Hlolweni*, Justice Moloto judgment, 26 May 2005, para 8(a).
27. Pityi interview.

REFERENCES

Beinart, William, Peter Delius and Michelle Hay. 2017. *Rights to Land: A Guide to Tenure Upgrading and Restitution in South Africa*. Johannesburg: Jacana Media.
Berry, Sara. 1993. *No Condition is Permanent: The Social Dynamics of Agrarian Change in Sub-Saharan Africa*. Madison: University of Wisconsin Press.
Capps, Gavin. 2016. 'Tribal Landed Property: The Value of the Chieftaincy in Contemporary Africa'. *Journal of Agrarian Change* 16, no. 3: 452–477.
Centre for Law and Society. 2015. 'Fact Sheet – Communal Land Tenure and IPILRA'.

Claassens, Aninka and Geoff Budlender. 2016. 'Transformative Constitutionalism and Customary Law'. *Constitutional Court Review* 6: 75–105.
Claassens, Aninka and Ben Cousins, eds. 2008. *Land, Power & Custom: Controversies Generated by South Africa's Communal Land Rights Act*. Cape Town: UCT Press.
Cousins, Ben. 2008. 'Characterising Communal Tenure: Nested Systems and Flexible Boundaries'. In *Land, Power & Custom: Controversies Generated by South Africa's Communal Land Rights Act*, edited by Aninka Claassens and Ben Cousins, 109–137. Athens: Ohio University Press.
Cousins, Ben and Aninka Claassens. 2005. 'Communal Land Rights and Democracy in Post-Apartheid South Africa'. In *Democratising Development: The Politics of Socio-Economic Rights in South Africa*, edited by Peris Sean Jones and Kristian Stokke, 245–270. Leiden: Brill.
Fazan, Sydney H. 1944. 'Land Tenure in the Transkei'. *African Studies* 3, no. 2: 45–64.
Kepe, Thembela. 2005. 'Magwa Tea Venture in South Africa: Politics, Land and Economics'. *Social Dynamics* 31, no. 1: 261–279.
Kerr, Alastair J. 1953. *The Native Common Law of Immovable Property in South Africa*. Durban: Butterworth.
Kerr, Alastair J. 1994. 'Customary Law, Fundamental Rights, and the Constitution'. *South African Law Journal* 111, no. 1: 720–735.
Mcauslan, Patrick. 1999. 'Making Law Work: Restructuring Land Relations in Africa'. *Development and Change* 29, no. 1: 525–552.
Nkonyeni, Archie. 2012. *Black Property Pioneer*. Johannesburg: self-published.
Nkuhlu, Wiseman. 1989. 'Regional Development in the Transkei'. *Development Southern Africa* 1, no. 3: 333–342.
Ntsebeza, Lungisile. 2006. *Democracy Compromised: Chiefs and the Politics of Land in South Africa*. Cape Town: HSRC Press.
Pienaar, Kobus. 2000. '"Communal" Property Arrangements: A Second Bite'. In *At the Crossroads: Land and Agrarian Reform in South Africa into the 21st Century*, edited by Ben Cousins, 322–339. Cape Town: PLAAS.
Sappi. 2014. 'Timber Control System Transaction Report', 26 November.
Southall, Roger. 1982. *South Africa's Transkei: The Political Economy of an Independent Bantustan*. London: Heinemann.

CHAPTER
# 12

# Restitution and Land Rights in the Eastern Cape: The Hlolweni, Mgungundlovu and Xolobeni Cases

**William Beinart**

This chapter focuses largely on ideas and arguments developed in preparation for the court case around the *Mgungundlovu* (Wild Coast Sun) restitution claim in Bizana, former Transkei (now Alfred Nzo municipality).[1] It was submitted in 1995 by claimants who had been forcibly removed from about 740 ha by the Transkei government in 1980 to make way for the Wild Coast Sun casino, hotel and golf course. The case was contested by Transkei Sun International Limited (hereafter 'Sun') but was legally settled in 2014, just as the court case was starting. The 106 claimants were successful and gained what most saw as a favourable outcome, including a cash payment and ownership of the land through a communal property association (CPA). The settlement did not, however, allow families to move back onto the land that they had vacated – at least not for 20 years.

Research and preparation for the *Mgungundlovu* case was a collective task. I served as a researcher, closely directed by the lawyers in order to support the legal ideas that they were pursuing. This chapter explores their priorities and how this shaped the focus of the work that was done (see also Fay in this volume). Interviews were conducted with Luvuyo Wotshela (co-researcher); the lawyers were led by advocate Alan Dodson and included Susannah Cowen and Apla Bodlani (advocates) as well as Norton Rose attorneys pro bono department (especially Nicki van't Riet). Dodson drew on earlier cases, notably *Richtersveld* (2003) the landmark judgment by the Constitutional Court,[2] and *Hlolweni* (2003) (see Chaskalson in this volume).[3] The latter case arose from a claim, also in Bizana, originally submitted in 1995 and settled in 2010 by the Land Claims Court.

My involvement began with Hlolweni in 2005 because the claimants' lawyers (also led by Alan Dodson) found *The Political Economy of Pondoland* (Beinart 1982) useful in outlining aspects of customary landholding in Mpondoland. Although the book was not quite as clear as I would, in retrospect, have liked for evidence in a court case, it helped to inform the arguments that the lawyers were pursuing. The fact that it was written before the claims were submitted enhanced its value for these purposes. I submitted a statement and was cross-examined as an expert witness in the *Hlolweni* case in 2009 and then worked with the lawyers on *Mgungundlovu*.

Among the many legal and historical issues that arose in these cases, some central questions were: who has rights to the land in the former African homelands of South Africa and what are the nature of those rights? Are these rights held by family heads, by families as a whole, by local communities, by chiefs or the state? Do they amount to a form of ownership and how do the layers of landholding and authority in these former communal or customary areas interlink? Does a form of customary tenure survive; how has this been affected by the land proclamations imposed on this area, and what is the status of those proclamations? These issues also proved potentially important in preparations for the Xolobeni case (*Baleni* 2016), again on the Transkei coast in Bizana, where African rural landholders were attempting to defend themselves against eviction by the state and a mining company.[4]

My affidavit in the *Mgungundlovu* case touched on these points and provided background to the political history of Mpondoland. However, tenure was not the only issue that arose: the lawyers asked us to collect testimony on the nature of the forced removal, the degree of consent, the extent of smallholder production and the historical depth of settlement by claimant families. This fed into the general preparation of the case as well as anticipated legal questions. Other researchers pursued related issues, including a more detailed questionnaire survey of agriculture before the removals, which was geared to calculating better the losses experienced, and an investigation of aerial photographs that showed both the settlement before the removal and the density of settlement in the areas to which the claimants had moved.

Critically, the lawyers themselves were able to get access to Transkeian government records, and the 1987 report of the Alexander Commission of Inquiry (see also Gibbs 2014), which revealed corruption in the first lease of land to Sun. Whatever the strength of the legal arguments, it is likely that one reason for the settlement of the case, immediately before the court hearing, was that Sun was concerned about the reputational damage that might arise from a fresh public airing of its payments to Transkeian politicians. If accepted by the judge, such evidence might also have affected its lease and operating licence.

In respect of research for *Mgungundlovu*, it seemed likely that certain evidence and interpretation would assist the claimants – for example, an emphasis on: the strength of customary land tenure; proof of forced removal and an absence of consent; a thriving smallholder economy before the removal; long-term settlement in the Sun site by specific families; and specific rights to land. To a degree our informants were also aware of this. We certainly did not have to invent any evidence, and of course it had to be sufficiently robust to withstand potential cross-examination by skilled advocates. But in preparation for these cases, a certain caution seemed necessary in the presentation of evidence.

Problems also arise in specifying the nature of customary tenure. Some overviews emphasise the strength of family rights over their residential and arable landholdings (Delius 2008). But such views are contested both by traditionalists, who assert the authority of chiefs and traditional councils, and communalists, who lay greater emphasis on communal and layered rights over land (Hornby et al. 2017). Historians are also attuned to evidence that rules, practices and customs change through time and vary from one area to another. The Constitutional Court has allowed for flexibility in interpretation of customary law, accepting evidence on living customary law as currently practised (see Budlender and Fay in this volume). Collecting evidence on living customary law is challenging and we found some differences even within the small area of coastal Bizana. Moreover, in all of these cases the relevant 'community' involved was a significant factor (Beinart, Delius and Hay 2017).

My engagement with these legal processes also helped me to refine arguments about the history and future of customary tenure and landholding. Current contestations over land are shaped by increasingly intensive competition for resources in the former homelands. Chiefs, the state, corporations, local accumulators and black economic empowerment (BEE) associates contend for resources. The rights of landholders can be threatened and, in this context, defining family rights in law seems to be increasingly important. Mining has become particularly significant in relation to contestations over land in the northern provinces (see Capps and Mnwana in this volume). This has been less evident in the Eastern Cape, but is directly relevant in Xolobeni. My arguments are influenced both by analysis of who *does* 'own' the land and who *should* 'own' the land.

## RESTITUTION AND THE COURTS IN BIZANA: HLOLWENI

After a long gestation, the *Hlolweni* case was heard in 2009 by Justice Bam at the Land Claims Court, sitting in the Tropical Nites Theatre at the Wild Coast Sun (see Chaskalson in this volume).[5] Some 900 families from Hlolweni and neighbouring settlements claimed about 10 000 ha in the Imizizi area of Bizana. The land was appropriated by the Transkei government to establish a sugar plantation and sugar smallholder scheme within the former homeland in the early 1980s. While sugar was successfully grown on some scale for 20 years, peaking in the mid-1990s, production dwindled by 2007 and remaining crops were damaged by fire. There were long-standing tensions over the scheme because only a small minority of those families removed were able to get sugar smallholdings.

Under the Restitution of Land Rights Act (Act 22 of 1994), the lawyers needed to establish that the claimants were forcibly removed from their land, but also that this was done under racially discriminatory legislation. The authority for this scheme came from the Transkeian government and the Eastern Mpondo paramount chief (or king), Botha Sigcau, who was also president of Transkei. The Transkei government had used the Agricultural Development Act of 1966, which gave wide powers to the state, especially in connection with the continued implementation of betterment. The lawyers believed that they had to show that neither the Transkeian state nor the Mpondo chieftaincy had the right to force people off the land for such purposes. They had to show that enforcement of this Act, by a black government in connection with African people, amounted to racial discrimination. And they were particularly keen to argue that customary law still governed landholding in the Transkei.

Alan Dodson thought that the Constitutional Court judgment in *Richtersveld* – a case contested to resolve issues that arose under the implementation of the Restitution Act – was applicable also to Hlolweni. The Constitution provides that where customary law applies, it should be taken into account by the courts. The court found that the annexation of this area in the Northern Cape did not extinguish customary or indigenous rights and that subsequent legislation and proclamations 'manifested an intention to respect land rights and not extinguish them'. The Constitutional Court judges accepted the idea, proposed by the claimant community's lawyers, that the word 'ownership' could describe indigenous or customary land rights. They wrote that the form of rights and occupation was 'akin to that held under common-law ownership'. They concluded: 'We have found that the Richtersveld Community held ownership of the subject land under indigenous law.'[6]

Although these precise words were not used in the Constitutional Court judgment, Dodson formulated the term 'communal indigenous ownership' and wished to establish this as the basis for African landholding in *Hlolweni*. My evidence argued that the Pondoland Annexation Act (Act 5 of 1894), analagous to the legislation for *Richtersveld*, did not specify that the state was taking ownership of the land. The key early land proclamations – 19 of 1899, 125 of 1903 and 143 of 1919 – recognised all previous allocations. The great majority had been done by customary procedures; this gave further weight to the idea that customary rights had not been overridden.

The outgrowers' lawyer did challenge the idea that the removal had been forced and noted that some of the claimants received plots. Certainly, promises were made in this respect. However, the claimants were able to present strong evidence about the coercion used and the legal team's research showed that only about 100 of the 883 claimants received plots (see Chaskalson in this volume). My evidence pointed to the Transkei's Public Safety Act of 1977 (passed soon after the South African government extended the formal status of independence to the Transkei), and other draconian measures that gave Matanzima the power to suppress opposition. Witnesses affirmed that the Imizizi chief, Chalara Mditshwa, was arrested because of his initial opposition to the scheme.

In the *Hlolweni* judgment, Justice Bam considered that *Richtersveld* had set a precedent and confirmed that the claimant communities had 'communal indigenous ownership' over the land. He used the term based on the arguments and affidavits presented, although this precise formulation does not seem to have become more generally established. Bam accepted the claimants' evidence that they had been forced to move and that the Transkeian state was, by this time, highly coercive. He came close to saying that no Transkeian legislation was valid because the Transkei was an illegitimate creation of apartheid whose government did not follow democratic practices.

Bam also agreed with the legal argument about the racial discrimination inherent in the Transkeian Agricultural Development Act of 1966. Its major purpose was to facilitate conservation via betterment, not to confiscate land for plantations. Moreover, the conservation laws applied to white South African landowners were by no means so coercive (Delius and Schirmer 2000). This difference constituted racial discrimination and thus this dispossession fell within the Restitution Act.

The judgment recognised that the claimants' collective right to the land from which they had been removed over-rode the Transkei government legislation. The paramount chief had no right to alienate such land without the consent of the communal indigenous owners: 'The chiefs' role was merely that of oversight in relation to the land'.[7] The judgment awarded the land back to the claimants.

This was an excellent outcome for the claimants, legally speaking – although less so in practice. Moreover, Bam in effect developed the idea of customary ownership. *Richtersveld* restored land to an undifferentiated group or community of Nama/coloured people. The whole community regained rights over the west coast area of land taken by the government in the 1920s and mined by the Alexkor company. The *Richtersveld* judgment did not identify any subset of claimants within that community. The whole of the Richtersveld community gained customary indigenous ownership over the whole of the alienated land.

In the Hlolweni case, the claimants were not an undifferentiated group of ImiZizi or Mpondo, but a list of 883 named claimants who had been specifically dispossessed by the alienation of the land. Bam in certain respects refined the content of communal indigenous ownership to mean a particular set of people who were not ethnically defined but defined by their shared historical 'ownership' of land and their shared experience of dispossession.

## MGUNGUNDLOVU: THE FORCED REMOVAL

Preparations for *Mgungundlovu* benefited from those for *Hlolweni*. However, the judgment in the Land Claims Court may not have set a precedent, particularly in relation to the nature of communal indigenous ownership and customary law, because these issues were not fully argued in the case. There were also significant differences. The 1966 Agricultural Development Act was not used as the legal basis for the forced removal from the Wild Coast Sun site. It would not have been appropriate for a casino and it proved difficult to clarify which law had been used. Whereas the ImiZizi chief had opposed the alienation of land, Chief Malungelo Baleni and the Amadiba Tribal Authority had supported the Transkeian authorities in taking over coastal land for the casino. Another difference was that the Sun corporation, to a greater extent than the sugar smallholders in Hlolweni, was able to brief highly experienced lawyers.

Interviews were done in 2011 and 2012 in Lurholweni, also part of the former Amadiba Tribal Authority. This is the area along the main road (R61) between Port Edward and Bizana town, now a dense settlement, where the claimants found sites following their forced removal in 1980–81. Mgungundlovu is the name of one of the two former administrative areas, which had their own headmen, within the Amadiba chiefdom. Only a limited part of this zone (740 ha), called locally Khimbili, was excised for the Wild Coast Sun and there were about 40 homesteads there at the time. The claimants numbered 106 because the households had fragmented after the removal.

Interviewing was organised by the claimants' committee, which called a general meeting to consult and then nominated informants who were thought to be most suitable. The chair, Elias Ogle, and vice-chair, Zodwa Langazana, attended most of the interviews. The committee had a long connection with the Eastern Cape Land Claims Commission Office and was also involved in the verification process of land claimants. Most of the interviewees expressed impatience at the slow progress of the claim, and felt that they had told their stories to previous researchers, such as those from the Commission, and lawyers. They did not fully appreciate the detail that we wanted.

There was a striking degree of consensus amongst those interviewed, indicating a strong social memory, although many also had distinctive individual recollections. We interviewed only sufficient numbers for the purposes of the case. People discussed in detail, 30 years later, their homestead sites and fields, and their access to resources such as shellfish and also fish in the Mzamba lagoon. In a coastal zone with high rainfall, many of these homesteads were site of agricultural activities. One of the most successful, Mgwigwi Miya, born around 1920, and still a fluent interviewee in 2011, was a migrant labourer for most of his life but said he had managed to consolidate a plot of 3.5 ha when retired. He claimed to have sold produce as far afield as Durban.[8] Miya played a significant cameo role during the site inspection before the case in 2014; his fields were still visible, terraced down a gentle slope.

Interviewees recalled that there was very little notice of the impending removal: they first heard about it when workers came into the area to position poles. A few recalled a meeting with the headmen, Qondiso Yalo, who was cautiously opposed to the removal. The meeting that stuck in informants' minds was called by Chief Baleni, late in 1979, at which he adopted an aggressive stance. One remembered: 'There were a few queries and even objections from some older men, but Baleni reacted angrily and dismissively ... He insulted people by insisting that they were "thinking like monkeys"'.[9] It seemed to them clear that the decisions had already been made, before any consultation. Baleni said their houses were worth nothing and if they did not vacate by April 1980, they would face arrest. This recollection about Baleni comparing people to monkeys rankled. Another interviewee mentioned that the chief said they were being 'slow witted, like a monkey chained on a tree ... He said of the Kuzwayo property, where they had only rondavels, where they were trying to cling on, they were not even worth R20.'[10] Employment at the Sun was promised in general terms.

An agricultural officer demarcated some sites in Lurholweni village, but these were much smaller than their previous landholdings and insufficient in number. Informants recalled no effective organisation for the move and a number were dependent for sites on the headman Qondiso (who still charged R10) and others in this village who shared their land. Late in summer, people scrambled to harvest some of their crops, as their homes were bulldozed. The government did not assist in the move. One local man, who had bought a second-hand tractor from a banana farmer in Port Edward, helped some families transport their possessions to bare plots. Many had to organise transport themselves, even walking the five km with valuable possessions and roofing materials in order to construct temporary shelters. Compensation was minimal, some did not receive it (because larger families split up in the relocation) and it was only offered for houses, not land, nor crops or fruit trees or other agricultural improvements. Some mentioned R35, although a few received more. An additional amount of R100 per family was apparently offered by Sun but it went into a collective pot and interviewees claimed that they received little or no benefit from it.

## MGUNGUNDLOVU: LEGAL ISSUES AND ADDITIONAL RESEARCH

The lawyers in the *Mgungundlovu* claim were uncertain about the implications of the *Richtersveld* judgment in respect of this case. The Constitutional Court had accepted that in Richtersveld, the same 'community' occupied the land before annexation and that annexation in itself had not extinguished their rights to a form of indigenous ownership. In Mgungundlovu, the problem of defining community was again an issue. The community in the Richtersveld case was in effect an ethnic community based on a pre-colonial polity or identity. It was therefore not difficult to show that, as a collectivity, they had inhabited the relevant area of the Northern Cape prior to annexation. This issue is not of relevance to many restitution cases in South Africa, because most claims have related to individuals, families, or specific groupings – for example, black people who had owned land privately in areas reserved under apartheid for whites.

In the Mgungundlovu case, the advocates were not appearing for the Mpondo kingdom or the Amadiba chieftaincy or even for the inhabitants of Mgungundlovu administrative area as a whole, but only for the 106 registered claimants who had been removed. As an expert witness, I could confidently state that this area was part of the Mpondo kingdom prior to annexation in 1894 and that the Amadiba chieftaincy had been mentioned in pre-annexation records. These are surprisingly rich because the Cape colonial state kept a careful eye on this potentially disruptive area beyond its borders, especially after the annexation of the surrounding areas of Transkei and East Griqualand from 1875. There is also a history, published in

1927 under the name of Victor Poto Ndamase, paramount chief of Western Mpondoland, and detailed magisterial archives from 1894.

Yet the wording of the *Richtersveld* judgment left some scope for uncertainty. Was it enough to show that the claimants had been forcibly removed or was it also necessary to establish that indigenous ownership was long-established and that the descendants of these claimants had occupied the casino site before annexation? As in the case of Hlolweni, we aimed to show that the Pondoland Annexation Act (Act 5 of 1894) had not undermined customary landholding. But the Constitutional Court judgment seemed to imply that the concept of indigenous ownership required historical depth.

Thus the lawyers asked us to try to establish not only forced removal without consent but also long-term settlement histories within the claimant community, as well as more detail about customary land rights. They wanted to show that land had passed between generations in Khimbili (the casino site) before the removal. They felt that it was not sufficient in this case to establish that people had permission to occupy certificates (PTOs) or similar documents, such as tax records, because the authority for PTOs came from state proclamations and not from custom. In fact, PTOs had not been extended to this area because Mgungundlovu had not been subject to betterment. In general, landholders had only received PTOs in Transkeian areas where betterment had been implemented – probably about 70 per cent of the area (excluding the districts in which individual quitrent tenure was implemented).

Ideally, the lawyers wanted us to show that 'the same patch of land was controlled by a family', rather than that families had simply been in the general area. We were simultaneously trying to establish who would be the best witnesses for the claimants in a court case. These would preferably be people who had a long-established family connection. They would also need to be articulate, clear and sufficiently confident to withstand cross-examination by seasoned advocates.

For these additional interviews, we returned to work with Zodwa Langazana and the claimant committee in December 2012. In this process we also mapped as far as possible the sites of the roughly 40 homesteads in Khimbili prior to the removal, together with the relevant family names. Sun gave us permission to visit sites and we found the scattered remains of buildings, and other evidence of settlement, as well as graves (see Skosana in this collection). Some graves were covered by a pile of stones and some, from the 1960s, if not before, had headstones in which names were carved. These named graves were potentially good evidence in a court case and the casino had been sufficiently sensitive to leave a number of them; they were hidden in thickets of vegetation adjacent to roads or the golf course. While initially it had been difficult for families to visit graves, Sun had been more relaxed about this in recent years.

The claimant committee had only anecdotal historical information about settlement; dates and places had to be reconstructed through interviews. The best example for the needs of the lawyers was our interview with Madodibunga Sonjica, born in 1948. He knew that his father was born in Khimbili. He did not where his grandfather was born, but he knew that this man and his four wives were all buried in Khimbili and all of his children were born in Khimbili. Family tradition related that they originally came from further north.[11] We were able to work back and establish that his father was born in Khimbili before 1910 and that his grandfather had children by two earlier wives in Khimbili prior to this time. This would likely place his grandfather in the area in the late nineteenth century.

The interview suggested that Sonjica came from a relatively successful family; polygamy on this scale was by no means the norm. Interviews confirmed that they were a core family in Khimbili and many others were related to them by marriage. Of those we interviewed, Sonjica had the largest site after the forced removal, which again suggests some connections in the surrounding area. His evidence was also useful in helping to show the linkages between generations in connection with a few sites. His grandfather's homestead was at the edge of the current airfield near the Mzamba gorge. His father had established his own homestead some time after marriage about two km away, close to where the current casino staff quarters are located. Sonjica was initially brought up at his father's place but as a teenager, he moved to his grandfather's homestead with his elder full brother by the third wife. His father's site was inherited by his half-brother who was a son of his father's second wife. Of the children of the first wife only daughters survived and they did not inherit. This was interesting evidence for us of the way in which family sites were inherited in complex patterns, generally amongst the men of the next generation. Sonjica established his own site at a little distance from his grandfather's after he married in 1975 when he was 27.

We could show that this and other claimant families had roots in the area or neighbouring parts of Bizana for over a century but also that the population was quite diverse, including descendants of traders, incomers from Natal and from the main Amadiba settlements to the south-west. We could not really show, on the basis of our limited number of interviews, that the ancestors of claimant families had been settled in Khimbili since time immemorial, though a few were probably settled there around the time of annexation and there was also a pre-colonial trading station in the area. This may not be surprising in that the coastal areas of Mpondoland were thinly populated in the pre-colonial period and some were intentionally kept vacant for use as winter grazing grounds. The coast receives particularly high rainfall, as well as sea mists, which keep the grass fresh in the dry winter months.

Our interviews went some way to meeting the lawyers' requests but the information was not always straightforward. Firstly, most interviewees remembered only as far back as grandparents. Secondly, this area was on the border of KwaZulu-Natal and there had clearly been a great deal of in-migration. We also came across significant changes in customary patterns of marriage in that some men from farms in Natal moved to communal land in Amadiba to marry and initially stayed at their wife's homestead. Historically customary patterns were patrilocal – women moved on marriage to the homestead of their husband's family (Hunter 1964). There were also cases of women who had applied for and received land in their own right – the first perhaps in the 1950s.

Interviewing was limited and ended when the lawyers decided that there was sufficient information for the court case. We videoed some of the follow-up interviews because the legal team was concerned that some of the older witnesses might pass away before the matter came to court. By this time, at the end of 2012, tensions were surfacing in the claimant group. Some, especially older people, were frustrated that they might see no compensation from this long process, started in 1995, before they died. Earlier negotiations had resulted in an offer of R30 000 per family – a total sum of over R3 million. This was not insignificant for those poorer, older claimants who depended largely on pensions, which were then about half that amount annually. The Eastern Cape Land Commission had encouraged a settlement along these lines.

The committee, however, encouraged by the lawyers and other advisers, was holding out for something more substantial, including restitution of the land; most of the key committee members were younger and better educated. They had financial support from the state, from pro bono lawyers, from the Eastern Cape Gaming Board and from an agent, linked with the African National Congress (ANC), who was interested in further tourist development on the land. Sun used less than half of the 740 ha. This strategy, however, carried with it the risk of further delay and a potentially protracted court case, with no guarantee of success.

Divisions within the community were exacerbated because a few of the office-holders on the claimant committee received small stipends as members of the Bizana Development Committee. This had been established as a condition of the renewal of the casino licence and received some income from Sun to distribute to projects in the district as a whole. When news of this became public, the office-holders were accused of using their position for personal gain while the poor were getting nothing. Two older women were particularly influential in these divisive disputes. Claimant meetings, supervised by the Land Commission, at which the lawyers were present, rejected their committee and replaced all the office-holders except one. The lawyers and community were having to cope with these divisions during the build-up to the court case in 2013–14. However, the new committee maintained sufficient commitment to the legal process to see it through successfully. It called for a great deal of consultation on all sides.

This additional research, tracking down the sites of displaced families in Khimbili, proved valuable during the site inspection by the judge, immediately prior to the beginning of the court case in 2014. The claimants' lawyers arranged for some of those chosen to give evidence to join the entourage and visit their old sites in Khimbili. Miya, over 90 years old, stood next to his former fields and reminisced eloquently about his agricultural success and the shock of the removal. It was a moving performance. Elias Ogle took the large party to his family's former homestead, abutting the Mzamba lagoon, where had fished as a youth. While explaining the settlement in detail, he walked into the ruins of a rondavel, barely visible in the grass, and plucked out a three-legged iron pot, holding it aloft to the audience. This had not been prepared by the claimants' legal team and was a memorable moment, which seemed visibly to move the judge and lawyers.

The judge and legal teams also visited sites to which claimants had moved. Sun's lawyers had argued that there was equivalence in these sites, and even had a soil survey done to show that the soil in the interior was as good or better than that in Khimbili. The claimants' lawyers in turn were able to show that the new sites were smaller, part of dense settlements and mostly unsuitable for agriculture.

## MGUNGUNDLOVU AND XOLOBENI: CUSTOMARY TENURE

The judgments in *Richtersveld* and *Hlolweni* were potentially good for recognising 'communal indigenous ownership' or collective customary landholding within the legal framework of the Restitution Act. However, they did little to specify the nature of that ownership in respect of the land rights of claimant families. There are safeguards for such rural landholders in the Interim Protection of Informal Land Rights Act (IPILRA) Act 31 of 1996, which covers customary as well as informal landholdings. IPILRA can be invoked by a community of landholders to prevent incursions on, or alienation of, their land; this Act also sees such rights as 'akin to ownership'. However, it has certain weaknesses. There is little administrative backup, which means that a community may have to go to court as a defensive strategy. This is expensive and generally depends on the support of pro bono lawyers such as the Legal Resources Centre. And the Act empowers a community to use land for development, even if this impinges on the rights of some families. Before the Maledu and Xolobeni judgments of 2018, it was not clear whether IPILRA was an adequate defence against mining on communal land if the chief and traditional council, which are often taken to represent the community, favoured such an enterprise (Beinart, Delius and Hay 2017: 29). The issue of consent becomes complex here and linked to the concept of community.

In the *Hlolweni* judgment, the named claimants achieved a collective right to the land as a community. Their ownership rights were vested in a CPA that would manage the whole area. Justice Bam did not assign families the right to return to their former sites. That is a decision that the CPA could potentially make, subject to resolving conflicts over the land with the Imizizi traditional council and subject to the consent of the Department of Rural Development and Land Reform (DRDLR), whose powers over post-settlement processes are not entirely clear (see Chaskalson in this volume).

In the *Mgungundlovu* case, the lawyers again prioritised establishing the nature of pre-colonial and early colonial customary rights, and accumulating evidence to show that these had not been extinguished. However, the relatively small group of 106 claimants did not conceive of themselves as a traditional community, nor did they wish to include the chief in their claim. They thought that if the Amadiba chief or a traditional council was involved, those who had actually lost their land would be bypassed.

For this reason, it seemed important to make a stronger and clearer statement of family rights to land in my affidavit. The expert summary emphasised that 'interviews with the claimant community affirm their understanding that in Mpondoland, families have strong rights to specific sites that are inherited across generations'. All interviewees articulated the point that 'once land allocations were made, Mpondo custom gave strong family rights to land'.[12] People spoke of being 'nailed to the land' (*isikhonkwane*). In interviews conducted in 2012, informants insisted that 'Mpondo custom is that once granted land, the family have it forever'.[13] Our interviews indicated strongly that this expressed the 'living customary law' (see Budlender in this volume) in the area.

This position was further developed for the Xolobeni case,[14] which was not a restitution claim. The landholders threatened with removal were living there. The area had not been subject to betterment and most families had sizeable arable plots adjacent to their residential sites. In their case, also, they do not make up an ethnic community or the whole of a traditional community, or even the whole of the local administrative area of Mgungundlovu. When the *Baleni* application to stop mining came to court, it was in the name of the headwoman and 128 people in the area along the coast for which a mining licence had been granted. Some of this is a distinctive zone of red soil, with little vegetation despite the high rainfall, containing titanium and ilmenite, a source of titanium dioxide.

In preparing for this case, it seemed all the more important to establish the rights of the specific families involved, rather than a general form of community ownership. The national government, the local ANC, Chief Lunga Baleni and his traditional council in Amadiba all supported mining in this impoverished area, from which many still migrate to work – arguing that it was a source of jobs and development. As noted in the chapters by Capps and Mnwana, the position is complicated by the requirement that BEE regulations require 26 per cent black ownership. Companies tend to solicit local chiefs as intermediaries and Baleni was directly incorporated as one of the BEE consortium. This was one (but not the only) reason why the landholders opposed mining, because their capacity to benefit may well have been bypassed. If, in this case, the legal community was deemed to be Amadiba traditional council, then the landholders threatened with displacement might have been in a weak legal position.

An argument for emphasising that customary land rights were primarily located at the level of the homesteads and families was one way of strengthening their position. A range of evidence supported such a view. Monica Hunter's ethnography of Mpondoland, *Reaction to Conquest* (1964), contained some valuable statements to this effect, and my reading of documents from the early decades of the twentieth century, summarised in *Political Economy of Pondoland* (Beinart 1982) reinforced it. In his review of ethnographic studies of southern Africa as a whole, Peter Delius (2008: 221) emphasises that 'household rights to arable and residential land were strong in pre-colonial systems of land tenure'.

Geoff Budlender, a leading lawyer for the Legal Resources Centre, who worked on land cases, emphasised with Johan Latsky (1991) that it was important to redefine African land rights, away from a loose notion of communal tenure and towards a more defined notion of ownership, because this would be valuable in strengthening and defending such rights. They cited Alastair Kerr on the customary law of immovable property (1953, 1990), two of the few substantial legal texts on this topic. This drew on Kerr's research into government commissions, anthropological work, consultations with experts, both black and white, and especially court cases. His reference point was mainly the former Ciskei but he tried to generalise.

Kerr noted that white commentators sometimes associated land with a particular chief. However, his sources revealed that the chief did not possess or own the land in his personal capacity, but on behalf of the chiefdom. The English word 'trustee' was sometimes used for the chief, acting in council, although Kerr considered this word problematic because it has specific legal meanings in statute and common law. The chief and council had some political and administrative authority over the land, but Kerr (1953: 17) confirmed: 'The chief is not considered as the owner of the allotted land'. Once allocated to a family for residential and cultivation purposes, it was generally secure. Kerr was clear that, on the basis of many of the sources, 'arable and residential land is not held in common' (1953: 25). Rights to occupy and use the allotted land were exclusive and he used the term 'ownership' (see Moguerane in this volume). Such homestead sites and arable land were generally handed down from generation to generation without interference of the chiefs. This allocated land was heritable within the family according to the rules for succession. Kerr's meaning was different from that adopted later by the Constitutional Court because they were referring to collective or communal indigenous ownership by a larger 'community'. The court has not ruled on living customary law in relation to family landholdings.

These arguments were not tested because the *Mgungundlovu* case did not come to court and *Baleni*, the Xolobeni case, was largely decided on other grounds, notably the provisions of IPILRA. Nevertheless, Judge Basson, in the latter case, did accept that the relevant community for the purposes of determining land rights were those who brought the application to stop mining, and were immediately threatened by removal, and not the whole of Amadiba or Mgungundlovu.

In preparation for the Mgungundlovu case, the lawyers were concerned to know whether the Acts and proclamations passed in the twentieth century to regulate and administer land in the former Transkei had a bearing on the case. The post-apartheid government's Communal Land Rights Act (11 of 2004) was invalidated by the Constitutional Court in 2010 and there was no clear alternative legislation on customary tenure. We investigated earlier proclamations in detail and argued that they had not displaced basic landholding rights. Much of the earlier legislation, including the proclamations by the Union and Transkeian government (from 1963), whatever their status, had ceased to operate. Government land registers have long been abandoned. Allocation by magistrates has not been practised for a few decades and these officials no longer have administrative functions.

After 1994, the state discouraged the issuing of PTOs, which had been central to many proclamations after 1919. In Mgungundlovu, PTOs had never been issued. In 1999 a report co-authored by an official in President Nelson Mandela's Department of Land Affairs, remarked of the former homelands: 'Generally, the systems of administration and record keeping have broken down and threaten a general collapse in rural governance. This collapse includes loss of records, doubts as to which laws apply and the unauthorised issue of permits and other documents' (Adams, Cousins and Manona 1999: 15). A detailed investigation in 2003, commissioned by the government, affirmed that land allocation and administration was becoming informalised (Mcintosh and Associates 2003).

In effect, a newly localised, hybrid system of land allocation and administration has emerged that draws, to varying degrees in different areas, on customary practices as well as some of the systems established under the land proclamations and betterment. It is an expression of living customary law and with respect to the Mgungundlovu and Xolobeni communities, there is a strong argument that this is the legal basis for landholding. Interviews affirm that a majority of informants put family land rights and a form of ownership at the centre of ideas about custom and practice. The state's expert witness on customary law in *Baleni* argued that the landholders held their land as 'lawful occupiers'. We strenuously disputed this formulation and argued that they hold their land as customary owners.

In *Baleni*, the Legal Resources Centre and Richard Spoor attorneys, working with advocate Tembeka Ngcukaitobi, prioritised a defence of community land rights on the basis of IPILRA. The wording in IPILRA, as noted above, is not entirely clear: 'community' is 'any group or portion of a group of persons whose rights to land are derived from shared rules determining access to land held in common by such group'. Justice Basson accepted that the 'portion of a group' who were directly involved as landholders constituted the community for the purposes of the Act. Basson called this the 'Umgungundlovu' community rather than the Xolobeni community but was careful to specify at the start that the relevant group was in fact the 128 applicants. The support of Duduzile Baleni, the headwoman or chief of Mgungundlovu administrative area, ensured that the Amadiba Traditional Council was bypassed. She was, in effect, challenging the authority of Chief Lunga Baleni; similar processes are evident elsewhere. Budlender (in this volume) argues that this has implicitly been recognised in the *Pilane* (2013) judgment: statutory authority accorded to traditional leadership does not necessarily preclude or restrict the operation of customary leadership that has not been recognised by legislation.

Basson agreed that the landholders' rights collectively merited protection under IPILRA. Read together with the Constitution, she argued that the broader intent of both IPILRA and Mineral and Petroleum Resources Development Act (28 of 1922) was to protect and enhance the rights of those who had been most disadvantaged. IPILRA required that the affected community of landholders should give full and informed consent to any mining. This was not an entirely predictable result but it was assisted by recent Constitutional Court judgments, particularly in *Maledu* (2018),[15] which also dealt with IPILRA. These two judgments are perhaps the strongest interpretations of IPILRA thus far handed down by the courts and have important implications with respect to who must be consulted and who must give full consent when landholders who have customary or informal rights are threatened.

## CONCLUSION

Questions of land tenure for those who do not have private, registered title are of great importance in South Africa at present and the rights of millions of South Africans are uncertain. The 1996 Constitution seemed to offer enhancement of tenure but this has not materialised in legislation. The Upgrading of Land Tenure Rights Act (1991, amended in 1996 and 1998) has allowed for some upgrading to title, very largely in urban and peri-urban areas, but it has not been widely implemented (Beinart, Delius and Hay 2017). There are protections for rural landholders in IPILRA and similar Acts passed in the 1990s, but they have limitations and little administrative backup. IPILRA is still temporary legislation, renewed annually.

The judgment handed down in *Hlolweni* (2010) extended that in *Richtersveld* by affirming that customary land rights survived and were akin to ownership. Partly because the communities involved in all three cases discussed in this chapter were not traditional communities under chiefs, the lawyers were keen to establish that such rights were held by affected landowners acting together. They wanted to advance notions of customary indigenous ownership and its legal strength separate from the claims of chiefs and traditional councils. I thought it particularly important to include arguments about the rights of families within such groups in order to bolster further the case for their claims to, and defence of, their land.

My research and affidavits for the *Mgungundlovu* and *Baleni* cases developed these arguments. I was guided by what I heard in the interviews done with Luvuyo Wotshela, and by others in Xolobeni. The lawyers also encouraged such evidence, although this was not their main concern. I hoped that such arguments might result in some positive statement by the courts that the primary rights to land in customary tenure lay with families and not with chiefs, headmen, communities or the state. These arguments were not explicitly tested. The *Mgungundlovu* case was settled after the site inspection and before arguments were made in court. *Baleni*, the Xolobeni case, was decided on other grounds and invoked IPILRA as a generalised, collective defence. The *Maledu* and *Baleni* judgments may imply enhanced rights, but do not make them sufficiently explicit.

The Mgungundlovu claimants for the Wild Coast Sun site were largely content to accept a settlement that disallowed their movement back onto their former land for the foreseeable future. Their rights were realised through a generous cash payment, three times that which had previously been offered, and membership of a CPA that became owner of the site and would receive annual rental payments. The CPA would also become a shareholder in Sun and have the capacity to develop new enterprises if they did not disturb Sun's operations. Each of the 106 claimants received an equal stake in the CPA and, in this sense, their rights to a form of ownership were recognised. As Raphael Chaskalson argues in respect of *Hlolweni* (in this volume), ideas about customary tenure are flexible. My argument here links with a broader discussion about moving towards a single system of landholding in South Africa, in which all have registered, secure and exchangeable rights (Beinart, Delius and Hay 2017). While ideas of ownership through private title may vary greatly amongst different landholders (see Kingwill in this volume), the fundamental value of ownership is that it provides the most secure legal, and arguably social, rights to land.

Court judgments emphasising the strength of family land rights in customary systems would be very valuable, but it would not be wise to depend on this route alone. Relevant court cases may not accumulate and, as each case is specific, judgments may not set general precedents. Views about customary law are contested and judges may not feel sufficiently confident to make a clear statement. The legislative route is probably more suitable, but is also contested. In 2017 the government circulated a new Communal Land Rights Bill for comment. This opened potential for upgrading the rights of customary landholders but only if their community (insufficiently defined) or CPA agreed to do so by a 60 per cent majority. There remains considerable pressure from traditional authorities for a formal role in customary landholding and for a different view of landholding. The government has not released a new version of the Bill, following the consultation stage, although further ideas about registration have been canvassed in the 2017 Report of the High Level Panel on Key Legislation and the 2019 Presidential Advisory Panel on Land Reform and Agriculture.

## NOTES

1. Mgungundlovu Community v Minister of Rural Development and Land Reform, Transkei Sun International Limited and Others LLC/10/2011 (settlement 2014) ('*Mgungundlovu*').
2. Alexkor Ltd and Another v Richtersveld Community and Others [2003] ZACC 18 ('*Richtersveld*').
3. Hlolweni, Mfolozi and Etyeni Communities v North Pondoland Sugar LCC 41/03 [2003] judgment, 2010 ('*Hlolweni*').
4. Baleni, Duduzile and 128 Others v Minister of Mineral Resources and Others 73768/2016 [2018] ZAGPPHC 829 ('*Baleni*').
5. *Hlolweni*, judgment (1 July 2010).
6. *Richtersveld*, judgment, para 102.
7. *Hlolweni*, judgment, para 8.
8. Mgwigwi Miya, interviewed by William Beinart and Luvuyo Wotshela, Lurholweni, Bizana, 17 February 2011.
9. Nomgcobo Elda Langazana, interviewed by William Beinart and Luvuyo Wotshela, Lurholweni, Bizana, 17 December 2011 (Langazana interview).

10  Albertina Simamane, interviewed by William Beinart and Luvuyo Wotshela, Lurholweni, Bizana, 21 December 2011.
11  Madodibunga Sonjica, interviewed by William Beinart and Luvuyo Wotshela, Lurholweni, Bizana, 19 February 2011 and 10 December 2012.
12  William Beinart, Expert summary prepared for Mgungundlovu hearing 2014, vol. 10, para 40.
13  Langazana interview.
14  *Baleni*.
15  Maledu and Others v Itereleng Bakgatla Mineral Resources (Pty) Limited and Another CCT 265/17 [2018] ZACC 41.


REFERENCES

Adams, Martin, Ben Cousins and Siyabulela Manona. 1999. *Land Tenure and Economic Development in Rural South Africa: Constraints and Opportunities*. London: Overseas Development Institute.

Beinart, William. 1982. *The Political Economy of Pondoland 1860 to1930*. Cambridge: Cambridge University Press.

Beinart, William, Peter Delius and Michelle Hay. 2017. *Rights to Land: A Guide to Tenure Upgrading and Restitution in South Africa*. Johannesburg: Jacana Media.

Budlender, Geoff and Johan Latsky. 1991. 'Unravelling Rights to Land in Rural Race Zones'. In *A Harvest of Discontent: The Land Question in South Africa*, edited by Michael de Klerk, 115–138. Cape Town: IDASA.

Delius, Peter. 2008. 'Contested Terrain: Land Rights and Chiefly Power in Historical Perspective'. In *Land, Power & Custom: Controversies Generated by South Africa's Communal Land Rights Act*, edited by Aninka Claassens and Ben Cousins, 211–237. Cape Town: UCT Press.

Delius, Peter and Stefan Schirmer. 2000. 'Soil Conservation in a Racially Ordered Society: South Africa 1930–1970'. *Journal of Southern African Studies* 26, no. 4: 719–742.

Gibbs, Timothy. 2014. *Mandela's Kinsmen: Nationalist Elites and Apartheid's First Bantustan*. Suffolk: James Currey.

Hornby, Donna, Rosalie Kingwill, Lauren Royston and Ben Cousins, eds. 2017. *Untitled: Securing Land Tenure in Urban and Rural South Africa*. Pietermaritzburg: University of KwaZulu-Natal Press.

Hunter, Monica. 1964. *Reaction to Conquest*. London: Oxford University Press.

Kerr, Alastair James. 1953. *The Native Common Law of Immovable Property in South Africa*. Durban: Butterworth.

Kerr, Alastair. James. 1990. *The Customary Law of Immovable Property and of Succession*. Grahamstown: Grocott and Sherry.

Mcintosh, Xaba and Associates. 2003. *Land Issues Scoping Study: Communal Land Tenure Areas*. London: DFID.

## CONTRIBUTORS

**William Beinart** is emeritus professor, St Antony's College, University of Oxford and senior research associate, University of Johannesburg. He was formerly director of the African Studies Centre. He has researched on land reform, as well as restitution and chieftaincy cases in the Eastern Cape and KwaZulu-Natal. Recent publications include, with Luvuyo Wotshela, *Prickly Pear: The Social History of a Plant* (2011), with Karen Brown, *African Local Knowledge* (2013), with Peter Delius and Michelle Hay, *Rights to Land* (2017), with Peter Delius, *Next Steps towards Land Reform* (2019) and, with Sonwabile Mnwana and Luvuyo Wotshela, on land reform and agrarian change (*Transformation* 102, 2020).

**Geoff Budlender,** SC, is an advocate in Cape Town, practising mainly in constitutional law, public and administrative law generally, and land law. He was previously the national director of the Legal Resources Centre, and subsequently director-general of the Department of Land Affairs (May 1996 to January 2000.) He has served as an acting judge of the High Court in Johannesburg and Cape Town. He appears as counsel in the higher courts in South Africa, including the Constitutional Court, and also in Namibia and Botswana. He was counsel in a number of the cases to which reference is made in his contribution to this volume. He is also Extraordinary Professor of Public Law at Stellenbosch

**Gavin Capps** is a senior lecturer in Economics at Kingston University, London. He researches the new political economies of 'customary' land and authority that are emerging in the mineral-rich zones of the former South African homelands, with a particular focus on the platinum industry. He previously led the Mining and Rural Transformation in Southern Africa (MARTISA) project, which was funded by the Ford Foundation and located in the Society, Work and Politics Institute (SWOP) at the University of the Witwatersrand (2013–18), where he remains a research associate. He has also acted as an expert witness for the Legal Resources Centre.

**Raphael Chaskalson** worked for two years in South Africa's non-profit sector, before studying for Master's degrees in Economic History and Development Economics at the University of Oxford. His chapter is a version of his dissertation in the former. His research interests include environmental history, economics and the politics of land reform. He currently works in London as a consultant for Vivid Economics, specialising in the economics of climate change.

**Thiyane Duda** is a researcher at the Land and Accountability Research Centre (LARC) in Public Law at the University of Cape Town. His focus area of research is traditional governance, living customary law and related legislation and its impact on the lives of rural citizens in the former Bantustans. Previously, Thiyane worked as a junior researcher at the Human Sciences Research Council in the HIV/AIDS, STI & TB unit and was involved in research on HIV and alcohol, HIV and men that have sex with men, HIV and gender-based violence. Thiyane has a BSocSci (Hons) in Social Anthropology from the University of Cape Town.

**Derick Fay** is an associate professor in the Department of Anthropology at the University of California, Riverside. His research is grounded in the political ecology of livelihoods, land and conservation in post-apartheid South Africa, and fieldwork around Dwesa-Cwebe Nature Reserve. He is currently working on the historical political ecology of customary and administrative law in the Eastern Cape, based in part on work conducted as a Fulbright Scholar in 2017–18 at the Land and Accountability Research Centre of the University of Cape Town School of Law.

**Rosalie Kingwill** is a research associate at the Institute for Poverty, Land and Agrarian Studies (PLAAS), University of the Western Cape, and an independent critical consultant on land issues, including research on land restitution claims. She frequently works with civil society organisations on policy-related research regarding land administration and tenure. She brings an understanding of emergent hybrid systems of authority and landholding in urban and rural settings. She is concerned with innovative approaches to formalisation and integration of land administration and tenure institutions in the context of legal pluralism, factoring in persisting customary social norms, kinship and family law.

**Sonwabile Mnwana** is an associate professor of Sociology at the University of Fort Hare. He holds a PhD in Social Sciences. He is also a research associate at the Society, Work and Politics Institute (SWOP) and at the Southern Centre for Inequality Studies, both at the University of the Witwatersrand. He is a former president of the South African Sociological Association. His research focuses on land, mining and rural social change. He is project leader for several research projects. Mnwana is also a research fellow at the Institute for Advanced Studies in the Humanities (IASH), University of Edinburgh. He previously held a visiting fellowship at the Stellenbosch Institute for Advanced Study.

**Khumisho Moguerane** is a historian of the European empire in southern Africa, with a current focus on colonial Bechuanaland. She is interested in what the (post) colonial archive in this setting has to offer for an interdisciplinary inquiry into nationhood, moral lives and subjectivity. She explores these questions through a study of everyday practice, especially on the land, and the language that mediates it. She is a senior lecturer in the Department of History at the University of Johannesburg.

**Ayesha Motala** is a research officer at the Land and Accountability Research Centre (LARC) at the University of Cape Town. She graduated with a Bachelor of Law and Master's in Environmental Law from the University of KwaZulu-Natal. Ayesha is an admitted attorney of the High Court of South Africa.

**Joanna Pickering** is a lawyer in ClientEarth's Climate and Forests programme. She previously occupied a research position in the Land and Accountability Research Centre's mining programme. Joanna holds a Bachelor of Arts and an LLB from Rhodes University, a Master's in European Human Rights Law from the University of Toulouse 1 Capitole, and recently completed a Master's degree in Human Rights and Humanitarian Action at Sciences Po, Paris. She is an admitted attorney of the High Court of South Africa.

**Dineo Skosana** is a researcher at the Society, Work and Politics Institute (SWOP). She holds a PhD in Political Science from the University of the Witwatersrand. Her doctoral research explored the contestations over coal mining and African grave relocations in Tweefontein, Mpumalanga Province. She has published extensively about the continued salience of traditional leadership in South Africa's democracy. She has research interests in indigenous politics, the institution of traditional leadership, as well as the politics of land, heritage and belonging.

**Janine Ubink** holds a chair in Law, Governance and Development at the Van Vollenhoven Institute (Leiden University). She has also taught at the law schools of University of California, Irvine, New York University and Australia National University and at the Lim A Po Institute for Social Studies in Suriname. Janine's research focuses on legal pluralism, traditional authorities, land management, gender, transitional justice and rule of law reforms, with a focus on Ghana, Namibia, Malawi, Somalia and South Africa. Janine is the president of the International Commission on Legal Pluralism.

**Tara Weinberg** is a PhD candidate in the History Department at the University of Michigan. Her dissertation explores a history of collective property ownership in South Africa. She has previously worked as a researcher on land reform at the University of Cape Town's Land and Accountability Research Centre (LARC). She has also worked on an oral history project about African immigrants to the United States. She has published and taught on questions of land, law and activism in southern Africa.

# INDEX

**A**
Abolition of Racially Based Land Measures Act 194
academics
   anthropologists 7, 8, 29, 32, 36—38, 41, 43, 44—44, 48, 50, 114—115
   court experts 6—8, 9, 28, 36—38, 44, 51, 193, 249
   historians 6—8, 32, 36, 112, 117, 166, 193, 249
activists 42, 193—194, 209—213, 221—225, 230
   lawyers 215, 217
   local 66, 69, 71, 72, 99, 125, 155, 214
Advisory Commission on Land Allocation (ACLA) 194, 216
African National Congress (ANC)
   land policies 1—3, 116—117, 208, 210, 216—217
   mining and 86, 89, 91, 239, 260
   traditional leadership and 3, 4, 5, 6, 9, 65, 147—148, 153, 155
African National Congress Land Committee 216—217
Agricultural Development Act 250—252
agriculture 2—4, 16, 183, 190, 232, 233, 238, 248, 253
   sugar 16, 229, 233—238, 240—244, 250, 252
Alexander Commission of Inquiry 248—249
Alexkor Ltd 239, 252
amaHlathi 142—144, 148—153, 158
AmaHlathi Crisis Committee (ACC) 144, 150—151

amaMfengu 143, 145—146, 148, 149, 152—155, 158, 160, 196
ancestors 13, 14, 45, 46, 47, 53, 107—111, 118, 145, 256
Anglo American Platinum (Amplats) 67, 70, 129, 137
anthropology; *see* academics, anthropologists
apartheid era; *see also* Bantustans
   chiefs 2, 15, 39, 62, 133, 134, 147, 152, 154, 212, 213, 219
   community authorities 145—146, 149, 157, 159
   customary law 24, 26, 28, 136, 230
   developmentalism 67, 231—236, 239
   ethnography 93, 220
   forced removals 4, 73, 113, 114, 143, 193, 194, 197, 208, 210—213
   land management 2, 62, 209, 210, 213, 214, 216, 218
   legal system 16, 21, 22, 26, 28, 112, 145, 194, 210, 225
   mining rights 67
   resistance 147, 143, 148, 193, 196, 194, 197, 216
   traditional authorities 2, 9, 62—65, 68, 74, 87, 122, 128, 129, 143
   tribal authorities; *see* Bantustans, community authorities
arable land 15, 16, 230, 231, 249, 259—261
Association for Community and Rural Advancement (AnCRA) 208, 209, 215, 219, 225

Association for Rural Advancement (AFRA) 208, 215—216, 218—220, 223, 225

**B**
Bafokeng 11—13, 33, 95, 232
   Tribal Authority 232
Bakgatla-ba-Kautlwale 72—73
Bakgatla-ba-Kgafela 10, 12, 33, 66—74, 121—125, 128, 220
   area 66—68
   Communal Property Association 73—76
   Traditional Administration 67
Bakgatla-ba-Sefikile Traditional Community Association 71—72
Bakubung-ba-Monnakgotla 33
Bantu Authorities Act 123, 133, 145, 148, 159, 231, 237
Bantustans (former) 4, 5,13, 60—62
   apartheid era 2, 4, 9, 61—62, 83, 145—147, 211—213, 231—236, 250
   Bophuthatswana 11, 64, 67, 76, 83, 91, 183, 209, 212, 232
   Ciskei 9, 10, 143—147, 152—154, 158, 195, 197
   community authorities 145—146, 149, 157, 159
   customary law and; *see* customary law
   institutional legacies 4, 9, 13, 17, 39, 87, 93, 122, 133, 142, 157, 159
   KwaZulu 233, 236
   land management; *see* betterment planning
   land rights; *see* land rights
   Lebowa 64, 129
   mineral resources 11, 13, 64—68, 83—86; 129, 249; *see also* mining
   post-apartheid economy 2—3
   Transkei 9, 15, 35, 55, 148, 155, 229—239, 247—255, 261
Bapo-ba-Mogale ('the Bapo') 11, 13, 33, 81, 82, 137
   leadership contestation 87—95, 97—99, 100
   mining and 82—86, 95—100
Barolong 16, 166—173, 177, 179, 182, 183
Barrick Gold Corporation 70
Barrick Platinum South Africa (Pty) Ltd 70
Beaumont Commission 177, 182
Bechuanaland 165, 166, 167—170, 174, 176, 179—182
Bennet, Thomas 40, 51—52, 55
betterment; *see* betterment planning
Bill of Rights 22, 23, 26, 28, 30, 52, 122
Bizana 9, 15, 16, 247—250, 252, 256
Bizana Development Committee 257
Black Administration Act 26, 133, 213; see also Native Administration Act
black economic empowerment (BEE) 3, 12, 65, 82, 84—86, 93, 97, 249, 260
Bophuthatswana (former) 11, 64, 67, 76, 83, 91, 183, 209, 212, 232
Border Rural Committee (BRC) 193; *see also* Grahamstown Rural Committee
Burke, Paul 36—38, 41, 43, 48—50, 54

**C**
Cala Reserve Planning Committee 156
capital 66, 83, 187, 205
capitalism 187, 189—190
cattle 69, 76, 134, 167, 192, 199, 212, 215
chiefs, chieftaincy; *see also* traditional leaders
   abuses of power 10, 25—26, 121, 124—129, 134—136
   apartheid era 2, 15, 39, 62, 67, 136, 145—147, 152, 212, 213, 219, 231—236
   claims, disputes 2, 5, 6, 9, 12, 26, 81, 132—133, 148—158, 263
   colonial era 29, 61, 62—64, 136, 164—170, 173—183, 196
   land disputes; *see* land claims
   local governance and 4, 5, 9, 64, 65
   mining and 3, 11—13, 66—68, 81—83, 87—93, 260
   powers, roles 1, 3, 9, 11, 12, 63—66, 136, 138, 141, 142, 147, 230, 231, 251
   pre-colonial 144
   resistance to 10, 68—77
   succession 6, 13, 14, 93—95, 99, 241
chrome; *see* mining
Ciskei (former) 9, 10, 143—147, 152—154, 158, 195, 197

Ciskei National Independence Party (CNIP) 146—147
Ciskei National Party (CNP) 146
claims; *see* communities; chiefs; land claims; restitution; traditional authorities
clans 168, 175, 181, 182, 196
   meetings 129
   royal 149
   section heads 144, 145
coal; *see* mining
collective ownership; *see* land ownership, collective
colonialism 114, 115, 164, 197, 254
   British Bechuanaland 165, 166, 167—170, 174, 176, 179—182
   custom and 28—29, 61—64, 75, 129, 136, 153, 196, 230
   governance 64, 144, 146, 153—154, 164—170, 174, 176, 181, 189
   land appropriation 112, 119, 158, 208, 210
   native reserves 61, 164—170, 174, 175, 178
Commission on Restitution of Land Rights 10, 150, 229, 236, 239, 242
   Eastern Cape 240, 253, 257—258
Commission on Traditional Leadership Disputes and Claims 124, 142, 150—151, 153
commonage 15, 16, 195, 200, 231; *see also* communal areas
common law 7, 22, 23, 27—28, 31, 43, 122, 186, 187
   *vs* customary law 7, 24, 42—44, 55, 196, 201, 239, 250
communal areas 2, 5, 64—68, 195, 213; *see also* commonage
Communal Land Rights Act (CLARA) 3, 4, 6, 17, 42, 65, 237, 261
Communal Property Associations (CPAs) 2, 4, 10, 195, 237, 239—240, 263
   beginnings 210—211, 214—219, 225
   conflicts 73—74, 76, 191, 219—221, 224, 225, 240—243
   constitutions 17, 30, 31, 209, 214, 215, 218, 221, 222
   functioning 30—31, 73—74, 191, 259

   land rights and 222—224
   politicisation 117, 211
   women and 223
Communal Property Associations Act 17, 30, 73, 195
   implementation 31, 38—39, 210, 214, 217, 237, 244
communities; *see also* amaHlathi, AmaMfengu; traditional communities
   claimant 6, 73, 117, 193, 197, 213, 216, 223, 238—244, 251
   concept 61—64, 189
   customary 24—26, 28, 33, 42—45, 51—53
   identification as 158—159, 220, 231
   'mine' 12, 66, 68, 84, 86, 119
   rural 5, 8, 9, 64—65, 112, 117, 122, 132, 136, 138, 142—143, 145—149, 153
   village 10, 155—157, 160, 263
Community Authorities 145, 146, 149, 154
community trusts; *see* trusts, trusteeship
Concerned Bakgatla Anti-Corruption Organisation (COBACO) 70
Congress of Traditional Leaders of South Africa (CONTRALESA) 8, 141, 220
Constitution; *see* South African Constitution
Constitutional Court; *see also* court cases; court judgments; South African Constitution
   appointments 32—33
   customary law and 5, 23—27, 28, 31, 41—43, 77, 129, 142, 153, 231, 239, 249, 250
   direction 32—33
   enforcement of rulings 123, 139
   legislation and 3, 136, 138, 142, 261
   limits 31—32
   *vs* lower courts 5, 10, 14, 75, 131—132, 135
   principles 23—26, 33, 128—129
   transformation and 21—22, 32
corruption 11, 33, 66, 68, 70, 71, 92, 123, 137, 154, 220, 249

court cases; *see also* Constitutional Court
  Bakgatla (2015) 30—31
  Baleni (2006) 248, 249, 258, 259, 261, 263
  Bhe (2004) 14, 23, 24, 25, 41, 129, 201
  Du Plessis (1996) 25
  Ga-Chokoe (2015) 129—130
  Gongqose (2012) 14, 35—36, 38, 42—55
  Gumede (2008) 23
  Hlolweni (2010) 15, 16, 229—231, 236—240, 242, 244, 248, 250—252, 258, 259, 263
  Hyundai (2000) 21
  Mahlake (2016) 133—134
  Makwanyane (1995) 21, 22
  Mayelane (2013) 23, 28—30, 50
  Mohlala (2014) 132—133
  Mgungundlovu (2014) 247—249, 252—259, 261, 263
  Petlele (1908) 25
  Pilane (2013) 10, 23, 26, 27, 32, 121, 123, 124, 128—132, 134—136, 138, 139, 262
  Ramantele (2013) 29
  Richtersveld (2003) 14, 23, 24, 27, 30, 41—44, 50, 55, 239, 248, 250—255, 258, 263
  Salem (2017) 6
  Shilubana (2007) 23, 55
  Sigcau (2013) 23, 26
  Tongoane (2010) 23, 42, 43
  Xolobeni; *see* Baleni (2006)
court judgments 9, 14, 32, 72—74, 121, 126, 129, 201, 242, 255, 262; *see also* Constitutional Court
courts; *see also* Constitutional Court
  colonial 63, 178
  High 23, 26, 52, 53, 70—72, 88, 89, 124—128, 135, 151, 156
  Land Claims 10, 73, 74, 236, 237, 240, 248, 250, 252
  Magistrate's 47—52, 123, 129—133, 156, 180
  Supreme 25, 69, 134, 170, 174, 178, 179, 180, 182
  Supreme Court of Appeal 23, 36, 52—55, 71—74, 126, 174, 237

customary law; *see also* living customary law
  academic research into 2, 6—8, 38—39, 230
  apartheid era 24, 26, 28, 136, 230
  colonialism and 28—29, 61—64, 75, 129, 136, 153, 165, 177, 196, 230
  *vs* common law 7, 24, 42—44, 55, 196, 201, 239, 250
  Constitutional Court and 5, 23—28, 31, 41—43, 77, 129, 142, 153, 231, 239, 249, 250
  contestations 2, 31, 94, 122, 125—126, 128, 130, 132—136, 151, 155, 237, 264
  development 31, 189
  distortions 24—25, 63—64, 69—70, 74—75, 196
  fluidity 5, 7, 13, 27—29, 31, 39, 187, 189
  formalisation 63—64
  *vs* legislative x, 14—15, 51—55, 123, 130, 139, 156
  marine resources and 44—55
  notion 39, 188
  official, rigid 61, 63—64, 77, 131, 157, 207
  women and 29, 23, 28—29, 31, 39, 165, 201, 202, 257
customary marriage 23, 28—29, 39, 165, 201, 202, 257
customary tenure 2, 42—43, 189, 190, 230, 231, 248, 249, 258—264
  legislation and 244, 261
  mineral resources and 33
  nature 38, 249, 264
  rights 15, 43, 263

**D**

D-accounts (development accounts) 67—68, 83, 90—91, 95, 97, 99
Daggakraal 214
Daggakraal Natives Committee 214
deeds; *see* title deeds
democracy 32, 33
  CPAs and 30—31, 75, 191, 195, 209, 220, 237, 244
  Constitution; *see* South African Constitution
  custom and 17, 26, 30, 127, 131, 142, 157, 194

South African 2, 3, 8, 11, 13, 21, 24, 26, 83, 116, 141, 225
traditional institutions and 8, 9, 26, 94, 128, 134, 142, 147, 156, 159
Department of Agriculture, Forestry and Fisheries (DAFF) 45
Department of Land Affairs (DLA) 39, 218, 222, 223, 236, 237
Department of Local Government and Traditional Affairs
Eastern Cape 152, 156
North West 67, 95, 137
Department of Rural Development and Land Reform (DRDLR) 211, 218, 220, 239, 240, 259
developmentalism 67, 231—236, 239
development accounts; *see* D-accounts
*dikgosi*; *see* traditional leaders
Dithakwaneng 208—210, 212—214, 225
Dintwe, Reuben 72, 125, 126, 127
dispossession; *see* land dispossession
Distribution and Transfer of Certain Land Act 194
Driefontein 209—215, 221, 223, 224
Dwesa-Cwebe Nature Reserve 14, 35—36, 44—46, 51, 52

**E**
Eastern Cape Governance Act 155—157, 159
Eastern Cape Land Claims Commission 240, 253, 257
economic development 2—4, 65, 86, 190, 232—233
environmental protection 52—54
ethnicity
conflict and 10, 116, 146, 160
mobilisation around 10, 62, 160
identities and 10, 13, 62, 115, 191, 212, 254
Etyeni 229, 233, 235, 236
evictions 173—178, 182, 210, 212—217, 224, 225, 248; *see also* forced removals

**F**
family tenure; *see* land rights, family
fiduciary control 91—93, 99

Fingoes 145, 149, 177— 178
Fingo Village 197, 198, 200, 202, 203
first-comers 191, 194
fishing 14—15, 44—48, 50—55
forced removals 4, 73, 113, 114, 143, 193, 194, 197, 208, 210—213; *see also* evictions
forests, forestry 231, 240—241
Framework Act; *see* Traditional Leadership and Governance Framework Act
freehold title 154, 175, 182, 186—187, 191, 194—200, 203, 205

**G**
gender inequality 5, 29, 40, 88, 183, 191, 197, 200—204, 223
General Royal Council (GRC) 94, 95, 98
Glencore PLC 13, 104—112, 116, 118
Glen Grey Act 144
gold; *see* mining
Grahamstown Rural Committee; *see also* Border Rural Committee (BRC) 215
grave sites 13—14, 104—112, 255
dispossession and 112—114, 119
as evidence 114—118, 119
Group Areas Act 220

**H**
headmen, headwomen 129—130, 144— 149, 153—160, 165, 177, 212, 231
Hlolweni 229, 231, 233, 236, 239— 244
Hobeni 35—36, 41, 46, 49, 51
Hobeni Communal Property Association 38—39
homelands; *see* Bantustans
homesteads 166—168, 179, 234, 253, 255—258, 260, 261
House of Traditional Leaders 94, 133, 150

**I**
identities 115
community 8, 117, 118, 119, 193, 230, 231
contested 66, 126, 166
cultural 45, 142, 190
ethnic, tribal 10, 13, 61, 62, 77, 115, 160, 165, 168, 191, 212, 254
family 201

275

identities *(continued)*
    group 60, 62, 68, 75, 188
    juristic 201
    social 196
*iinkosi; see* chiefs, chieftaincy
ImiZizi Traditional Authority 236, 241
immovable property 201, 260
individual tenure; *see* land tenure, individual
inheritance 14, 17, 23, 39, 41, 165, 172, 196, 199—205; *see also* succession
interdicts 124
    against meetings 26, 70—72, 124, 127—132
    traditional authorities and 88—90, 132—134
    against transactions 84
Itereleng Bakgatla Mineral Resources (Pty) Ltd (IBMR) 70
Interim Protection of Informal Land Rights Act (IPILRA) 18, 222, 243, 258, 262
Intestate and Succession Act 201, 202

## J
Judicial Service Commission (JSC) 32—33

## K
Keiskammahoek 10, 143, 145, 153—158, 198
Kerr, Alistair 15, 230, 260—261
*kgosi; see* chiefs
kings 141, 150, 160, 239
kinship 114, 190, 191, 197, 200—205
KwaGcina Traditional Council (KTC) 156
KwaZulu (former) 233, 236

## L
labour tenants 104, 105, 109, 110—114, 117, 149, 215, 223, 224
land administration
    CPAs and 211
    contestation over 11
    hybrid forms 191, 194, 262
    informal 261
    state 192, 195, 232, 261
    traditional authorities and 3, 5, 10, 40, 65, 136, 174, 230, 232

community authorities 145—146, 149, 154, 157, 159
land access
    communal 31, 191, 192, 214, 217, 222, 262
    customary 77
    families and 16, 17, 166, 197—205
    gendered 17, 197—205
    mediated (by chiefs) 1, 11, 66, 166
    unequal 1, 166, 189, 211
land allocations 41, 213, 231, 262
    colonial 165, 168—171, 176, 180—181, 251
    CPA Act and 214, 222, 223
    to families 259—261
    to individuals 16, 231
    by North Pondoland Sugar 234—236
    traditional authorities and 17, 29, 39, 64, 149, 154, 171, 180—181, 213, 232, 234
Land and Accountability Research Centre (LARC) xii, 243
Land and Agricultural Bank 70
land cases; *see* court cases
land claims 6—8, 10, 12, 33, 37—41, 77, 187, 188, 191, 193—194, 263
    Bakgatla area 60, 71—77
    Bizana 252—258
    Hlolweni 229, 236—244, 250—252
    Hobeni 41
    Rietfontein (Molopo Reserve) 16, 171—173, 178—182, 210
    Rustenburg (Bapo) 82—86, 100
    Tweefontein Colliery Complex 13, 109, 115—119
Land Claims Commission; *see* Commission on Restitution of Land Rights
Land Claims Court 10, 73, 74, 236, 237, 240, 248, 250, 252
Land Commission, Bechuanaland (1886) 168, 169, 171, 172, 173, 181
land cultivation; *see* agriculture
land disputes 4, 5, 10, 12, 16, 68—77, 172, 180, 193, 197, 200, 210, 240, 249
land dispossession 187—190, 203—205
    apartheid and colonial 2, 6, 61—63, 76, 112—114, 119, 197, 198, 211—213, 238, 239

through indebtedness 199
by local elites 3, 12, 18, 158, 172
mining and 12, 14, 18, 77, 105
protection against 16, 18
resistance to 211—215
land management; *see* land governance
land ownership; *see also* land rights; land title,
  collective, communal; *see* commonage, communal areas; Communal Property Associations
  common-law 239, 250
  concept 186—187, 192, 198—199, 204, 260, 261, 264
  customary 7, 15—18, 30, 39, 61, 151, 250, 252, 254, 255, 258, 263
  disputes *see* land rights, contested
  exclusion; *see* dispossession
  family, household 63, 196—205, 222, 239, 260—261
  hybrid, fluid 5, 15—17, 24, 41, 186—187, 192, 196—198, 201, 204, 214, 230, 248
  immovable property and 201, 260
  individual 195, 196, 197, 199, 217, 222, 230
  private 16—17, 117, 187, 199, 264
  state 4
  white 4, 6—7, 174, 210, 211, 212
landlords 86, 97
  chiefs 16, 165, 166, 169, 170, 183
  colonial 174, 177—178
land reform 2—3, 6; *see also* land tenure laws
  activism 194, 208—210, 215—221
  apartheid era 194
  failures 117
  implementation 225, 240
  law 17, 117, 194—195, 210, 211, 264; *see also* land tenure laws
  policies 193—195
  politics and 116
  programme 1, 4, 116, 118, 193
Land Restitution Act; *see* Restitution of Land Rights Act
land restitution, redistribution 1—2, 4, 17, 114, 116, 119, 193, 210, 221, 229, 237; *see also* land claims

land rights; *see also* rights
  commodification 60
  communal 2, 8, 17, 43, 44, 63—64, 250, 254, 258, 259, 262
  contested 4, 5, 10, 12, 16, 68—77, 172, 180, 193, 197, 200, 210, 240, 249
  customary 15, 17, 23—25, 29, 30, 39, 42, 44, 60, 61, 64, 77, 188, 210, 243, 244, 263
  dispossession; *see* land dispossession
  familial 15, 16, 62, 63, 166, 192, 205, 215, 221—224, 230, 231, 234, 239, 259—263
  individual 195, 197, 205, 215, 221—224, 230, 231
  mediation by chiefs 68, 71, 75, 212—213
  occupation, occupational, *see also* permission to occupy (PTO)
  overlapping 6, 15, 178, 192, 193, 230—231, 234, 248
  protection, restoration 18, 32, 73, 116, 119, 188, 193, 208, 209, 217, 244, 260, 262
  registration 192, 195, 217, 218, 219, 221, 244
land tenure 16, 44, 60, 61, 117, 190—191, 217—219, 223, 225, 240, 263
  customary; *see* customary tenure
  collective, communal 38, 44, 62, 154, 164, 181, 187, 188—190, 214, 230—231
  disputes; *see* land rights, contested
  fluid, hybrid 5, 13, 17, 190—192, 196—197, 204
  homestead-based 166
  individual 61, 144, 190, 213
  informal 4, 43
  laws; *see* land tenure laws
  policies 193—195, 244
  permission to occupy (PTO); *see* permission to occupy certificates
  pre-colonial 196
  quitrent 154, 194—196, 222, 255
  reform; *see* land reform
  security 116, 205, 211, 232
  upgrading 2, 194, 263; *see also* land tenure laws; Upgrading of Land Tenure Rights Act

277

land tenure laws
 Abolition of Racially Based Land
  Measures Act 194
 Communal Land Rights Act (CLARA)
  3, 4, 6, 17, 42, 65, 237, 261
 Communal Property Associations Act
  17, 30, 31, 38—39, 73, 195, 210, 214,
  217, 237, 244
 Distribution and Transfer of Certain
  Land Act 194
 Glen Grey Act 144
 Interim Protection of Informal Land
  Rights Act (IPILRA) 18, 222, 243,
  258, 262
 Provision of Certain Land for
  Settlement/and Assistance Act 217
 Upgrading of Land Tenure Rights Act
  (ULTRA) 194, 263
land title (formal) 12, 187— 190, 192, 205;
 see also land ownership
 collective 17, 191—195, 209, 214, 217,
  218, 221, 222, 224, 239, 244
 deeds 117, 183, 198, 209, 210, 213—218,
  222, 225
 family 190, 191, 194, 196, 198—203,
  205, 222
 freehold 154, 175, 182, 186—187, 191,
  194—200, 203, 205
 indigenous 239
 individual 16, 191, 194—197, 205, 210,
  213—217, 222
 native 38
 private 16, 17, 197, 244, 263, 264
 tribal-title-trust-regime 197
Langa, Deputy Chief Justice Pius 21, 25
lawyers, role of 4, 7—8, 10, 11, 18, 24,
 28, 30, 32, 75, 193, 210, 213,
 215—217, 225
Lebowa (former) 64, 129
Legal Resources Centre (LRC) 8, 38, 42, 44,
 54, 144, 213, 216, 218
Lesetlheng village 66
lineages 11, 46, 85, 94, 116, 174,
 199—201
living customary law 5, 7, 24, 39, 77, 187,
 197, 259; see also customary law
 determination of 28—30, 249
 fluidity of 31, 39, 55, 262

jurisprudence 10, 14—15, 24, 28, 33, 35,
 38, 41—45, 54, 55, 128, 261
landholding and 15, 16, 29, 201, 224
concept 24, 41, 55, 63, 77
vs 'official' 61, 63—64, 129
local government 5, 9, 67, 95, 123, 137,
 143, 149, 152, 156, 159
Local Government and Traditional Affairs
 (LGTA) 67
local histories 6, 7, 12, 46, 66, 75, 82,
 158—159, 168, 172, 224, 255
local politics 5, 10, 85, 93, 231—238
local practice 9, 14, 24, 29, 40—41, 44, 45,
 47, 52, 249
 custom and 31, 43, 55, 142, 178, 190,
  196, 234, 262
 land and 16, 40, 41, 165, 168, 178, 187,
  192, 196, 234, 262
 traditional leaders and 122, 129, 153,
  156, 165
Lonmin plc 65, 81—86, 88, 89, 93, 95—99

**M**
magistrates 45—52, 131, 144, 154,
 170—172, 176, 177, 180, 181, 230,
 232, 261
Mampuru, Chief (*Kgosi*) Billy 132—133
Marikana Commission of Inquiry 81, 86
Marikana massacre 12, 65—66, 82, 86
Marine Living Resources Act (MLRA)
 46, 48, 52
Marine Protected Area (MPA) 46, 52—54
marine resources 14, 15, 45, 46, 48, 51,
 52, 54
Mashego, Chief (Kgosi) Mo 133
matriliny 201, 203
Mditshwa, Jongamampondo 236—237,
 241—243
Mfolozi 229, 233, 236
Mgungundlovu 252, 254, 255, 259—263;
 see also court cases, *Mgungundlovu*
 (2014)
 community 254—255, 261—263
migrants 5, 61, 104, 105, 112—114, 167
Mineral and Petroleum Resources
 Development Act (MPRDA) 3,
 11—14, 33, 65, 84, 104, 117,
 119, 262

mineral resources; *see* mining
mining
    chrome 2, 88
    coal 2, 6, 13, 104, 105—112
    disputes; *see* mining disputes
    gold 10, 11
    platinum 6, 11—13, 60, 62, 64—70, 81—86, 97, 125, 129, 137, 232
    revenues 11—13, 64—68, 70—72, 75, 77, 83—85, 88, 90—91, 96, 124, 220
    rights 11, 13, 33, 77, 84, 86, 239
    titanium 2, 260
Mining and Rural Transformation in Southern Africa (MARTISA) research project 81, 100*n*1
mining disputes 8, 10—14, 18, 33, 232, 249, 259; *see also* court cases, *Baleni* (2006)
    Bakgatla-ba-Kgafela 68, 70—75; 123—135
    Bapo-ba-Mogale area 81—93, 97—100
    Tweefontein farm 106—112, 118—119
Mogale, *Kgosi* (Chief) Bob Edward 87—89, 98
Mogoeng, Chief Justice Mogoeng 32, 127
Moruleng 69, 123, 136
Moses Kotane Local Municipality (MKLM) 67
Motlhabe 66, 72, 73, 77, 121, 124—128
    Tribal Authority 125, 126
Mpondoland 229, 232, 233, 240, 248, 254—256, 259, 260

**N**
National Heritage Resources Act (NHRA) 13, 104, 105, 110
National Land Committee (NLC) 193, 216
National Movement of Rural Women 223
National Traditional Leaders Framework Act 94
Native Administration Act 16, 26, 145, 166, 181—182, 196, 201; *see also* Black Administration Act
Native Affairs Act 179
Native Affairs Commission 179—181
Native Commissioners 69, 165—166, 174, 181, 182, 238
Native Farmers' Association (NFA) 214

Natives Land Act (1913) 16, 62, 112, 174—180, 182, 211—212
Native Locations Act 169, 179
Native Trust and Land Act 62, 198, 212
natural resources 11, 14, 15, 35, 44, 45, 51, 63—64, 65, 136
newcomers 149, 169, 176, 177, 179, 191, 195, 214
Nhlapo Commission 6, 9
non-governmental organisations (NGOs) 4, 42, 144, 193, 208, 210, 216, 243
norms
    customary 25, 27, 41, 51
    democratic 195
    landholding, tenure 16, 40, 41, 198—199, 214, 221
    patriarchal 40
    social 190
    succession 14, 23, 29, 40, 41, 190, 201, 202, 261
    transmission of titles 190
North Pondoland Sugar (NPS) 233—236, 238

**O**
Office of the *Kgosi* 94—98
*Oorlamse* 76
oral evidence, histories 7, 8, 36, 46, 66, 105, 117, 119, 210

**P**
patriarchy 25, 28, 29, 39, 40, 181, 196, 201, 204
patriliny 40, 46, 199, 200, 201
peri-urban areas 2, 5, 263
permission to occupy certificates (PTO) 17, 195, 213, 232, 255, 261; *see also* land rights, land tenure
Pilane, Chief (*Kgosi*) Nyalala 67—73, 75, 123, 124, 126, 127, 220
Pilane, Chief (*Kgosi*) Ofentse 76
Pilane, Chief (*Kgosi*) Tidimane 68—69, 76, 134
Pilane, Jacob 69, 134
Pilane, Mmuthi 125, 126, 135
Pilane, Tlhabane 125
platinum; *see* mining

plots 187, 230, 232
   arable 15, 16, 178, 223, 230, 231, 234—236, 241, 251, 259
   residential 15, 16, 198, 200, 204, 230, 231, 254
ploughing 69, 165, 171, 177, 178, 183
Pondoland; see Mpondoland
Pondoland Annexation Act 251, 255
post-apartheid era; see democracy, South African; post-apartheid legislation
post-apartheid legislation 12, 66, 72, 195, 230, 261
   Communal Land Rights Act (CLARA) 3, 4, 6, 17, 42, 65, 237, 261
   Communal Property Association (CPA) Act 17, 30, 31, 38—39, 73, 195, 210, 214, 217, 237, 244
   Eastern Cape Governance Act 155—157, 159
   Interim Protection of Informal Land Rights Act (IPILRA) 18, 222, 243, 258, 262
   Marine Living Resources Act 46, 48, 52
   MPRDA; see Mineral and Petroleum Resources Development Act
   National Heritage Resources Act 13, 104, 105, 110
   National Traditional Leaders Framework Act 94
   Promotion of Administrative Justice Act (PAJA) 52
   Restitution of Land Rights Act 6, 8, 9, 119, 195, 197, 208, 210, 217, 236, 238, 250, 251, 258
   TLGFA; see Traditional Leadership and Governance Framework Act
post-colonialism 61—62, 114, 153, 158
pre-colonial period 54, 62, 64, 143, 144, 145, 158, 256, 259, 260
Presidential Advisory Panel on Land Reform and Agriculture 18, 264
Professional Grave Solutions (PGS) 105, 106
Promotion of Administrative Justice Act 52
provincial governments
   Eastern Cape 9, 10, 136, 147, 148, 150, 155, 158, 159, 241

   North West 11, 13, 68, 81, 88—94, 98—100, 137
Provision of Certain Land for Settlement/ and Assistance Act 217
Public Protector (PP) 91, 137
Public Security Act 238

**Q**

quitrent 154, 194—196, 222, 255

**R**

Rabula 157, 197—200, 203, 204
Ramaphosa, Cyril 3, 82, 86
Rapulana lineage 166, 168—173, 176— 179
Ratlou lineage 168, 171
Ratshidi lineage 166, 168, 170—173, 176— 179
reforms; see land reform
restitution; see land restitution
Restitution of Land Rights Act 6, 8, 9, 119, 195, 197, 208, 210, 217, 236, 238, 250, 251, 258
rights; see also land rights
   commodification 60
   constitutional 10, 23—26, 28, 29, 52, 73, 75, 121, 126—129, 131, 135, 136
   legal 105, 106, 108, 117
   citizenship 112, 142
   customary 10, 14—15, 17, 23—29, 35, 45—50, 52, 54, 62, 121, 137, 139, 166
   democratic 157, 159
   environmental 54
   family 15, 16, 17, 18, 203, 204
   frozen 54—55
   inheritance 201, 202, 205
   to marine resources 14, 44—47, 53, 54
   mineral, mining 3, 11—13, 33, 65—67, 81—84, 86, 104, 238, 239
   popular 1, 3, 14
   socio-economic 8, 14
   succession 29, 190, 201, 202
   universal 2
   violations 10
   women's 23, 29, 39, 204
royalties 12, 65, 67, 70, 83—85, 90—91, 96, 220, 232
rule of law 2, 63, 128, 242, 269

rural economies 2—3, 4, 11, 61, 190, 205, 232—233, 236; *see also* mining
Rustenburg region 12, 67, 81, 82, 83

**S**
Sefikile village 66, 77
segregation 12, 16, 24, 62, 112, 145, 164—166, 169, 170, 174—176, 179, 182, 197—198
Sinawo Community Property Association 237, 240, 242, 244
Social Darwinism 61—62
social differentiation 189—193, 196—197, 203—204, 224
social reproduction 165, 192, 198, 204, 224
social units 64, 167, 188, 189, 191, 197, 231
Society, Work and Politics Institute (SWOP) xii*n*1, 11, 81, 100*n*1
South African Development Trust (SADT) 218
South African Constitution; *see also* Constitutional Court
  Bill of Rights 22, 23, 26, 28, 30, 52, 122
  customary law and 2, 5, 14, 22—24, 26—31, 40, 42, 44, 49, 52, 63, 122, 128
  tenure reform and 3, 17, 194, 209, 215, 263
  traditional authorities and 8, 40, 72, 128, 134, 135, 138, 141, 147
  transformation and 21—22, 27, 262
South African National Civic Organisation (SANCO) 144, 149, 235
South African Native National Congress (SANNC) 173, 175
Standing Committee on Public Accounts (SCOPA) 92
succession; *see also* inheritance
  chiefly 6, 13, 93—94, 99, 241
  property 14, 23, 29, 40, 41, 190, 201, 202, 261
sugar 16, 229, 233—238, 240—244, 250, 252
Supreme Court of Appeal 23, 36, 52—55, 71—74, 126, 174, 237
Surplus People Project (SPP) 208, 216, 217
surveys 154, 198, 204, 242, 248, 258

**T**
taxes 134, 181
  hut 168, 177
  mining 13, 83, 232
  records 255
tenants 105, 109, 110, 112—114, 191, 194, 197, 200, 211, 214—215, 222—224
  in British Bechuanaland 165, 169, 172, 177
tenure; *see* land tenure
titanium; *see* mining
title; *see* land title
title deeds 117, 183, 198, 209, 210, 213—218, 222, 225
Traditional Affairs Bills 32
Traditional and Khoi-San Leadership Act (2019) 3, 12, 18, 137, 138, 142
Traditional Authorities (TA) 12, 83, 236, 241
traditional communities 62, 123; *see also* communities; 'tribe'
  amaHlathi 142—144, 148—153, 158
  amaMfengu 143, 145—146, 148, 149, 152—155, 158, 160, 196
  Bafokeng 11—13, 33, 95, 232
  Bakgatla-ba-Kautlwale 72—73
  Bakgatla-ba-Kgafela 10, 12, 33, 66—74, 121—125, 128, 220
  Bakgatla-ba-Sefikile 71—72
  Bapo-ba-Mogale 11, 33, 81—85, 87—90, 97—100, 137
  Barolong 16, 166—173, 177, 179, 182, 183
  Batlokwa 132
  judgments and 73, 74, 87, 90, 121, 125, 128
  legislation and 26, 65, 137, 155, 157, 159
  Mapela 129—130, 137
  Moruleng 123
  rights 25, 26, 121, 126, 127—128
Traditional Courts Bill 32, 65, 142
traditional councils 3—5, 18, 65, 77, 82, 87—88, 135—138, 142, 155, 237, 259
  Amadiba 260, 262
  Bafokeng 13
  Bakgatla 71, 72, 74, 121, 123—126, 220
  Bapo 88—100
  ImiZizi 243, 259

281

traditional councils (*continued*)
    KwaGcina 156—157
    Moreipuso 133—134
Traditional Courts Bill 65, 142
traditional leaders 141, 210, 213; *see also* chiefs; headmen; kings
    apartheid era 136, 142, 147, 152, 154, 158—159, 213, 219
    abuses of power 134—136, 218—220
    in Ciskei 144—148
    Constitutional Court and 23, 25—28, 32, 40, 121, 122, 126—129
    disputes; see chiefs, chieftaincy, disputes
    influence 8—10, 141
    powers 8, 14, 64, 66, 72, 87, 122, 136—139, 142—143, 225, 262
    provincial houses of 9, 147
Traditional Leadership and Governance Act (provincial)
    Eastern Cape 155—157, 159
    Limpopo 130, 137
    North West 88, 126, 137
Traditional Leadership and Governance Framework Act (TLGFA, 2003) 3, 8, 9, 26, 122, 142, 151, 153
    traditional councils and 9, 65, 126, 136—137, 237
    village head elections and 155—157
transactions
    land, property 199, 230
    mining 11, 70—71, 84—86, 88, 93, 96, 97, 99, 124
    rents 177, 179, 181
Transkei (former) 9, 15, 35, 55, 148, 155, 229—239, 247—255, 261
Transkei Agricultural Corporation (TRACOR) 232, 233
Transkei Agricultural Development Act 238, 251
Transkei Development Corporation (TDC) 232
Transkei Public Safety Act 251
Transvaal Rural Action Committee (TRAC) 208, 215, 216, 221, 224, 225
Transkei Sun International Limited 248—249, 252—255, 257, 263
Tribal Authorities (TA) 87, 125—126, 143, 145, 149, 152, 154, 158

Amadiba 252
Bafokeng 232
Bapo 82—84, 87
ImiZizi 233
Motlhabe 125
Nqgika 157
tribal trust accounts 67, 83, 87
'tribe' 142, 179; *see also* traditional communities
    colonialism and 26, 62, 63, 167, 168, 172, 180—182, 212
    tenure and 12, 13, 64, 230
trusts, trusteeship 4, 12, 13, 39, 63, 67; *see also* tribal trust accounts
Tshidi; see Ratshidi lineage
Tshintsha Amakhaya 42
Tweefontein Colliery Complex 13, 104
Tweefontein farm 104—106, 109, 113, 116, 118

**U**

*ubukhosi*; *see* traditional leaders
Union government 61, 169, 170, 173—174, 261
United Democratic Movement (UDM) 147—148
Upgrading of Land Tenure Rights Act (ULTRA) 194, 263
urban areas 4, 5, 192, 195, 198, 263
urbanisation 192, 199

**W**

Welgeval farm 75—77
women
    customary marriage 29
    inheritance 14, 17, 23, 39, 41, 165, 201—205
    land rights 23, 29, 31, 39, 40, 201—204, 223, 257, 261
    lineage 174, 200— 201
    traditional councils and 9, 87, 88, 142, 223, 237

**X**

Xolobeni 259, 262; *see also* court cases, *Baleni* (2006)

**Z**

Zuma, Jacob 3, 242

www.ingramcontent.com/pod-product-compliance
Lightning Source LLC
Chambersburg PA
CBHW020902080526
44589CB00011B/401